Suffer Less in Life & Work

THE ACCEPTANCE OF HUMANNESS IS A PEACE-CREATING GIFT TO SELF AND OTHERS.

A guide to finding greater peace, exploration, and reward.

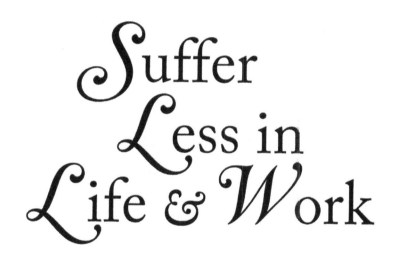

Suffer Less in Life & Work

Vincent Dodd, R. N.

gatekeeper press

Columbus, Ohio

Suffer Less in Life and Work: A guide to finding greater peace, exploration, and reward.

Published by Gatekeeper Press
2167 Stringtown Rd, Suite 109
Columbus, OH 43123-2989
www.GatekeeperPress.com

Library of Congress Control Number: 2021952744

ISBN (hardcover): 9781662922817
ISBN (paperback): 9781662922824
eISBN: 9781662922831

Dedicated to you. My colleagues, bosses, patients, clients, defendants, strangers I have met, lovers, family, friends, and foes; thank you all for the good we shared, the tasks we have accomplished, the joys we created and felt, the people we helped, the pain and struggles we helped each other through, the laughs in grocery store lines, even for the not so good times when we did not get along so well. Great, good, or bad, thank you, because we learned, experienced, and grew.

Because We Are Stronger Together:
20% of all proceeds from the sale of this book will be donated to
The Yandle, John D., Sheehan, and Daigle Foundation
a.k.a. "The Human Bonding Foundation"
website: humanbonding.org

Strangely, dedicated to Randy, Jack, Jessie, Cooper, and Maggie. Wise dogs that helped me write one of the more important yet beautiful paragraphs in the chapter on politics while I was house sitting with them on and off over the past year. They tried awfully hard to teach me a few other important things, but I am not on their higher level, so I missed most of it.

TABLE OF CONTENTS

My love of quotes comes from my understanding that life is teamwork, and every fresh angle, especially from those with much greater wisdom than I, helps me see myself and the world with greater clarity and understanding. Albert Einstein is one of my favorites. His humanistic mind was equally powerful as his scientific mind.

"As a single footstep will not make a path on the earth, so a single thought will not make a pathway in the mind. To make a deep physical path, we walk again and again. To make a deep mental path, we must think over and over the kind of thoughts we wish to dominate our lives."
—Henry David Thoreau

"You will learn a lot about yourself if you stretch in the direction of goodness, of bigness, of kindness, of forgiveness, of emotional bravery."
—Cheryl Strayed

"Just because I disagree with you, does not mean that I have to hate you.
We need to relearn that in our society."
—Morgan Freeman

Warning:

The title is correct, this information explores some causes and solutions to human suffering and may stir memories and emotions. You are about to begin a journey that will infiltrate the *deeper core* influences of life's discomforts, frustrations, and outright pains of being a human being. *Suffer Less* is not "Sufferless." We can never dissolve the balances of life's ups and downs, good and bad, happy and sad, content and scared, love and fear, or successes and failures. Although some are hard to hear, this book is filled with gems to help you suffer less. People told me getting through *Suffer Less in Death* was hard, but they also expressed there was no doubt it greatly helped them suffer less concerning the dying, then death of loved ones and pets, and eased their fears. If you can read the hard to hear about death and tell me it helped, then I know you can read this at times hard to hear information about self and life, and then find the benefits for yourself. The greatest way to suffer less is to go inside yourself and do a little work, and that is exactly what we are about to do. However, this page is a warning, if you find some deeper feelings or past traumas coming to the surface and pushing on you too hard, please seek help. Maybe talk it out with a trusted friend if it is mild, or perhaps find a qualified counselor if it is lasting or deeply affecting you. Please remember, the human mind is an amazing and powerful yet limited organ in every one of us. Seeking help is not a sign of weakness, but rather a sign of courage and strength. It is saying that I have the courage to be honest with myself on a deeper level. Be proud to work with your mind, not ashamed or embarrassed. It only makes our exploration of self and life easier.

CHAPTER 1

THERE HAD TO BE A BETTER WAY

"I always wanted to be somebody,
but now I realize I should have been more specific."
—Lily Tomlin

My Ego is Rarely My Friend

My ego is a thief
It wants to rob me
Worse yet, it wants to rob others

My ego is strong yet weak
It wants to dominate
Yet weak to truths and self-honesty

My ego lies to me
It tells me it wants to protect me
But denies me raw self-exploration

My ego is abusive
It suppresses my self-knowledge
It blames others for my mistakes

My ego is not my pride
True pride is deserved and welcomed
False pride is my ego still lying

My ego is unavoidable
But can be tamed
My ego is rarely my friend

When I was eight, we moved to the semi-suburban bayous of South-East Louisiana. I throw in the "semi-suburban," so you don't get a false vision of me being lucky enough to paddle a pirogue (Cajun canoe) to school and fish on the way home. But we did live on a bayou that was about 30 feet from the back door, and I did go fishing when I came home from school. We just didn't have a pirogue; we didn't even have a cypress tree. The only South Louisiana classics we had were water moccasins, a periodic alligator, and so many mosquitoes that they sounded like an interstate a few miles away filled with eighteen-wheel trucks doing eighty. All my new friends had bikes, so I asked my parents if I could have a bike. They said, "sure."

A few weeks later, when I asked them when I was going to get my new bike, their reply was, "Have you saved any money?" I was the youngest of six, so money was an issue. I thought to myself, "Ooohhhh, so, that's how this works." I asked if I could do a few more chores and get paid for some of them. I already had chores: taking out the trash, scooping up our basset hound's poop from the backyard (which was probably the reason I did not mind becoming a nurse), and my four older sisters demanded that if I used the kitchen, I had to clean it before I ate the peanut butter and jelly sandwich I had just made. My parents said yes, and my first paid job in life was cleaning out and organizing the garage. If only all my bosses and jobs could have been like my parents: rarely home, complimentary, and no taxes! I also boldly knocked on the doors of total strangers in the neighborhood and got a few more hits for a few extra dollars. I started researching my bike options, the ones I could afford, saved my money, and after a few months, I was able to buy that bike.

That was the beginning of my love to work, and in a way, it was also the beginning of life. I say that because life is work; we work all our lives, and work is not solely what we do to exchange our time, knowledge, and skills for monetary compensation. Work is also what is required to remain alive and even helps us feel alive. Life is also work, and becoming more so every day with increasing social, financial, and economic pressures. That type of stressful work is holistically hard and unfortunately can damage us physically, mentally, and emotionally.

That expenditure of my time in exchange for monetary compensation to buy that bike was fifty years ago. I still love to work, whether at a job, outside, or the daily chores to keep life moving forward. Please don't get me wrong. I have had a handful of jobs that outright sucked, and a few periods in my life haven't been so great either, usually self-inflicted, but not always. One of those "not always" moments would be the frequent and paralyzing migraine headaches that strained my childhood until they went away in the eighth grade. But as my personal philosophy of the bad jobs and bad periods of my life, if that is my place in the big and little picture, then let me work giving it my best. Except for the few times the situation was too far off-balance to find enough to be positive and I had to walk away for my well-being, when a task is before me, I choose to find a way to enjoy something about it. Finding something positive about spraying acid on multiple layers of dried barnacles on the hull of a sailboat, then trying to scrape them off is not an easy joyful job to find positive. But I did it for a summer and somehow, I enjoyed that job too. I'm not always going to paint a picture of puppies and Easter baskets, but I do love to work.

Over the years, I have had a respectable number of people tell me they also learned to love their life and work more after hearing and seeing how I approach life or work, or how I worked with a tricky situation or difficult person. The only real energy required to carry out most of what I am going to share is within thought, with just a little expenditure in actions.

Attempting to resolve an issue only at the surface does not address the core origin of the problem. It is the difference between apologizing to someone for saying something poorly, instead of working on the core issue that caused you to say something that caused a bump in the first place, therefore decreasing the number of times you say something poorly, and increasing positive statements prevents issues from occurring in the first place. For a more physical example, it's like repeatedly cutting yourself with a chef's knife and continuing to put on Band-Aids, as opposed to watching a video on how to sharpen and correctly use one, then rarely cutting yourself again on any kind of knife you use for the rest of your life. I am hoping to save you a lot of life and work-related Band-Aids.

Other lifelong benefits to such an approach are the internal and external rewards of less bitterness and conflict, greater and much easier teamwork, and productivity. All equal greater peace and profit at work, and time and money saved in your personal life. One more benefit is more humor and laughter. Stress and conflict love to block our potential for more joy and laughter.

I initially started to write two books, *Suffer Less in Life* and *Suffer Less in Work*. As I was working on the outlines, I quickly realized there was so much overlap. It also dawned on me that not only is our professional and daily maintenance required for life, but all life is work, and work is a constantly integrated part of all life, rather than "just" your job. Does it not sometimes require work to move the clothes to the dryer and fold the ones that are finished? It does not matter your socioeconomic range, poor or rich, is it not work to walk to the kitchen and back if you have the flu? From our teen years to our death, isn't it sometimes work to get out of bed, meet an obligation, hear sad news, watch the news, do homework or after-hours work, do the dishes, or deal with cable or IT issues? Because our personal, social, and financial strains are intensifying, daily life requires higher and deeper levels of work we all must do, mixing the boundaries of why work and life are the same in many ways. Both also require constant work with our normal everyday emotions and imperfect thought processes, which is heavy work all on its own.

Finding better ways

Just as I looked at how we notified family members of an unexpected death and thought to myself there must be a better way, that is exactly what I have done by looking at the origin of life's struggles with first ourselves and our relationships to avoid unnecessary energy consumption and conflicts, and to increase our peace and reward. I developed, tested, and applied these tools in two highly stressful and challenging careers, for almost thirty-five years. They worked well for me and for others that have trusted me with their occupational and personal life frustrations. I also respect that they may not work for all people or situations. Let's strengthen the test of functionality even further. This information was tested during the stressors of lifesaving tasks for twenty-one years in large teaching hospital emergency departments, three of which were in Intensive Care Units, and for over twelve years in a uniform and marked car in law enforcement. They were tested further because both fields are filled with dominant, staunch, no-nonsense personalities, and nearly every person needing our help was in some level of crisis. My development and use of these slight changes in thought process and approach was inspired and applied equally towards both colleagues and the public. A reader can take this material and make their personal or occupational life much easier; or a team can apply these internal tools and make everyone's lives easier, profitable, and personally rewarding. Even though the chapters require some internal work and self-exploration, everything you will read has been harshly test-driven and pushed to the edge of challenge. Not just by me, but by many others who have told me that applying these gems has made their lives easier. Both careers forced me to keep exercising, fine-tuning, and redirecting some internal thoughts and some external application, but the time and energy saved is significant. Life never gets easy, and I never get it perfect, but it can get easier, wonderfully wider and deeper, and funnier and more joyful.

An often-undervalued positive contributing factor in group dynamics is the calmer and less frustrated a person becomes, the calmer and less frustrated the surrounding people become, making it easier for everyone to be calmer and less frustrated. It is one thing to be inspired to want a calmer life, but the accomplishment of that goal, day in and day out is harder as the surrounding personalities become harder and our life stressors increase. I know creating a positive cycle makes life easier and easier with every completed cycle. Yes, it never becomes a perpetual motion of its own. It will always require some effort on our part. The longer a person or team accomplishes this, more positive human dynamic awareness and application together, whether at home, roadside, restaurants, office cubicles, hospitals, or boardrooms, the amount of energy required to keep it going becomes less and less. Calm or tense energy spreads like the flu; it is up to each of us to use our free will and choice to decide which energy we choose to spread. The benefits of choosing to spread calm, productive, solution-oriented energy will start that positive cycle by first easing life for yourself, then easing it for those around you, which then eases it right back to you. Win-win and win again.

The spreading of either positive or negative words and actions can have a huge effect on both you and those around you in your personal and occupational life. The width of that statement has no limit. Don't ever think that your actions are benign or that you don't make a difference. Our attitudes and the treatment of each other spreads, and some will stick. Because some of your words and actions do stick and self-perpetuate, you have the free will and choice whether you want to spread negative and potentially damaging actions, or healthy contributing actions that will have a positive ripple effect.

An actual physical death is not the only part of us that can die from unhealthy relationships in life and at work. Unhealthy settings and relationships also began to kill parts of our being, or as some may call it, our peace of mind. This whittling away from the inside of us does not only occur to the recipient of unhealthy relationships, but also to all involved, including the sender. The research is overwhelming: for all parties, whether personal or professional, lower-level employees to CEOs, stress eats away at our mind, bodies, and life. High blood pressure, infertility issues, cardiac disease, gastrointestinal disease, anxiety, depression, suicide, and addictions are all contributed to by unhealthy relationships. The research is not one-sided with the workplace or the home; the healthier the employees, the healthier the company, and likewise, the healthier the individuals that make up a couple, the healthier the relationship.

So, what gets in the way? Money, power, pleasure, and personality, all can be painfully powerful and destructive forces in our day and time. As Russia invades and is killing the people of Ukraine as I type these words in this very last edit. These forces are not new to humans. Quite the opposite, they are as old as the first person who realized their life could be "easier," more comfortable, and filled with greater pleasures by the dominance or control of others. What makes these modern times so much more powerful is the magnitude of wealth, the over-development of staunch personalities, the collapse of family structure and support, a population forcing a level of competition to stay on top like never seen before, and the list of stronger forces is endless. Our homeless population is just one indicator of that fact. Our mounting stressors can be witnessed in the escalating numbers of addiction and mental health issues. Most of these factors and influences pressure each of us as individuals, families, companies, communities, and cultures can be influenced into new positive directions. Giving up first with our thoughts, then attitudes, then our negative or lack of positive actions, or ultimately, giving up in exasperation will only accelerate our failures.

What is the proof that we can change and grow? Couples counseling has a fluctuating level of greater than 60% success rate. We do not need research to prove this in our occupational lives, who has not witnessed a department or company damaged by the arrival of an emotionally unhealthy person on any equal or higher pay level? Who has not witnessed the revitalization and growth of a department or company by the arrival of an emotionally healthy and humanistically intelligent person's arrival in the team or management? The conclusive proof that we can change and grow from any point of an outright tough situation is that 72% of couples that remarry each other for a second time stay together. If we can get this positive statistic out of marriage, then some level of change for the best is almost always possible. The more wisdom than humorous old joke, "How many counselors does it take to change a light bulb?" has more wisdom and guidance than we've ever given it credit for beyond "so true" after hearing the answer of, "just one, but it has to want to change."

If two humans, that once had to divorce for their peace, can grow, change, and appreciate seeing life and the other person from healthier new angles can have a greater than 70% second try success rate! Then I know we are capable of change that can bring us more peace and productivity.

Changing angles

I went into law enforcement at the age of forty-three as a second career for a handful of reasons. I considered it in college, but my friends talked me out of it, saying, "You have way too strong of a sense of justice to go into law enforcement, and your thought process is too non-traditional, you will not be happy." They ended up being right, but I accomplished over twelve years anyway. Yes, they were painfully right. After graduating from the academy, I made it to the interview stage with a large, highly respected department, twice. They did not hire me on the second try either. A friend of mine that was in the department knew someone on the second oral board interviewing me. He called me a few days later and told me why they did not hire me: "Your answers to their questions were far too encompassing. If they ask you one question, give them one answer, not three answers from three different directions." As we were laughing at me, he closed with, "I know this is going to be really hard for you, but attempt to keep your answers under three sentences."

I followed my college friends' advice, and my heart, and went into nursing. I never regretted that choice. I went into law enforcement to challenge my mind, slightly to answer my old curiosity question of whether I should have gone into it after college, but also because I knew law enforcement was heading towards trouble. I wanted to gain experience from the inside to help. I wanted to study its layers and influences on and within law enforcement. I also went into it to attempt to prevent crises from occurring. Once someone arrives in an emergency department, the crisis has already occurred, but on the streets, some prevention can take place. The last reason was to see if the same de-escalation techniques that worked so well for me in the emergency department would work while I was in a uniform. They required some modifying, but they did work.

I am much more a nurse than I ever was a cop. Even while in the uniform, for the most part, I approached the job as a nurse in a police officer's uniform, with the authority of an officer but the knowledge and skill sets of a nurse. So, both the nurse and the officer in me witnessed the dangerous traffic violation. The authority granted to me as a commissioned officer of a state and a department moved the little switch over that turns on the overhead emergency lights, that interrupts and inconveniences your day. Which is basically a momentary detention, and the written citation, also known as a "ticket," is basically a mini arrest, and the officer directing you to safely drive away is your legal release from non-jail. That is the part many people forget, being pulled over is a big deal. It is the police officer that activates those lights that make our heart race, but it is you, the people, and all three branches of government that trained that officer, granted them the authority, and expects them to detain you, then ticket or warn you, for placing others in danger. Then the officer in me handled the roadside and personal safety, while the nurse spoke with the driver. The team approach worked fantastic. Even the few times I received the rapid immediate verbal attacks, they were thrown off and calmed because I did not escalate. Unfortunately, there is a small percentage of society that wants to see the officer escalate. I also know luck is involved in every traffic stop, I also got lucky.

That cop nursing team was incredibly effective and rewarding. Those years assured me there is more than one functional way to approach our social issues, and a percentage of our judgment towards law enforcement. I had been told by many cop acquaintances through my emergency nursing years not to go into their field. Yet, I wanted the experience, and I considered it research into one of the hardest, often no-win situation careers. Thankfully, it was also mixed in with often highly rewarding moments of social contribution. One of the first interesting things I heard in the academy was, "You will save lives and prevent crimes that you will never know about because you cannot record a non-event." An example would be pulling over a car for reckless driving and excessive speeding in medium to high traffic. Had the officer not pulled them over, they may have caused a major fatal crash in the next few miles. If events were prevented, then how would we know, or how could we document something that did not occur? I know I made a slight difference, and I will never regret those challenging and educational years.

Change is possible, research proves it, and so does our past. We may not be able to record one non-event, but we can prove many. Such as decreasing a speed limit on a curvy mountain road, then observing its long-term effects. The levels of strife or peace in our life are measurable also.

Something that can never be stated or thought too many times, especially since so many no longer believe they can make a difference, is: If small and large negative actions can bring a person, group, community, country, or culture into distress, then logic and history prove that positive actions, both large and small, can pull us away from distress and back to being healthy and sustainable. That is an affirmation that can change our lives, our relationships, and our communities and further.

Don't get the wrong picture

Let me set the record straight, as I did in the first paragraph. I don't want you to get a false vision of me responding to emergency calls all day and night long. I always want to paint as near to correct pictures for you as our human minds allow. For almost all my years in law enforcement, I mostly only enforced one very peculiar court order called a Writ of Execution. It is basically a great court order that is often rendered relatively worthless because most deputies won't enforce it or spend much energy past the minimum required to send it back to court with nothing accomplished. Instead, I used all the skills I had in me and turned it into a highly functional piece of paper. I was told "Thank you" more often from the defendants that I enforced it against, than from the plaintiffs that financially benefited from my efforts. I will tell you more about it later. But I was in a uniform and a marked police car for a little over twelve years, and I did a little speck of everything, even traffic stops. I just did not write anyone a ticket for the last six or seven years. This is how differently I approached being in law enforcement. I did not activate the overhead lights and pull someone over for all infractions; it had to be infractions that the twenty-one-year emergency department nurse in me knew could truly cause one of those hundreds of deaths from car crashes that took their last breath before my eyes. You were not going to get pulled over by me for going 5 miles per hour over the limit on a medium to light traffic highway. Here is where even traffic stops get a new angle. After introducing myself and stating the reason for the stop, I would ask, "I will let you decide: would you like a ticket, or would you like a talk?"

Of course, after I developed this technique, I only heard, "Really?! I'll take the talk!" I would then say, "Okay, talk it is, but only under one condition: you agree to not drive off and say, 'Ah-ha, I got away with it!' but that you agree to drive off and say to yourself, 'He gave me some good information; I need to try and do better.' Deal?" Not only did they all agree, but the number of people that thanked me for stopping them at the end of the stop was significant. With great responses, such as, "Thank you for backing up your information with statistics," "I don't have to think about it, you are right, I forgot that I am human and can make mistakes that end up hurting others."

One of my favorite responses was from a man that created so many infractions and so aggressive that, as people sometimes do, a few drivers rolled down their windows and gave me a thumbs up for pulling him over. I always loved it when the public let me know they had been pushed past their limit too and gave me those thumbs up or yelled a

"Thank you!" After I finished informing him of the many traffic laws I saw him break and gave him my standard talk on the minute-to-minute responsibility of driving, he also thanked me. Then he added, with a rather sad look on his face, in a low-clam-embarrassed tone, "I have become the asshole driver that I accuse others of being." I was in shock at his honesty, all I could think of to say was, "Well, that means there is great room for improvement, and I can't thank you enough for wanting to be a safer driver."

Please don't tire of me using our driving as examples throughout the book. Our driving is a direct reflection of our deeper human behaviors, both as an individual and as a society. I will also reference it often because forgetting how dangerous driving is, and driving by habit not momentary awareness, makes it even more dangerous. The always-a-nurse in me also cares to attempt to keep you alive, or at minimum save you time, inconvenience, money, property damage, or serious injury.

This "educational break" the driver received would not completely work for everyone, because a percentage of people either cannot or will not change dangerous habits. Since I like to keep things accurate and balanced, the financial assistance that violators provide local and state governments are also significant. Also significant, is the fact that many serious criminals are caught during traffic stops. But if an officer, or even a whole department, came up with an effective educational talk to citation ratio policy, then perhaps they'd only write a criminal traffic citation every other or every third violator they pulled over. Officers do have this flexibility, but if it were a policy, they would be more protected to handle traffic violators this way. The rest get a meaningful statistic filled educational talk. Which one do you think would make our roads safer in the long run?

I share this with you in the first chapter, so you can see how I have spent my life attempting to find not easier ways of doing things but better ways, which also means more effective solution-based answers to issues at their origin. Easier often follows, but what follows is alleviating many of the problems that cascade out from the initial origin of an issue. There are so many functional and easy changes that can be made within law enforcement, and in the public's perspective and actions also, that would create safer driving yes, but could help many of the interactions between police and citizens. Creating healthier conditions and a more rewarding outcome for all parties involved, is obtainable. Most cops would rather you just move along safely and respectfully down the road than have you put others in danger. I have discovered that a rather sizable percentage of officers are tired of the public judging and hating them for doing their job.

I shared this example for many reasons. One is to present an issue from the base of a problem up, not the top down. What you just heard is the product of my twenty-one years in teaching hospitals, where knowledge is being traded in every direction with one goal: to heal human body issues, not with surface bandages, but with teamwork to find the origin of discomfort, pain, injury, and illness, and then fix it from the origin out.

I have looked at life's personal and occupational "illnesses" for fifty years, since I had to figure out the most efficient way to clean out and reorganize that garage, and then to attempt to resolve life-threatening issues at teaching hospitals with that same approach. What is the origin of the issue, what caused that issue, and how can we not only fix the problem, but prevent it from happening again? Working with the inside of the human body is not always easy; is it appendicitis, or a right ovarian cyst, or a right Fallopian tube pregnancy? Is it a cardiac issue or an aortic aneurysm? Working with the human mind, behaviors, groups, and social dynamics are even harder. Add in money, profit, job stability, a family to care for, the human ego, and resistance and manipulation to protect special interests. It all becomes a block to accomplish true resolution to any damaging issue.

We have become a culture that only wants to accept solutions to our mounting problems if those solutions fit into our preexisting beliefs and preset agenda. Statistically speaking, it is impossible for all the best solutions to all our issues to be ones that line up with any one person or group's beliefs. Not every healthy solution will be easy to hear, but many things can get easier if we allow ourselves to hear and accept the healthier and more functional big picture answers. The dash camera first started being installed in police cars in 1981, it was a great big picture answer to many problems. That advancement worked in favor of protecting all parties: the officer, the citizen, and you the taxpayer. The computer in the car, body camera, pepper spray, and the taser have taken that even further for the good of all. When someone is injured before or during an arrest, they often must be cleared by the local emergency department before being accepted into central booking. Starting in the early 1990s, with the introduction of the taser, I saw a significant drop in the number of people with serious injuries having to be cleared by us before lockup. There may be those that are critical of the taser, but it has prevented thousands and thousands of serious injuries. Even just its presence, even if not drawn from its holster, used, or not, prevents incident and injury, as well as your tax dollars saved. To carry the taser, the officer must receive training, and the officer is tased in that training. It was one of the most amazing and strangely painful 5 seconds of my life.

Before the dash camera, police brutality was a much larger issue than it is today. Once police started being recorded, the percentage of police that used excessive force were placed at a higher level of check and balance. Because I always attempt to approach contributing factors with balance, it also cleared many officers because they were, in fact, meeting a high level of resistance or assault, and their actions were highly appropriate. Even on a traffic stop that required no physical intervention, the dash camera forced a higher level of professionalism and appropriateness from both the officer and the citizen. The bigger a solution is, the closer it gets to the origin of the problem, the more time, energy, and money it saves us all, and the more peace it provides.

I experienced this phenomenon by adding one piece of equipment to my uniform. My job required me to do a lot of work between defendants and attorneys. This increased my personal liability exposure, and the dash camera microphone did a poor job of recording conversations. So, I added a dash camera microphone extension, a small microphone with a tiny anti-wind noise foam cover clipped on my shirt between the top two buttons. It was a much clearer recording to help protect me concerning what I did and did not say, which would potentially save you the taxpayer, had someone complained or brought a civil suit against me or the department. It made it very clear you were most likely being recorded. The body camera now accomplishes this in-your-face notification that you are being recorded. But I was amazed how adding that highly visible little microphone to my uniform significantly increased respectful conversation, and thus allowed me to help more defendants get this headache out of their lives.

Here is the balance that is hard to hear: we as individuals and as a society have become hyper-defensive toward our behaviors. I could activate my dash camera if I saw a violator placing everyone's lives at a high level of risk, such as extreme, excessive speeding in morning traffic, no blinkers, tailgating, weaving in and out of lanes with unsafe movements that force cars to break over and over. My dash camera even recorded the people's brake lights coming on over and over because the violator was repetitively cutting back in too close. Before I could catch up to that car, I observed and recorded ten or more violations.

The nurse in me could see the potential for other innocent law-abiding drivers lying dead on a trauma room stretcher, then I see the physician and I walking out to the private death notification room to inform the family. Then the driver quickly says, "Why did you stop me?" Then when I list off only the clear violations, I hear, "I was just . . ." followed by a myriad of excuses usually involving "late" or some other stressors in the excuse. One consistent interesting observation I noticed was nine out of ten excuses were a reason to drive more cautiously, not more reckless. Such as, "I just have so many things going on with my work and family that I wasn't paying attention." The dash camera helps law enforcement and the taxpayer from several angles at that moment. Officers may periodically get reprimanded for unprofessional behaviors, and fired if egregious enough, but you, the taxpayer, are constantly paying for the issues between citizens and law enforcement. Periodically it is the innocent who fights a traffic citation, but often it is an accrual violator, and the dash camera has proven that over and over. Dangerous habitual accrual violators are a significant danger to you and your loved one's lives when driving near you.

Although we are looking at driving, I will give examples throughout, unrelated to our driving, of how we are all directly, and indirectly, affected negatively by people who refuse to accept the responsibility of their behavior in several ways. The officer was not available to get to your 9-1-1 call as quickly because they were delayed, or completely unable if the traffic stop turned into an arrest. Chronic violators will often take a citation to court because they know they may receive a reduced fine or to keep a violation off their insurance or driving record. The down the road cost of the behavior, then the long-term effect of not accepting the responsibility, and the worst part is the crashes, injuries, and deaths. It boils down to your tax dollars, your time, you and your family's safety, your property, your wellbeing, and maybe life.

I know a very professional early grade-school teacher who at the beginning of every school year, for the purpose of teaching proper classroom behavior, will ask the scholars this next question to teach their part of classroom management, by teaching them the concept of doing the right thing for the right reason, "Who can tell me why you wear your seat belt in the car?" "So my parents won't get a ticket!" is the number one reason they give. With, "To protect me if we get in a car crash," sometimes not being heard for a year or two. What is hard for officers to watch is when a parent has their child in the car, especially a driving age teenager who witnessed the violation, and the parent denies it. Is this teaching the child or teen it is acceptable to break the law or rule, and it is acceptable to lie about it? Is it better for both ourselves and those around us, to simply accept our responsibility for our actions? Unrelated to only simply avoiding consequences, the benefits are significant and multi-directional.

Please know I know this is hard to hear, but the only way life can get easier for the individual and society is if we accept our responsibility and not assume that we are not contributing to problems. This is one of the reasons this book starts with a warning.

I share my experiences with traffic stops because seeing a little more clearly, the cause and effect of our behaviors on those around us is important. Thank you to all the people that recognized my peculiar face, who came up to me in coffee lines or restaurants, introduced yourself, thanked me for pulling you over in the past, and told me that I made a difference in your driving. Thank you also for your ability to care and grow. I especially appreciate those of you that had the honest self-review to tell me, "Had you written me a ticket, I may not have changed my driving behaviors." You are all very welcome. It was my pleasure to serve you all.

A few months into my career in law enforcement, the people I worked with realized their preconceived notion that I was a nurse in a white cap turned into the realization that I had seen and dealt with a barrage of human tragedy, violence, and the need to restrain physically dangerous people. On any night, maybe in just two hours, several cops in the north area of the city deal with an active assault that turns into a foot pursuit through a neighborhood that ends with two people being injured. On the east side, several cops handle a major car crash with one fatality at the scene, and the other trauma being air-lifted out. On the west side, several cops deal with spouses that stabbed each other in an argument. Your local emergency room staff most likely treated all those people in the next few hours.

The minefield and candy store

Life is balanced and expecting anything else will be a difficult expectation to meet. Yet most moments are indeed an opportunity to feel accomplishment and periodic joy as we step through the minefield and candy store known as our life.

Work is no exception; we spend one-third of our life at our job. We might as well not live in a mindset that means 33% of our life is going to be filled with pain, frustration, disappointment, resentment, and anger. For the great majority, work is a mandatory requirement, but that does not mean it has to be more painful than rewarding. Even if you are not doing what is in your heart's desire for your income, you are mostly contributing, and helping other humans. If you are in the food industry, know that your role is noble. You are feeding people. You, like our drivers, pilots and flight crews, the train industry, and the shipping industry, keep this world moving. All of us that mostly contribute help keep society "moving." Thank you for what you do.

That figure of 33% is below the percentage of your life that will be spent working, because "work" encompasses so much more than the job you do that returns a monetary payment. Work is any activity that involves mental, physical, or emotional effort done to achieve a purpose or result. This is why the title is *Suffer Less "in" Life & Work*, not "at." We are immersed in work and the routines of life; caring for a family member with Alzheimer's, taking out the trash, or standing in line to get your driver's license renewed in the state you just moved to, it is all the work of life. So, a more exact way to look at that percentage is 33% of your life is spent resting and the other 66% is spent working. Even vacation, play, and sex are work, because it is spending energy to achieve a purpose or goal, even if the purpose or goal is pleasure. The good news is that your entire being is not only designed to carry out enormous amounts of work, but we also benefit from it on many levels. Expending energy creates energy.

After my first job cleaning and organizing the garage, my next few jobs required my mom to drive me. My first "real" hired job was after school in the seventh grade, Tuesdays and Thursdays, for two hours, at an old gas station that still worked on cars in Slidell, Louisiana. I would clean the bathrooms, sweep out the two garage bays, sweep out the inside, then mop the inside. If I completed everything, I could move onto the highlight of my "shift," and squeegee a few car windows before mom picked me up. To top off that excitement, I made $2 an hour! I thought to myself that times have really come a long way, because I knew my dad's first hired job was $0.50 a week as an usher at a movie theater in 1940. Before that, he gathered wood scraps that fell off a conveyor belt that crossed a public road to sell to the folks in town for firewood. I loved that gas station job; those guys were so nice to me. I'm laughing because I just this second realized they were nice to me because they didn't have to clean the bathrooms or mop the floor, and although squeegeeing car windows was unbelievably cool to me, they were probably sick and tired of it. But I loved that job, and it was good for me during a hard time in my childhood. My mother was smart to get me moving, busy, and accomplishing.

Even though data shows that 53% of the workforce admits they are unhappy at their work, thus potentially adding to someone's unhealthy state, sometimes just changing the angle of approach in our thought can increase our rewards. I am not unrealistic that everything in this book is magic dust. I also fail at being able to accomplish this all the time. We all have a limit to what we can take. I have reached that limit a few times in life and had to walk away from a job I loved, but it had become unhealthy. I had to take care of my health, happiness, and well-being first.

If an issue is human related, there is rarely a black and white answer. To add further complexity is the fact that the influences that created those issues are normally shades of gray also. That's a human mess of gray. I don't care how solid and steady you believe yourself to be, the human mind is an inconsistent, fickle organ, filled with strengths and weaknesses. Being realistic and gentle with yourself and others is one of the foundations of less suffering. Just because someone owns a company, or is promoted to management, has a title behind their name, or even has become wealthy, does not mean their minds are not still subject to the same fickleness of the employees or a partner or friend in our personal relationships.

Great bosses, friends, and intimate partners know they make mistakes, know we all need and benefit from teamwork, and will accept the input of those working with and under their direction. I have always reminded people to be realistic and gentle with themselves while they attempt to change a habit in life. We are not a light switch that can be simply flicked on or off, but rather we are more like a dimmer that is rolled as one works to stop or start a behavior or learn a new endeavor. Although some behaviors may need to change immediately, most, such as eating healthy daily, are more gentle brightening or darkening of the behavior or thought process we wish to change. Expecting light switch changes in ourselves or others is another hard to meet expectation.

The gift to ourselves of rational detachment

Expecting light switch changes of others or ourselves will only lead to unfair judgment and disappointment. Attempting to practice the functional, and sanity-saving, concept of rational detachment is not always easy. Applying rational detachment is helpful for anyone dealing with other human beings or stressful situations, translating to almost all of us. There are many explanations for the concept of rational detachment, most deal with how we respond, and are equally important definitions. I have created a definition that deals with the deeper first sparks of an issue and deeper solutions.

Rational detachment is the ability to remain personally separate from a difficult or potentially damaging person or situation, even though you must interact with the person or situation to help find a resolution. Rational detachment does not mean turning away from the problem, and nor does it mean not caring. However, it means attempting to not let it upset you, trying to not allow it to stir strong emotions, and trying to not react in a nonproductive manner. Rational detachment means attempting to keep yourself whole and healthy, even though someone may be insulting you, angry, attempting to manipulate you in any way, or even violent. Rational detachment with someone who wants to physically hurt you looks like protecting yourself and stopping the violence as needed, but not hating the person or physically hurting them more than may be required to stop the threat. My repetitive use of "attempt" and "try" is another example of why we are more like rolling dimmers and not on/off light switches. We humans are emotional beings, those emotions can be scary strong. Some people are fantastic at getting under other people's skin, or the situation is too sensitive to not be affected. Therefore, rational detachment is never 100% obtainable. However, it is about getting less of the "mess" from the person or situation on you, or worse inside of you.

"Inside of you" is more than just a momentary upset. It is when we lose hours, days, weeks, or years to a person's behavior or situation.

You are worth more than another person's normal human crisis, or the outward projection of someone's weaknesses, fears, judgment, and insecurities. You are worth so much more than the damage someone else's unchecked ego may want to cause you.

Rational detachment is about not giving someone else your good energy, even though they want to take it from you while you attempt to work alongside them or are trying to help them. If one can get better and better at practicing rational detachment, it leads to less strife and greater calm when someone wants to pull your spirit down while you must help resolve a negative situation. The harsher application of this concept can be taken from most emergency departments. Please excuse the language and the magnitude of the graphics of these two examples, but they are actual examples of the self-protective application of rational detachment and its periodic inability to always work.

Nurses in emergency departments get MF'd on a fairly frequent basis. Between pain, intoxicants, psychiatric crises, long waits, and the periodic refusal to prescribe narcotics, we get "MF'd," as we call it, all too often. Before I ever learned to name the concept of rational detachment, I realized, even though I was the one receiving the verbal, and sometimes tried and accomplished physical assaults, the person was not actually personally angry with me. The application of rational detachment allowed me to calm myself with, "This person doesn't even know my name. They are angry for a plethora of legitimate reasons and few that are not; they don't sign my paycheck, they aren't going to ask me to dinner and a movie, and I won't be asking them for a reference letter for my next job, so what difference does it make if they are cursing me up one side and down the other?" It is my job to get them through their issue. That is why I went into nursing, and why this hospital hired me.

So, rather than saying one defensive word back to them, I tell them I don't blame them for being angry. Get them a ginger ale to get their blood sugar level back up, I bring them a warm blanket from the warmer, and quickly present their case to the upper resident or attending, write the order sheet for the equally busy doctor, tell them why I would like to start an IV, order an X-ray, and give them some pain medication. I have just calmed someone that could have potentially escalated to the point that we had to restrain them, creating a potential for someone to be hurt, including a patient or family member.

Unfortunately, emergency departments are very unstable environments, due to all the stress factors I listed above. I spent my first three years in the emergency department at Charity Hospital in New Orleans. I quickly realized that arguing with patients or their family members during crises was an assured effort in futility, and that I don't win the moment protecting my ego, but I win the shift if we all go home at the end unhurt. I did not win all my shifts, but I started to get better at deescalating people by validating them and then meet their needs when able. Life, and moments, got much easier and safer.

The second example of rational detachment that has its limits is during a pediatric critical event. One role of the charge nurse is to delegate the nurses that are to work on an inbound trauma. Most emergency department nurses do not really gravitate towards pediatric trauma, and I don't blame them. I would be in the medication/supply room with three other nurses drawing up medications or gathering supplies for a procedure and the charge nurse leans their head into the room and says, "The helicopter is fifteen minutes out with an x-year old ejected from a car crash, apparent multiple fractures, and an older brother fatality at the scene. Who wants to work it?" I looked around and I could have sworn there were four of us in here, and now I stand alone. "I guess that leaves me," I say, and the charge nurse says, "I'll go find you two more." The child arrives and an entire trauma team works trying to save the child's life.

At that moment, we are all using rational detachment, still doing our best, but not allowing the magnitude of the tragedy to get in the way of our professional knowledge and skills. The child dies. But the person in room 7 is having an active heart attack and the cardiac catheter lab is ready for them, and a seventy-year-old is having problems breathing in room 15 so we all keep working. Thirty minutes later, the rest of the family arrives, and the attending and I go out to talk with them. It's devastating. Their lives and families are shattered. After the family spends time with the child. I go with a nurse's aide to transport the child's body to the morgue, so they don't have to do it alone. A few hours later, on the drive home, for the second time in my now long career, I pulled over because the vision of the child and the spirit-shattering news of informing the family their second beautiful young child also died came rushing back, and I can no longer see to drive through the tears. Rational detachment allowed us to give fast, efficient, exceptional care, everyone did everything right, and both children's fate was sealed at the moment of impact. I didn't stand a chance to override the appropriate powerful release of tears and sadness that *every* front-line worker deserves to periodically have experience and release if they feel the need. The visions I had while crying that morning were like a slideshow of horrors changed every 1/10th of a second. I let out so much more than just that night's tragedies that morning. I did not even attempt to stop it. I let the tears roll until they were done on their own.

Rational detachment helps

After someone comes to me and shares an issue in which rational detachment is part of the answer, I usually hear the following statement after they get back to me with a follow-up, "That is much harder in application than I expected, but it helps."

"Harder than expected, but it helps," is an initial key to everything I am about to trust you with from my life to assist you in suffering less. No matter what, life requires a little effort. Expending some upfront energy prevents far more pain and frustration than the larger energy spent repairing a situation or relationship of any type. It is also healthier and calmer to our spirit to prevent than to constantly repair. As long as we are breathing, our peace, contentment, and happiness will always remain fleeting. That is balance. Yet spending upfront energy helps keep the balance leaning towards less bad.

Although the constant balance of good and bad can never be removed, we try. Such as, although never obtainable, we will often work to a detrimental level to experience only joyful emotions. Our difficulty accepting that life is filled with balance, with ups and downs, failures and accomplishments, bulls-eyes and mistakes, sets us up for high levels of disappointment and even some disrespect. Getting mad or upset with all the inevitable not so good is hard on the self, and those around us that get upset at unavoidable balance. We are all victims of this type of thinking, and we are all capable of these thoughts and behaviors when we are upset with setbacks. Our levels of peace and productivity increase through the acceptance and practice of realistic expectations of human capabilities and with accepting balance. This can be accomplished with a minimal upfront expenditure of time and energy to move towards greater prevention. Peace and rewards in almost every aspect of our life can follow when we accept that the bad happens, too.

WIDER ANGLES:

THE DIFFERENCE BETWEEN TOUGH AND STRONG

Over the years, I have developed some creative, simple wider angles to help me see myself, others, and some tougher subjects with greater acceptance, tolerance, understanding, and forgiveness. My theories usually bend textbook definitions or other standards, but help me to further understand the human condition in an easier way. I figure anything that can help make working with our complexities easier is worth doing. I know these angles are not set in stone, mostly subjective, and flexible. I was a teenager when I came up with my first one—I first practiced with this one of whimsical humor.

I was walking in the pasture of my grandparents' place. I would ride my motorcycle to go visit them from college, maybe a two-hour ride. My grandfather, Daddy Whit, cracked up when I told him, "I think cows possess the answer to all the world problems, but they just can't tell us." He knew me well enough to know I was joking. The wild thing is, I have grown to wonder if I wasn't onto something. This is not the wider angle I am about to share with you, but it is the obscure first one I cut my teeth on.

As I stood in the pasture surrounded by the cows, watching their behaviors, I thought maybe cows possess the answer to all the world problems, but they just can't tell us. They are, for the most part, calm but paying attention. They will defend themselves, but would rather avoid trouble, and their tail calmly swishes attempting but knowing it will only partially help rid the flies. The only things the female cows seem to care about is peacefully eating quality grass and their offspring's well-being. Those behaviors appeared rather accepting and self-aware to me, maybe they know . . .? The next person I told my thoughts to after my granddad was my grandmother. Being a no-nonsense nurse her whole life, she immediately furrowed her brow and said, "Are you kidding me? Cows are so dumb they won't even move out of the way of a train." She huffed and said, "You really have to pick a major other than sociology fast, it's warping you." The next time you are close to cows, give this one a go.

The actual wider angle I would like to share has nothing to do with cows, but has to do with separating the difference between "tough" and "strong." Remember, I am bending definitions for ease and simplicity to help with our humanness, and to help make potentially or difficult situations, thoughts, and emotions easier.

I believe that being tough is a hindrance to self-exploration and growth, however, being strong aids in those. I fine-tuned this wider angle through watching myself at times be afraid to be imperfect, or being unnecessarily self-protective, or not wanting to admit I had made a mistake. Tough is like a thick, solid piece of leather that is hard to get through, but strong is like a flexible piece of bungee that can stretch and bend to accomplish a task yet remain a flexible, strong bungee.

It is the difference between saying, "I'm so tough I can handle anything," but then deflecting or suppressing our more painful emotions. As opposed to a strong person who has the strength to experience their more painful emotions, then learn and grow from them. "Bring it on, let's take a look," more accurately describes strong. I've never understood the label assigned to a man crying, sometimes being called a wimp, baby, or weak. When that person is showing the strength to allow a powerful emotion in, to experience a sensitivity, then grant a deeper self-exploration to fully experience a sensitive moment. That is true strength.

Labeling someone as weak or not tough enough to deal with life because they are seeing a counselor is really the extreme opposite of those stigma labels. It takes strength to first be able to say, "I need help." Then it takes further strength to sit down in front of a counselor and say, "Let's open me up and see what's in there," without the tough walls of rationalizations or painting a picture of perfection that you have never made major mistakes that set you back or hurt others. Strength is what allows you to take those difficult steps to raw, bold, and beneficial self-exploration.

I also believe that being tough is a setup to miss a percentage of our life, while being strong is having the courage to say, "Let me experience all my life, let me look at and sit with some sad, hurtful, mistaken or imperfect parts too. So I can help make the weight of life easier."

CHAPTER 2

ALLOWING YOURSELF TO REMAIN A STUDENT

"If you are not willing to learn, no one can help you.
If you are determined to learn, no one can stop you."
—Zig Ziglar

Our everything

Your entire life is experienced by the same organ that is processing these letters into words and an organized thought: your brain. Although our lives are experienced through our five basic senses and then interpreted through our mental, physical, and emotional aspects of our being, ultimately, whether pain or pleasure, happy or sad, love or fear, every part of the processing of your life is carried out in your brain. Our brain is the organ, our mind is the brain functioning. Our mind keeps us safe, yet also gets us into trouble. Our mind's hand us our ups and our downs, our loving actions, and our selfish ones; it can be our best friend in pleasure or our worst in depression, narcissism, or suicidal thoughts. We know so much about the human mind and there are still recesses left uncharted, but not as many as we used to think. Thank goodness the old myth that we only use 10% of our brain was discovered not to be true. Magnetic resonance imaging (MRI) research shows us that we use most of our mind, even when we sleep. I'll miss the 10% myth; it gave me a great rationalization for some of my mistakes in life.

Rationalizations are at times important gifts and some of the widest lies our minds produce, with the brain's average count of 80 billion nerve cells. That is not a typo. We rationalize when we use self-protective reasoning to explain or justify an inappropriate or unhealthy behavior, action, or attitude. Rationalizations have their place; they protect us from an overload of our imperfect humanness. But just like our ego that drives our rationalizations, they can rob us of our opportunities to explore our minds and life, grow and do better. I loved a scene in the great 1983 movie *The Big Chill* between Jeff Goldblum and Tom Berenger, which truly sums up the frequency and importance of our rationalizations. They are discussing what is the most important thing in their lives. Berenger thinks it's sex, but Goldblum thinks it is rationalizations. Goldblum says, "Don't knock rationalization. Where would we be without it? I don't know anyone who could get through the day without two or three juicy rationalizations. They're more important than sex." Berenger says, "Ah, come on. Nothing's more important than sex." Goldblum replies, "Oh yeah? Have you ever gone a week without a rationalization?"

Why do we rationalize and how does it contribute to our unhappiness? To do that, let us first go back to Sociology 101 and the theory of Johari's Window. Like all life, the application of this self-awareness, and thus peace creating theory, is harder than only knowing its explanation. This theory was created by two psychologists in 1955, by the name of Joseph Luft (1916–2014) and Harrington Ingham (1916–1995). The name Johari is derived from them blending their first names. Johari's window is a square with four squares in it that looks like a four-pane window. Each window represents a level of self-knowledge. The first pane is what we know about ourselves and what others also know, the second pane is what we know about ourselves, but others do not, the third is what others know about us, but we do not, and the final pane is what neither we nor another know about us. In most discussions about this theory, it is healthiest to work to increase the size of the first two windows and shrink the two windows that hold information about ourselves we do not know.

To accomplish this greater self-awareness, we must be willing and able to hear input from others about ourselves to help downsize what others know about us, but we do not, and we must be able to dig deep inside ourselves to help downsize the window of what others don't know about us and nor do we. I remember about the same time I learned about this window; I was walking to the cafeteria on campus with three of my friends and we stopped to talk to some women leaving the cafeteria. As we walked away from them, my buddies said, "How come you always rub your eyes when you talk to women? I've seen you do it frequently." By them telling me that and I being willing to hear it, I moved something about myself from the "what others know about me, and I do not" to the "what others know about me, and so do I" windowpane. They were right. I paid attention and noticed I was doing it, and accomplished stopping the nervous behavior rather quickly. That was a relatively easy bit of self-knowledge to accept. However, over the years, hearing information got tougher as I found myself in relationships, both personal and professional, that forced me to hear what was being presented to me about myself. To this day, my ego and my ability to rationalize can stop me from hearing or processing painful self-information; yet my fear of having my faults and weaknesses being pointed out has diminished over the years. I can only work on what I have the courage to see.

Although the information about myself became harder to hear as it began to expose deeper faults and weaknesses than just rubbing my eyes, life became easier because I had more accurate self-awareness to work with. My efforts to work with these flaws, those I could acknowledge anyway, decreased many problems inside myself and in my relationships. I am still human and some days it is easier to work on myself and accept input than other days. Although sometimes it is hard or even disturbing to hear, if we look at ourselves and don't reject it or rationalize it away, but instead work with it, the ability to hear someone else's input about ourselves only makes life easier and less painful.

All living organisms share characteristics that are required to stay alive, thrive, and continue to reproduce their species. The characteristic known as variation and adaptation is why foxes learned to live in cities, why viruses mutate into various strains, or why birds learned to migrate south to find more food. If organisms do not vary and adapt, they will die, and their species will perish. For us humans, variation and adaptation is also incredibly important in almost every aspect of our life, including ease and growth.

We humans are included in these amazing characteristics that are required to stay alive physically. We also have many levels to our being that can also become damaged or die, besides death of the entire body, if we do not continue to vary and adapt. A harsh but realistic example is living in the presence of any type of abuse, whether physical, mental, emotional, financial, or sexual. If the victim does not vary and adapt by leaving, even if the victim does not die, parts of their spirit can die. Bullying by an abusive boss or colleague in the workplace can produce the same weakening of a part of a person, unless we also learn mental and emotional adaptation to keep our spirit alive. In some less dangerous examples, that ability to adapt could be as simple as changing how you allow that person to affect you. This connects back to applying rational detachment to decrease the effect negative people or situations have on us. Using this often only means one must adapt their thought process, so the less than ideal anything has less of an effect on you. Or, if needed, adapting and varying by walking away from a job or relationship altogether if needed for your well-being.

A friend of mine was great at this on an impressive level. This person had a boss that was very threatened by their intelligence, experiences, and capabilities. Their boss would show shunning and punitive behaviors, completely wasting this capable person's full potential, and would assign them menial tasks, such as moving the contents of a storage room to another storage room. This wise, flexible person knew they only had to hang in there for a few more years, but then had another option brewing. "Okay!" in an excited, happy tone became their chant every time the boss assigned one of these highly underutilizing tasks or, if left idling, they would take online courses during the shunning periods and further accelerate their already high knowledge level. My friend has a rather strong personality, firm in convictions and consistent as a day-to-day person, but able to maintain peace within and outwardly by the application of variation and adaptation. This friend made it through this potentially rough period and has moved onto those much greener pastures that awaited.

The education of life, self, and better

One of the easiest ways to accomplish increasing variation and adaptation, in all aspects of your life, is to consider yourself a student of life and humanness until the day you die. Many have grown to hate, fear, and dread change, but constant change is one of the few constants in our life and is necessary. So why not embrace it? I had the joy of having eighteen of my years in nursing occur in teaching hospitals. How the field of medicine does things is constantly changing, varying, and adapting due to the ever-changing findings of medical research from around the world. Your entire life is no different for two reasons: you are always growing and changing, and the world and people around you are also in constant flux. I think it is one of the contributing factors to our high rates of divorce in the twenty to thirty-five age groups as we change so much during those years. I know I was changing a noticeable amount every three or four years through my twenties to mid-thirties.

Still at fifty-eight, I know every five years or so I seem to be a slightly different person, and I want to be a different person. In college, I dated a woman who summed it up with a passionate response to me attempting to give her a compliment. I said, "Don't ever change," to which she replied without hesitation, "Why in the world would you wish that on me!?" After age forty-five or so, besides the gray hair and easier weight gain, I became calmer inside, more accepting, my view of life and society became even wider, and the shades of gray became wider, too. The wider shades of gray brought me more peace, not less. By being able to adapt and change the way I saw life and the world around me, everything inside of me became more peaceful, not more turbulent. After its only minimal initial disruption, change brought me peace.

Human behavior, as an individual or in group dynamics, has so many influences. Most are difficult to clearly label, or even sometimes to say which influence was the strongest driving force. The human condition is messy and multifaceted, and when it comes to why we did something frequently, "D, all the above," is far more often the answer. When we only assign one influence for why we did, or did not, do something, we are often leaving out a significant percentage of influence and potential growth. While arguing, we are often quick to assign one reason to our partner's behaviors for something they did that we don't agree with. Why are our personal inconsistencies and individuality so varied in the little picture, but so alike in the big picture?

If the average human mind is made up of over 80 billion neurons, that would mean each person is guaranteed to be wired differently from every other person. I love to play chess, and I have played for a long time, but I am only an average player because my mind has its limits and strengths. I play to continue to exercise my mind and because no two games are the same. Just like no two people or two days of our life are the same. The chess board has sixty-four squares and thirty-two pieces at the start of the game. In the first three exchanges in a chess game, there are over 9 million potential moves. Now consider the strengths and weaknesses of every human mind, the fact that those 80 billion neurons will never line up the same, and now attempt to fathom the potential differences between two minds, or all minds. What would the chess possibilities skyrocket to if we doubled the board and chess pieces to one-hundred-twenty squares and sixty-four pieces? That is still only a minuscule fraction of the 80 billion neurons composing our brain, which is the foundation of each person's unique processing abilities, which are likely to have a considerably greater combination of potential strengths and weaknesses between any two individuals than a game of chess.

I share these ridiculous astronomical number combinations with you to give us all reasons to never stop exercising or being gentle with our minds' assured imperfections or the minds around us. In no way does this negate the periodic need for each of us to protect ourselves from some of those minds when needed. The factors for the variations and compatibility of more than two minds skyrocket even further if discussing group and social dynamics, every person added to the group increases the factor by another 80 billion neurons.

Yet another important contribution to who we are, how we were influenced or not, and how our minds receive and express information: is, of course, nature versus nurture. Nature is what you are born with, and nurture is how you were raised and influenced. Neglected or nurtured, criticized or praised, or coddled or encouraged to accomplish on your own all fall into nurture. Other layers of influence are our family, friends, culture, ethnicity, race, government, resource availability, religion, media, social media, and the social norms and morays of your region.

The reassuring thing in this myriad of influences on who we are and how each unique mind operates is, for the most part, a percentage of the human mind is malleable. There are parts of our mind that are indeed hard or impossible to rewire, but lucky for us, a percentage is flexible. We can adapt for our health and peace. Not only is our mind capable of change and growth, but it thrives on it when encouraged. It is this percentage of your amazing brain that wants you to remain a student of life, self, others, and of better. It is this percentage of your mind that is willing, wanting, and seeking to never stop filling your life with greater exploration, peace, contributions, and self-reward. Your 80 billion neurons are always wanting for more. It is only our ego and staunch, self-protective emotions that lie to us and tell us we are done learning and growing.

The willingness and excitement to embrace this spirit of new growth is giving yourself the gift of deepening your exploration, and greatly increasing your ease in so many directions. Accomplishing graduation from high school or college should be seen as graduating school, but not the end of your education. Mahatma Gandhi summed it up well, "Live as if you were to die tomorrow. Learn as if you were to live forever." Our graduation from our education should be considered our last breath of life, not a diploma.

Although I love to learn, school was not easy for me, quite the opposite. Until the eighth grade, school was damaging me, and almost succeeded. I should fine tune that. School was not bad. My issues were making school difficult for me. I grew up with horrible migraine headaches several days a week and a few learning disabilities that had me struggling at the bottom of my class. I somewhat missed the first seven years of school. To this day, I joke in seriousness, and only slightly exaggerated, that I carry my driver's license so I can sign my name correctly. I am an extremely poor speller. The mistakes you see in this book are because I foolishly made changes after the final professional edit, while practicing what I preach, "I can say that better." One of my learning disabilities, I was told from testing when I was younger, is phonetic deafness. In my case, that means that I do not hear the short vowels correctly. That is just one weakness in my very imperfect brain.

In the eighth grade, the headaches started going away, and I let go of worrying about a ranking compared to others. That combination did the trick, and off I went, loving to learn for the first time in my life. Off I paddled down the bayou of life with greater rewards. Remaining a student is not always easy; there is homework, and very few of us loved the homework. Yet if you want the true tangible rewards, one of which is greater ease throughout your day, some practice will always be required.

The difference is listening to a TED Talk or a fantastic sermon in church, nodding your head in agreement, telling yourself, "Yes, that will make my life easier and more fulfilling," then walking out the door and applying none of what you just agreed was applicable life-enhancing information. Life enhancement does require effort, personal homework, and a little daily practice to accomplish beneficial change. But first one must accept that all lessons are not going to be easy to hear or accomplish at first. I knew an interesting lady, many years ago, who lived across the street from a huge church. Every Sunday, she would leave to go to her church service while this big church's parking lot was emptying cars from one of its services. She would sit at the end of her driveway, with her left blinker on, waiting, and waiting, but no one would stop exiting the parking lot long enough to let her make her turn. She had the funniest monologue about how they had forgotten the sermon between walking out of the church and leaving the parking lot. She would go on about how she knows for a fact they did not teach self-centered driving in the sermon. "Application, application, don't just hear it, apply it, let me have a turn to get out of my driveway, do unto others as you would have done unto you . . ." Then she would say, ". . . and if they did teach self-centered driving in the sermon, then shame on that pastor, but they sure did listen and accomplish the application of that sermon, didn't they?"

Information that is not easy to hear is often the information capable of helping us the most. Just as the surgeon must sometimes cut before healing can occur, we too periodically can accelerate self-growth by also opening ourselves to painful self-information. The interesting thing about opening these rawer parts of the self is that part of you can then often heal stronger than the original trauma. As fibers form to heal a broken bone, they crisscross, overlay, and "cement" together, often forming stronger tissue than before the trauma. Trauma to our being is no different, it has the potential to make us stronger. I am going to give you an example that will be a little gross to hear, equaling "trauma" to your ego, or the damage an unhealthy person can cause an individual or to a group. Yet hearing and applying this truth can strengthen you and increase your peace after the initial "trauma" of hearing unpleasant words and a hard self-awareness. By the nature of the human mind, we all have hypocrisies and double standards. The human mind is not consistent and self-honest enough to see itself or its outward expression with perfect accuracy. We are incapable of always being and saying externally what beliefs we feel or hold inside. That is hard to hear, even for me; I hate my hypocrisy and double standards, unavoidable but still embarrassing. One example is that I teach to let people finish their thoughts and sentences, but I too sometimes interrupt people with my excitement while they are talking. However, by me doing the painful work of hearing that, then accepting its truth, I am then opened to look out for them, and hopefully catch a few more than I would have never caught had I told myself, "No way, I'm not a hypocrite. I never do such things." "Growing pains," sum it up.

I'm laughing as I read what I just wrote, that's a harsh paragraph. But I am, and we all are, hypocritical to some degree. This is normal and okay, and is one of the reasons this work is so hard at first. If one can accept this hard to hear reality of humanness, then one can be mindful to catch a few more hypocrisies and double standards before they slip out. As I like to say about many subjects related to human behavior, it never gets easy, but it can get easier.

The ability to be professional about all our messed-up humanness varies. In periods of my life, I have been great at not getting my humanness on others, and at other times my humanness spilled all over other people. I feel trusting to share this with you because I know only humans will read this, and so I am not alone. We are all amazing, faulted, strong, slightly confused, more confused at other times, insightful, wise yet foolish at times, walking and periodically stumbling through this life. With brains capable, imperfect, awesome, unique, and, at times, stubborn. Our minds want to be fed and stimulated to do better. Allow yourself to accept there is so much more to learn, even in your professional field, and throughout our daily life.

What stops us?

Looking at some factors that hold us tight to resisting change, growth, and expanded self and social knowledge can help us remove some of these limiting blocks. Again, our ability to vary and adapt is innate in all living organisms, we are made for it, and for the most part, it is good for us. If constant change is here to stay, which it is, resisting is futile, and another set up for frustration and trouble. We resist change for several reasons, but basically it boils down to a few categories: fear of an unexpected outcome produces anxiety and creates some limited control, and we don't like to give up control. Pushing past this fear is going to require us to expend more energy at first. Unfortunately, change is often accompanied by unnecessary criticism. Constructive input during change is a completely different subject than criticism and should always be welcomed.

Input and criticism are two completely different subjects; input from staff or a partner is incredibly important during change, and for daily input and improvement potential. It shows by example that, whether a personal relationship or you own the company or manage it, remaining in the frame of mind that we remain a student in life and work pays off in unlimited directions. The greatest bosses, most functional, and healthy companies or departments I ever worked for accepted huge amounts of input from the staff before, during, and after implementing change. The worse ones took no input from the lower levels and made the huge mistake of thinking their way was always right. Narcissism and narrow-mindedness in business or management is often detrimental to profit, productivity, and peace. This type of one directional thinking created both an unhealthy work environment and management often had minimal respect from their staff. Thank goodness the great majority of my supervisors were fantastic; still human, still made mistakes, but fantastic in so many aspects.

I have a good friend that opened a very successful company many years ago. I love her philosophy on remaining a scholar from a productive and holistically rewarding angle, even in the workplace. I know for a fact she retained the attitude of a scholar of life, too. It shows in her ease, humor, peace, and ability to change directions in her personal life when humanness was preventing growth and exploration. Although wishing to remain anonymous, because the company is still in operation, she shares this:

"The most important objective in starting our company was to create an environment where people would have fun working and finding a way to be creative with their career. My business partner and I always felt that the top-down philosophy of making policy decisions was ill-conceived. In the past, we had both been on the receiving end, as top management passed their new policies down the chain, expecting unequivocal acceptance as well as efficient and prompt implementation of the new policy. We witnessed firsthand the resistance of our peers by such management mandates. More times than not, management became frustrated as their new policies failed to function as intended.

We wanted the bottom-up philosophy to be available to all company personnel. Our primary objective was to empower our team to feel respected as an important part of the company, and, most importantly, to empower the individual to act in ways that would enhance the company's viability. We wanted all team members to know management welcomed and encouraged their creativity. We felt this was the best way to not only feel we cared about their career and place in the company, but to know we cared. Our reward for such a relatively easy and respectful way of looking out for our employees' higher level of well-being was, they also looked out for the company holistically.

A company that accomplishes this kind of individual empowerment for their staff to create their own destiny, creates an environment that enriches all concerned. Of course, when owners and employees of a company are happy... guess what follows? Yes, the clients... and they are willing to pay premium prices for premium work. It's a profitable situation and a healthy work environment. The staff provides exceptional customer service from their nurtured, but mostly self-built, pride with joy and ease, not from surface written policy stating they need to. Sadly, corporate America has forgotten how this works, and fewer employees of today have ever experienced such a functional, inclusive, and rewarding environment."

Their approach has worked well for fifty years and is still going strong. I share this because it reinforced the forever a student philosophy. It also shows that even though they were the owners, they wanted to learn from any and every direction possible. That holds true for any field on any level, including our personal life. I have always found it interesting that we often feel being a professional is limited only to our work. I wish to spread my professionalism into my personal life and relationships also. I want to attempt to be a professional human being, not only a professional at my work. Granted, this can be harder in our personal or intimate relationships, and family can be a whole other level of discussion. Our more personal relationships can have sensitive hair-trigger buttons that are embarrassingly easier to have activated, and unfortunately, so much harder to reset. One of many criteria to being a professional is ongoing education in your field, and I hope in your life also. I don't want to be self-limiting by only being a professional in my occupation, I want to be a professional in life, and in being a human.

Learning to step out of ourselves

The ability to step out of your thought process and into someone else's has its most positive results when it is for the purpose of problem resolution. It is a hard exercise, but it produces several rewards for our efforts. It not only alleviates a percentage of my suffering in life and work, because of how it creates calm and solves problems in my immediate presence, it also allows me to extend myself to helping others. One other benefit is I feel less alone in my fears and hopes when I step outside myself. I see most have many of the same fears that I carry. Our inability to even care to place ourselves in another person's place has become a contributing factor to the detriment of individuals and society. It has become an exercise that we only do for the purposes of defense, potential manipulation, sales, or profit, rather than using it also for the good of all. It is 50% of chess strategy, or any sport. Yet, still, there again that is for defense or to win, the benefits can reach much further than self-gain.

It can help in an immediately unstable situation, as seen in someone losing rational control, whether in the hospital as a nurse, on the streets in law enforcement, or for anyone anywhere. This technique works no matter what your role; customer service, call centers, checkout counters at the grocery store, or just walking down the road of life. The exercise of stepping into someone else's thought process can be active or passive. Active is the easier way, if they will cooperate, just ask them what their immediate need is. Some people won't help you that easily because they share little of themselves, or some because they are in a high-level crisis and can't. Passive is harder and leaves more to chance, that is trying to figure it out on your own.

Without knowing, I first learned to apply this one average eventful night in my second year of nursing, still at Charity Hospital in downtown New Orleans in the mid-1980s. Eventful was Charity's normal. Our voices often rise in volume when we are headed into crisis, so emergency nurses become very attuned to escalating voices. It could mean one of your fellow workmates is about to be in danger, and we all move towards the sound to help and protect each other. I worked with two tall nurses that matched each other in extreme stature. If they were facing each other and talking, you would question if you were looking at two six-foot five-inch men standing two feet apart or two roman columns.

One night, the three of us were on a shift together, working up a patient who just arrived in the trauma side of the department known as "The Accident Room." We heard male voices escalating and all three of us quickly stepped into the hall. At the other end of the hall was an extremely large naked man with three huge hospital police officers bladed off in front of him. He was screaming, "Back off man, don't you f*^*^ing touch me!" The three of us headed down the hall and these two giants were in front of me. I pushed my little skinny self through them and jokingly said, "I've got this." As I squeezed through them, without missing a beat, they both grabbed me under each armpit, lifted me up and placed me back behind them. I kept my legs in a walking motion while in the air, and down the hall in the origin formation we went. Before we arrived, this giant of a naked man turned and pushed out the backdoor into a hallway that led either to the front of the hospital or back around to the emergency waiting room. The five of them ran after him and I turned around and went back down the hall to head him off in the waiting room. I now realize, had I arrived first, I would have been easily flattened by this man. They had already run through the waiting room and out onto the back ramp by the time I made it to the waiting room, past all the obstacles and people in the hall.

As I stopped at the front of the large waiting room, I saw they had caught up to him and more police were there also. Remember, I was only twenty-two years old, so there were fewer filters. I attempted to ease what had just occurred before the eyes of a waiting room full of people and I asked the waiting room, "Did anyone see a huge naked man run through here with a bunch of cops chasing him?" knowing good and well they had all witnessed it seconds before my arrival. About thirty of them said nothing, but held up their right arms, and pointed to the door with dropped jaws.

Thank goodness, two seconds later, they all started to laugh. Double thank goodness, it was New Orleans, naked does not surprise that city.

The man was rolled back into room 5 a few minutes later, now restrained to the gurney. I started to let him know I only wanted to help him and asked him what happened. He was appropriately very angry and said with a throat clenched in anger, "I've got to pee. I told her I have to pee, I still have to pee." I immediately helped him urinate, since he was restrained. The second the urine starts to come out, his voice calmed only slightly, and his eyes teared up just a little, and he said to me, "All I had to do was pee, and now look at me. I kept telling her I have to pee, look at me now, are they going to arrest me?"

I felt so bad for so many reasons, the first being I could tell he was a gentle spirit. I reassured him he would not be arrested, he calmed, and

I cut his restraints off since they were normally just three-inch strips of sheets we had torn at the beginning of the shift. We unfortunately had to restrain several people a night, and if no one was seriously injured, Hospital Police did not arrest. Nor did they have the time to arrest people. I wasn't wasting this preventable situation; I went and asked the X-ray tech about her side of the story. She felt bad it happened and admitted she had kept saying, "One more X-ray, we are almost done," and told me she often had to say that. She too, like me, was young, fast experienced, but able to remain a student and said from now on she'll start asking, "Can you wait until we are done?" I'm surprised that tiny X-ray room didn't catch on fire with how many X-rays it took every twenty-four hours. I respected her rush too.

But I did not stop there. I dug into myself also. It was after that night that I started getting out in front of that wall of people ready to restrain during escalating situations to attempt to talk to the person starting to lose rational control. Being one of balance, I am realistic, human behavior does not always allow for these approaches. If time allowed, I would attempt to step into the perspective of that person's thought process. Or just outright ask them what they need. More often than not it worked. It paid off in law enforcement too.

Even though in law enforcement I did not deal with the same volume of crisis as most 9-1-1 responding officers, all my years were in a uniform and a marked police car. Most of those thirteen years I worked alone, often in rural situations, and unfortunately, I did upset a lot of people by informing them of the court order I was assigned to work against them for ninety days. I calmed initial anger hundreds of times, with only needing to call for backup maybe six or seven times. By the end of those years, I was working over 350 court orders a year. Being able to place myself into their thought process kept me safe repeatedly. It works well, especially if the action of balanced compassion immediately follows, until it can't for my own safety. The attorneys were great to work with and often thanked me for helping them resolve a difficult and often long-standing situation. I just treated all parties with respect and remained neutral while working towards resolution. By professionally doing my job with holistic compassion, I had helped every party involved resolve a few thousand civil cases: the plaintiff, the defendant who had no idea they had options to resolve their predicament, the attorney wanting to collect for their client, and the courts were cleared of all those unresolved cases. Over the years I even had a few judges thank me for my work. The work was hard, but highly rewarding and helpful to so many. Although I worked alone, I did not accomplish it alone. It was teamwork involving my sergeant and corporal, and a fantastic bunch of clerks back at the office that professionally helped me daily for all those years. Thank you all, fantastic teamwork! If we include all parties, together we helped thousands of people get a major headache out of their lives'. Thank you all for your persistent hard work! I could not have done it without you.

That night's hospital crisis changed my approach to escalating crises when time and behaviors allowed. I could not have made it to that man in time to ask him what he needed to make everything okay at that minute, he had bolted before we arrived at the end of the hall. But what if someone else had slightly dropped their defensive posture and asked how they could help him? What did he need? Before that night, I would have just joined in the wall of people ready to restrain him. Remaining a scholar, and attempting to experience someone else's reality, allows me to evaluate, learn, and attempt more effective resolution. There are almost always more ways to resolve an issue than first appears. After learning this ability to step into someone else's point of view, everything got easier, it was empathy in action.

"There is a better way for everything. Find it."
—Thomas Edison

Whether someone is at a low level of anxiety or a high level of crisis, once you discover their thought processes and needs, if safely, legally, and appropriately possible, tell them you will meet that need if you can, and then do so as soon as possible. As well, attempt to validate their fears and needs that you can without encouraging fantasy or dangerous thinking. It is as easy as letting someone go ahead of you in a grocery store line because it is your day off, you are not rushed, and you have heard them sigh twice, and they are restless waiting in line behind you. Or drive as if you are surrounded by friends and family in the other cars. Isn't it meaningful when someone is bluntly courteous and helps you move into a busy lane of traffic by letting up on the gas to open a space for you? At most, that positive contributing action of kindness took three seconds to accomplish. One act, and not only did you accomplish something positive but who knows what negative you prevented, or how much did your easy giving action mean to the receiver? Perhaps you prevented an accident, a road rage incident, or maybe you helped restore a speck of someone's faith in humanity. The desire to suffer less in life and work is greatly aided by helping those around you suffer less also. Our go-to mantras of today, such as, "That's not my problem," "I am not responsible for how others feel," or "I am not part of the problem," are a detriment to the well-being of individuals, community, and yes, to ourselves. One quick litmus test to reinforce this; does it upset you if someone tailgates you, cuts you off with an unsafe lane change, or interrupt you while you are sharing a thought or idea and tells you your thoughts or beliefs are wrong? We do affect each other, you can make a positive difference every day with minimal effort or compromise, and some days you can make a substantial difference.

Life and work will keep getting easier, personal rewards will grow in many directions, and you will continue to make a difference on a wider scope, if you commit to remaining a student of self and life.

CHAPTER 3

MAKING LIFE EASIER WITH THOUGHT, NOT FORCE

"As a single footstep will not make a path on the earth, so a
single thought will not make a pathway in the mind. To make
a deep physical path, we walk again and again. To make a
deep mental path, we must think over and over the kind of
thoughts we wish to dominate our lives."
—Henry David Thoreau

(I am sharing this quote a second time because it is so
helpful to more peaceful thoughts. Please forgive my often
intentionally repetitive nature. I am that way with myself, too.
I do so because this quote is accurate.)

My next job after cleaning the gas station bathrooms was stocking
shelves at a drugstore during the summer after seventh grade. Then
came the acid application and scraping of the dry, rock-hard barnacles
off the bottom of sailboats, the summer after the eighth grade. I'm not
going to list all my jobs, but I will introduce you to the ones that had a
more notable influence, some positive and some negative. Even the ones
with some crummy aspects helped me navigate life, bosses, workmates,
internal compromise, outright abuse, and handed me some positive
rewards also. Only somewhat unfortunately for me, none of those
rewards provided me with impressive financial reimbursement. Due to
discovering a key to my own personal happiness at a young age, I have
always chosen to pursue social contribution as my career as opposed
to big bucks. My bank account has suffered for that choice, but the

personal growth and rewards have far out-shined the lack of monetary reimbursement. I know CEOs with salaries that could cause even Pavlov's dog to drool, but admit to me, they have trouble sleeping due to the choices they have made in the name of profit and stock dividends. The number of people that have shared this type of statement with me is significant. They admit they are starting to see the longer and wider effects of profit over people, or the issues caused by shaving expenses that negatively affect society, customers, and employees. Some directly share this internal conflict, and some passively share this by saying they are jealous that my careers helped people daily. Saying something along the lines of, ". . . sometimes I wish I had made a choice to help people like that." Most are older, with more time to look back with greater clarity that is less about profit and more about cause and effect. Thus, I can promise most bosses are not heartless, even if their action in the name of profit, or at times actual company financial stability, outwardly appears to give them that label. Those trusted confessions, like so many from all walks of life, are another reason I am inspired to write. They also remind me there is not a human demographic that is not strained, to some degree, by the many stressors of our complex times.

Many people express unhappiness at work, painful thoughts concerning human behaviors and frustrations with life in general. I know we feel and are affected by these strains even when we hold them in. Thank goodness most of us do express ourselves and are both the sender and receiver of these needed trusted verbal expressions of catharsis. Also, adding to our daily stressors is the present-day high levels of self-protection, displayed in quick defensiveness, that so often is lightning fast, harsh, often out of proportion, or outright unnecessary.

The across-the-board stressors that unite all of us in further commonality is many. It is a good thing both appropriate self-protection and looking out for others can be pursued at the same time. It may not seem like it on the surface, but our youth are figuring that out, and giving their time and energy to causes their hearts can support. Many companies are encouraging their staff to pick a non-profit to support both with hands-on volunteering preferably, and financial support if they wish. Some neat feedback that further inspired me is I have also had a few of those same high-level executives come back to me later and tell me my tidbits of advice greatly helped them. They informed me they found ways to merge the two and are finding greater reward in their heart, and better sleep at night. I would like to thank all of you over the years who have trusted me with their life and work stressors, and then told me the new angle of approach helped you see a situation from a less distressing perspective or different corrective actions. Your self-awareness, honesty, encouragement, desire to keep learning about your humanness, and your trust in me, helped me also.

For I am human with clear eyesight as to the harsh realities, I too could become pessimistic about my feelings and actions. Seeing with my own eyes decreased stress and increased joy and reward in someone that want to try something simple and positive to improve their spirits health and hearing the feedback from so many people accomplishing positive change, instills in me further belief in us humans. Your trust and your feedback encourages me to never give up.

Texas has some seriously high flyovers at its interstate intersections. One morning in my first year, I saw a car stalled at the top of a flyover slowing and backing up traffic. I activated my overhead lights and pulled up behind it. We are in a single lane sharp right curve; I am guessing two-hundred feet off the ground, there is minimal space for me to stand between the passenger window and the concrete side barrier, and cars pass to the left of our cars. When I first pulled up, I thought the car was unoccupied because I could not see a silhouette. The driver is a small elderly woman, in total fear, white-knuckle squeezing the steering wheel as if she were falling off the flyover at that moment. She informs she ran out of gas. She is only a few feet from the crest of the top. I inform her I am going to push her car with my car just a few feet. I will then stay behind her, and she will roll down the flyover to a parking lot on the right that I pointed out to her. She tells me she understands. I watch her put her foot on the brake and place the car in neutral. I tell her when my car touches her car to remove her foot from the brake. I go back to my unit to accomplish this task. But her car does not budge. I realize she does not have the courage to take her foot off the brake. I squeezed back to her passenger window and asked her how many children and grandchildren she has. The number was high. I informed her, "If you have the strength and courage to raise that many children and grandchildren, through their teen years, then you have the courage to take your foot off the brake and do this." She does, and down the ramp she glides. When she gets out of the car in that parking lot, I have never received a hug so tight in my life. I had no idea my neck could take that much pressure, and her makeup and perfume were all over my uniform.

That was over fifteen years ago, and her big tight hug still encourages me to want to make a positive difference.

Learning from mistakes, and an outright discussing analogy

When I look back on my life, the dumbest, hardest, and wildest job I ever had was the summer after I learned to drive, I was only fifteen. In Louisiana in 1979, you could drive at age fifteen and legally drink at eighteen. Washington wisely guided the state into changing that up to sixteen to drive and twenty-one to drink by threatening to hold back federal highway and transportation funding if the state did not bring those ages up to the standard of the other states. I was hired by an older friend of a friend to be a subcontractor to install cable TV from the pole to the house, through the attic, down the wall, and connect it to the cable box and then the TV.

I have no idea how I lived through that job; I guess my saving grace was some level of half-smarts in my complete stupidity, and a lot of luck. If you are a teenager reading this, you need to know I am embarrassed of the following, and please, please, use way more common sense than I did in making these poor choices. I, too, was a victim of my own, "It can't happen to me" syndrome.

The cable company that hired this creative entrepreneur had no idea this man was actually a pot dealer and had given me, and I think other teenagers, his equipment and cable supplies to do his job for half of what they paid him. Half of what they paid him was still more than I ever made in the few little jobs I had worked. But the wildest, and dumbest part was that I accepted half of my salary in cash and half in disgusting cheap, moldy, compressed pot that had been smuggled in the hulls of the cargo ships arriving into the Port of New Orleans. Maybe the equally dumbest aspect of my choices was that he was huge, probably a size twelve or thirteen foot, and I was this little skinny, hairy kid that maybe had a size nine foot. He gave me his pole climbing spikes and safety harness that were extremely, dangerously, way too large for me.

Let me tell you just how skinny and hairy I was. In my tenth-grade yearbook, there is one picture of me that is not the official school photo. I finally had a social non-portrait picture of me in a yearbook! Yay! Oh no, it was only a picture of my right arm in a short sleeve shirt, taken at the annual school fair. When I first saw this picture, I was finally able to accurately describe just how skinny and hairy I was. Imagine taking a toothpick and smearing glue on it, waiting until it is almost dry, then rolling it back and forth on a new black shag carpet until you can barely see the toothpick. You are now looking at my arms and legs though my teen years. My arms aren't much bigger now, except you would have to roll the toothpick in brown and gray carpet.

It is the middle of the summer in South Louisiana, I'm by myself, I have a list of addresses, and a trunk full of cable supplies. I had gone on maybe three jobs with this man to show me how it is done. I can promise I was highly under-hydrated considering the gallons of sweat that poured off me crawling through attics and up utility poles, and let's not forget an abundance of cheap moldy pot to smoke between addresses. I was a self-assured, lucky, careless, inexperienced idiot having the time of my life thus far.

The man who hired me had more time to play Pong, which was the first home video game, didn't have to crawl in a single sweltering attic, and still drew a greater than 50% salary. No wonder he was so nice to me also! But I learned an important life lesson that summer: duct tape the pole spikes to your boots with three wraps around the shoe before you start climbing. I learned that one the hard way. But I discovered you can get back down a pole with only one spike if you can hug the pole with all your might, between each step down with the one remaining spike! Thank goodness I wasn't past halfway up when it fell off. My heart is racing just remembering that event. All that hair on my skinny little arm most likely created some increased friction to help me not slide down the pole with each replanting of the one spike back into the wood on the way down. Yep, half-smarts in total stupidity.

In talking with a handful of friends about writing this chapter, each who knows me and knows how I attempt to walk through life, told me I should include it because it was the foundation of what helped them pull everything together that I have shared with them over the years. They told me if I had not first shared these angles with them, to help them drop defensiveness and control their ego. They would never have accepted the good stuff that has been so helpful to them. One friend told me when I expressed my fears about this chapter, "If they have gotten to your third chapter, it means they get you and the deeper richness of your tools and sharing, and those people will continue to read. So, trust."

According to *Forbes* magazine article from 2016, authored by Liz Ryan, the top ten reasons people hate their job are:

1. They are not respected as people at work. They are viewed as production units, rather than valued collaborators.
2. They don't have the right tools, equipment, information, and basic operational requirements they need to do their job. When they ask for tools or guidance, they get yelled at or ignored. What kind of company would impede its employees' ability to do their jobs, then get mad at them for asking?
3. Their employer disregards their personal life and has no compassion for their obligations outside of work.
4. Their immediate supervisor is a tyrant, unqualified for their job, or both.
5. They are tired of being lied to.
6. They have no visibility into the future and no confidence in their leaders will do the right thing, either from a business standpoint or a human standpoint.
7. They are tired of dealing with the politics in their workplace.
8. They are underpaid and overworked.
9. They go to work every day and push a rock uphill, trying in vain to get forward motion on their projects. They're tired of pushing.
10. They have to watch every word they say and every move they make, because the knives are out, and they could get in trouble or fired for almost any reason.

As I read over these, I see that each of the ten in its own way correlates to life outside of work, to how we are treated by society, groups, some personal relationships, and the percentage of politicians that put special interest before the good of the people or the planet. Those ten can even apply to how we look at and suppress our own lives just by a negative attitude or outlook.

Before I continue, I must clarify something with a caring disclaimer. Anytime I mention "cut to heal" I am not referring to, or encouraging, the self-destructive behavior of "cutting," or any self-mutilation. I am only referring metaphorically to something that must have exploration with potential pain before it can heal. I have cared for many people in the emergency room that have cut themselves on purpose. Most told me they were doing it for just that reason, "To let the pain out, for some relief, and hopefully to start healing." That person's pain was most likely inserted by the actions or words of another. We do affect each other, and this chapter is diving into that fact. If you are self-mutilating in any way, please seek help so you can start to get the pain out and heal through a deeper and more lasting release of healing than self-mutilation can ever bring you. You are not alone, and there are many professionals out there that want to help you.

Just as a surgeon must first cut into the human body before some types of deeper healing may begin. Sometimes we must first open our hearts to our true deeper selves to heal, is what this chapter is going to involve. I warn you that I am about to use an absolutely disgusting, but extremely accurate, analogy of an abscess in the body that must be cut and is painful, before it can heal. Just like hearing the tougher stuff about ourselves that is painful but has a great long-lasting positive effect if we can hear it and work with it. A further correlation to unhealthy situations in our lives is if this condition is not cut, it will not only not heal, but just as unhealthy, unhappy work or life issues, it will fester and spread, spread to other organs, and eventually sicken and then kill the body. An untreated abscess is capable of killing the entire body. In some cases, these unhealthy situations kill a part of our spirit and damage a part of the body. Many gastrointestinal diseases have physical, mental, or emotional stressors as their major contributing factors but do not physically kill us. At least not at first, how many deaths from heart disease or stroke had the contributing factors of life's stressors involved?

An abscess, also known as a "boil," is a localized bacterial infection in the body that will grow and spread deeper and wider into the surrounding tissue unless stopped. I warned you it was a gross comparison, once a nurse, always a nurse. Just like unhealthy situations and conditions in life are "communicable" to others, they also can be infectious and will eventually spread into one's spirit, and unhealthy people are no different. Eventually, the infestation leaves your thoughts, enters your spirit, meaning significantly affecting your mental and emotional well-being, and eventually causes your body and your entire life to become increasingly "infected." An ulcer inside the stomach cavity can be brought on by psychological and emotional stress, such as an unhealthy, abusive personal relationship, unhealthy occupational relationship, or even a one-hour commute in heavy traffic every morning and afternoon. Abscesses start when bacteria get under the skin, often starting in a hair follicle, sometimes with an ingrown hair. The people we work with, their statements, and actions also "get under our skin" then fester and spread just like bacteria growing in an abscess. We may allow anything from waiting in a line or the temperature to get under our skin. Sadly, and poorly reflective on them, some people want to get under your skin for pleasure or manipulative gain.

Before we cut, let's look at a few aspects of the anatomy of an abscess. There is no pain-free way to relieve and heal an abscess with just the little prick of a needle, they must be cut open. An abscess, just like an unhealthy issue in life, is not just localized under the area of redness and swelling. As the untreated bacteria multiplies, it literally eats healthy tissue for its fuel and continues to eat tracks of tissue like the spokes of a bicycle spreading outward from the center. Correlating to an unhealthy personality spreading damage though the workplace, family, community, or culture, and feeding on healthy people. As the infection caused by unhealthy people creeps further outward, it causes more extreme pain, affecting more and more people. If the stressor continues, it causes more pain, then increasing disruption as it travels further into each person affected. Just as we are eventually driven to seek medical attention to cut out the infection, as we become more and more sensitive and less tolerant to any situation or person that is unhealthy, we eventually reach a point that we either become sicker and weaker or we seek some type of help or relief. Untreated abscesses only become larger and more painful, the same way an unhealthy person or situation can become larger in our lives and more and more sensitive, painful, and eventually dangerous to our well-being.

Here is the rough painfully further raw correlation: the local anesthetic known as lidocaine really doesn't seem to work that great around abscesses, correlating to attempting to "numb" a bad situation in life often does nothing to help the unhealthy situation either. Emergency departments see a lot of abscesses; in 2005 over 3 million people visited emergency departments to have an abscess opened and drained. In my twenty-one years in clinical nursing, I helped care for many of these creatures. Lidocaine is often unable to completely block the pain because the area is so inflamed. For many, there would be less pain if they just cut it, roughed up the tissue inside to break up those tracking outward spokes of infection, packed it with gauze, and be done.

A few times in those twenty-one years I observed doctors wisely explain that the local anesthetic is often ineffective and give the patient the choice to receive the lidocaine injections or not. Interestingly, those people who choose not to receive it often handled the pain of the procedure better than those who received the lidocaine. I personally think they were not only prepared for the pain, but they also did not have an unrealistic expectation of no pain. Abscesses are so inflamed they really hurt. I share this because I can't give you lidocaine before you read this book, or you have to work with an unhealthy person in your life. But just like an abscess, once you get to the other side of the cutting and digging out, it is all going to get easier and hurt so much less.

The opening of an abscess, also known as a lancing, is accomplished by a decent sized incision made right across the top and down deep into the pocket of puss. Just like a bad situation in life or work, the pressure that has built up forces a percentage of the stinky mess out on its own. Again, the correlations are uncanny, and just like a situation in life or work, it stinks. The bigger and badder the number and type of unhealthy bacteria, the worse the stink. This would correlate to the difference between a boss that is only just defensive and lacks healthy management skills stinking only a little, as opposed to a manager with narcissistic tendencies that are abusive to the staff, causing a greater stink. After the initial cut relieves the first primary pocket of infection and pressure, the doctor still must dig deeper and break up those further infected tracks of infection that have grown out and are spreading into surrounding tissue. Correlating to you also gently opening some deeper pockets inside yourself too. Then the doctor literally inserts a closed hemostat into the wound in every direction and opens the hemostat to open those spokes or "fingers" of infection tracking outward that want to keep eating healthy tissue and spreading further and further causing more and more damage.

Abscesses and unhealthy people and situations in any aspect of your life are an illness that wants to damage the healthy parts of you, a company, or a community. Both will continue to spread and damage faster and greater unless stopped and healed, or in the case of a person or situation, change with the situation or how you look at it, or walk away from the unhealthy. Both require some effort to stop the stressors that are consuming the good and healthy and then begin to heal.

The same thing might happen as you read; more than just one thing causing the stink might come out. You may meet a few parts of yourself that may be a little red and sensitive. Honest self-review causes some pain too. Many have trouble holding still or want to reach down and stop the doctor from opening the hemostat a third or fourth time to open more infected tissue. I'll often validate their pain, then encourage the need to finish, so healing can begin, so less ooze and more ease may enter life. The human condition is messy. Thinking about the other people's messes that got on you might get tough as you read also.

An actual abscess can happen to anyone. But the research shows those already challenging their health, immunity, and wellness have a higher chance of getting abscesses. I hope you will continue to develop a stronger, healthier "immune" system to the unhealthy people around you and develop fewer difficult people "abscesses." I also hope you will feel lighter in self and life for having lanced a few of your own internal abscesses. That internal work may lead to you lancing a few of your external abscess too, meaning creating a healthier life around you.

A few general big picture issues

Our present-day work and business models are far-off balance making it harder to accomplish business, workforce, and balanced economic sustainability. The problems are multifaceted in causes, effects, and solutions: prices are increasing for the business as well as buyer, labor and supervisory issues, poor customer service from some, and a few poor customers, too. All are pushing on and stressing each other. We are like a slightly angled pinball machine, with no exit hole or flippers, only bumpers, so the game never ends.

I would like to start with a compliment, that unfortunately is one of the causes of the detrimental direction our present work and business paradigms are leading us. The business industry, especially big business with large capital to leverage, is too good at what it does. From academic training to fine-tuned application, they have learned to shave more and more off the cost of doing business and maximizing profit and growth. The only problem: at what cost, and detriment, has being too good at business caused to both the individual and to society?

Sustainability is not just a new awareness related to ecology and the earth's well-being alone. Sustainability is also a consideration we benefit from when we begin to pay attention to it in every aspect of our lives. Profit, and greed are no exception. Profit at any cost will continue to erode the relationships between more companies, their employees, and the customer, if we don't start to break the cycle.

That trilateral relationship, company-employee-customer, is also being affected by changing individual and social attitudes, and is a negative vicious cycle, yet partially avoidable. There are so many companies, employees, unemployed, resources, and customers with unlimited needs and wants on the earth has created an attitude from all three sides of the trilateral relationship of seeing each other as a dollar sign made or paid out rather than a human being. When the reality is, all three sides benefit from mutual respect and effort. Unfortunately, the greater the consumer's need for the product, sometimes the less the company cares for the human being.

Don't get me wrong, there are many small, large, and gigantic businesses out there that are still attempting to hold true to this fading more caring model but are hindered by the employee that does not feel this way, or the consumer they must protect themselves from. It holds true in the opposite direction, too. Look at the caring professional call-takers that must apologize due to their employers' policies that are no longer customer service-oriented, but are completely profit-oriented. It may be easy for that increased profit decision to be made in the boardroom, but on each end of the phone are two humans having to enforce and accept it, or not accept it and blame the messenger. As is the case with the often rightfully angry customer, it is just not rightful that we take it out on the messenger. To complete the triangle, there are also consumers who can be unrealistic in their expectations of the business or the employee. Call-takers must apologize profusely because they put us on hold for only twenty seconds is telling. As soon as anyone, on any level, thinks they cannot be a part of these larger problems, that person becomes a bigger part of the problems. Remember, if you are not open to even thinking you make mistakes, then you will not catch a greater percentage of the ones each of us is guaranteed to make. Each of us, by our brave, empathetic awareness of the effects of our actions and omissions will make a difference. Cause and effect are all-encompassing.

I know profits must be made, and the health of our entire system and the economy is based on that fact. But the present-day behaviors of a percentage of the business realm, and individuals, are shooting all of us in the foot, including the businesses. I use a huge, heavy rolling ball to describe our modern-day healthcare system, to say it is a powerful force that can be hard to control. Although that big ball cannot be stopped on a dime and turned, everyone's actions can tap on it to speed or slow its direction, power, and negative or positive effects.

The owners and upper administration, board members, stockholders, and investors known as "The Top" may say, "Why in the world would I care to change the force and direction of business, when I am happy and rolling?" While the employee and consumer repeat something along the lines of, "I feel like a helpless victim of the system with no hope of getting ahead or being treated as a valued employee or customer that will ever see change." Feelings of hopelessness and helplessness is never a good sign, symptom, or indicator.

I also know people at the top that shared feelings of being victims of their positions and the expensive lives they have created for themselves. Far from all bosses, owners, and investors are uncaring, and I once again thank those of you who have trusted me with your mixed feelings. The answer has to do with seeing the bigger picture of cause, effect, and consequence. If all three sides will actively start to do their part to return healthier relations from their directions, since most of us are two of the three parties involved, then healthier business relationships in all directions can return. We are in a vicious cycle from all three directions—corporate, employee, and customer—each side truly capable of aiding in turning that large ball into a more positive, sustainable direction. Companies won't send an email acknowledging they received an application, or that you did not receive the position, so you wonder if they even received the application. Yet, businesses say they have a genuine problem with new hires not showing up for work on their first day and not letting the company know their new hire accepted a position at a different company. Then there is the customer that will buy clothing, or a power tool, use it, and return it, knowing that was the plan all along. Although fairness is not always obtainable, nor is it a constant in humanhood, working towards it with effort is still beneficial for long-term growth and stability. Yet, deeper fairness feeds the morale of people and the spirit of communities and nations. One of many answers will look like everyone bumping up general respect towards the other two directions. If it comes from all three sides, then we all benefit.

Pointing fingers of blame won't change the loss of basic human, business, and social courtesy from all directions. The blame approach has never accomplished resolution of the true origin of an issue or needed healthy change. Blame also gets in the way of accepting our part in an issue.

However, it is important to identify the origin of an issue, but only for educational reasons, not blame. Then we must immediately move to solution-based efforts. In the short and long run, it saves time, money, energy, frustration, and anger, while returning nothing but goodness.

Returning to doing the right thing, or even a little more of the right thing, helps slow and change the speed and direction of this massive rolling ball, known as our present big picture issues. Those issues could fit into an exceptionally large yard cauldron, but if you boiled it down for hours, the sticky stuff left at the bottom would be a lack of mutual respect and appreciation.

Slowly increasing respect and appreciation is an achievable goal. When slow remains steady, it becomes significant.

There is too much bad, my actions can't possibly matter or help

We too often feel that because so many powerful and bad things are happening every day that we are powerless. Yet we are not powerless, to acknowledge the people around us as human, to help another feel noticed, requires seconds per day. You too will receive more of that basic human respect if we change how we see and treat each other. If being treated as invisible, or bullying from all directions, for all reasons, and from all ages, had not occurred to us throughout our lives, would we feel so invisible, helpless, hopeless, and undervalued?

There are a percentage of businesses and people that will hurt, steal, con, and manipulate whoever they can for the purpose of gain over good. It is easy to forget for blunt reasons that this world is not filled with those people and businesses. Basic human response and social forces tell us if negative careless actions, both large and small, got us digging this hole, then positive caring actions both small and large can help us fill that hole in. That is a theme I will chant a few more times, it is too important and functional not to. I know how much joy and reward is in someone's voice and spirit when they tell me of a positive action by a stranger that was shown to them. Likewise, I also know the tone of joy and contentment when someone tells me of doing something positive for a stranger, too.

I know a woman who has been through her fair share of personal tragedies, to the level that it could have closed her down, but she continues to see these big pictures of cause and effect. She recently told me of a young person checking out her groceries that she knew to be a polite, consistent, studious, and hard worker, and she noticed their glasses were being held together with tape. She handed this young person a $100 bill and suggested it be used to get some new frames. That giving action also filled her heart, and there was such deserved joy in her while telling me of this random, spontaneous, positive action.

I had a very good friend die a few years ago from brain cancer. A beautiful, humanistic, self-reviewing, and optimistic person, who remained all of those through his illness and to his death. We had amazing lunches with wide social and humanistic discussions, often dissecting ourselves. If I were sharing one of my self-inflicted messes, I would periodically receive the following wise advice: "The first thing you do when you find you have dug yourself into a hole, is stop digging." We have dug ourselves into a hole. Let's stop digging. At least, whether a business, nation, community, culture, or individual, let us at least stop digging so fast.

What is getting in our way?

Why has it become so hard to accomplish simple positive actions in this day and time, even when those actions create immediate and long-term benefits for ourselves and others? What is the pathology behind a growing percentage of people contributing to the downside, not the upside? I can admit, I also periodically feel the desire to stop expending energy. I sometimes have to fight "first thought, wrong thought" thinking, "Why pick up that piece of trash and put it in my pocket for the rest of my walk when someone else is going to throw down ten more pieces this week?" Or "Why let that speeding driver into my lane when they are probably going to drive aggressively the rest of their lives?" Then I remind myself, I have hindered, and I have helped. I push past those moments of pessimistic thoughts of futility by remembering it is not only about me, that I want to keep trying to make a difference for all of us, especially the children.

The last humbling thought I have to help me is a strange one; I remember I am the problem too, I have accidentally littered, and I have hurt others in my confusion or outright selfish thinking or behaviors. It gives me the drive to not give up, to not give in, and to remember if I have hurt, which must mean I also can help. Even though I have been part of the problem, I never want to stop trying to be a part of the solution also. You have that same power to help or hinder, you are not powerless. I respect you feeling that way. Just don't stay there.

Those are the surface thoughts and behaviors. What is the deeper pathology of our feeling of futility that allows us to say, "It doesn't make a difference, so let me do it to them before they do it to me," or "It doesn't matter. There is so much bad, mine won't make a difference." The deeper origins of our behaviors are not all bad, either. They are initially innate to help keep us alive, and they do still attempt to keep us alive because there will always be robbery, theft, harm, and killing. The key for me is to remember the bad is not everywhere. I am not the only person shoving a piece of trash in their pocket on a walk. I am not the only person that isn't trying to figure out how to screw another person or business over in the world. I am not the only person that will extend myself to people and groups.

I remember that in my years of driving, people have let me in when the traffic is heavy. As well, others have even waved a "that's okay" to me when I started to move into their lane, and they had to break and honk.

Because the moment I did it I waved to them a peace sign, then placed my hand on my heart, and mouthed "I'm sorry" with an exaggerated mouth movement so they knew I was sorry. Because I am that sorry, my moment of normal human error could have taken that person's life. That is worthy of a big apology.

This world is not all bad, most people are good and want to do the right thing for the right reason, it's just harder to see and feel because the bad is louder and more in our faces than ever. However, I think we can all agree, the ratio of good to bad needs to be moving further towards higher good numbers. We accomplish that through positive actions. It is those positives over negatives that feed us the strength and courage to keep pulling the good up from our deeper self. It is how we feel and experience hope.

Are more and more people thieves and uncaring in society when it did not seem that intense years ago? Or is it still the same ratio of good to bad, but the increase in population has made it appear worse? The inundation of identity thieves, online scamming, and telemarketing cons is just one category of proof that something is increasing. Or has the internet made thievery easier, or has its anonymity enticed more people into theft? Why is doing the right things for the right reasons sometimes so hard, even when a part of us knows it is the right thing to say or do, or what we do not say or do most times? Some of the origins of why are for good reasons, and some are not.

Let's return to the ever powerful will to live, one of the innate characteristics of all living organisms. It is what drives our basic needs that I like to call the work of life. It is the reason we need to find food, clothing, shelter, and to defend ourselves when needed. Your will to live is why you can so quickly move over, but hopefully not hit the car on your right, when someone tries to come into your lane from the left. But the will to live can also drive the bad. Sometimes that bad is a shade of gray, such as the true need to eat, forcing someone to steal. However, all too often it may be more of an internal drive for excess, excitement, greed, or an addiction to pleasure or escapement behaviors, such as any of our addictions, whether sex, money, unhealthy relationships, food, gambling, or intoxicants.

The will to live does not always drive bad actions, it can also drive the omission of an action to help someone. We have all heard someone say, "Why should I . . ." followed by a reason to not help others, that has to do with not wanting someone else to get ahead. It all stems from not only our will to live, but also the mentality and fact of nature known as survival of the fittest, or painfully even our escalating issues with entitlement. In the same paragraph, all these behaviors that can potentially damage us and those around us, are also required to keep us alive. It is up to our free will and choice when and how to exercise a great percentage of them.

Please remember, as I give examples of human behavior, I am not passing judgment. The human mind is faulty, strong, weak, powerful, and requires control and exercises. Without that effort to exercise and control the mind, it very much grows and bulges out in the directions that it wants to. The direction the unfiltered mind will gravitate towards is power, pleasure, and perceiving and reacting from our emotions, not our rational thoughts. As we watch our youth grow, we hope sooner than later they embrace, "Hold on, this is not good for me or those around me, I may have more control of my thoughts and actions than I have been giving myself credit for." Most of us are guided to this higher level of personal and civil awareness, control, and responsibility of thought and action as children. Hopefully our parents, mentors, and teachers planted these "right from wrong" concepts in us. Hopefully, once instilled, we can grow these concepts within ourselves.

Our ability to receive, comprehend, and then apply this less self and more societal awareness input from our adult mentors varies for each person, everything from the quantity and quality of early childhood input to the emotional and cognitive ability of the individual to receive and process the input provided. Textbook labels of good and bad are often generalized and inflexible to the various strengths and weaknesses of each of us as individuals. Without either the proper guidance or ability to use that guidance from others, we develop towards the actions that are driven purely by our emotions or that feel good to us, but have long-term, highly disruptive effects. Sometimes these influences move us towards unchecked pursuit of self and hyper-individualism. As a rookie, I received an encompassing summary of this spectrum by a mentor officer in relation to chronic traffic law violators: "Some people drive in a manner dangerous to others because they are antisocial and have no concern for the well-being of those around them. Some people are dangerously self-righteous and think they cannot cause an accident, major injury or death to another person. Then some people drive as carelessly as they can afford to. Their wealth makes a traffic ticket and increase in insurance ineffective, and that decreases their ability to care for those around them, believing driving is a monetary responsibility not a life and property damage responsibility. Such as the teenager of a wealthy person being given a new car because a crash they caused totaled their first car, but not being aware the person they hit is a single mother struggling to make ends meet, that now is hindered from getting to work without a car that she cannot afford the deductible to get it fixed." This officer said, "Then you have the people that just understand and care that they are responsible for controlling and maneuvering a large dangerous, powerful mass of steel among other people, and they care to care."

Some people only want more without giving back to others, without caring to help those around them, and some people with little give back and care for those around them with hearts of gold but wallets of little. One can never judge a book by its cover, and nor should we humans be judged by anything external other than our words and actions, with a little intention thrown in. Our prejudice towards skin color, gender, sexuality, and even the wealthy are too often inaccurate, hypocritical, detrimental, and outright archaic. I have known criminals who walk into poor churches and leave large donations in the collection box to help renovate the roof, and I have known wealthy people that will cheat the lawn person because they know they are in the country illegally and have little recourse. Criminal or not, some people give back in action and some people will not. The unchecked will to live, and rationalizing survival of the fittest, is dangerous when it comes to excess or greed. Some people can say, "I have enough, let me help others," and some people are driven for more and more comfort and security at any cost to those around them, and even to themselves.

Robert Smith is an excellent example of that mixed goodness. He was recently found guilty of significant tax evasion on millions in income and is now working with the IRS to resolve his transgression. Yet, in 2019, while delivering a commencement speech to the graduating class at Morehouse College, he stated he would pay off all their student loans—a $34 million gift to a huge group of people he does not know individually, but only by association. Everyone should listen to the speech he gave before making that statement and gift. He may be a powerful businessperson, but he also has a heart, and that heart sees a bigger picture. I would guess that was not his first charitable gift to society, and I doubt it will be his last.

We should never stop being aware of the parts of people we may need to protect ourselves from, but that should not stop us from helping people or believing in the goodness of most people. If we have an influence or opportunity to help people directly, indirectly, or even to make the right choices, we should if it is safe and welcomed. But we should stop throwing people away because parts of their being needed some fine-tuning or redirection. I don't know Robert Smith, but he can't be all bad. It is just not right, and somewhat hypocritical, that we label and see people for their mistakes, but we ourselves only want to be judged for our good intentions. I know I don't want the world to throw me away because of my past humanness or outright mistakes. I don't have to feel safe to tell you all about forgiving mistakes, because I know every one of us has gotten your mess on others too, and each of us hoped to be forgiven and not discarded.

Not one of us will always make the right choices throughout life, and none of us wants to be discarded or overly judged because of it. If you ever get a chance to listen to Robert Smith's commencement speech, it is moving, educational, obtainable, and inspiring. He is talking to the graduating class of Morehouse College, so he is talking Black history, progress, and future hopes and strengths; but his powerful, amazing talk is a truth for all people and all cultures. He is very right; we must start reaching and lifting each other up, no matter what race runs through our blood or what culture someone identifies with. He is a powerful businessperson, but he is also obviously emotionally-, humanistically-, and socially intelligent, as well as giving.

Perhaps he became addicted to making and saving money, that too is an addiction issue across the globe, but he is still a good and contributing human. We have become a society of blame, fast harsh labels, and pointing fingers at others, so we don't have to look at our own daily mistakes and even slight negative contributions. We must stop throwing people away for only being human, or we will all end up on a heaping pile of discarded humans.

What has such a tight grip on us?

I have been the victim of crime a few times in my life. I had my car stolen by a bunch of teenagers that took everything in it. Joy rode for about an hour, and a witness from their front porch watched them bail out before they intentionally let it run into a brick wall. Hell yes, I was upset, I'm human. Even though they were never caught for that crime, I still hope they turned their actions around and became contributing members of their communities. I also hope they do not continue their behaviors and end up in prison. That is just how my heart works, but yes, if they continue the criminal behavior, then give them a consequence. But would it not be better for them and society if they changed their ways and never stole again?

I mention this as a personal example of the title and content of this chapter. I could have spent a huge amount of my energy, time, life, general well-being, and happiness being angry that my car was stolen and ran into a brick wall for the fun of it. By working to see the bigger picture, I let go of more external events which I cannot control, in that case, theft of a car that I had no choice but to park on the street. My first thoughts of anger, blame, and generalized outright wrong were becoming tiresome and unproductive. I made life easier by only changing my thought process. No, it wasn't easy at first. They stole and destroyed my car; but a few days later I got to that bigger-picture and a less self-destructive place.

Had I let it continue to upset me or affect me, they would have succeeded more than once in damaging my peace; first without my help by stealing the car, and the rest of the time with me helping them run internal parts of me and my peace and happiness into that brick wall repeatedly in my head, maybe for days, weeks, or years. We are human, so we can't just turn off thoughts of injustice, yet still actively try not to help people succeed in damaging parts of you past what they already accomplished damaging with their initial negative action. Your life, growth, and peace are worth more than the little picture actions of others.

Are "they" wrong, or are "they" different?

Another of many origins of our periodic difficulty to do the right thing, or not do the wrong thing, that cannot be overlooked is ethnocentrism. Ethnocentrism is holding the belief that because a person, culture, or race does something different from the way you, your culture, or race does something, that the other way is not only different, but also wrong. There are so many considerations here as to why it may be, but what we can look at is what are the problems ethnocentrism causes us.

Discrimination and oppression are some of many byproducts of acting on ethnocentric thoughts and then turning those thoughts into actions. Everyone has the right to think someone is wrong in their thoughts and actions, although different is more often a healthier way of looking at another's unique ways of doing things. It is even good to share those opinions and discuss these differences for the purpose of expanding knowledge, resolution, collaborative problem-solving, as well as individual, professional, community, and world peace. When our healthy differences leave the realm of education, positive change, or peace creation, is the beginning of us headed into trouble. As long as no one is getting hurt by these differences, does it really make a difference?

A beneficial part of welcoming these differences, not shunning them, is that we could benefit from the fact that others see situations and issues differently than we do. Just as an individual or group will never be capable of 100% accuracy in their beliefs, neither will a race, culture, or nation accomplish always having the best way. Therefore, ethnocentric thinking and actions only hamper. Scientists and musicians from all walks of life have already figured this out and are great at international collaboration. When music is playing, food is being eaten, or scientists are discovering more, skin colors fade. The non-profit organization Playing for Change is an exceptional example, their videos are fantastic, moving, and important. Our potential to solve some of the greatest issues of our time would be resolved quicker if collaboration across all cultures, races, nations, and communities was a stronger standard.

However, for too many, it has become the standard to point out our differences as an issue rather than a strength. The need to tell others they are wrong is too prevalent, especially when no one group is capable of thoughts and actions of perfection. When I was much younger in nursing, I used to think other nurses should do things the way I do. I realized again, as long as we are not doing something dangerous, but only different, does it really make a difference? That self-honesty made life and work so much easier. But we get into serious trouble when we believe that we know the right way to do something all the time, and worse, if we push it aggressively or violently on others.

Whether someone is a professional in the medical field or elsewhere, we should all be striving for a better way. Accepting the status quo, "This is the way we have always done it," creates a stagnancy in our minds, spirits, communities, and cultures. Eventually creating more issues than balanced, aware, planned, implemented, then evaluated attitudes, thoughts, and actions. Not accepting the status quo is why our computers are so small and fast, and why the medical field has advanced as far as it has, because people said, "Let's not accept this level, let's do better." It is also the reason I know we as individuals and groups, large or small, are capable of improvement and change. Please let us all continue to find the courage to keep wanting to look inside without rose-colored glasses and expend energy to continue to be solution-based in our thoughts, words, efforts, and actions. It's daunting and overwhelming, but it all starts with the minimal expenditure of energy in thought at first. With time, the positive actions will not require as much energy to carry out, but the returns will remain broad and exponential.

WIDER ANGLES:

YOU NEVER REALLY KNOW SOMEONE UNTIL YOU BREAK UP: WHETHER INTIMATE, PERSONAL, OR BUSINESS

I started forming this wider angle after my first year or so in college while watching myself and friends end relationships. Heading into college, I had only dated two women in high school, and the later one lasted close to two years. Both of course had ended, as our first relationships are often proximity-chosen and not always by compatibility, but they had not ended with horrible anger or too much mess. I was fifteen and seventeen, so I was highly on autopilot. More peace and less emotional strife in a breakup should always be the goal. Sometimes there is a lack of cooperation towards obtaining that goal. However, if healthy love or respect is not present, some effort may be required. Or worse, if anger is also being released, it may require much more effort to exit in peace. By the time you have had a few relationships, you know endings are on a continuum, and sometimes we do great and walk on as friends or acquaintances, and then sometimes the terrain is a little rougher. People seem to have rougher endings and the need to blame seems to be increasing. Yet also, more are learned to cut and run fast. A few decades back I formulated this theory: You never really know someone until you break up with them.

In all fairness, I have to say when marriage, attorneys, assets, children, or emotions, such as anger, jealousy, or vengeance, are involved, endings can become a whole different beast. Please, work harder for an amicable ending when children are involved.

The reason I believe you never really know someone until you break up with them is you find out how much love, real love, is in their heart for you and vice versa. How we end a relationship, unless personal safety is an issue, is an indicator of how our hearts really felt for someone. Have they been showing you true healthy love, or were they in love with what you did for them or in love with controlling you? If the relationship ends and they can treat you with a level of respect and understanding, even though they might want you back or express some anger, yet for the most part, they let you go with closure and grace, they loved you and were realistic with themselves. Realistic, either about their part in the relationship's breakdown or that it just no longer is working. We don't have to hate someone because we grew apart, or because the initial infatuation was strong, but the longer compatibility was just not there. That alone sums up the innocent, great percentage of relationships until we meet the one that really clicks. Great initial infatuation and connection with a later discovery of less long-term compatibility than originally thought alone does not deserve blame and hatred. Even if it was a good run for many years.

Hey, you got close, right? We should thank each other for confirming each other's hope and reminding each other that connections are possible. Walk on in peace. Another good reason this type of relationship should end amicably is because we might have many while we wait for the one that lasts. There is no need to have a rocky ending to all of them. If someone can't or won't allow a peaceful ending, no matter how hard you try, that's a positive sign you are doing the right thing to walk away. Peace is a gift to ourselves that we should never feel guilty or ashamed for creating, even if it means protecting yourself from someone's unhealthy thought process and actions at the end of a relationship.

I believe when a relationship ends and one or both feels a strong need to blame, belittle, attempt to assign 100% of the fault, stalk, or attempt punitive/vengeful acts or direct physical abuse, they did not genuinely love you to begin with. You provided them with something, and they are now angry that you will no longer continue to feed them whatever it was that was benefiting them. Or the feeding they received was the control of you, and they are angry you can no longer be controlled.

Another hard and painful, yet beautifully giving side to this wider angle is formed by looking at what I call part of the definition of genuinely loving someone. I believe if we genuinely love someone, we will want that person to live their life to the fullest and happiest they can find. If I am no longer that person, I should let that person go be their happiest to their fullest potential. This doesn't mean we always give up on the first sentence and walk away, although sometimes, please do just that if needed. This doesn't mean I can't feel hurt, pain, and grief that it ended or that I want that person not to walk away. It means I will do my best to go through those emotions without turning my pain, grief, and even mistakes and failures on the other person to attempt to hurt them or help ourselves feel better about our percentage of the breakdown. We all must do some work at the end of any relationship. Sometimes, that includes turning away fast, and we move on easily and sometimes, that requires some serious processing for a while. Yet, always attempt to let go of the person with minimal discord, even if you must be firm. In this day and time with finding the right person taking longer and longer, we should continue to learn how to break up peacefully, or at least exit peacefully and quickly, if needed. I know I have failed on a few endings, stumbled on a few, and did respectfully okay on a few.

Some of those failures to a picture-perfect ending were required to protect myself from dangerous behaviors. Yet, some of my less than perfect endings were because I am human, and love can turn us upside down, it can confuse us and can weaken us away from what normally would be the best of our ability. If you ever want to read the most accurate and balanced description of love's ability to create and humble, or to ground or unravel us, just read the short section "On Love" in Kahlil Gibran's *The Prophet*. I read this piece every few years, just like several good writings that I reread every few years. His short writing about love is that helpful. It calms and grounds me to be reminded it is normal that love is just sweetness and that there are benefits to its pain. It makes love easier for me to know that love's balance is normal. Another reason I reread some pieces is we all need periodic reminders to help us be more aware, gentle, and peaceful. To this day, I am sorry for my part in the times of our messiness, with various degrees of culpability, did not allow us to assure a relationship ended with the total peace our hearts felt towards each other.

As the years went on, I realized this wider angle applied to most relationships. Whether a business associate or someone in your personal life, unless there was abuse, thievery, or one person just outright used or blatantly and intentionally wronged the other, we should try to part ways with a little more respect if there was a mutual working relationship at some point. Mutual, also comes into play when both sides mutually falter and make mistakes. If we are brave and look inside ourselves with clarity, we can usually see that the end of most relationships is a 40–60% fault spread. Sometimes there are shades of gray as to who was 40% and who was 60%. There is much peace, humbleness, and growth in learning to own up to your percentage; it is that self-honesty that prevents us from making the same mistakes over and over, or from the wrong of trying to get someone else to accept our percentage of responsibility. That is not love.

For me, the hardest and most important lesson is to remember that I am also the one showing my true level of love if a personal relationship, or my level of respect and admiration if it is a social or business relationship. Seeing ourselves in any relationship can be one of the most rose-colored glasses lies we ever feed ourselves. It's okay, I've worn those glasses too. Learn, forgive yourself and the other person, then walk on. It's one of the ways you let them know you appreciate them for the working relationship, or that you loved them, and you want to show them one last time by doing just that, walking on in peace. It is also one of the ways we show ourselves love, respect, and peace.

CHAPTER 4

EMOTIONS

"Someone once asked me, if I were stranded on a desert island
what book would I bring. . . 'How to Build a Boat.'"
—Steven Wright

Working with our emotions, and the emotions of others, is at times
some of the most exciting, hurtful, challenging, scary, invigorating,
frustrating, enriching, and, yes, even dangerous daily work we do
with our lives. Our emotions can be one serious wild ride. Our ride of
emotions can be an all-out gallop, hopefully many pleasant calm trail
rides, and even a little refinement of dressage thrown in. But for the
most part, at least for me, it's a rodeo.

We give our emotions an unfair reputation by labeling them
"good" or "bad." I agree completely that some emotions feel good or
bad, and I will go further to say that some feel incredibly amazing,
and others feel scary as hell. But emotions, positive or negative, are
normal. It is what we do with them, and how they affect us, that can
make them good or bad. Those good and bad results are influenced
by the actions, omissions, fast reactions, or calm responses we have to
our normal emotions. There is no question that emotions can wreak
havoc. I am not talking about the more extreme diagnoses such as
chronic depression, anxiety, or anger disorders, to name a few, which
I leave to the professional counselors and psychiatrist. Rather, I am
talking about learning to work with our everyday emotions at a lower
level, shortly after they first appear. Learning to check an emotion is a
wonderful gift to greater peace and stability. We can then knowingly
realize that even though we may not be able to control what emotions

hit us, we can learn an increasing level of active control of what we do with those emotions. Working with our emotions is also the work of life, not a monetary reward, but you will reap rewards. I just realized that many monetary deals have been lost due to emotions, so maybe there will be rewards in that category also.

Greater calm and less turmoil can be achieved by learning to work with emotions before acting on them. It starts with trying to identify what brought us to an emotion in the first place, and evaluating what led us to that conclusion, and whether we processed it correctly. For example, you turn the corner to pick up your partner at work and see them half-squatting on an open car's foot bar, hugging a person sitting in the driver's front seat of a car you don't recognize. Our first emotion might be jealousy, sending us to the emotions of anger and fear that your partner may be having an affair. You get closer and realize they are not stopping. Your second thought is that they are in love and all three strong emotions intensify. You get out and walk towards them but, as you get closer; you see, they are both crying. Your partner looks at you and says, "They just got a call that their mother died unexpectedly at only sixty." You also add more information and realize it is someone you have met, they are not having an affair, and they are giving appropriate and genuine crisis support. Granted, not all can be redirected so clearly or easily, but just as our first thought can be a wrong thought, and it often is, a first emotion can also be the wrong emotion. Crimes of emotional passion are a huge issue. Even if not a high-level emotion such as jealousy, anger, or fear, less intense emotions can still give us a bunch of little unnecessary bumps in a day. Learning to identify and understand potentially harmful emotions can help us redirect those emotions more quickly.

From the lowest to the highest emotions, they are one of the powerful things that bond us as humans and help remind us that we have more in common than we do not. Emotions have the power to elate or damage us, and those around us. The best part of the scary wild rodeo ride they put us through is that we are not total victims of their damage, or their ability to lie to us, or to hurt others. We do have a level of ability to work with our emotions. I realized this and began the exercise of learning to redirect them a little more. I am still a victim of my emotions, I'm human, and I can't change that, but a decreasing percentage of the turbulent ones still affect me. My emotions can scare or fool me, but I still welcome them. I have no choice, I have never in my life stopped an emotion before it arrives, but I do have options once it enters. This chapter is me sharing a lifelong, hard, often painful, look at how I actively diminished a chunk of my suffering in my work and life that some of my emotions were causing.

Before getting into the fine-tuning of emotions and the varying degrees of being able to work with them, an understanding of a conditioned response must come first. A conditioned response can affect emotions just as fast as it can a physical reaction. The difference between an unconditioned response and a conditioned response is that the unconditioned response, let's call them reactions, occurs naturally in all of us. An unconditional reaction can be the first time you heard fingernails drag across a blackboard—you had never heard it, but it still had a cringing effect on you. Due to the popularity of the dry-erase board, that sound/feeling is something our younger generations may never experience. A conditioned response, again let's call it a reaction because we are going to build on that, is an experience programmed into us. Such as, once you have experienced the nail-chalkboard sensation, you immediately cringe if someone puts their nails on the chalkboard and threatens to drag their nails, but doesn't. Or the immediate rolling of the eyes of a teenager when a parent starts to talk, even though the message is about to end positively. This is important to help learn whether you are having an emotional conditioned reaction that is not appropriate, but only occurred out of habit or assumption. This first quick check should be part of the evaluation of any potentially disruptive emotion. We can have some of the fastest, most inaccurate, conditioned reactions in our intimate, family, or daily relationships. It seems the more important a person or subject is to me, the more I must pay attention to this.

Please don't beat yourself up for conditioned reactions, but don't give into them either, as they may be lying to you. It is not easy to reprogram conditioned reactions, but it is possible; don't ever give up on the human mind's ability to be flexible. There are several important reasons that variation and adaptation is a characteristic of all living organisms. If something is damaging a part of you, you most likely do have the ability to change the thought process or behavior. We all have been gifted with some level of variation and adaptation, so practice it with honor and peace, not resistance. It is another key to an easier life.

To those of you who have read *Suffer Less in Death*, I will try not to repeat myself. When I mention something that was covered in the first book, I will work to present a new angle or direction. I am working to keep overlap to a minimum, but sometimes a little is required for a bigger picture. For example, I previously introduced my suicide attempt in my early teens for the purpose of prevention. Yes, I will always mention it to help prevent suicide, but I am about to use it for the purpose of emotional awareness and the ability to work with natural emotions, and thus prevention follows. I want to do this, so hopefully we can have our natural depressive emotions and thoughts, but they don't lead to chronic depression, anxiety, addictions, hopelessness, or suicide. I cannot stress enough that I am talking about early tools to help us work with powerful, typical, normal human emotions only. Please seek professional help if you are having trouble with emotions in life that are causing any increased levels of pain or disruption to self or others, even if you just want more self-awareness as another life tool. Counseling does not, by any means, need to occur only when there is a problem. The entire basis of this book is that we are among each other to stay, that we are different but the same, that we affect each other, that we are capable of internal change to give ourselves greater peace, that we all need the help of others, and that we can make a difference in each other's lives. So please seek help if your normal everyday emotional speed bumps are turning into potholes or roadblocks.

Every one of us periodically needs others to help us literally get back up, whether from events like car crashes, heart attacks, major addictions, or suicidal thoughts. Please seek help if you are finding any emotions stealing your life, especially the big and frequent ones such as depression, anxiety, anger, hatred, or jealousy, to name just a few. Any emotion, positive or negative, may lead someone to an unhealthy place inside themselves or in their life. Even love can become troublesome in our lives.

The emotional and rational parts of our brain

We experience our entire life in basically three ways: physically, mentally, and emotionally. The physical is both the receptors that feel and the health and well-being of my body. It is everything from our senses, to giving or receiving pleasure, to our health or illnesses. Emotions are the feelings of our being. The actual part of your brain that deals with emotions are known as the Limbic system. The mental is where our entire life and being is received, processed, learned from, calmed or escalated, and acted upon through words, actions, or omissions.

I admit the immediate hole in this simplified outlook. Except for some reflexes that occur in the spinal cord before reaching the brain, our entire lives are really only experienced through the mental channel, because both our emotions and physical reactions are processed through the mental aspect. My heart can pound with excitement and my chest can feel strange because the emotion of excitement, fear, danger, or attraction, stimulates a release of adrenaline. Yes, my heart rate rushed, even the strength of its contractions increased, all because my body released adrenaline. Yet, my awareness of that physical reality was still actually processed in my brain and experienced via thoughts— all experienced mentally. I choose to look at how I will experience my life in these simple three processors because it helps me work with each by separating them. It empowers me with just a little more control of my chaotic 80 billion neurons that create, experience, and act on my emotions.

Admittedly, these are hypothetical rough estimates, but if I experience a third of my life mentally, a third physically, and a third emotionally, why would I want to deny myself half of my emotions because they are not the ones that feel good? Denying or blocking myself from the not-so-good-feeling ones would be denying myself roughly one-sixth of my potential life experiences. I especially don't want to deny, or at least I want to look at, negative emotions since a percentage of them will be incorrect due to wrong or a lack of total information. I don't want to mislead myself. I would rather experience and work with an accurate negative emotion than I would deny, suppress, or regress an inaccurate or accurate negative emotion and it continues to affect me. Yes, denying, suppressing, or regressing an emotion can affect us long term. But I also don't want to deny the not-so-good ones because they have lessons in them also, or even some potentially good side effects.

My own example that helps me is one way I learned to work with my own periods of depression. Although I rarely experienced depression for prolonged periods of time since learning to work with emotions, my sensitivities and awareness do lead me into periodic depression for a few hours or a day or three. I accept these down times as my spirit taking what it needs, even resting aspects of my being during down times. After my suicide attempt, short little periods of depression for me became a rest on every level. Even though I am processing sad thoughts and emotions, my brain and body also slow down. To this day, my entire being feels rested when I come back up from the down time of processing all this world hands me. There are reasons to be depressed with the realities of the world. I found it helpful to stop and sit with them, as opposed to trying to suppress them or cover them up, which would cause them to stay around longer and increase. Personally, I found that when I would just stop and be with my depressive thoughts, or the harder parts of our real world to digest, that alone helps weaken the strength of the world's harmful effects on me. My depressive thoughts and emotions then have less of an effect on me. I'm not giving into the emotion to pull me under for a lengthy period, but I will take an appropriate pause to sit with and ponder if something or an emotion knocks me over.

This is not my technique. It was taught to me a long time ago in reference to grief related to death or the end of a relationship. That attempting to push grief away, or attempting to cover or force it away, only makes it stronger or forces it out somehow in other unhealthy ways. That is one reason I call grief "The Monster of Grief," you can't push away, cover, or suppress a monster. We either fight it and it stays before us, or we befriend it in health and do the work until it chooses to walk away.

This does not mean we welcome "negative" emotions to stay for an extended period, or to pull us farther down than a natural emotion can appropriately do on its own. Paying attention to workable early emotions is beneficial to almost every aspect of life. Even with effort, they will periodically jump up fast and cause us some problems. Trying to prevent or block the more unpleasant emotions is more futile than accepting that our natural emotions will come, and then hopefully they will go. This attempt to block or suppress emotions rather than working with them, is another major contributing factor to high levels of addiction and abuse of self and others. Yes, some emotions are harsh, and that is hard, but accepting that most of the time we are having normal emotions to the realities and injustices of life and society gets rid of a percentage of our struggles. I once saw a bumper sticker that summed it up, "If you aren't angry, you aren't aware." Yet, if we work with emotions first by acknowledging the emotion, then looking at it before we act on it, greater control and peace is obtainable.

Some emotions can be calmed quickly and easily with one first rough filter, which is often the only check and balance needed to settle an upsetting emotion. Is the emotion accurate or authentic? Do I have the complete information or is my perspective of that information incorrect? As the example above in the parking lot, do my emotions have the facts straight?

If that quick check does not help to dissipate or calm an upsetting emotion, then I need greater refinement. I accomplish this last delineation by working to move my emotions from the areas of my mind that I label the "emotional" and into the "rational" part of my mind. It helps me to think of the emotional area as the origin of emotions. Unfortunately, this emotional part of our brain has much power to control and can react too quickly. That is how our emotions push us into trouble. The area known as the rational part of my mind is where I attempt to move upsetting or unsettling emotions to help me process them further. Rational thought is led by the evaluation of calmer, more factual thinking, not emotional reactive thinking. Now, you can see why there would be so much less violence and abuse if anger and jealousy could be worked with in the rational part of our brain before it is acted upon as rage or revenge.

By practicing this awareness with daily, and admittedly sometimes hourly, exercise, I can keep safe positive emotions in the emotional part of my brain to play with, enjoy, and grow from. Yet, I can also move the not so healthy emotions more easily into the rational part of my brain to work with them on a firmer foundation. It keeps me from acting on the more "negative" emotions to move them into the calmer, safer, more workable part of my mind. This exercise shares something with rational detachment; we can get better at it, but perfection is unattainable.

A few of our more frequent emotions are fear, sadness, anger, excitement, disgust, surprise, awe, satisfaction, contempt, guilt, shame, feelings of awkwardness, anticipation, hatred, envy, jealousy, pity, disappointment, admiration, empathy, remorse, regret, and emotional pain. That last one can be a whopper.

A peculiar emotion that I have always found helpful in action, but only recently learned in name, is called sonder. The emotion of sonder is allowing yourself to feel the reality and empathy that every person on the face of this earth has an entire life, just as complex, emotional, with pain, and joy, just as you do. I mention this awareness, not the emotion by name, often in my writings, because it is no longer a natural emotion in us for several reasons. First, our ego and even normal low levels of narcissism can prevent us from getting the emotion of sonder to the surface. Also, social, and our way of life, changed dramatically in the past 140 years; have decreased many of the bonds of community, and hand in hand teamwork, that existed and were required since our beginning. Those decreasing human bonds significantly contributed to our increased isolation from others and is a major contributing factor to us being clobbered with skyrocketing numbers of mental illness, addiction, anxiety, depression, and suicide since turning into the twenty-first century.

Feeling the emotion of sonder is profoundly helpful in not feeling alone, picked on, entitled, or overly self-serving. The emotion of sonder is a true pillar to peace and the resolution of many of our troubles, including government, community, judgment, and even personal and worldly issues. Even many painful disruptive emotions could be calmed or resolved with more movement of those emotions into sonder. Sonder also creates an easier path to empathy and compassion. Both of those return goodness back to us and start positive cycles.

The pendulum swings to the other side

One of the more interesting emotional responses or behaviors we are seeing more of in this second wave of woke generations is a continuous powerful drive not to recreate the emotional stifling that the older generations were taught. This second wave of woke generation is mostly correct—too many previously attempted to suppress natural emotions. We can't suppress them forever, they come out somewhere, often in unhealthy releases or numbing actions, or they keep eating us inwardly. However, emotions can be over-released too. Many effective solutions-based discussions and then corrective actions are being missed because of over-releasing emotions. So many now feel it is okay to allow all their emotions out as a right, as a statement, or even a feeling of urgency for change, or worse, to prevent change. This problem is wide-reaching now too, from our politicians and special interest groups to our intimate relationships. Some cannot help their over releases, that I respect, because it can happen to all of us. Taking stock of an emotion before it is released is a basic human consideration that we should all strive for. I know I am embarrassed of the times I vomited my emotions on others. I also wish others had not vomited theirs on me quite a few times as well. There were times I needed that unleashing of someone's emotions too; my perspective was off, and I needed the harsh redirection from someone else to snap me out of my self-righteous, self-absorbed, inappropriate, or just outright wrong thinking or behavior. I respect balance as everything human is mostly shades of gray.

Every one of us, in some way, shape, or form, continues to cushion a percentage of our emotions and more painful awareness. That normal and self-protective need to calm, suppress, or deny our emotions is the core reason for our natural defense mechanisms. Self-medicating with intoxicants is another way we cushion or escape ourselves and our emotions. Our ways of not seeing and feeling are hardly limited to defense mechanisms and intoxicants; the excitement of making money or gambling, the pleasures of tasty fat grams and simple sugars, or our addictions to shopping and materialism are a few big ones that are attacking many of us from the inside out, because we don't want to feel the normal periodic unpleasantries of life.

My mother summed this up well when I was a kid. She said to me, "It is often the most sensitive and aware that become addicted to intoxicants or other escaping behaviors. It may start with experimentation and the exploration of euphoria, but all those escapes from our feelings, pains, stressors, and realities often become an addiction to continue to numb those of us gifted and cursed with high levels of awareness and sensitivity." When she told me this, and I had not yet attempted suicide. But after my attempt, her having said "gifted and cursed with high levels of awareness and sensitivity" suddenly made sense. Except for the very low percentage of people who were born without compassion, remorse, or guilt, or have had it trained out of them by either conditioning, neglect, or abuse, that "high level of sensitivity and awareness" she mentioned pretty much includes all of us.

Being aware and sensitive for each of us is also on a spectrum, with each person's level fluctuating at various times. Our fluctuating levels are influenced by many factors, such as the subject and who is stimulating the emotion. Awareness and sensitivity are definitely a curse and a gift for all of us on some level. Both sensitivity and awareness, painfully at times, had to be present for me to care and attempt to help. It is the reason I have spent my life attempting to help others and attempting to work with my emotions. I found that once I saw how sensitive and aware I was, then contributing in a positive way back to society, helped it all clobber me less. One of the good sides of sensitivity is it drives me to attempt to make a difference. But I also know for some it can be paralyzing. It also seems to have helped me see that for the most part everything is more okay than I originally perceived. I have known people of all ages that are hit hard by their sensitivities and awareness, leading to higher levels of depression and anxiety. I encourage them to start volunteering or choose a path in life that is a hands-on helping career, such as going into the healthcare field or social work. Many have told me it helped decrease the pains of their sensitivities and awareness on many levels; from a student to a retired person volunteering a few days a week, positive is the only feedback I have ever received. Getting my sensitivity and awareness busy is what my mother was doing when she helped me get that job at the gas station after my suicide attempt. It worked for me then and it still helps.

Depression was the first emotion I realized needed to be actively worked with. I grew up with learning disabilities and severe frequent migraine headaches two to three days a week. My migraines were so bad that nausea and vomiting often occurred. It would hurt to hold my head up, but it also hurt to rest it on the pillow. Even the pillow was too much pressure. My parents did not ignore my issues. I was tested from a few different directions for both the headaches and the learning issues. Everything from an EEG (electroencephalography, to measure electrical activity in various regions of the brain), to IQ and academic testing at both Tulane and S.E. Louisiana University in Hammond. Everything came back basically "normal" apart from dyslexia and something they called "phonetically deaf" at the time, which in my case, meant that I did not hear the short vowels correctly. When I would go up to the teacher's desk to ask how to spell a word and they would say, "Go sit down and sound it out," they were sending me away to an exercise in futility. To this day, if I spell a word correctly, it is by habit, or I have finally memorized it correctly, for now anyway. Between the headaches and the learning disabilities, I basically missed the first seven years of school. Between those two setbacks, and a teacher picking on me, I took a bunch of pills one night in the seventh grade and woke up in the ICU the next day.

That attempt to end my physical, mental, and emotional pain turned my life around, and I was so glad I failed. For the first time in my life, failing at something was more than okay with me—I lived! I realized nothing and no one was worth that. I also began to believe my mother's chant that she had said to me a hundred times since I first started falling behind in the second grade, "Knowledge is relative, and we all have strengths or weaknesses in academics and development. Einstein got lost walking around the block; you are bright, and everything will compensate, you are ok."

I still can't spell, but everything did compensate out okay. If you are young, or have a young one struggling with academics, please believe this and remind yourself, and repeat to them, that everything is okay, and it will all compensate and balance out in the end. One of my favorite t-shirts when I was younger said "Slydexics Untie!" I didn't get it until one of my sisters told me it was spelled wrong.

About a year after the attempt is when everything really started to get easier for me, both personally and academically. I would get off the bus, drink a glass of water (thank goodness I had figured out my headaches were affected by dehydration), and my German shepherd and I would walk off into the woods and marsh and not come back until dark. It was my escape from people and the sadness I could feel in their presence, but not my escape from thinking about it. It was so bad that I could get depressed seeing a dog in someone's backyard that was in a tiny pen or on a short rope. That sensitivity and awareness, and the depressing and hopeless emotions that followed contributed to me giving up a year before. I knew I had to learn to work with sensitivity and awareness, which pours out in the emotions of sadness, helplessness, and hopelessness.

We woke up real fast I tell you!

It took me a good fifteen years from that point to get to a very real and solid way of looking at my periodic depression to be able to decrease its effects. Wanting to learn more about why depression, anxiety, addiction, and suicide were escalating in the world meant digging into the changes that may have contributed. In looking back over the last century, I discovered a handful of major contributing factors to our wide-reaching spikes in depression and anxiety. Until the Vietnam War there had never been as many freelance and media sponsored photographers and journalists covering a US war. They sent the world uncensored graphic pictures of war and human atrocities at a volume never witnessed. Before the Vietnam War in the US, our war coverage was mostly filtered and then presented to us by the military's paper, *The Stars and Stripes.* Censorship of what we saw back home was gone from the early 1960s on.

Of interest, *The Stars and Stripes* newspaper was founded during the Civil War in 1861 by a bunch of Union soldiers who found an empty newspaper office in Bloomfield, Missouri. They printed a newspaper about what they had been through, and the publication continues to this day.

The explosion of freelance journalism in the Vietnam War was a heavy load of reality after the "on the surface wholesome" years of the second half of the 1950s. That was followed by a huge explosion of self-awareness through the 1960s and beyond, and I am not just talking about the drugs. If you look at the concepts of "self-help" or "self-awareness," in the form of available knowledge through literature, those sections in bookstores were maybe a few feet wide, if that, going into the 1960s. Over the next ten to twenty years, those few feet on a shelf turned into entire bookstores, and a seminar industry of self-awareness also exploded. Counseling and mental health awareness also began its needed long climb to becoming more accepted and less shameful, with more resources and help available.

If we look at a timeline of humans and look at what happened in just the twenty years of the 1960s and 1970s, that was a level of raw, naked, social, global, and self-awareness like no other woke period before it. Those generations were the first wave of "woke." It needed to happen, and was bound to eventually happen, but a part of our beings and society was just not ready for it in some ways. I believe that we became not a depressed society, but rather we became highly aware and informed of the broad spectrum of the potential hideousness of individuals and society, along with the deeper than ever meeting of ourselves via self-awareness and exploration. We have seen human badness since the beginning, but this was a new barrage of intense harsh realities in our faces that deeply and intensely stirred our emotions. We became aware to a new depth and width, and that contributed to the depth and width of our depression.

Are we depressed? Or are we painfully aware, and that is depressing? We could ask the same question about the more recent increasing number of people with anxiety. Much of what we are aware of has reasons to cause anxiety also. This delineation is only to validate and add to our tools that may help even just a little.

Just as the media of the 1960s and 1970s television, newspapers, and magazines led to those two decades of assault on awareness and depression, I believe we can look at the internet moving into phones in everyone hands, including our children, as a major contributing factor to our rapidly escalating numbers in our youth experiencing debilitating anxiety. They are clobbered with an even more intense awareness in their face than previous generations. Yes, they are experiencing anxiety on a new level. Compounding their anxieties are groups of people that will suppress or bend the truth, without caring if they are spreading lies for their gain, not the good of all. Then our youth must deal with being told climate change is not an issue by a sector of society that shamefully ignores science in the name of profit margins. When their young eyes and smart brains have too many facts to be fooled. They see skin cancer numbers, increasing hurricane intensity and frequency, increasing wildfire volume and faster spread, ice sheets the size of states breaking off, sea levels rising, rain falling less and less, and our beautiful origins of life and the earth's balance being affected by the oceans being harshly disrespected with pollution and overfishing. Yes, I would be screaming in frustration, confusion, anxiety, and even anger also if I didn't have years of tools inside of me to help calm those same rightful emotions.

I once had a wise and wonderfully forward-thinking teen ask me, "Even if they believe that climate change is not human action influenced, why wouldn't they want to do everything they can to slow it down for their kids and grandkids?" I could have given a long encompassing answer of many influences, but I did not have a satisfactory answer that would not have been obviously pacifying. Our teenagers are already angry with the levels of blatantly pacifying answers they are receiving concerning so many troubling issues. I had no answer for this teenager, because beyond contributing factors, I don't have a good answer to that wise question.

At least when the older generations were receiving the pioneering first wave of wokeness through the 1960s and 1970s, we had to turn on the TV or choose to pick up a magazine or newspaper to have the raw assault of human indifference and violence enter our brains. Now it is in the palm of so many children's and teens' hands, so of course they are experiencing anxiety, depression, and suicidal thoughts and threats, and sadly too many suicides have been accomplished. We need to help them feel real hope, and honesty and positive unselfish actions are a good start.

On top of that assault, we must add in the layers of bullying, criticism, and judgment that are being handed to youth and adults alike, both in person, in school and work, and streaming right into the devices in the palms of our hands. When do we get a break from anything now? At least for previous generations, their day of being bullied stopped when they stepped off the bus, well, except for siblings. Now the younger generations stay awake at night voluntarily allowing themselves to be guided, judged, and bullied engaged in social media until late into the night.

We allow our autonomous life and our peace to be robbed worrying about what other people think of us.

It is not only the news, bullying, and social judgment and pressures that are hard on the emotions and development of our youth. The barrage of online pornography at too young of an age is also emotionally hard on our children and young teens. It is not the exposure of learning the facts of life that is the issue, nor is it the books in our school libraries, but rather it is the Internet's onslaught of raw sex that is robbing them of their childhood by introducing complex sexual behaviors that also add fear, confusion, and anxiety. They are dealing with complex and sometimes even upsetting sexual behaviors before they have even figured out how to kiss. Some of the online porn subjects even upset me, and I'm a nurse from a very promiscuous city, New Orleans. !!Wow!! . . . that's a thing?!? No way! They are far too young for that level of unfiltered raw. The sexual attitudes, raw materials available, and the emotions our youth are being hit with are all seriously heavy pressures for such youth. It does not stop at our youth either, pornography is setting the bar too high for our mature adult intimate relationships too. It can cause serious emotions of inadequacy in both directions, "My partner is not enough for me," and "I am not enough for my partner," leading to detrimental vicious cycles. This insatiable and inadequate thinking is damaging the bond, intimacy, and longevity of our relationships.

What does help

Depression is a major issue around the globe and often requires and deserves professional help. But never forget the well-known basics that are also known to help with lifting depression: sunlight, hydration, increasing exercise, sobriety, proper hours of sleep, and healthy nutritional intake.

Rest is important, yes, but sometimes when experiencing longer periods of depression, we are already lying down too often. Exercise helps return our bodies to normal sleep ratios and quality and can also return everyday energy even if we are not depressed but just "tired all the time." Frequently exercising and keeping busy, not more rest, are the keys to feeling less tired. Your body creates more energy the more energy you burn, so keep going. Often a better answer to feeling tired is more exercise, not more rest. It is extremely important to remember that expending energy creates greater energy. Move your being.

Taking actions to help decrease our emotions' ability to cause issues in our lives has a wonderfully large investment to return ratio. It requires not only effort, but also the belief that you are capable of changing how you process some emotions. As time passes, we start processing input the same way we start driving—by habit and assumptions, not by minute-to-minute focus with appropriately reasoned responses.

Your entire life is only 2.2 billion moments, and most of those moments are safe

Before anxiety first appeared in the DSM-III as a diagnosis in 1980, it was obviously an increasing issue, or it would not have become a diagnosis in the first place. Anxiety, before we realized it could consume us, was a definition known simply as: fear of the unknown. Fear of the unknown is not new to humans. However, the intensity of anxiety has begun to overwhelm and is significantly escalating. This issue is not generational either, anxiety in all ages is increasing, which tells me fear and anxiety is affecting all of us. It also does not help that there is so much political manipulation and some of our news intentionally further frightens us. Sometimes those two are one and the same, intentionally fear based slanted for the sole purpose of manipulating us. Returning to the emotion of sonder, remembering we all experience these complex emotions, can be helpful and reassuring. Our intensifying urgency in so many realms are driven by personal and societal anxiety. From politics to environmental stability, to the anxious gobbling of wealth, we are an anxious society. So how can we work with our escalating daily anxieties?

What seems to work for me and seems to work for the people I share it with is not my strategy. I have been taught this technique from so many angles and people in my life. Everything from stress reduction classes to people management courses, from eastern religions to half the self-help books I have read, and from counselors to even my father who, unlike me, was a man of very few words. If it is so widely known, why don't we use it more often? That is a life enhancing good important question.

Our anxieties and fears, both potentially devastating emotions, are usually occurring because we are thinking of the past or conjuring up our tomorrow, and we are forgetting to stay in the here and now. Take a minute to sit with the joy and comfort of here and now. At any given moment most of us are safe. It is what every second of your life really is, the here and the now. For much of the world, but not all, at any given moment we are protected, warm, fed, sheltered, rested, and our basic needs are met. It is not always easy for me either, but when I come back to my moment, I have no unknowns and therefore no need for fear and anxiety.

Our moment is not always safe. Yet the vast majority of our moments are safe. This does not negate the fact that many areas of the world are not as safe as other areas. Hunger is a huge issue across the globe, war and social unrest is always in flux, and violence can be as random as dementia. That has been the reality since the first human hit another human or experienced hunger, and that will remain. So even the basic definition of the emotion of anxiety, fear of the unknown, is slightly off. For it is known that bad things will happen to all of us. Perhaps, a slight altering of the definition would make it more accurate, applicable, and easier to work with inside ourselves, in both thought processes and preventative actions? How about we change the definition of anxiety from: fear of the unknown, to fear of the rare but guaranteed periodic bad things that will happen to all of us?

That slight change in definition may allow us to stop losing moments to an emotion that has some accuracy to it, but still robs too many of us of an undeserving loss of a percentage of our life. Anxiety is valid, and the ability to release a percentage of it is also obtainable. When I talk about fearing dying then death or avoiding the subject, I use the analogy of hoping the sun will not set if we close our eyes tightly and turn our heads. The sun will set and all of us will die. Anxiety is that exact opposite, it is hoping the sun will not set if all day long you fear it setting. I am not making any level of fun here about anxiety, it is not as clear as that; the human mind cannot just say, wow he is right, I am going to change that. But because I am talking about early lower-level tools to work with our emotions, the awareness may help. Anxiety is not a joking matter, it has been an increasing issue in numbers and severity, and it is stealing too many people's life, comfort, security, and moments.

I know there are no magic tricks to completely alleviate our anxieties. Although easier to write than apply, it helps me to remember that fear and worry will do nothing to eliminate the amount of periodic inevitable bad that will happen to me, but rather it is the application of energy into prevention that creates less bad.

If our emotions are normal, and for the most part, valid once we have evaluated them further, and we know what we do with an emotion can be good or bad in action or non-action, then which parts can we control? Let's use anger again since it is consistently one of our more sensitive and dangerous emotions. If someone has a healthy stimulus of anger from an injustice, or an unhealthy stimulus such as political slant, causes us anger, this is where exercising our choice comes in. If more people could learn to move anger from their emotional brain into their rational brain to work with it, how many fewer shootings, stabbings, child abuse, assaults, and outright murders would I have seen during those twenty-one years in emergency nursing? Anger is a natural but extremely dangerous emotion. Even if it does not push us to hurt others, it damages the inside of us. It holds the top of the pyramid of dangerous emotions, with fear, jealousy, and envy, vying for second place.

The ability to move an emotion quickly into the rational part of our brain, where safer, slower, and gentler things can happen, is truly lifesaving. A considerable number of the car crash patients I have cared for in the emergency department volunteered that they caused the crash because they were "upset and not paying attention."

I have always been a strong promoter of free will and choice, if those choices are not disrespectful to others. We exercise and empower our free will and choice when we move our emotions that may not have benefit for us, into the rational part of our mind for closer examination. When our emotions lead us without a second examination, they steal our free will and choice.

Dangerous reactions and calmer responses

There is no question about it, my life is so much more peaceful when I remember to respond after consideration, as opposed to reacting quickly directly from the emotion when it first arrives. This too may seem like a strange delineation, respond versus react. Our often-reflexive split-second reactions are becoming a bigger and bigger problem to us as individuals and for much of society. You may have noticed in the beginning of this chapter I interchanged "reaction" and "response" a few times. I think it is a major contributing factor in our issues with law enforcement today, from the officer, the public, the media, and the politicians. As always, the balance to this is especially important, because as law enforcement knows all too well, the ability to react can literally keep you alive. However, there are few critical situations in life that will be handled more efficiently and appropriately if your response comes from rational thought rather than reacting quickly from emotions. Even when an officer must react in a split second, it should be from training and muscle memory. It is the reason some boxers and fighters can truly give their opponent a genuine hug after the fight: because they keep their emotions out of it. They were not fighting from personal emotions; they were fighting with professional responses and calculated lightning-fast reactions. Many great fight trainers teach the same thing—emotions in the ring, whether fear or hatred, literally consume more energy and quicken fatigue. Life is no different, high emotions burn great energy.

Careful though

Although I say that emotions are not good or bad, but normal, there are exceptions. Emotions can be very bad if recurring, we act on them in violent or controlling ways, or we become addicted to them. Love addictions are devastating to all involved. The emotion of love is also capable of fooling us, especially when we are young, but its trickery is not limited to our youth.

Whether an intimate, personal, professional, or social relationship, jealousy is another emotion capable of control and abuse if not worked with. Although jealousy is a natural age-old emotion, in this day and time, acting on it with too much force can reveal thoughts of ownership. Whether driven by emotions that hurt others, or when we stay too long in an emotion such as depression, anxiety, fear, or anger, they are capable of damage to both the person with the runaway emotions as well as those around them. We all have had our emotions run away from us; it happens. Yet please, pay close attention to even low levels of stalking, controlling, assumptions or fears turned into accusations, or the wide range of other damaging or controlling behaviors our emotions can pull us into.

Hatred, and retaliation are also emotions that turn damaging. Both trust and distrust, although also building blocks to safety and protection, are also emotions that are instinctively important but can lead to damaging actions and behaviors. Fear and insecurity are also emotions to pay attention to. Fear is, at times, important and appropriate, but it is so capable of grave unnecessary damage. Some politicians, political groups, and news outlets intentionally play on our susceptible emotions of fear; social media and biased news coverage are all an escalating issue driving our politics, anger, fear, and anxiety.

Please don't get tired of me saying this for an especially important reason but seeking professional help with our emotions can be lifesaving and life enhancing. I know my parents, or a school counselor, would have found me help had I told them that I was suicidal. Maybe seeing a professional counselor could have helped me see how normal and okay everything already was, since I obviously did not believe my wise and accurate mother at the time. Maybe what I figured out later, I could have learned, accepted, and embraced before the suicide attempt. It would have been so sad if I had succeeded. I have had a wonderfully balanced life of joys and pains, mistakes and success, even lots of friends and few enemies. I would not trade one of my hundreds of migraine headaches as a child, each one helped me become me. However, I also wish the world's pain, abuse, and neglect did not have to occur. It has been an amazing life, and I never stopped finding rewards in helping my fellow humans. Or accepting help when I needed a hand up when knocked down. My emotions of depression, self-doubt, and fear almost stole over forty-seven amazing years from me. We are now watching too many emotions steal life away from a huge sector of the world. Anger is a form of suicide of our spirit or soul. Anger can also kill parts of our being or spirit, just as it can kill the entire being.

I bring up anger one last time in this closing paragraph because of its force on too many parts of the world, from politicians to voters to rioters (peaceful demonstrations should not be included here, around the world, that should be everyone's inalienable right), to political and social injustices. Of course, included are the ones that affect us the closest: anger decreases peace in our heads, hearts, and homes. Anger, as are all emotions, is a potentially healthy motivator, or it can set us far back.

Our unchecked emotions are consuming our individual and societal peace, and hinder the rational thoughts, actions, and the accomplishments that can follow. Those accomplishments, and our increased peace, are so needed.

CHAPTER 5

MY GREATEST INTERNAL BATTLE AND THIEF

My damaging ego versus my healthy pride

Knowing I was in a ridiculous situation with the cable installation job, and after nearly breaking my neck halfway up a utility pole, I walked into a Waffle House in Slidell, Louisiana, where one of my sisters had waited tables in high school and filled out an application. I liked to cook, how hard can it be, right? They called a week later, on a Saturday at 6 a.m. and asked me if I still wanted the job, and if so, could I be there an hour ago. About an hour later, I walked into what appeared to be chaos, and what turned out to be a needed positive milestone in my life.

What I walked into was a very loud packed restaurant with people standing, waiting to be seated. Two no-nonsense ladies were handling the food preparation. Talking across the packed counter, one of them quickly and forcefully introduced herself as the regional manager, handed me a uniform shirt, and said, "Thank you for saying yes, put that on over your tee shirt and come around the counter." The other person was the manager of that location. They told me all they wanted me to do was make toast, waffles, and put lettuce, tomatoes, onions, and pickles on every plate they put a mayonnaise packet on. She made eye contact with me and said, "Start listening to and watching everything that is happening, like you never have in your life." I stayed behind that counter for two years.

With goodness not sadness, I just teared up writing that last sentence because of how life-changing those years were for me. At that time, I was getting my feet under me and was slowly starting to believe in myself; school was getting easier, but I was also still flailing in a few departments. I was only fifteen years old that morning, and I was also overwhelmed, intimidated, shocked at the speed and efficiency of those two women as they professionally grill danced with each other as they turned out plate after plate of beautifully cooked eggs, as they quickly pulled down empty plates to fill the empty spaces of the four that just left the line, as they broke eggs with one hand in a split second without breaking yolks. To top that off, I had never realized the cooks at Waffle House don't get a ticket to reference. The waitstaff call out the orders, "Order on three, one scrambled, with scatter, smothered covered, one over medium, grits, one sunny with grits, two bacon out like one, one sausage, two ham, two waffles, make one pecan, one quarter cheese plate also scattered, smothered covered," and walked away. They were remembering the orders! I'm thinking to myself, "I can't even keep up with them making toast, how the hell can I do this?" The orders never stopped coming. Today, the cooks at Waffle House can call out to have the waitstaff hold orders until they get caught up, that wasn't a thing in Slidell in 1979.

I was doing what they told me, soaking it all in, picking up a method to the madness. I remembered almost nothing being called out, though. I suddenly realized there was another assault on my senses in progress. I had shut it out seconds after walking in the door when I started to receive directions, but behind me I hear a blending of forty or fifty people talking louder and louder in competition with each other, and Eric Clapton's "Cocaine" blaring from the jukebox, at least once an hour for the next two years. I hear cursing, and the waitstaff's main theme is openly complaining about the third shift not doing their stocking prep work. That song and those complaints eventually became the material of my dreams. I still periodically walk into a Waffle House for a flashback meal and all-encompassing memories. I will go once or twice every year or three, to honor the goodness it gave me. I still love their burgers with hash browns spread out with grilled onions in them, "Quarter plate, scattered and smothered." To this day, the complaints of the previous shift can still be heard across the counter.

I am grateful as I recall that accomplishment in relation to how unsure of myself and my intelligence I was. Yes, I put out some under par food with mistakes for a few months. But then it started to click. I was cooking. I was remembering the orders for approximately 40 seats with a fairly fast turnover. They even created a special thirteen-hour shift for me that started when I finished school Friday and then back again Saturday night. After about three months, I was handling those thirteen-hour night shifts without a second cook. The wait staff started to compliment my consistency and easygoing work attitude. I had to learn how to periodically deescalate two drunk people from fighting at three in the morning, when all of them could have easily crushed my hairy little skinny toothpick self. But I did it, I accomplished my first difficult occupational challenge of my life. I could accomplish and grow; I was a whole capable being. I realized I was going to be okay; I was compensating.

Later that first morning, I found out both of those women were long time Waffle House managers; they were great to work for and excellent teachers. The place didn't have an empty seat until about 1 p.m. that afternoon. Then they had me on the grill and breaking eggs that afternoon for the last two hours. They were my first true professional occupational teachers, pushing me right into more and more tasks, but patient too. They would not just tell me to do something, they also taught me the reason for doing it. They encouraged me by telling me stories of their first few months of cooking and their screw-ups. They set a fantastic foundation for a life of professional learning and teaching that I work to hold to this day.

That first morning was really the first major challenge my "pride and ego" ever presented to me, at least that I had blatantly noticed. My "pride and ego" had been a bit crushed academically until the eighth grade, and then it started to build. Back then, I had no way of labeling it, because I had not yet begun to academically study humanness. I put "pride and ego" in quotes because we are about to change their meaning a little. I quickly began to see the difference between my ego and my pride, because the mistakes were knocking my ego down, but the fact that I was getting better and having fun was building my pride.

It was not until after obtaining the terms and their meaning in college that I paid attention to the pros and cons of both ego and pride, well by textbook definitions anyway. Having to meet more of myself in my first long-term relationships after college also helped me get to know my ego and pride on a different, more painful level. Staying in relationships, healthy ones anyway, is a great pusher and humbler of our ego, yet builds true pride. I began to slowly stop using the firm textbook definitions. I also began to further delineate pride into false pride and true pride. That first morning, walking into that packed busy restaurant, I was thinking there is no way I can cook under all these challenging conditions, including my own disabilities.

My main concern was my ability to memorize information. If I learn something, I usually have it trapped in there, but if I try to only memorize information, it falls out the other ear. It is why I did so well in nursing, I wasn't memorizing anatomy and physiology; I was learning it. I was enthralled, so I learned about the body's organ systems rather than just memorizing information for a test. I was a sponge and knew it after hearing it, I did not have to memorize most of it. It is also why I did not do so well with criminal law in law enforcement but excelled in civil law enforcement. Civil law made sense to the wiring of my 80 billion neurons, but criminal law had more details to remember for each offense and fewer concepts. However, at the Waffle House, I had to memorize those orders, no ticket, and another order being called out right after the next so frequently. I was filled with thoughts of "I can't" that first morning, but by the afternoon I was accidentally thinking a few "maybes." Their encouragement showed I had a reason to feel overwhelmed, but still they believed in me and that greatly helped.

About four or five months later, when it all started to smooth out, my pride began to really rise for the first time in my life. For the first time, I felt pride that I did not quit during the first few weeks. I had several decent rationalizations that I could have easily used to talk myself into quitting, but I stuck it out. I'm grateful I didn't quit, those years were filled with rich experiences, learning, and growth.

I had been paying attention to how my family interacted and got along ever since I watched my first argument between my sisters, which may have impacted my curious little being. It wasn't the first one I heard, that one most likely occurred while I was still floating in amniotic fluid in the uterus. But this first one that I took pause with, I bet I was in diapers while I held and drank from the bottle that I wouldn't get rid of for years stuck in my mouth, with wide eyes, holding onto the side of a chair or couch, wobbling, and barefooted. I held onto that bottle until I threw it out the car window when I was maybe three, then I screamed for Mom to go back and get it. "No, you made your choice" is what she told me she said.

Being the youngest of six children in ten years, I got good at observing group dynamics, and how each person affected that group at a very young age. Those skills brought me some peace in my childhood; I learned from watching my siblings to do things right and do things wrong. I too, ended up doing right and wrong things for the rest of my life, but I found a higher level of ease by not choosing to make some of the mistakes I had observed by watching my siblings grow ahead of me. Yep, I am proud to say, I made all my big mistakes without anyone's help!

Before my first solo shift, I had not really had major consequences for making mistakes while on the clock. I turned out some bad food the first few weeks, and a few rounds of not so good food over the next few months. Most of the waitstaff and customers could look over to see that a rather young person just cooked this meal, or should I say just attempted to fix their meal, and they would just send it back and have me try again. But I also got hit with plenty of consequences too, from the top down and the bottom back up, waitstaff also. Painful and mean as some of it was, it sure forced me up to par fast. Being admonished for mistakes was new though. I had had a handful of jobs working for and with other people at that point, but no one had ever not been nice to me. I just realized the difference! Before, if I screwed up, it might have cost myself or the owner a little time and maybe money. This time, if I screwed up it would cost the waitstaff precious income, and somebody had to spit out my mistake in a napkin!

That early moderate pressure ended up helpful down the road in high pressure roles, and in life in general. Every shift was getting me closer to my first shift without a mistake! That job was my first true core education in learning to work with my pride and ego; forty-three years later, I have landed in a healthy place with those two aspects of my being, but ego still requires daily checks and balances.

Healthy pride and humbleness are compatible, but not so much with ego

I don't look at my pride and ego exactly as the textbooks taught me. I simplify them also to get a little better control of my ego's desire to damage. Ego especially needs some reining in. It is strong and tricky in its ability to fool, stunt, get in the way of progress, and just in general get in the way of all of life. False pride can be troublesome too, but for the most part our true healthy pride is goodness.

In the textbook definitions, pride and ego are different and both contribute positives and negatives to our well-being. Most popular sayings or general descriptions usually combine the two, just as I did above, "pride and ego." Or they are used interchangeably. I too separate them out so I can catch a few more of the moments my ego is not being my friend.

Throughout the rest of the book, I am going to be referring to pride and ego from this personal angle, which at times will vary slightly from the textbook. My goal is functional daily tools to bring greater peace to our spirit, not to regurgitate textbook definitions. I know this read requires hard self-honesty, but I also know the lasting calm that can wash over after the honest look, especially if followed by acceptance and a willingness to be ok with your humanness being a lifelong rewarding project. You are a wonderful, whole, and perfectly imperfect person, just like every human you will see or hear your entire life. Breathe, you are just right, and you have an amazing ability to keep exploring and growing yourself.

I made my ego my constant internal villain in life, and I took the few textbook good things out of my ego and gave them to my true pride. My ego rarely used those few good things the textbook told me about anyway, so I felt my pride deserved them. Pride I could trust more, but only if it was true pride. My false pride is my ego trying to have something, anything, to show for its unhealthy efforts. False pride still gets the lies that ego gets past me, even though I try to pay attention. I also moved back into ego the few not so good things that pride had in its textbook descriptions. I really don't have to check in with pride or false pride too often, since completely separating all bad into ego and all goodness into true pride. Ego is now kept in easier and greater check, and my pride is now fed more factual information. That separating and assigning of good and bad helps keep both pride and false pride in its place, both fairly quiet and out of the way.

Healthy pride does not mean being outwardly prideful. It means allowing it to be a healthy internal motivator for better. This is how pride and humble are compatible. But I still keep a little eye on my false pride because its name does include the word false.

I have been taught at various times in life that pride can get in the way of healthy, important humbleness. I clearly see how ego and false pride both can get in the way of humbleness; but true pride helps with humbleness, because true pride never feels a need to use bravado. Humbleness is an important attribute to peace. However, it is okay to feel pride and even share it; we should be proud of true pride. Simply by paying attention to both of their influences on each other will help us find a balance between humbleness and pride, and I think they can get along and be good for you. Your entire spirit has a right to be proud of your goodness and your accomplishments. It is an unchecked ego that unnecessarily inflates false pride. Our spirits need and deserve to feel true pride, and deserved self-appreciation delivers a calm and non-inflated self-assurance in us that can help supply significant peace. Healthy pride can also help weaken insecurity and self-doubt.

The above slightly changed angles of approach are also designed to help simplify working with the three: ego is not to be trusted or ignored, well-deserved pride is good and helpful, and try not to let ego feed false pride.

I have things in my life I am not so proud of, but I have many that I am proud of. I have accomplished, and I have failed, but I am okay with my moderate pride, I really don't even have to spend too much energy on it. My pride holds my accomplishments in life, and strangely even some of my failures. For our failures mean we at least tried, and hopefully learned. It is so important for the growth and development of our children that they see periodic failure as both normal and an opportunity to try again, not failure of their being. To tell a child they cannot or must not fail guarantees self-disappointment, over-protection of ego, and actual direct destruction of their pride when they do normally periodically fail. We teach them the same destructive lessons when we as adults cannot admit to our mistakes and failures, or they see an inability in us to apologize.

Being a giver and contributing is great for our pride, and pride even encourages it. My pride would rather build with communal accomplishments than those of self-promoting accomplishments. True pride wants us to solve our personal, occupational, and worldly issues. Pride wants you and the world around you to create and find peace. Ego is not going to be this easy to comfortably sum up, but it really doesn't care if you find peace. It actually doesn't want you to find peace.

Ego is the origin of all those little tools we use to not get too much self-honesty all at once, also known as our defense mechanisms. Your ego thinks you can't handle meeting yourself, so it wants to guide you away from seeing the real you far too often. That has some validity too, because the scariest thing I ever did in my life was to look inside myself. The challenge is to look inside myself while not trying to convince myself I have done everything right in my life. The kind of looking inward that hurts to see, especially the looking in where you see that you have hurt others. Not accepting responsibility is often the ego stealing moments and opportunities for you to stop blame cycles that are lies or distortions of reality.

Your ego doesn't want you to find your faults for two reasons. The first is that your ego is self-serving. The more you accept your human faults and imperfections, and work with them, the weaker your ego becomes and the more appropriately strong and healthy your pride can become. Ego knows this and does not want you to find self-review and peace, they wreak havoc on its job security.

Your ego doesn't know acknowledging your faults is a strength not a weakness, it foolishly spends your life trying not to appear weak. Ego would rather lie than celebrate your humanness. It is our ego that prevents us from saying we made a mistake, and we are sorry. Ego hates that.

It is just those behaviors of our ego that makes it abusive to ourselves and others. It is abusive to others when ego prevents us from owning up to an error and allows, or worse yet pushes, the blame onto someone else. Low levels of this behavior are human, higher levels are another classic behavior of narcissism. Our ego is one of the contributing factors to the slight and constantly fluctuating level of narcissism in all of us.

The power of our ego to stifle, upset, or even damage so much of our lives is the reason I started Chapter 1 with one of my simple pieces of poetry about ego's destruction and lies. Really, I should more accurately call them "writings in stanza kind of thingies," not poetry. Me calling my writings poetry is an excellent example of ego feeding false pride. I placed that piece first in the book, the bow, the cutting edge, because without grasping how destructive your ego is, you will miss chunks of life and this book will be less helpful. Our egos are a primary destructive force in all our lives and relationships. Ego prevents true intimacy in the sharing and accepting our responsibility in forgiveness or apology. Ego loves blame, and its main of many self-deceptive mantras is, "That wasn't me!"

Our ego wants to control us and everything around us. Our unchecked ego is not a team player. Team players want the team to win, your ego only wants you to win. You can build pride when you care to see the people you work with grow and excel. This is opposed to your ego wanting to see them fail so it alone looks good, which causes a hindrance of personal and team success. The ego's general ignorance and lack of big picture vision is a major contributing factor to stress in the workplace. Correction, ego is a major contributing factor to stress in life. Ego is a lying scaredy cat that is in fear of your strength to look inward and grow, or even to apologize. It thinks it is protecting you, but it prevents growth and amazing exploration of the self, especially exploration of the faulted self—remember, that is its job security and its strength. Our egos really don't care or want our lives to be more peaceful.

When I separate my ego as bad and my pride as good, my self-review also became more honest, and even easier and safer. I started to get embarrassed by my ego's past behaviors. I've wasted moments of my life defending the self-lies which my ego convinced me were truths, which led me to argue even though I was wrong, or even just not meet in the middle and apologize for my part. I am so sorry for the times I defended my wrongs. This awareness that hit me, and is still shaking me, is not a way of saying it wasn't me doing these behaviors. I am not blaming my ego so that I do not have to take responsibility, it just helps me look at the cause of my behaviors. It was my ego that caused those foolish defenses; therefore, the embarrassing behavior was mine and mine alone.

I can feel proud knowing I am sorry for a human error and accepting my part has become easier for me. I protect fewer of my ego's lies than I used to. I word it that way, so I do not drop my guard. Ego is too strong for any of us to completely suppress, so I must keep a vigilant eye out for its future flexing. Some will still get past.

Down ego, down

The greatest way I have found to keep my ego in check, and stop it from its insecure trickery, is to accept my limited human abilities, always seek as much self-honesty as possible, and feel good about working with it. My ego loses much strength when I keep working to accept myself.

CHAPTER 6

PAIN, SINCE IT'S UNAVOIDABLE, LET'S FACE IT AND WORK WITH IT

"That's the thing about pain . . . It demands to be felt."
—John Green

No, wait, come back

I was formed and born
One day I kind of just noticed I was here
I'm a thing
Then I had to start to figure that out

I quickly noticed it was not always easy
Trying it is and trying I am
Still, I'm little even now
Moderately maneuverable, mostly manageable

Wait a minute
Reality and daily existence
It does get painful at times
Painfully painful

I am back and experiencing again
I made it to the other side
Hey great to see you
Joy and Laughter are stopping by more

There they go again
Not Pain again
Awareness helps
Pain comes less frequent and easier with acceptance and time

Why must Joy and Laughter go
Can't they stay
Please
You two are softer and feel better than Pain

Oh, Balance is here too
Now I understand
Yes, then I accept
See you soon

One of my sisters helped me get my foot in the door at a job at a very nice restaurant in Uptown, New Orleans. This sister part is important for the story; she was dating the general manager who gave me a shot at a prep cook position. I was seventeen and knocking those orders out at the Waffle House like the whopping two-year experienced kid I was and getting it right a high percentage of the time. I loved working on timing. Timing is the ability to have everything on the plate finish cooking at the same time, so nothing cools off waiting on anything else to finish.

Because I had started my lifelong process of growing up on the North Shore of Lake Pontchartrain, a high school friend of mine let me stay at "his place" in the city. Which means his mom's place, because he was only seventeen too. I was supposed to be going into my senior year of high school, but my mom made me an offer I could not refuse. She knew I was loving the Waffle House work every Friday and Saturday night, had a great girlfriend that was helping me mature, and kept me out of normal teenager trouble. Mom could also see I was starting to disconnect from school again, not disconnecting from education and learning, just from school. She came to me halfway through my eleventh-grade year and said, "Vincent, you are not going to learn to spell in your last year and a half of high school, and you seem ready to go. How would you like to get your G.E.D. and start college next year instead of a senior year in high school?" I jumped on the offer and started college ten months later. I was excited to learn again in the classroom setting. I missed sitting at a desk and being fed information that I knew would be enriching to numerous aspects of my life.

Off I went to live in New Orleans and put in forty-plus hour weeks at a high-quality restaurant and with a great group of people to teach me and work with. Those chefs took me under their wings and pulled me behind the line to help them every chance they got. The head chef was great to work with: positive, very funny, creative, and rarely grumpy or temperamental as has become the standard vision of the head chef. He had a positive crew, he would shuffle across the slick kitchen floor and do a fantastic loud impersonation of the Wicked Witch of the West, "I'll get you, my Pretty!!" with the perfect laugh to follow. But then trouble hit.

My sister stopped dating the general manager. Remember how I told you I did not have a mean boss? Well, that still didn't change, he didn't get outright mean, but he started to give me some manure. It would be eight at night, peak hustle hours, usually I was down at the end of the line responsible for the steamer, and half of the broiler. If anyone wanted to walk away for a break or to prepare something, I would fill that spot while they were gone. Sauté and broil I liked, the frying was always harder than I thought it should be. We flowed, the humor, the lingo, the rhythm. They were impressed with my timing for being seventeen. Although they knew the answer, with almost nightly repetition, one of them would say, "Babe, what timing! Where did you work before here?" Polishing my fingernails on my shirt I would say, "The Waffle House, Babe!"

"Babe," was the term of endearment for anyone working in a kitchen in New Orleans at the time. The general manager would walk into the back from the front and, sometimes but not always, he would look at me behind the line and yell, "Dodd, get out from behind the line, I hired you for a prep cook, peel shrimp!" Most of the time, he would come back and stay five to ten minutes before returning to the front, but sometimes he would say "Dodd, peel shrimp!" and make a big, exaggerated left leaning U-turn, to basically non-verbally admit he openly was just riding me for the fun of it, and he'd head right back out the door. The few times he cracked us up making the big funny theatrical U-turn, I didn't move, and we kept cooking. If he said it and stayed in the kitchen, I'd go peel shrimp because that was an endless need in a New Orleans restaurant. "Peel shrimp!" has probably been echoed off the kitchen's walls of New Orleans since the first log and mud shack eatery. He would exit back to the front, and I would go back to cooking.

Mother's Day morning rolled around, the busiest and most prestigious of mornings for restaurants across the city, across the country, and the person who handles the steamer, the broiler, and four of the sauté burners didn't show up. My manager comes to me and says, "Get behind the line," then turns and starts to walk away. I said, "Hey, hey, wait up a minute." He turns and takes a step and stands rather close, like a drill sergeant in someone's face, and says in a quiet voice, "Yes?" I would bet my voice was shaky, but I did not back up. I said, "Well, I have a question. Are you asking me now because of need only, or tomorrow do I get to stay behind the line?" I'm nice, but I do stand up for myself and others. He did not answer the question, he was just looking at me for maybe ten seconds when he said in the same soft quiet tone, "Okay," and he turned and walked away. I only stayed another three months or so before heading to college, but I stayed behind the line, and we got along just fine.

Mental and emotional pain

It was painful leaving that restaurant: the people, the fun, the onslaught of culinary and life education I was receiving. I was so torn, but I knew staying would have been the wrong decision. I was hit with a second pain. My sweet, funny, intelligent, and easy-going girlfriend of two years started seeing someone else shortly before I left for college. I had no idea an emotional punch to the stomach could hurt that badly. I felt the first empty hole in my chest and abdomen in my life. The huge hole of grief, with a decent chunk of emptiness and loneliness mixed in, I know you know that feeling. I had heard about that empty feeling, but now I felt it. I was devastated, even though I knew I was young, would survive, and this was normal, age-appropriate situational pain. I was aware I was only seventeen and, unless you stay with your high school love, it's practically a first rite of passage to deeper pain and growth. But as painful as it was, it only took me a short time to realize I had done this to myself. I had not talked to her enough about me going to college and her choosing to stay there. My inaction, I am sure, had been an enormous influence on her choice to move on. I don't blame her; I already knew she was an incredibly well-rounded, balanced, and intelligent person. I was young and did not know about the importance of communication.

So, in a few weeks, I had the emotional pain of the loss of an amazing ten months of real-life experience, life education, laughs, friendship, challenges, and my first hard and painful love lost. I confess, it knocked me over a little. I even stopped holding doors open for women for a few weeks. I can say that now, because if my mother had heard that while she was still alive, she would have given me one of her combination validating and disapproving looks. Yes, she could do both in one look, moms are great at those. Thanks to an out-of-the-box nonlinear mom and four older sisters, I was raised to hold the door open for women. My mother was also a medium-level feminist with several degrees and a career. She taught me I am not opening a door because a woman can't open her own door, you open a door for both women and men as a social courtesy. But arriving at college righted that situation quickly. No, it was not the six-thousand female undergraduates. It was the educational atmosphere, courses, and the instructors that I fell in love with. I read, I watched, and I applied it all to myself and the world around me. But I also learned more about pain. All pain. I did not realize pain had so many layers of destruction and lessons. I knew there was enough wide and deep pain to greatly damage people and society. I had gone that low only five years earlier.

I would say the most important truth that I learned, then applied, that took the most punch out of my pain was that not only can we never get rid of all pain, but we can damage parts or all of ourselves trying to stop all pain. We can learn ways to decrease pain, to see things so that it doesn't even produce pain, or at least not as much, and learn to work with the pain we do have.

Besides my personal pain, the pain that people have trusted me with in confidentiality, the pain presented by the news of our human doings, people's acute pain in front of me for my years of emergency and intensive care units, and years in law enforcement, have all been my training grounds for learning to work with pain. People normally arrive at emergency departments because of one or more of the major types of pain that we feel: physical, mental, or emotional. As a nurse, I heard, saw, and worked with healing the pain of people's trauma, illness, tragedy, and discomforts, while hearing their expressions of grief, remorse, or sorrow, and I was almost always completely welcomed to help. In law enforcement I also heard, saw, and worked with people's tragedy and pain; but in that role, I heard their expressions of injustice and anger, and I was only partially allowed to help. I was often limited to help with pain on many levels; be it the individual not believing I cared or could help, the public also had its ways of setting limits on my ability to help, mainly a lack of trust. The liability limits of the role or the standards of law enforcement also limited my ability to help with pain. Both of those roles gave me a wide range of experience working with the pain of individuals and society. Having been exposed to human pain has allowed me to study pain to help to decrease it.

If we bury our pain, it is still inside of us. If we go inside and find where we have hidden it, then we can get a percentage of our internal pain to the outside of us.

Since we cannot stop all the pain from entering, how do we work with it? First, by talking about it to learn how it works and looking at a few of the diverse types of pain. Having this knowledge then helps us with its application during pain. I have learned that when experiencing pain, whether myself or working with someone else's pain, it is also important to validate it. Pain does not have to become stronger when validated. Often, just identifying pain alone may weaken it.

Good pain versus bad pain

Since we can't stop all our pain from entering, we should look at some of it as an experience. It's extremely difficult to imagine physical, mental, or emotional pain could be good for us. I'm sorry we experience life's discomforts, especially the pain that comes from abuse and neglect. I also remind you to please seek immediate professional help from many directions if you are considering suicide to end your pain.

It is important to divide pain into good or bad. Yes, even a little periodic discomfort can help us with lessons, grounding, and growth. One example would be the pain of love lost, which is filled with growth, strengthening, and confirms that you have loved, and you will love again. That chest-ripping pain reminds you that your heart can still feel. Love pain can be bad if we cannot experience it, welcome it, but then move on when healthy grieving has accomplished is hard important goodness. Love pain denied has no benefits and may cause self-damage, just as most pain denied or suppressed, has the potential to damage further. Love pain turns bad if we cannot calm it with a healthy grief, or we hurt ourselves or others with it. Love pain is bad if we shut our hearts to more love because we absolutely do not want to ever experience that beautiful, powerful shearing pain again. Not wanting to ever feel the pain of love again is denying that love, like everything, has balance in how it gives and takes. Just like the action of loving someone, including yourself, involves both give and take. Not having the energy or desire to go for a walk when your partner asks you to is human, pushing yourself to go anyway is the giving energy of love. Our love pain is good if each time it teaches us to love better, again starting with ourselves. Not all pain is bad. We have a choice of how we work with a percentage of it. Love pain can also be felt as too much to bear, or the magnitude of the pain can be seen as a beautiful representation of the elevated level of love, respect, and appreciation that was or still is there. How intensely we grieve the death of a person, pet, or relationship correlates to the same intensity we loved, connected, or professionally respected that which has died or walked on. The greater the love, the more intense the grief will be. See, pain can be for a good reason.

If your thoughts are relentless, filled with fear or hatred, unsettling, aggressive, uncaring, overly controlling, outright abusive, self-damaging, or if you just want life to get easier, find professional counseling that fits you. I have never regretted the times I knew I needed caring support to help me see deeper inside, and a wider safer picture of what was happening both inside of me in thought, and to help me see the many influences with greater clarity. Or, if you don't think you need that level of help, do you have a safe friend that will listen and not judge, truly understands the meaning of confidentiality, and won't use what you share against you later? If so, call them, they may need someone they can trust on those levels too.

Try not to feel frustrated with a counselor that won't tell you what to do unless you are in an abusive or unsafe situation. A counselor will ask questions to help you find your own answers for yourself. They will also explain human behaviors and influences, so you learn more about both your unique blueprints, and your shared blueprints as a human. Because of those unique blueprints we all have, don't get frustrated if your counselor tells you little about their own life. They may share a little to validate, to let you know you are not alone, or that they are human too. Most counselors will not compare their life or their personal strategies with you because they know what works for them may not work for you. I am not a counselor by any means; I share what works for me, and what I have witnessed in others, as a human peer. I know my life tools may not work for you, and that is why counselors don't share their worlds too much. It would be like trying to start a Chevy with a Ford key. Meeting our deeper self can take time, and if you are digging out of a hole, that can take a little more time; be patient and gentle as you meet more of yourself.

Whether you find the courage to see someone because of a situational crisis, meaning an internal or external situation that is causing a temporary crisis, or you want to look at a deeper part of yourself, when it is time, give yourself permission to laugh. When it feels right, attempt to give ourselves the gift of less self-criticism and unnecessary self-protection. If I couldn't have laughed at myself, I would have missed a life enhancing large amount of both laughs and material to help others laugh. No, not all situations are a joking matter, none of us need to be reminded of that. Being strong, not tough, is how pain is worked with, weakened, and used for the good of self and all. We are all beautiful messes, none of us are alone in our humanhood. Being tough prevents feeling emotions. It tries with futility to block them or push them down. Strong is having the courage to feel and work with pain.

Since the subject is mental and emotional pain, let's look at one more aspect of seeking professional help, the difference between a counselor and the M.D., whether a psychiatrist, neurologist, internal medicine, family practice, or pediatrician. This is an important delineation to understand in this day and time with so many medications being prescribed to help with our mental health, wellness, and focus. Focus deserves mention, with the equally high numbers of attention deficit disorders, ADD, in the pediatric and the younger populations being treated with medications. "Counselors" come in many forms, and each state has slightly different requirements to become licensed. People who call themselves "life coaches" can be fantastic and helpful in sharing tools to motivate and to help find greater peace. Psychiatrists are M.D.s specializing in the mind's processing and coping abilities. They prescribe medications for mental health, and various attention deficit disorder medications, such as Adderall. Although most doctors will refer their patients to a psychiatrist for mood stabilizers or antidepressants, some neurologists, pediatricians, internal medicine, and family practice doctors feel comfortable prescribing some of these medications to some people, depending on the situation. Most ADD drugs are strong stimulants and addictive, so seek help if you find they are causing issues in your life. It is important to remember that most are derivatives of methamphetamine. These drugs can also lead to seriously dangerous side effects and are highly worthy of caution.

The role of the psychiatrist has partially turned from counselor to prescriber. This shift is not by their own choice. Often forced by the sheer numbers of the people they must routinely see and do brief check-ins to continue to prescribe the medications that are working for someone, or to adjust medications to try to get them working optimally for each unique individual. Psychiatrists are artists, painting peace and serenity onto the canvas of each person's unique mind, which has unique mental, emotional, and physiological responses to these medications. Their medium is medication instead of paint. Every person's "canvas" is a different shape and texture, so balancing those medications is not as clear-cut as one may think. They must also see the patient they are prescribing to periodically for important check-in on the medication's effusiveness and how you are handling it. This is why counselors are so important and great at helping people look in and develop healthier life skills. Psychiatrists are capable of this type of functional helpful calming of the spirit and teaching functional life skills to help us; they often just don't have the appointment availability to accomplish weekly or biweekly sessions. Weekly or biweekly has been proven to be the most helpful during acute crises, or when first starting to build a new counseling relationship.

Medications definitely have their place, yet the talking to get it out, the non-judgmental help to smooth out our humanness, and gaining helpful internal tools to ease our everyday life is just as important. I believe if someone is prescribed psychiatric or ADD medications, which are powerful too and can turn a life upside down as quickly as they can help, they should also see a counselor regularly too. Why not seek tools in life to help the medications? I wish more doctors would make seeing a counselor at least twice a month a condition to continue to prescribe these medications and then periodically follow up with the counselor. I think it would be another win-win. Receiving these medications without regular counseling is like taking medication for a high cholesterol level but continuing to eat red meat three meals a day; the medicine may certainly help, it can give people back their lives, but it will not supply the life skill tools to help lighten the problem at the origin of the issue.

Pain walks with us

Our first pain and discomforts start shortly after birth. We go from a warm, dark, hopefully safe, floaty environment to bright lights, rough rubbing to dry us off, a hard suction bulb being stuck in our nose and mouth to clear secretions so we can breathe, ointments in our eyes, injections, a heel stick for blood sample, and maybe even an IV and more blood drawn or a tube into the lungs to help us breathe. Those first few minutes are most definitely a serious, harsh reality check, and an immediate indoctrination into the pain and discomfort of life. Thank goodness balance begins immediately also; we get wrapped up in warmth, held, and told we are beautiful. From our first breaths, balance and the ups and downs of life will walk with us to our last breath.

Our pain hopefully won't end for nine or ten more decades. Hopefully, we will take some of our guaranteed pains and learn to accept them as not only being alive, but also the reassurance we can feel. That ability comes in handy during life. No, pain is not something we should seek, although a percentage of our pain is self-inflicted due to our choices. But pain will arrive without looking for it. Whether a broken bone, periodic or chronic depression, grief, emptiness and loneliness, or anxiety, pain is one of the many human experiences we all share. I am repetitive about encouraging professional help, not only because it helps ease humanness, but also because all types of pain can push us to addiction, depression, isolation, and suicide.

Working with the pain of our minds is a lifelong rewarding endeavor. Whether we hit or sink into crisis for a period or walk with struggle, we are not alone. Reach out to all the potential levels of help and reassurance that are out there. I recently listened to a podcast called Mental *Health, Hope and Recovery*. This podcast is so moving and reassures us that we are not alone in life's difficulties, or our sea of hope and joy that we get to float in also. The beautiful and functional aspect of this podcast is that it comes from the firsthand experiences, lives, history, and tools of two open and trusting people that share their own experiences with their mental health and their journey to, and maintaining, wellness and joy. "Onward," as they say.

Physical pain

There is a difference between physical pain that is bad and good. The separation of these two is paramount for pain management to get off pain medication after surgery quickly, and to increase the speed of rehabilitation progress after surgery or injury. Yes, physical pain can also be good. It too reminds us we are alive; it reminds us we have been injured to humble us and to help prevent injury in the future. Before I continue, I acknowledge there is nothing "only" about pain, especially emotional pain. Physiologically, pain is only a nerve transmission, which is only chemicals moving in and out of the micron space between millions of nerve cells in a line between what hurts and your brain. Emotional and mental pain is basically the same nerve transmission, except it all takes place in the brain creating difficult thoughts and feelings. Unless it is a reflex, physical pain is a message that is sent from somewhere in your body up to your mind. Not all reflexes go all the way to your brain, many only go to your spine, then shoot back to the extremity that withdraws from the hot burner in a fraction of a second. But your interpretation of physical pain really is completely inside your head. I have fractured a bone three times in my life, and I know physical pain can hurt badly, I am not calloused to severe pain.

When experiencing pain, I ask myself whether it is good or bad. Bad pain is not to be ignored, and can come from a medical issue or physical, mental, or emotional trauma. Bad pain hurts to motivate you to seek help. Good pain, on the other hand, means the issue has been fixed, is healing, or you are preventing illness before it occurs. A pain may occur with self-honesty.

A frequently occurring trauma that is a great example of good versus bad physical pain is someone falling and fracturing the hip. Not always, but often, that means a break in the neck of the femur bone just before it goes into the joint with the pelvic bone, where it sits and rotates as we walk or stand. The outside of the bone is wrapped in nerves. Broken bone edges often either pinch those nerves, if it is a small fracture, or have torn them and are poking those nerves and other tissue structures, if a larger fracture has occurred. This is bad pain, and one must seek attention right away; this pain is the body saying, "Something is very wrong and must be fixed." Hip fractures can bleed so much, so fast that death can occur from the blood loss. Into a complicated surgery you go; they cut through layers of skin and muscle; they touch and move tendons and ligaments that really don't like to be touched, much less stretched and moved, and they literally saw off the femur bone below the break. The bone is cleaned out to make room for the prosthetic structure to be inserted, the prosthesis is "cemented" and/or screwed into place in the bone, and they then work the new ball top back into the joint, then they start backing out stitching layers as they close you back up.

Yes, you are going to have serious pain when you wake up, but what was bad pain before surgery is now good pain. You are alive! You have lived through a major bone being broken that is capable of bleeding out your blood volume, you have lived through a rough surgery, but you have been repaired. The collective knowledge, skill, and experience of the entire team that gets you through trauma or any surgery is amazing. The new structure may feel like you are going to fall apart, but it is so much tougher than you think. Yes, if it is right for you to accept the pain medication, please do. I confirm the magnitude of even the good pain. It is still a significant pain.

However, in a few hours, the staff will come to first sit you on the side of the bed and dangle your legs. Push through your fear of pain, don't say, "No! Wait!" over and over and become paralyzed. Tell yourself, "Yes I can, this is good pain," and do not listen to that good pain parading as bad pain telling you "No." Stand when they think you are ready and tell you to do so. If you tell yourself this and follow their professional directions, your good pain will leave you faster because you will heal faster. I believe you when you say it feels like you are damaging the doctor's skilled work. Yet, the great majority of post hip replacements do not damage anything after surgery due to the rehabilitation work.

By beginning to see pain as a message on a nerve path, or a thought, or emotion, that often can be worked with a little, as opposed to something we are complete victims of, empowers you and your choices to handle all of life's pains a little stronger. I know what it is like to have recurring painful thoughts, especially when I feel I have been wronged or it involves the injustices of our times.

A good pain that prevents future and greater pain, expense, and health issues is having your teeth cleaned or a cavity filled. Yes, it can hurt. Yes, they are poking and picking at your teeth and gums with sharp instruments. Blood may appear in your spit or the suction line, but they are trained professionals helping you keep your teeth. Something surprising my dentist taught me was that I could have part of a tooth drilled out without first injecting a local anesthetic, also known as numbing medicine, such as Lidocaine or Marcaine. To help me understand further, he reminded me that my teeth do not have nerves in the actual tooth material. If the drilling is not to the root nerve, it would not hurt to drill without a numbing injection first. He also taught me that he can't push the drill too hard or keep it in one place for too long without allowing the tooth to cool, because it would cause too much friction that produces heat, and if the root gets hot, then I will feel pain. So, he touches the drill for what seems like two to three seconds then lifts it off for two to three seconds to allow it to cool back down. My dentist was right and has since done several drillings over the past fifteen years without local anesthetic. I was not in pain in the least. If I had not trusted, I would have had four or five times where I had to experience the pain of a needle being inserted into my gums, and the momentary burn of the medicine being injected before it started to numb a second later. All for no reason, except to numb my fear. It takes trust and teamwork to accomplish this feat. There are times to listen to your pain and the fears that our instincts surround pain with, and times to conquer your fear and pain.

I was respectfully put in my place

Because I like balance, I'll share a great answer given to me after I had shared the above information about good and bad pain. John, who I introduce further in the *Suffer Less in Death* chapter, "Promoting life in a book about death," was a wonderful friend and life mentor to me through our nine-year friendship before he died at age ninety-eight. In his mid-nineties, he ended up in the hospital, for the third time since we met, this admission was for a small spinal compression fracture that was stable. Stable, meaning no risk of spinal or neurological damage with movement. It is day three, and he is still hitting his PCA button heavily. PCA stands for Patient Controlled Analgesia, and it is the best and worst thing to come along in the world of pain control since sliced bread. You push a button, and it delivers you intravenous (IV) pain medication at a rate no greater than the maximum dose the patient can have, which is controlled by settings entered by the nursing staff to match the doctor's orders. This device is great in several ways; streets should be named after the inventors. It can be programmed to give a set amount automatically at set intervals, such as X mg every Y minutes.

The next excellent feature is that it gives you the freedom and flexibility to give yourself a small dose periodically as needed. Instead of X-Y mg every two hours, one can give themselves, at the push of a button, 0.X mg every Y minutes. These more frequent smaller doses prevent huge peaks and valleys in pain. This takes away those two hours or more of steady rises in pain until the nurse is allowed to give your next dose. However, the downside of the PCA pump is over-sedation, less motivation, an unrealistic expectation of no pain through a rehabilitation period, and the high potential for abuse that can continue for the pleasures of euphoria rather than any real remaining levels of pain. We know people abuse this device for a few reasons.

The first reason is nurses get good at reading direct observation of pain's signs and symptoms correlated to what we are being told by the patient. But the objective way we know is at the end of every shift, the ongoing nurse and the off-going nurse check the PCA pump together. One thing the pump tells us is how many times the patient pushed the button, even though it will only give a dose every so many preset minutes. Pushing the button before those preset minutes have passed gets you no medication. Sometimes the number of times someone pushed the button is in the thousands at the end of a shift. A PCA is a beautiful thing, but it is a good idea to get off it, and encourage other people to get off it, as soon as appropriate, decreasing pain levels and healing allows.

John is a very self-motivated man, nothing to this point of our friendship can keep him down. On day three, he asked me, "How come this time it is harder for me to get up and go? Aside from my age, I am not getting up and pushing myself like I normally can." I answered by validating his age and injury and told him that crushed bones do indeed cause severe pain. Then I gave him the same pain talk I had before when he was in the hospital, and that I just gave you above, ending with, "If you want to get up and go, then push the pain medication button in your hand less!" He had been looking at me the whole time, as I finished my ten-minute too wordy answer, he raised his eyebrows, and with three days of PCA pump comfort in his eyes and voice said, "Well that's all well and good, but they aren't your neurons, they're mine." After we finished laughing, I realized he had gifted me a grounding I needed, and I accepted.

He immediately stopped pushing the button as often as he had been and was discharged a few days later.

The deeper pains we can't completely dissolve

I feel I would stop short if I did not talk about our deeper pains from the greater traumas, mistakes, regrets, and injustices that occurred to us, and that we carry. The fleeting and fluctuating greater one known as emptiness and loneliness will walk with us the rest of our lives. Emptiness and loneliness partially leave us when we find companionship on various levels or extend ourselves in healthy friendship. Whether your loneliness is from isolation or a lack of connections to others, emptiness and loneliness are painful and can affect every aspect of our being. Loneliness is so powerful we can feel it to a devastating degree surrounded by a hundred people. I admit it is difficult that emptiness and loneliness never leaves us. However, once I accepted that emptiness and loneliness will always be with me, they started visiting me much less often and less intensely.

The feeling of emptiness and loneliness is one of the most gouging pains, and our life's work with it is a tough deal. To attempt to avoid these feelings, some people reject that they have a need for others on any level. Others swing to the opposite side of the pendulum and surround themselves with all levels of contact to keep busy and hope that emptiness and loneliness will enter less, or not at all.

Even though most of us walk our lives with companionship on some level, we must accept that we all carry a void in our chest and gut of varying sizes throughout our life. Building healthy relationships is one of the ways we keep this void to a workable size. Those relationships could be intimate, a friendship, occupational, family, or our relationships with exercise, work, or your god, and hopefully your spirituality. All healthy relationships are good and healthy, except they can fool us, especially new intimate relationships.

Expecting another to fill or remove your emptiness and loneliness, when they have their own to walk with, is unfair and a setup for issues. Yet thankfully, all types of healthy relations do help us decrease these pitted feelings, and thankfully, there are people wanting to help each other. Where we are initially set up for failure is that sometimes a new relationship can completely cover that open space for a short period of time. The painful truth is that open space can never be completely filled. It can be covered, partially filled, but never eliminated. Whether a deep and lasting connection or an intense infatuation, the empty and lonely feelings may start to come back, even in healthy, happy relationships. Accepting this admittedly difficult reality of the human spirit can save a lot of problems and may even decrease the frequency of feeling emptiness and loneliness. On the surface, it might look like not being angry or disappointed in others that we still sometimes feel emptiness and loneliness. Or the natural slowing of a relationship as the infatuation eases to a calm comfortable glide is not seen as something wrong with the relationship or worrying that the initial spark calming is the end of the goodness. Accepting that emptiness and loneliness never completely get resolved does not mean love and intimacy cannot remain powerful, passionate, and ever evolving.

It is human to want to avoid or cover the fact that we all must walk with a certain level of emptiness and loneliness. Addictions only cover up emptiness and loneliness when we are partaking in the addiction.

When the reality is more often the reverse occurs, true addictions add deeply to emptiness and loneliness because our addictions often cause shame and isolation, whether legal or not, or involving intoxicants or not.

Oftentimes, accepting a painful reality can decrease its negative effect on us. The acceptance of a slight to periodic medium level of emptiness and loneliness weakens its ability to squeeze the chest and gut region as hard as it once could when we expect it to be gone and never return. To be able to say I will walk my life with a low workable percentage of this pain has been freeing. I no longer blame my relationship or feel there is something wrong with me when I periodically feel it.

Friendships help decrease pain

True friendship is harder to find as we become a more me-oriented society. I always fall back on the pillars of acceptance, tolerance, forgiveness, and understanding to discuss any healthy relationship. But true friendship requires a few more specific heavy hitters. The adage of quality over quantity comes into play when we talk about friendship. Personally, I noticed my deeper pains are lightened by true friendships. I have slowly developed a few criteria for a close friend. Yes, friendships can hurt, yet they also can be helpful to our healing, growth, and stress reduction.

Healthy friends will not try to be perfect, and they too will share their faulted humanness. I have found that my true friends do not judge me when I trust them with my mistakes in life. My true friends are too busy looking out for their own faults and weaknesses to judge others. I have discovered my true friends understand the meaning of confidentiality and will not share with others what I have entrusted to them. I feel I can trust a faithful friend and display my softer spots; a loyal friend will not try to hurt me with it later. My friends will show me their humanness, that helps me feel less alone and less faulted. Nor will they try to outdo me, and they will attempt to let me finish my sentences. I say "attempt," because friends should be excited to talk with each other, and a respectful friend will not make me feel like their next statement is more important than me finishing mine. These are hard to get perfect, which is why I am still actively working on being a better friend. Being a better friend is how we bump up the friendships we have, or find better friends, then our deeper friendships can become richer and more supportive. Friends should be able to laugh at their humanness together, they should be safe for that healthy goodness.

I am sorry bad things happen to us

Our past traumas are major contributing factors to our deeper pains. Most of us have experienced trauma in our lives that falls into the realms of direct abuse, assault, neglect, being the victim of crime or manipulation, or the confusing self-doubt trauma of being the victim of narcissism. I know of very few people that have walked any real distance in life that has not experienced mental, emotional, or physical trauma. Sexual assault and abuse at any age is yet another hell on earth, especially involving children and youth. Our traumas remove our trust and security in those around us. Trauma steals parts of our being and life when it stops us from experiencing people or places due to damaging our trust. Such as people that are unable to drive again after a major car crash, distrusting the other drivers around them, or fear walking into your own home after being the victim of a burglary. Just as the teamwork of an entire hospital gets us to the other side of major physical trauma, it may take professional help to get to the other side of the mental or emotional trauma. The pain of past traumas is deep, wide, and is so invasive into too many areas of our being. Dealing with trauma can take a lifetime, but it does not have to take a lifetime to start getting parts of ourselves back. The above referral to the podcast *Mental Health, Hope and Recovery* is filled with amazing stories and tools to gently walk with and lighten some of our traumas.

I wish I had, or had not

The last type of pain I would like to touch on is one that often grows with time. All other pains can often weaken with time, but this last one seems to have a reverse correlation with time, that being the emotion and pain of regret. The pain of regret can become stronger as we realize with every passing year that we cannot get our minutes, choices, words, actions, or our lack of positive actions back.

The pain from regret also has its origin in our lack of acceptance of our beautiful, imperfect humanness. We regret either an action or an inaction, yet our humanness at that given moment is why we did or did not act. Does that mean we regret being an imperfect human? Then what would the opposite of that look like? If you have read *Suffer Less in Death*, you know that I have talked to many people about their mortality and their fast-approaching death. Regret quickly became a common theme.

Something powerful changes in us when mortality shakes our core. That is often when we realize our life has an approaching time limit, we slow down the use of the rationalizations we used to paint the pictures of our lives prettier than the reality of the unfiltered truths. When these powerful events, such as cancer, major trauma, or advanced aging occur, regret can gain strength and twist us up tighter. Just because you are young, please know these paragraphs on regret are for you also. Seeing the benefits of positive actions today will help you have fewer regrets tomorrow. Or, if we choose acceptance and peace with our human limits, also known as our past poor choices or outright mistakes, then acceptance can allow us a gentleness with life's choices, as

opposed to regret. In these deep, beautiful conversations, I have heard
the most interesting and powerful regrets. My favorite was very wide
and nonsensical, but only in literal meaning. But oh, how it allowed me
to drop my shoulders further into relaxing and trusting, "I regret that I
did not exhale more than I inhaled." I am still not through allowing that
one to help me.

Most tell me they don't regret their life in its totality, but many do
regret some of their choices. It all adds up to reasons to live our lives
with goodness each day, because I have never once heard someone say
they regretted doing something in their life that was of goodness. The
most common theme was those two little words I like to tack onto the
end of sentences: omissions and in-actions.

Regret squeezes us harder, causing a sharper, longer pain, as years
pass. Many people have expressed great regrets concerning someone
who has died. The pain of regret can start to get right up close as our
days become slightly more clearly numbered. Do-overs become harder,
periodically even seeming impossible if the do-over needed to be with
someone who has died. Yet, it is never too late to get all or part of our
most regretful subjects partially corrected, even if death has occurred to
the person we wish to make amends. However, when we cannot make
direct amends to someone who has died, or gone from our lives, it can
leave us feeling incomplete or again regretful.

It is never too late to weaken regrets even partially. You may
think it is too late to change a regret that you have towards someone
who has died, such as wishing your last words were not harsh, or
you had encouraged someone to a goal before an early death. Even
those seemingly hopeless feelings of painful regret could be partially
righted by more kind words to others or supporting someone else
towards a dream. There are those we cannot apologize to for one
reason or another, even if death is not the reason, maybe anger or
mental wellness prevents discussions. But we can partially make it up

to them by learning, growing, doing better, and in general giving back to others.

I have witnessed the proof that it is never too late to weaken or resolve the pains of regret. I have mentioned these two to you before, they both did something to prevent an inaction regret. I met a resident working the medical side of the emergency department at Charity Hospital shortly after I started. This driven woman was in her late sixties. She had raised her children, helped raise her grandchildren, and had always wanted to be a doctor. She wisely did not let that create a regret and entered medical school in her early sixties. About twenty-one years later, while in the law enforcement academy, I met a man who did the same sort of action. He had retired from a successful career in the world of finance in his mid-sixties and wanted to keep accomplishing his goals and continue to contribute to society. He graduated from the academy and went to a department as a reserve officer. It was an honor to train next to these people that set out in action to weaken their life's regrets.

We all have the potential to feel greater pain when we look at the choices or statements we made and later discover we were wrong. The pain of regret has an extra strong bite when we find the courage to admit we hurt people, whether with intent or by accident. Self-honesty shakes our core, and that helps break up our more deeply embedded darker places to help us get them out. It is not my place to say what your dark places are or even if you should shake them up to get them out.

We may have regrets about the times we ignored wise words of wisdom that attempted to prevent our mistakes and wrongs. The list is endless for the length and magnitude of a human's mistakes, or our list of wishes or experiences missed. However, it is a deep core gift to yourself, and will bring peace today and fewer regrets tomorrow to accept and embrace the following truth. We will do many things right and many wrong, we will see and do much, and there is much we will never see, accomplish, or learn. Yet, wisdom, peace, and tranquility can be found in the gentleness of knowing most of what was not our best, and all that we will not get to experience, is very okay. Especially, if we are grateful for, and can deeply experience, all we will see, will feel, will learn, and will accomplish.

WIDER ANGLES:

MY MOUTH

I believe my mouth is on my chin for a very important reason. This location moves it 4 to 5 inches away from my brain. You see, if my mouth were on my forehead, there would be less than half of an inch between my thought and my spoken word. Instead, with my mouth a few inches away on the chin, it gives me one second to filter what I am going to say. Now, I know one second is not long enough to help 100% of my more embarrassing poor choice or arrangement of words, but it sure helps decrease some of the stuff I wish I had not said. Pathetic, I admit, but I think my mouth would have to be on my knee for me to accomplish a higher margin of safety.

I finished sharing this absurd visual with a very special friend who said, "What if our mouths were on our hearts?"

CHAPTER 7

RELATIONSHIPS

"Coming together is a beginning, keeping together is progress,
working together is success."
—Henry Ford

There are a handful of things we absolutely cannot choose throughout our lives: parents, birthright nationality, race, the body we are born into, sexuality, falling in or out of love, periodic random tragedies, and the socioeconomic level we are born into. One step further, nor can we choose our family or order of birth. This is another great reason to stop holding such unavoidable demographics against each other and move onto healthier relationships. I always had trouble understanding people who hate the people of a race, nationality, or even the wealthy, when not one person can choose what body or region of the earth they are born into. The title of Trevor Noah's book *Born a Crime* sums it up well. He had zero control that he came into this world as a newborn of a white father and a black mother, in a country where it was against the law to marry and have children with someone whose skin color did not match your own. Not one of us had a speck of control over the who, where, or what we were born. Similarly, we are not able to pick completely who we must have a relationship with, such as a work relationship, a neighbor, a customer, or a classmate. But we have a fluctuating amount of free will and choice in how we choose to work with most people we meet.

I worked my way through high school and college. I had a wonderful hodgepodge of relationships due to all those jobs, bosses, workmates, classmates, professors, friends, and acquaintances during those years. The people, and the relationships I had with them, just kept coming at me. I had no idea all those relationships were warming me up for an onslaught after graduating and going to work. Just a few weeks after graduating nursing school, I was walking into the emergency department and seeing patients, trying and failing to keep their families updated, working with the hospital permanent staff, and the rotating LSU and Tulane interns and residents. I was inundated with new relationships every shift. I found out quickly that some of those relationships were not going to be easy, whether a short-term relationship with a patient or family member, or a long-term relationship with a staff member, resident, or attending. I thought to myself, if I have a life of this amount of great and sometimes bumpy relationships with people, I want to get better at the not-so-easy ones. I began to exercise what varying influence I could have on helping to create more peaceful and productive relationships in my life. Just as with every subject in life, my success rate fluctuates.

Don't get me wrong, I am no angel; I upset people. We all upset people. If you have a brain, a personality, and a way to communicate, you will upset people. Every one of us can rock the boats of the people around us, it just happens. It correlates to the wise old construction saying, "If you are not making mistakes, you aren't building anything." Until the day you no longer have a way to communicate your personality, you will continue to periodically upset people. I consider it a major win-win when the number of people I upset goes down, and the number of people I get along with goes up.

I also know people that just don't want contact with others past what is required for work and life. They have a wide range of reasons why they prefer to keep people at a distance. I do not know that person's life, I have no idea what traumas they have endured. I do not judge. They may have good reason to keep so many people at bay with a shield of one type or another. Then, unfortunately for them and all of us, there are some people who enjoy some type of reward by actively not getting along with the people around them. For balance, sometimes past traumas or deep insecurities also influence this behavior. Although, I think most of us would rather get along in the relationships in our lives. There are three rewards to being flexible and aware of mutual responsibility and teamwork in all cohesive relationships: peace, profit, and productivity. Profit and productivity have a much wider meaning behind them than only dollars earned, or units produced.

Our relationships can be amazing in many wonderful directions, or laser-burning difficult. Of the thousands of relationships that you will have in your life, whether the checkout person in the store, a client, colleague, or intimate partner, you do have an active influence on its outcome. Granted, some people are just outright difficult, and some of the most peaceful and understanding people in the world have relationships that stumble. Always allowing yourself room for self-review and improvement can bring greater calm and less conflict to your relationships

Relationships can turn tense quickly

The healthcare field has a wonderfully old, incredibly important, yet never outdated saying concerning a major medical or trauma situation. This saying is not reserved for the moment of death of someone at the end of their long life, but rather this saying is for the nineteen-year-old in the car accident, or the fifty-six-year-old having a major heart attack way too soon in life who just coded, and CPR is starting: "The first pulse you take is your own."

Those eight little words have the potential to change our world, and at that moment, the life of other human beings, literally. When someone's eyes roll up in their head and they make a loud grunt, it can often mean their heart is no longer in the correct electrical rhythm, and the clock just started ticking to the potential for brain damage from a lack of oxygen or actual death. It happens so fast sometimes. Hopefully they are already in the cardiac room, and the defibrillator is a few feet away. But what if they are in the walk-in clinic for knee pain, and they aren't on a cardiac monitor? "Code!!" You call it loud and clear! "Code in walk-in clinic room 9!!" Do you start CPR there? How busy is the entire department? Or do you take the breaks off the bed immediately and roll them around the corner to the cardiac room? Are your buddies inbound to you with a code cart with the needed defibrillator? Or are they tied up with another trauma or cardiac arrest? You decide to roll, a nurse-aid drops the railing and kneels on the bed to start CPR as you are rolling, the cardiac room is open, the staff is arriving as you hook up the defibrillator monitor. It is ventricular tachycardia, the defibrillator charges and alarms, another nurse already has the defibrillator paddles in hand, and yells, "All clear!" and checks to make sure no one is touching the bed, looks at the monitor one more time to make sure the cardiac rhythm still needs to be shocked, and Boom! The defibrillator discharges. The patient's arms jerk towards the center of their body, the rhythm converted back into normal sinus rhythm, the patient opens their eyes immediately. They are confused, "What happened?" You calm and inform them, but you all keep hustling because there is work to be done immediately for further stability care and diagnostics. Everyone took their own pulse first. Everyone knew what to do, and a good level headed call by the nurse to roll the patient to the cardiac room. Their brain went less than 20 seconds without CPR, and 60 seconds before the shock of the defibrillator restored a normal heart rhythm, and thus oxygen is moving in the body again. All because of rational thinking, with trained professional calculated responses, not disorganized emotional reactions.

Taking your own pulse first is the key to all of life's relationships. If you want greater peace in your relationships, that fast self-pulse check is the difference between having a reflexive fast emotional reaction as opposed to a peace-creating rational response. A fast self-check, often involving a fast down-ego-down, can potentially deescalate the slightest bumps to the steepest mountains in relationships. Granted, the closer the person is to you, the more they are in your life, the closer the required contact, whether by personal choice or occupational infliction, the more challenging this can be. Also, the more we respect and care about a person, or feel a responsibility to help and protect them, then not allowing a bump to turn into hills or mountains can be harder. Such as your children or an aging parent making questionable decisions. I have been guilty of losing that needed easygoing weekend to saying the wrong thing, or to having a conditioned reaction move across my face. It is daunting the number of factors that can derail a relationship and damage our peace, productivity, and profit.

The big key

There is a great lasting way to make almost all relationships much easier, and as strange as this may sound, the answer is forced on all of us. Even if you walk into the woods to be reclusive, to not see another person for years, you cannot get rid of this human relationship. It is the hardest, scariest, but most rewarding and yet potentially peace-filled relationship in your life. I guarantee it will also be the most deceptive and potentially manipulative relationship of your life. It is the relationship you have with yourself.

The real growth, smoothness, and ease come from remembering you are hopefully 50% of the connection and influence on how each of those relationships unfold. I say hopefully 50% because I am realistic that sometimes that percentage can drop far, depending on the personalities and the type of relationship. You can have a great boss that is not insecure and is broad minded in scope, does not have control issues, and is emotionally and humanistically intelligent enough to know that keeping you at 50% autonomy in the working relationships keeps you creative, happy, and highly productive. If a boss is not capable of that for a myriad of reasons, then your influence percentage is going to be much lower than 50%. You can be a 100% self-motivated, competent, capable, contributing to the team type of person, but their position and personality forces you far below 50%.

Except for the less-than-optimal relationships, the good old standard of a 40–60% fluctuation rule will normally apply to the amount of influence you have on a relationship. We all have days when we are not at our best, that is normal human fluctuation. Yet, our relationship with ourselves affects how we react and the level of flexible peace we contribute. Are we appropriately trying to bring calm, productivity, and function to that relationship and moment, or is our ego responding with unnecessary defensiveness or aggression? My relationship with myself will ultimately decide if I will allow my ego to respond or if my calmer, more secure, peace-creating, and rational self will respond.

After I left Charity Hospital in the late 1980s, during most of my years in teaching hospitals' emergency departments, I mainly worked twelve-hour weekend nights. I routinely worked with the same people also on special weekend night plans. I started doing fast post-incident reviews, or debriefings, after we had to go hands-on and restrain someone for the safety of all. If it was the same team, we discussed it less because we knew to self-evaluate, but if a new person joined the team, we would add a few back in. We would go over how the escalation might have been prevented, because not all can be prevented. We would look to see if there was a point that a simple action could have prevented what became a physically dangerous situation. We would all learn to drop the ego's defensiveness and say, "You know, they came out to the nurse's station twice and complained about the wait time, maybe I could have taken an extra minute to validate and move their care along." Inevitably, there would be a new member to the team who initially could not do this review without ego, "I could not help that outcome. She called me so and so and kept walking into the rooms while I worked with other sicker patients telling me...." We would let the new person know that we do these reviews periodically, and it is a moment we all look back to find somewhere early on that the relationship with that person could have been assisted to a calmer level. That is our job to see and attempt to deescalate hills and mountains while they are still small rocks on the path. Once new nurses had witnessed us being able to find the point the relationship may have been improved, they too would learn self-review.

Granted, most situations do not turn as potentially physically harmful as they can in frequency in hospitals and on the streets for EMS, fire, and police. But it is happening more and more—workplace violence, shootings, and mass killings have been an increasing fact for a few decades now. How you treat others does have some level of immediate and down-the-road culpability for someone's behavior. We have had a great injustice perpetrated on us over the last few decades. It was self-perpetuating with our attitudes and reinforced by social behaviors. The trending and destructive belief that we are not responsible for how other people feel is easily disproved in one question. Do other people say and do things that upset you? Yes, every one of us can be triggered by the behavior of others. From the inconsiderate driver that cuts you off, to the unrealistic boss, to the bluntly selfish actions of our partner, kids, parents, siblings, or coworkers. We upset each other; we do have some level of responsibility for others' feelings. Yes, ultimately, we are responsible for our own emotions as far as what we do with them. Yet, at the same time, denying we affect others is not conducive to smoother and easier.

How we evaluate our past also has an influence on our relationships. Our past has created many conditioned reactions. A percentage of those may have been formed out of necessity to keep us safe, but many become unnecessary and are now robbing us of our peace, and even our free will and choice. Our relationship with our past has created conditioning that may cause us to unnecessarily or inappropriately react to something said or done that does not deserve the conditioned reaction it caused in us. Thank goodness many conditioned reactions can be partially or completely unconditioned. We may not be able to unlearn them all, but we may accomplish decreasing the frequency and intensity of the automatic place we go when a button is pushed.

Reconditioning or working to change a conditioned reaction is not easy, they are often in place for an accurately perceived need for self-protection. Anything we developed for protection, whether accurately perceived or not, is normally a deeply ingrained defense. Fear, insecurity, inflexibility, control, anger, jealousy, and even greed, to name only a few, can create lightning-fast reactions in us that are often far more powerful than is appropriate for the situation. How much conflict in our lives could be avoided by not quickly reacting or even slightly reacting to what someone is saying? This does not mean you do not share your thoughts on a subject if appropriate or helpful, for that is another way we lift each other up. Looking at how often we are unnecessarily defensive to input or even just brainstorming is a good start. Once we become comfortable being imperfect humans, and we add in an open desire to never stop attempting personal growth, then defensiveness loses much of its unnecessary flexing. The gem of decreasing defensiveness may be hard to start working on because ego will try so hard to block your progress. Once you get more of your free will and choice back, continuing to decrease unnecessary defensiveness rapidly becomes easier and easier. This gem is a seriously important key to suffering less.

In truly dangerous situations our fast reactions can literally keep us alive. However, during the other 99.99% of the time, those lightly fast reactions can ruin a moment, day, or relationship.

I admit, accomplishing that in a police uniform was a little harder than accomplishing it in hospital scrubs or plain clothes, but I proved it can be done for over twelve years. To have a driver start a traffic stop by aggressively accusing me of this or that for this or that reason, and by the end of the traffic stop they apologize for both what they did wrong and for how they treated me, is pure gold and proof there is a better way to do everything. That person drove away with a positive interaction and outcome, to a no fun relationship that started off with red and blue lights in their rear-view mirror, and a crummy emotional, aggressive, and accusatory start towards me. By the end of the stop, they were truly relaxed, comfortable, from the core out more aware of their driving, and would often apologize for their unnecessarily aggressive start. By applying rational detachment, I was able to not allow their emotional response to control our relationship. Which may have contributed to the roads being one person a little safer for you, they may have gained slightly more respect for law enforcement, and hopefully they share the experience with others to multiply the goodness. Even though their initial aggression could have triggered an emotional response in me, I applied rational detachment and delivered a rational response.

When any relationship begins to escalate, I *attempt* to tell my ego it can't talk. If ego gives me input, I normally do the opposite. It does not matter what your many roles are in a day, mom, manager, friend, or intimate partner, our ego is potentially reactionary in that role. Our ego is worried about how it will look tomorrow, not how safe, peaceful, productive, and profitable you are today. My rational thoughts have a much higher rate of appropriate calming responses.

Human but trying to be professional about it

Around the end of my first year of nursing I had an awareness come to me that first led to being more realistic with myself, and then led to great conversations and team building. I displayed this awareness by wearing a name tag throughout the rest of my nursing career that I would modify slightly. I would write or tape the initials "H.B." after my name and title of R.N. The team building came from the existing staff initially asking, "What does the H.B. stand for?" Patients, family members, and new teammates would also ask about the H.B. I would reply with pride and seriousness, "It stands for 'Human Being,' it is my highest degree, and the reason I wear it is that my nursing abilities are limited to my human abilities." I then followed that with, "It is just as much a reminder to my colleagues as it is to patients and family members." I did notice a difference in the team's gentleness with themselves and each other; it gives everyone permission to drop a peg in self tension. It clearly allowed for increased professionalism. Ego and professionalism have a negative correlation; as ego goes down, professionalism increases.

Since we are all limited to human ability, should we not all be wearing "H.B." on our name tag, door, desk, and title? The name tag is not as important as the application of the concept. For this awareness to truly bring benefits, it must first apply to yourself, then to any person you will interact with in life and work. Pushing yourself, or someone else, past human ability will lead to rough relationships, failure, frustration, burnout, and can even fall into the realm of abuse. Functional, optimal, long-lasting, productive relationships and teams come from realistic expectations of human ability. This does not mean we do not "push" ourselves and each other to always strive for better.

There is also nothing wrong with periodic short-term productivity pushes, "We need 200 units produced and delivered by Friday." Pushing individuals or teams past human ability is not optimizing relationships or potential future productivity. Strong productive individuals make up strong teams, and strong teams wisely know to keep the individuals strong and cared for too. This has been a practice by the most balanced societies of the world since the formation of tribes. Try to not only evaluate cultures by their "development;" many cultures have never stopped being strong and healthy in this mutually supportive understanding. That deserves recognition and respect.

Too much self-gain beyond healthy instilled self-care and security by any team member will upset the balance and united strength of that team's potential and healthy longevity. That unhealthy team player can be the owner, boss, or a peer. This historically significant mutual relationship dynamic is being challenged and ignored as we become a society more and more focused on self-gain only, leaving out balance, longevity, and sustainability because they are "Not my concern" according to many. The pursuit of security and wealth is not the issue, that is an inalienable right of all humans. The issue is the over-focus on self-gain that disrupts the balance of teams, groups, communities, and countries. I recently heard in conversation, "The pursuit of freedom is not necessarily a concern or drive across the earth, but the pursuit of power is." Too many supervisors use that power to treat their staff with uncaring disrespect to make themselves and their "numbers" look impressive. Then they wonder why their turnover is so high. This is not a small issue, with great workers and the general health of peace, productivity, and profit, suffering because of it.

There is a lengthy list of criteria that should be met to be considered a professional. To name just a few, training, knowledge level, teaching, self-review, peer review, ongoing education, and displaying a high level of professionalism, even under challenging situations. One's daily words and behaviors are very much a part of that earned and worthy title. I have known surgeons who have wonderful, mild bedside manners with patients and family, but literally throw tantrums and objects in the operating room if a nurse hands them the wrong instrument. I have seen nurses who would rather argue to be right, then to be calm, understanding, and treat the patient and family members with flexible professional respect during their momentary crisis. I have seen staff members place their ego before their professional responsibility, who inflame patients or family members to the point of verbal or physical violence, resulting in the patient or family member being restrained or escorted from the hospital. Pulling all of this together is why I believe that it is not the title that makes someone a professional, but rather *how* they are doing that job that should proudly earn the individual the honor of being a professional human being, not only a professional at one's occupation.

Various relationships: friends, occupational, personal, and family

Once my close inner circle found out I was including a chapter about relationships, people started giving me input: "Include bosses," "Include teenagers," "Include difficult customers," and painfully, I forcefully once heard, "Include moms!" That one I could have done without. I write about my mother's humor and outlook, but I would rather not write about her dynamics in relationships. The only one I hated hearing more was, "Cops, you need to write about cops, we need a better perspective." I added to the list any relationships I could think of that either were frequent relationships or difficult to one or both parties, such as a phone call to customer service or technical support. As any good comedian or comedy writer will tell you, always start off making fun of yourself, it lets the group know you're human, faulted, and have no trouble going first.

Myself

I am primarily driven by the same characteristics of all living things, and a few more bonus ones, and a few not so bonus ones. Those characteristics of all living things are worthy of mention, they bond us all, and that human bond is important to me. I know we need each other, and everything that bonds us is important.

The deeply ingrained what and why of parts of my being are strongly influenced by the following characteristics of all living organisms. I am made of living cells, that I, too, must work to keep alive, healthy, and regenerating. My cells' DNA was passed down to me; that DNA makes me hereditary, and my parents and long lineage are in me. I am one big metabolic function; I must consume nutrients and water to provide energy to my physical body that carries my being, and I also must be able to feed my spirit, mind, heart, and soul throughout my life, or parts of my spirit will die too. I must be able to regulate myself or I will die. I must be able to grow, my cells must be able to reproduce, and our red blood cells are very good at it because they only live about 120 days. I have a need to eliminate—some people say I am full of elimination— and once again I find a bond in knowing we are all full of elimination. I have a characteristic in me to reproduce, though I overrode this characteristic with a vasectomy at the age of twenty-seven. However, the drive to attempt has never left this organism. In humans, it also shows itself as a desire to touch and be held, and I still have that characteristic too. I have a need to breathe in oxygen and exhale carbon dioxide, plants have the same need to exchange gas to live, except in reverse. Thank goodness they like making oxygen for us animals and they like our carbon dioxide just as much, a needed mutual relationship. I have the ability and need to be mobile; movement is good, as well as required.

My last two living characteristics are my favorites for the big wide wonderful reasons of promoting life within. I have an ability to change and adapt, meaning I am instilled with an ability to stay alive by changing habits and behaviors. The ability to change and adapt is also the ability to be flexible and figure out new and better ways to not only stay alive but feel alive. The ability to change and adapt hopefully keeps me from making the same mistakes over and over. Well, . . . and over. I expend a lot of energy exercising this characteristic. I also share the ability to interact with other living organisms, whether that interaction is other humans or all other organisms. The ability to interact is required to stay alive and to be challenged and stimulated. My lifelong practical experience and observation of this characteristic has brought me great pain, joy, growth, humor, knowledge, and challenges.

Besides those ten, I have a few other innate drives that seem to have been in me from an early age. I have always had a strong drive to contribute in both large and small ways. I pursued helping fields because I know they help me too. My sensitivities and awareness of the pain in the world also drives me to attempt to help. It has been a drive in me I have never regretted, and it has given me just as much as I have given, perhaps more.

I have always been self-motivated to learn and accomplish, both personally and professionally. Perhaps I am compensating for missing the first seven years of school to those migraine headaches and learning disabilities; but I have a brain that desires to never stop evaluating how something is done and just looking to see if it can be done in a better, more efficient, or more peaceful way.

I am an optimist on the outside but a realist on the inside. Even though I painfully know the dangerous magnitude of human behavior on an up-close personal level, I refuse to give up on us humans. The people that give up don't seem as joyful in life as those who keep believing and contributing.

Working with me is relatively easy. I just want to know that you know we are both human. Since I can assure you that our relationship will have mutual mistakes and imperfections. I have a limit, and I will protect myself and others. I have taken two vows, in nursing and law enforcement, to be an advocate for the people and to protect others. I have gotten into trouble with bosses because I cannot leave those oaths at the door of my work. But I had that problem before I ever went into nursing. In eighth grade, I was discretely punched in the stomach on the school bus for telling a ninth grader he was being rude to his girlfriend. My mother and four older sisters trained much of that into me at an early age also, and I am grateful for that influence.

How would you have written this subsection for yourself?

Friendships

Our friendships should be our glue. We are not as sensitive to our friends' words as we can be hearing our intimate partner state the same words. It can still get a little sensitive with friends at times, because a strong bond grows if it is a healthy relationship, and even friends can hit bumps. We should be a counselor to our friends, and they should counsel us too. Friends should not be yes friends; I painfully have periodically needed my closest friends to show me tough love. As a fun nursing buddy loved to say if I presented some sort of rationalization for my actions that she could see right through, "I call bulls*#t on that." I hate that she was too often right. That's what a friend will do; attempt to correct or push me out of harm's way, even when harm's way is my own dangerous way of thinking. Our friends sometimes see the situation more clearly than we do, but sometimes their caution can hold us back from accomplishment. True friends say things I don't want to hear, sometimes about me, and sometimes about the world, or even their political or social views. If everyone stays respectful, I welcome opposing views from friends, as we are all periodically a little off or wrong. I would rather have a friend point out the error of my ways than continue to err.

Friends want to teach each other how to be better friends. When you really care to be a good friend, you will work to be the friend they want you to be, and not only the friend you think you should be to them. It's a mix. Sometimes if these don't line up, true friends will respect that the friendship is growing apart. A true friend will be good with that and let it grow apart with peace and respect.

Poor friendships have red flags, some painful ones. Bumps in friendships happen, those are not red flags. When a pump occurs, a true friend can apologize and accept their part of the breakdown. This should hold true for all healthy respectful relationships, even professional ones.

Friendships are our glue because they are capable of holding us together when we are getting close to falling apart, have fallen apart, or just need steadying. They are also glue because they hold up with the passage of time. Or, if the friendship left off in a personality bumpy place, after a rest period, its bond holds, and the friendship rebuilds and continues to walk onward.

The Mentor

The mentor is a tricky relationship with important responsibility and great rewards. It is a waning vital relationship of society. Our youth depend on mentors to guide them with the respect of truths, facts, encouragement to think on their own, and the separation of facts and opinions. Both are important. For the student's sake, facts and opinions must be labeled honestly and correctly. Our youth deserve and need to have both labeled honestly, out of fairness and respect to the student and the well-being of their tomorrow. History shows the wider the knowledge of the youth, the greater the potential and strength of a society's future.

The mentor to the much older student, meaning into adulthood, is also a trusting relationship. It is harder for the older student to say, "teach me." It shows teamwork and commitment, it selflessly might even mean you want your competition to succeed. Sharing your knowledge is the mark of the professional, the mark of the caring, and of being secure in yourself. It means you care about bigger pictures than yourself, and that someone else's well-being and tomorrow is important to you also. That is noble.

The healthy mentor will not knowingly manipulate. They may share scary knowledge, but they will not use it to scare others to attempt to manipulate their thoughts. The wise and healthy mentor will say "Here is my knowledge," not "This is what I want you to do with the knowledge." As Margaret Mead said, "Children must be taught how to think, not what to think." We adults should be their greatest mentors, so try not to fade or feel defeated by the media and social pressures. Throwing your arms up in futility should never be a choice. Keep tutoring the youth, even when they scream "Shut-up, shut-up, shut-up," and their bedroom door slams. Some of your input absorbs and helps them. They need your balanced, wise input more than they will ever thank you for.

After parents, the mentor role falls on all of us next, as the youth are watching and listening. We are all their mentors by example: they are watching us drive, they are watching how strangers treat strangers, and they are watching how other parents raise their children. Please, help the children and our youth to learn, grow, succeed, and thrive. It is the responsibility of the mentors to see the bigger picture of what the student is working with today and what they are walking into their future, not what the mentor's past was made of. That type of thinking will only get the trusting young person into our yesterday, not their tomorrow. We need to remember their reality is not the reality of yesterday, before we tell them they can't read a book because it teaches them about today's realities.

Our educators in the classrooms of the schools are our commissioned mentors. Never underestimate their role, even though society wants to undercut their value and their commission. You already knew you were following your heart, not your wallet. I only remind you of that as a reason to continue from the heart, not as an excuse for your low financial compensation. I hope society sees the magnitude of the energy teachers must spend daily to help raise our children. I am pulling for you all; I hope society sees you are worth more than you are being thanked. I also know teachers need help in their classroom, the behavior issues by a few students fatigues them and detract from the other scholars' education. This issue is only half about the special needs of that child and the teacher, the other half is related to the education of all.

What you say in your classroom, in the halls, and outside, students do hear. So please choose your words from consciousness, not judgment, habit, or frustration. Never think they don't hear you, and never think you can't make or break them. I painfully know for a fact that your words can be the straw that breaks the student's back. Remember professionalism, do not become stagnant. "That is the way we have always done it" is accepting stagnation. Never stop educating yourself from every direction, you are leading by example. What if a scholar said to you, "That is enough, I don't need to learn anymore, I've got this." Change grade levels a few times in your career, learn the curriculum in the grades before and after your favorite grade. It will help you help your students. Never forget, it is not about what is easier for you, it is about the growth and development of those entrusting you with their minds and spirits. Keep yourself in check and balance; teachers can be bullies too, to students, and other teachers. I come from a family of educators, and I have heard the rewards and the pitfalls. Treat other teachers with professionalism, the students and parents are watching, they see and hear. Parents need to double check this one too. What you say about your friends and neighbors is how your children will treat their friends and classmates. Being a mentor is not self-chosen, we are all mentors to our youth.

Thank you to all the mentors in our lives. Please never stop working from your heart, and never stop sharing the healthy encouragement that helps another human stand taller and more autonomous and independent. Knowledge is freedom. Yes, our youth are our tomorrows; but it is your time, energy, and input that is helping to build tomorrow's hope and strength. When you empower someone with wider and deeper knowledge you empower both a life and everyone's future.

The Bully, the Narcissist, and Hyper-Individualism

This relationship is another one that starts with an honest look in the mirror. We all have the potential to be a little of each of these; if we can accept that truth, we can work to keep them in check and balance. If that statement alone upsets you, beware.

These are the relationships that sometimes literally kill people, by suicide or homicide. These relationships also frequently kill the spirit of other humans, with daily wanton disregard for those around them. These are the people that inhale you and exhale themselves.

These are the people that are our only true enemies; not political parties, not the wealthy, not a race, not a sexuality, not a nationality, but the self-blind to their ways, behaviors, and wants at any cost. Yes, these people can be found in all demographics. Yet please, do not discard whole races and cultures as bad; that is unfair to the undeserving good people in every region of the earth. The cyberbully must be given their own mention, due to their rapid proliferation since the internet landed in our homes, and then into our hands. With only a vague username and rarely even a photo, they have become the judge, jury, and executioner of our normal everyday human imperfections.

The bullies are ageless and exist in all areas of life, from schoolyards to the government, family gatherings to assisted living facilities, to those typing their harsh, judgmental social media opinions. Bullies are insecure, this is textbook; they build up themselves by attempting to knock others down. They are often painfully good at it. Bullying is sadly a learned behavior, but I also believe it has a pack mentality. One bully can get others, that normally would not bully, to join in. Bullying can be unlearned too. Parents, with self-honesty and involvement, can teach more appropriate ways of handling feelings and responding to peer pressure and conflicts. Parents, I respectfully ask to always remember your power. We teach our children as they hear us talk about our colleagues, neighbors, and acquaintances, and that is also molding them.

Katie Hurley, who is a social worker specializing in bully behavior and recovery, has this to say about bullying:

"Bullying, at its core, is a learned behavior that is used in response to stress. Bullying is an attempt to gain superiority or control over another. Bullies do tend to have a few things in common: Immature social skills. Lack of compassion and empathy. Poor impulse control. Bullies are not born; bullies are raised. We have the opportunity to raise children who will choose to be empathetic, kind, and loyal friends. All we have to do is teach them those skills."

Bullying is not a schoolyard matter. Research shows the schoolyard is only the tip of the iceberg leading to other antisocial behaviors of all degrees: drug use, skipping school, shoplifting, and vandalism. Rebuilding these young spirits seems to be the key. If this person can develop social skills, executive functioning, and self-awareness, then antisocial behaviors and bullying often decline.

We cannot forget the other side of this relationship, the victims of bullying, both the target and the price society at large pay. Since mass killings are escalating at an alarming rate, we should look at that which we can prevent. According to a study by the Secret Service, most perpetrators of mass killings were victims of bullying. Bullying is now creating victims out of all of us, from cyberbullying to road rage, from the office to the family, and into the news and our politics. Bullying is now in everyone's presence. Even the bullies of politics are making us all pay with decreased productivity, by setting poor examples, and a lack of balance in laws. Politicians now bully to get their way. Unfortunately their way is not always what is good for the masses.

The consequences the individual victim of bullying pays can be compounding and devastating. Victims of bullying often become loners. This withdrawal behavior increases isolation, leading to decreased contacts and friendship. They often began to show a decreasing connection to their schoolwork or occupation, or trouble following classroom or occupational expectations. Victims begin to take on some of the same feelings as the bully, such as feelings of not fitting in. The emotional and psychological stress will take its toll, increasing their risk of depression, anxiety, substance abuse, and emotional problems, including, but not limited to, psychosis or suicide. These struggles can escalate further into a lack of emotional control and stability issues. It can become a vicious cycle; they react more intensely to the bullying, often leading to even more bullying. It is not uncommon for the victim to start lashing out to bully others, starting the cycle over again. Research has found that even on school grounds, victims of bullying are more likely to carry weapons. It is not uncommon for these victims of bullying, and victims-turned-bully, to have trust issues, pessimistic outlooks, nervousness, hyper-vigilance, unfriendliness, and even hostility, again leading to greater isolation and fewer friendships.

To discuss narcissism, we should first differentiate between having narcissistic traits, which we all have on hopefully lower levels, and the psychiatric diagnosis of narcissistic personality disorder (NPD). Mayo Clinic's definition of narcissistic personality disorder is, "One of several types of personality disorders—is a mental condition in which people have an inflated sense of their own importance, a deep need for excessive attention and admiration, troubled relationships, and a lack of empathy for others. But behind this mask of extreme confidence lies a fragile self-esteem that's vulnerable to the slightest criticism."

Inflated, excessive, and extreme are all in the above definition, and unstable, outburst, overwhelming, and inappropriate are other descriptors that will often appear in the difference between the diagnosis of the disorder and the fact that all humans have a little narcissistic trait in us. A little is normal and is not the issue.

It is not uncommon for narcissists to have an excessive drive for admiration, showing a disregard for others' feelings, often lack empathy, have an inability to handle any criticism, and carry a sense of entitlement. Grandiosity, callousness, and uncaring traits are often displayed in actions and statements correlated to, "I don't care....," or the next level up, "I don't give a. . ." even if their opinion has nothing to do with the issue presented except control.

Just as I discussed in *Suffer Less in Death*, I believe most mental health issues should be on a continuum, not just autism. Even low levels of narcissism fluctuate on that scale. Narcissism is woven through our ego. It is another natural, important trait in all of us that has pros and cons. If we can acknowledge our potential for even low levels of narcissism, it can be worked with and kept in check. If not, just like our ego, whether the diagnosis of NPD or not, our narcissism is capable of disruptive, controlling, and damaging behaviors to the relationships in our lives. It is also significantly disruptive to teamwork, productivity, profit, and our personal levels of peace, joy, and self-worth. It is not the person with NPD disorder who wants to dominate, suppress, and abuse those around them, but rather a medical disease of the mind that wants to do those things to others. As the old saying goes, "Don't throw the baby out with the bathwater," that does not mean you may not have to protect yourself from someone with NPD, or even moderate levels of the traits. As you can imagine, narcissists are hard to work or live with. Unfortunately, narcissists, as with most personality disorders, are often hard to get into counseling, someone who thinks they are more "together" or smarter than the rest of the world is not the type of person to seek out or welcome counseling.

Having compassion for the person with higher levels of inflated self does not mean you do not have to protect yourself from these people's thought processes and behaviors. The narcissist can be a danger to the wellbeing, free will, choice, productivity, safety, and sanity to those around them. I once heard a great prayer to sum this up: "God, give me the strength and courage to always seek the truth, and protect me from those who already know it." Narcissists always have a fast answer across the board. This is not a comparison to asking questions of a professional in their field—many people are highly knowledgeable and do have many great fast answers. You can feel the difference.

Narcissists have trouble leading or being a healthy part of teamwork and are often micromanagers. Even on a team, the narcissist will have a challenging time giving credit to those that deserve it and will steal the ideas of others, but reword it or attempt to manipulate credit for self-gain. Narcissists are not easy to work for or with, as they like to create instability in their staff or peers because keeping people off balance or fearful makes them easier to manipulate. Of course, it is also shooting themselves in the foot, because doing that to your staff or teammates will decrease individual and team stability, and increase general unhappiness, which ultimately decreases team productivity and profit, or peace in the home. Even if that decreasing peace is in the minds of those around them.

Hyper-individualism and toxic individualism are fairly new terms to me. Both terms accurately sum up these dangerous personality and group traits. A group of people can also have the same characteristics as a hyper-individualistic person. Becoming aware of these traits should help us double-check and balance ourselves as well as attempt to protect ourselves from the hyper-individualist, and groups. World War II is an excellent example of a group moving hyper-individualism into global action. Russia invading Ukraine a few days ago is hyper-individualism still being played out on a large scale.

Hyper-individualism is the thought process and actions used to act in a highly individual way, without concern for others or their detrimental actions on society. The driver committing reckless endangerment to those around them is hyper-individualism. The speed limit is already 70 mph, traffic is heavy but moving, and the hyper-individualist is trying to get ahead, speeding, changing lanes, tailgating, not using blinkers, and people are forced to brake to allow the repetitive lane change cutoffs. That person is literally putting your life in danger. Even if a death or major injury does not occur but an accident involving several cars does occur, that person's actions still affect others by causing multiple injuries, property damage to the cars of multiple innocent safe drivers, and potentially causing several thousand people to be late for work.

On a lower level, but still contributing negatively to individuals and society, they are saying their time and destination is more important than the other thousands of people trying to get to work in a large metropolitan area. Another way to look at hyper-individualism is to be aware of the difference between self-care and selfish behavior. That line can get a little blurry for all of us at times, but the hyper-individualist does not care to even try. That painfully accurate saying applies, "It's their world, we are just living in it."

Toxic individualism is also worth mentioning. It is hyper-individualism on a large scale. Painfully and accurately, the world has been labeling the United States with toxic individualism for decades. Unfortunately, we are proving them correct at a faster and faster rate. Toxic individualism is the attitude and actions of everyone out for themselves.

I mention these hyper-self-personalities because the bigger subject is less suffering. If we don't start to look at our own behaviors and even attempt to gently, and always safely with respect, help others see the consequences of their behaviors, we all will be suffering more tomorrow. We all make a difference; we just need to believe we do. Hyper-self-personalities and groups are already difficult to bring back to the middle. These hyper individuals or groups don't like it in the middle; it's gray there, and the middle requires compromise. Compromise is something the hyper-selfish do not really like to do.

The Boss

I have had some amazing bossing in my life. I've only had a few bad bosses; the few bad ones had heavy narcissistic tendencies and should never play poker because they had billboards on their foreheads displaying fears and insecurities. Bosses can have, or develop, narcissistic traits without keeping themselves in check. People apply to move up the occupational ladder for a variety of reasons, the difference between confidence and competence comes into play, money of course factors in.

Bosses can definitely cause a huge amount of pain and suffering, or they can be the amazing guiding coach that can pull a team together, nurture it with healthy fuels to grow and keep the team running, and lead by example by never asking a subordinate to do something they could do themselves. That was always a big one for me in nursing. I would never ask a nurse-aide to do something I had the time to do myself. I've watched a few bosses lose a huge amount of respect by over-delegating, which was sometimes a competency issue.

I have almost always appreciated my strong healthy bosses and have never had trouble telling the good ones that either. Part of me can even appreciate the few bad one on some level, because I don't want their job either. I know management is much like the field of law enforcement, far too many no-win situations. I have respect for management and owners, living between a rock and a hard place, is not an easy place to live. I have profound respect for their role and multi-directional pressures.

I wish some bosses wouldn't lose respect for the role and stressors of the employee after promotion, mainly meaning their human limits. I encourage you to give your boss a break until they prove they don't deserve one. Just make sure you keep your judgment realistic for their human limits and their pressures to keep profit and productivity high. Some do not know, or cannot comprehend, that knowledge of the workings of humans increases productivity and profit far higher than manipulation, force, threat, or the authority of their title. Keep yourself safe from the unhealthy ones, as they can be dangerous to your employment or well-being. If you have a healthy, humanistic, and emotionally intelligent boss, who stays realistic and appreciates you for doing your job well, appreciate them back.

The Really Bad Boss

To be fair, the really bad employee is a subject below. This is a category of its own because unhealthy people, that happen to be our boss, can get too much of their unhealthiness on us. I was inspired to include it because of all the support I have given to friends and family over the years that had these types of bosses. This also includes peers that think they are your boss and have many of the same markers you will read below. The terms I have most commonly heard, stated by those trusting me about really horrible bosses, are abusive, lazy, narcissistic, liar, narrow-minded, bully, hypocrite, favoritism, self-serving, and self-righteous.

My other inspiration for including this section is because of my love for many of the articles in *Forbes* magazine. I don't go after *Forbes* articles for the money-making aspects because my brain doesn't work that way, and I am not financially investment savvy. This fact of my weakness is one reason I have respect for the ethical big moneymakers. The main reason I appreciate *Forbes* is because they devote some of their articles to the dynamics and psychology of the relationship between the employee, management, and the company. *Forbes* seems to care about the well-being of employee satisfaction, they publish articles to help raise the employees' level of awareness of their role and responsibility to the company and to their own job satisfaction. In February 2020, Terina Allen wrote a fantastic article, "10 Things That Horrible Bosses Secretly Believe About Employees." This bold article sums up these bad bosses well. I am only going to give you her first two paragraphs, the synopsis of the first belief that bosses hold, and then I will list the other nine. I'll warn you, her article hit the nail on the head. Ms. Allen states:

"If you work for an ineffective boss—a really bad one—you likely know the difference between an inexperienced or incompetent boss and a truly horrible one. You likely appreciate the normal imperfections that supervisors have and realize that most every supervisor will fall short in one area or another over time. But you also know that the worst ones have the audacity to work at it. There are people who actually work at being horrible and then substantiate their efforts by relying on deeply negative beliefs that they hold and espouse about employees.

Horrible bosses compel good employees to leave because they are more than ready to advance their own poor and ineffective leadership and will create a completely chaotic and toxic organizational culture to do so. The result is that the entire organization suffers as employees become more and more disengaged while delivering less-than-optimal performance. Here are 10 things that some of the most horrible bosses believe about their own employees.

1. Horrible bosses really believe that you are less important than they are. They aren't interested in your needs or the needs of your colleagues, and so they won't invest in you. They don't concern themselves with your professional development needs. They won't be bothered to consider what benefits or resources you might need to be successful. Horrible bosses believe that their needs are more important than yours, and they believe that what they care about is far more important than what you care about.
2. You should be held to a higher standard than they are.
3. You are inferior to them in almost every way.
4. You don't add value and are easily replaced.
5. You could never be as smart as they are.
6. You don't have a right to question their authority.
7. Ethical behavior and respect are optional.
8. You are to blame for their failures.
9. You should kiss up to them and rub their egos.
10. You deserve to be micromanaged no matter how good you are at your job."

I share these to reassure you are not imagining the feeling you had or the statements you heard. Yes, you probably have had at least one really bad boss in your life. I commend Ms. Allen for her courage to write such an exposing and confirming article. Thank you, Ms. Allen, you have summed up the impetus for what is being termed "The Great Resignation." The Great Resignation is a mass exodus from the workforce increasing in the past decade and not showing signs of letting up. Surveys are showing repeatedly that it's happening due to the number of people who no longer want to be mistreated and taken advantage of by disrespectful bosses and companies. I don't point out our issues to belittle bad companies and bosses, I do so to help everyone's long-term peace, productivity, and profits.

Most of the people that have talked to me about bad bosses are not real complainers, and I have found all were quite open to accepting their part of failure in a working relationship. I know these people to be competent professionals, with a desire to do their job well. A one-frame cartoon joke I had on the wall of my cubicle the past ten years sums up horrible bosses well. It is a simple drawing of a steep incline, a solo person leaning head forward, pushing with all their might, a huge ball, twice the person's size, up a hill. They're working hard, leaning into the task at hand, with exaggerated sweat flying off their forehead, but the ball has hit a desk facing down the hill with a little figure sitting behind it, doing nothing, and the plaque on the desk reads "Management."

The Employee

Although the employee is often made to feel expendable and undervalued, they are the movers and the shakers of keeping everyone in this world in motion. As soon as you think you don't need anyone's help in life, I encourage you to remember it is estimated that it takes over fifty people to get one head of lettuce from seed to your kitchen table. Unrelated to the periodic need and right to discipline or discharge low contributing employees, those fifty people are the employees who hold up the world, and they should not be made to feel any less.

The employee is also a human being with thoughts, feelings, limitations, and needs. There is no question there is room for improvement in how many are treated. Yet, at the same time, the employee holds, and should accept, their share of the responsibility of the breakdown in the relationships between the company, which in this case, includes management, owners, and shareholders, and the employees. Both sides hold responsibility for the steady decline in mutual respect between the two, and there is little question respect is one issue causing the deterioration of healthy companies and the relationships within them.

Since this chapter is about relationships, let's reference a culture that has had respect, mutual respect, paramount in their working relationships for a long time. The Japanese expend great energy in their business traditions to maintain productive, mutually beneficial, and profitable working relationships built on mutual respect and professionalism.

These traditional efforts to maintain bilateral working relationships have relaxed in Japan over the past few decades. They, too, have had a huge increase in startups and extreme growth into the international trade markets that have not always worked to maintain as high a level of effort as traditionally held. However, it is clear their efforts continue to pay off in longevity, profit, and workplace stability. For balance, they also still have traditions that are problematic, such as many female employees are hired as temporary workers, so they do not have to provide benefits. Japan also has a low rate of women moving up the management and executive ladder.

Other than that major disrespect, their respect and professionalism are present through all levels within a company. Their levels of respect are so high, they even have a formality in how they exchange business cards, how they are seated at a business lunch, and how they treat each other among peers in the workplace. Although I am about to simplify the big picture, there are innumerable ways they show respect to each other in the workplace.

The Japanese understanding of the need for maximum productivity within a company is the cornerstone of their philosophy. The company respects the employees, and the employees respect the company. In the US the norm appears to be the exact opposite. Too often neither side feels respected, and everything falls apart after that. It is a vicious cycle that my research shows began in the mid-1940s, then started gaining more speed in the 1960s and 1970s and culminated after the turn of the century. No finger-pointing is necessary because the contributing factors are wide and far. But it all ends up with our occupational relationships suffering. Ultimately, we all and the company pay the price. Over the past few months, I have compiled a list of various complaints from articles that employers have of their employees. This is where the worker needs to accept that they too can improve. All of these are a two-way street. I picked these subjects because I read Japan actively spends energy to address and weaken the following counterproductive issues.

Lack of communication skills: Japan emphasizes professional and respectful communication, including a preference for face-to-face communication as often as possible, not text or emails.

Dishonesty: A significant part of dishonesty is an inability to accept responsibility when we have done something wrong. We have become a society of blame and any cost. We have no issues even using a horrible phrase to describe how harshly we will blame others for our part in an issue, "Throwing someone under the bus." Japanese culture appears much more open to accepting responsibility for a mistake, whether personal or occupational.

Lack of loyalty: This is the two-way respect I mentioned above. Everything from kitchen theft in a restaurant, to stealing clients on the way out the door. This one is wide and far. There is also mutual responsibility for this two-way street. Such as when a significant injustice has been done to the employee, so they take a few clients out the door. Many employees couldn't care less about the big picture of the health and wellness of their company, or their colleagues' success. But this is also a double-sided edge and major influence on the damaging reciprocating negative cycle we are in. The other side there are employers, owners, investors, and boards that also care little for their staff. It is a horrible vicious cycle that many are caught in. I have known small business owners that will hang onto a failing company to the end out of loyalty to the welfare of their staff. On the opposite side, years ago, I heard of a large hospital system CEO who said they have, "Little concern for the complaints of the nurses and doctors because, nurses and doctors are like gumballs: put in a quarter and out pops another one." I wonder if that CEO still feels that way after the COVID-19 pandemic strained and severely taxed the staff? We are trapped in a cycle that only both sides caring to expend energy, respect, and loyalty to each other can start to change the negative cycle direction into a positive direction. I have to say it again, but it is true, the top must set some profit aside to show their top-down desire to change their negative contributions, and the employee must put their reasons for rationalizing disloyalty aside also. Mutual respect is gained through mutual respect actions. More finger-pointing will not only accomplish nothing, it also creates or adds animosity, and feeds the vicious, negative, nonproductive cycles.

The Japanese know they need each other and treat each other with the mutual respect that keeps that positive cycle engaged.

Lack of dependability: Not showing up to work on time is a huge complaint of companies of their employees. Not being hungover is another one that I hear often, when owners and management tell me their issues. Not smelling like cannabis is an increasing complaint, except in a few of the managers of creative thinkers. Dependability is another wide one, but no matter the subject, just ask yourself as the employee, "If I was my boss, how would I want my employees to show dependability?" This self-check question works for all subjects and both sides. Managers, owners, investors, and board members need to ask the same question, "If I was an employee how would I want to be treated?"

Lack of teamwork: A cliché I know, but employers wish they could see "less me and more we" in departmental teamwork. They can often tell when ideas are being stolen, or when fault is not being admitted by the proper person. It is important to remember a team is not just a sub-group of people assembled to accomplish a goal, a team is the entire company, and everyone's healthy positive efforts create a solution where everyone benefits for every person in the company. Strife among various departments within a company also prevents strong teamwork.

Inflexibility: This one I could write a chapter on. Inflexibility is a powerful and considerable influence on all dysfunctional relationships, and a respectable amount of life's strife. Inflexibility in either thoughts or actions create enormous amounts of pain, loss of productive compromise, and suffering across the face of the earth. We are suffering from human inflexibility. Our inflexibility is a huge source of our unhappiness in every direction. We are meant to be flexible and were gifted with that innate characteristic of variation and adaptation we talked about early on. The more we can apply flexibility, without compromising our core being, the fewer pumps we have in a day. Just like loyalty, inflexibility is trapped in a vicious negative cycle, leading to the same in the other party in the relationship, and around and around it goes with less flexibility accomplished every cycle as one reacts to the other. Not surprising, our ego often drives our inflexibility. Our inflexibility is even a damaging influence on our political productivity to accomplish solution-based resolutions to our issues. One of the hardest things that is so painful to watch, is the loss of greater peace, productivity, and profit that inflexibility blatantly produces. Being flexible as often as I can has worked for me for most of my life, but the real proof is that the most joy-filled, peaceful, and calm people and workplace environments I know are also the most flexible.

Lack of eagerness to learn: Often displayed as an unwillingness to learn new or improved information or ways of doing something, not wanting to take part in continuing education, or the training being criticized or skipped out on altogether. In Japan, the ongoing training is highly nurtured, with even upper management and owners joining in to stay updated on all levels. The employees have a level of respect for upper administration joining them on the production floor to attend the in-service on how a new piece of equipment works. The greatest nursing supervisor I ever had was very much a boots on the ground eager to learn type of person, including working one or two complete shifts in the emergency department every week. Because of her eagerness to learn next to her staff and work with us, the respect she had from us, and the desire we had to do better for her, was incredible. Even though she ran a sizable department, with high patient volume numbers with serious pressures from all directions, and managed a large staff, she still had an amazing sense of humor and was realistically

grounded in her expectations of each of the staff members. If you asked
to attend advanced training, she sent you.

Lack of work ethic: Our work ethic is the belief, followed by actions,
that effort to accomplish in both quality and quantity have benefit and
an inherent value to build our character, ability, productivity, and pride,
with a resulting side effect of success. Classic signs of a strong work
ethic can be seen in one's level of dress, attendance, attitude, personal
and occupational character, communication, flexibility, cooperation,
productivity, time management, continuing education, professionalism,
teamwork, a wide-reaching overall respect, and a positive outlook. Each
of those are highly beneficial to the individual and the big picture of
creating positive occupational cycles. If our work ethics are positive in
all directions, then what might some of the wide-reaching benefits of
"life ethics" be?

Lack of overall ambition and responsibility: Responsibility includes
everything from treating fleet automobiles and company equipment
with respect, to picking up a piece of trash by the front door as you walk
into work. Life-ethics would be standing over a spill in a grocery store,
so no one slips while an employee goes to get a mop and a caution sign.
Ambition and responsibility are knowing that a problem in front of you
is everyone's problem to help correct, not someone else's problem. You
could have slipped on that spill, or your elderly parent. That grocery
store spill could cost someone their well-being to work and support a
child, or even their life in the case of a head injury or hip fracture. You
may be a customer in the grocery store, but that water on the floor is not
necessarily someone else's problem. Being preventative and proactive in
every direction shows ambition and responsibility. It looks like parking
your cart over the spill and finding someone to get a mop and wet floor
caution sign. Ambition and meeting responsibilities does not look like

a title on your desk, car, or large home; those are goals. This is also a key characteristic owners and managers like to see in people they promote or consider when it is time for salary increases. Having responsibility initiative shows that you not only care about the well-being of the company, in the bigger picture it shows you care.

The Unhappy or Underappreciated Employee

A simple tool an employee can have to empower themselves, no matter how unhappy they are in relation to pay, position, or how they are appreciated or not by management, is to know you make a difference. Exceptional customer service is also self-rewarding—doing the best job you can is nothing but good for the self. Negativity creates more negativity, even internally, so place the goodness inside of yourself that begets more goodness. If you feel you have a good gig, appreciate your employer for that environment and hopefully all of you will keep up the good mutual efforts. Let's see if we can slow down the great resignation, or we will all continue to feel the consequences.

Being a responsible employee is the backbone and muscle of the company, community, and society. It also has a huge ability to appropriately build your true pride; you are vital, needed, you help nurture everything! Whether you are openly appreciated or not, find some level of reward in knowing you are helping society function. The voice that comes through the speaker at the fast-food drive-thru is not and should never be made to feel unimportant. That voice could be someone who just showed up to do another job. Or, that voice is a person, a professional, a part of a noble profession feeding us. That person, and the entire team in that building you are driving around to grab and go, feeds the other employees of the world, humans who are building our roads, constructing our homes and office buildings, caring for the sick, or who are a parent raising kids and holding a household together. That voice is another person helping our world to turn. No matter what your role or title is as an employee, work to be a professional at what you do, and find a way to take pride in yourself and your work. Even if it sucks, and you are looking for another job, you are most likely helping someone's life somehow.

If you are unhappy at work, do your part to make it better, and I hope the stressors that are pushing on your unhappiness and under appreciation figure out their negative contribution, or they will do the same to the next person who takes your position.

The Really Bad Employee

You all know this person; you must work harder and protect yourself because of them. They will steal your ideas and in the same slip of the hand attempt to make you look incompetent. These people are thieves: they steal time, productivity, and profit from every direction they can. Their idea of a team involves only them on the inside and sometimes they even show it outwardly. Often with narcissistic traits, sometimes very charismatic and friendly, but their true self eventually bleeds through. They are often gossipers, judging others and leaving piles of hypocrisy and double standards so big even they slip on them. Yet, they can't see it as their own doing because their ego has already blamed someone else. They have a knack for great reasons not to do their work, and often get others to do it for them. They are often unprofessional in other ways also: non-supportive, boss-bashers even to good bosses, staff-bashers, backstabbers, even punitive and vengeful if they feel an injustice has been done to them. Yet, they are great at schmoozing the right people. The defense mechanism of projection is usually alive and well in this person. The only thing required to not have much of this in us is to have a strong work ethic, and to remain open to being honest when looking inside.

Just like how all bosses should keep an eye out to make sure they don't have a little horrible boss in them, so must the workers keep an eye out for this character trying to get out. Don't think this person gets away with it either. They normally spend more energy avoiding work than they actually would doing the work. But the biggest price they pay is again a waste of moments, and the only pride they build is false pride. Protect yourself well from this type of person and attempt to use copious amounts of rational detachment to keep yourself safe. Your spirit and peace are worth so much more than what their personalities want to take from you. Just because someone wants to sell you the short end of their personality, doesn't mean you have to buy it.

The Harsher Customer, Client, and Patient

The average or good customer is hopefully the role every single one of us play nearly daily, but then along comes the not so good customer. Is the customer always right? Should you always work to make them feel right? Most of the time, yes, but not always, respectful, appropriate redirection is sometimes required. That doesn't mean you should have to take customer abuse; but know that most of it is only abuse if you take it personally.

Our healthcare and first responders require high levels of flexibility and understanding, we know our "customer" is already in some level of crisis, or we would not be in front of them. It is our job as crisis public servants to have higher levels of patience and tolerance, we signed on to handle the tough and the rough. That does not excuse the uncalled for abuse we must take. I never minded when someone in an acute crisis insulted me, but it was sad when it was a much more relational person's frustration being flung at me. Especially if I was trying to help them as a nurse, or they had done something wrong that initiated the contact when I was in law enforcement.

I think some customers feed off abusing those attempting to help them. As if paying for a product or service includes discharging their life's frustrations on an employee. Think of the abused call takers in service centers who are so roughed up by a percentage of their customers. Any time I talk to a call taker, I first ask them about their day, and if everyone has been nice to them. I know they can't answer that question with unfiltered honesty, but the pause is always telling. They remember script guidelines and answer with something mild and vague. It is not uncommon by the end of the call that they are a little more open. I often use the fact that if they put us on hold, even for fifteen to twenty seconds, they profusely apologize for the wait when they return. I'll tell them in humor, "It was only twenty seconds, but thank you for the profuse apology. It is very telling about how impatient the average caller must be." That is when they will sometimes say something like, "You have no idea."

A call taker once pointed out to me something that I had already figured out about aggressive drivers. This person explained that callers get to higher levels of anger and aggression because they are not face-to-face, so it's easy for them to get to an exaggerated level of anger than they would normally have in person. This person said, "We call takers sometimes get the full brunt of the person's lifelong built-up unhappiness with poor customer service, because I am faceless and nameless to them, and I can't fight back." I took a pause on that one, that was painful to hear, I felt even greater compassion. Driving presents the same level of perceived anonymity. When we get in a car, the apparent anonymous position can make some people bolder, and they no longer feel as exposed to the personal consequences. As if I am no longer Vincent, but rather I just transformed into just another car. Therefore I am not being judged personally. Talking to a call taker has some of that separation involved.

I think this is one of the contributing factors to why so many people deny the traffic violations I have clearly recorded on the dash camera video; it's a dissociation from personal responsibility. The toughest part the harsh customer presents with their pressure is that the call taker often has absolutely nothing further they can do beyond the policies and procedures they must follow and inform you of.

Customers deserve elevated levels of care and service. Yet whether a customer, client, patient, or anyone we are interacting with somehow, is the basic we should all strive for: treat all people how you honestly wish to be treated.

The Good Customer

You don't deserve poor service or to be disrespected by the business. Keep up the proper excellent work. Thank goodness so many businesses and employees care about you and the service they provide.

Owner, Corporation, Board, and Investors

Don't even think these people don't have heart, they do. But they also have a job to do, and that must always be respected. It's like hating attorneys for being good at their job, that is just outright unfair. I had the pleasure of working closely with many attorneys in the civil field across the state of Texas during the years I worked in civil law enforcement. I enjoyed those relationships. I had two attorneys in twelve years treat me poorly, three if I count one on the roadside, and I could just feel the first two were attempting to bully me due to a lack of skill or knowledge. At the same time, I respect that not all officers feel this way. Criminal defense attorneys spend their careers trying to discredit law enforcement to defend their clients, and prosecuting attorneys will not always press an officer's criminal charges against a violator. I went down that attorney rabbit hole to show the title a person holds is not the issue, it is what they do with their position. Equally important in how we judge the top is the angle we are looking from. Let us not be prejudiced toward the top of the corporation because they have the ability, capital, knowledge, and then follow thought to create the large corporations we work for, or purchase from. They were hired or came together to make money, how they make it is the true marker.

These people at the top are human too, making big money just happens to be their job, and that can get in the way of humanness at times. Many owners, CEOs, and board members who have had open discussions with me admit they feel stuck in a difficult situation. As I shared with you in the first chapters, the friends and acquaintances I have had that were big money makers would express to me, especially as they got older and were approaching their normal life review with advancing age, that they often felt torn between profit and their internal humanistic pull. Many stated the number one thing that helped them was to create a human relationship with the employees, such as learning the name of as many as they could and stopping to talk with them. One told me, "Start with the custodial workers." Another CEO years ago told me she liked to ask random employees to join her for lunch as she was headed out the door to a restaurant, stating the knowledge and respect both people would gain during those lunches was immeasurable.

I realize "owners" can have a wide range of meanings. Whether the owner of a twenty-crew roofing company or the owner of a 2,000-crew corporation, the pressures and goals remain the same. They must make and keep that company successful, and they need your professional help to accomplish that goal. Being larger should not make it more impersonal, but often it does.

I do have a hope for the top, that making money and still being humanistic can be done at the same time. That doesn't mean you don't fire people that need to be fired or cut back staff when it must be done. But at every corner remember you are the leader of people, humans with needs, children, and feelings, and the same goes for the customer. Yes, investors want and deserve to make money, that is why they opened their wallets in the first place, but at what costs? Such as, how much will "The Great Resignation" end up costing in profit? "At what cost" is much wider, deeper, and far more important than those three little words can convey. Please, never forget the big picture of your actions in the name of a dollar.

This is where I plead for both sides, and I give an apology to the top. I am sometimes hard on the people at the top, but it is for an important reason. I am sorry, and I am not; please let me explain. Employees, customers, and we, the public, cannot be upset that our business world is good at making money. But I request the business world to check and balance yourself. What are the long-term effects of your current practices, on the people, the environment, society, the long-term stability of our economics and our general individual and social morale? I also hope you will not smirk, rationalize, and write these pleas off as nonsense, or worse, rationalizing survival of the fittest.

You, like all of us, make a difference in the little and big picture. Except your difference is greater in some ways. When I remind people that we all make a difference in how we treat each other, I am aware that most I encourage are making a difference to one or a few people at a time, but still have a positive effect on the world, from the bottom up. My plea to you is on a bent knee, for your actions and choices can affect thousands and thousands if you include employees and customers. You hold the power to make a difference from the top down. Our elected officials also fall into this same powerful and prestigious humanistic position. I beg you to consider much wider pictures than only profit. Your great-grandchildren are depending on your free will and choice. Please, for your heart's peace, and everyone's tomorrow, begin to see pictures that do not always involve only dollar signs, and act on them. I deeply thank the companies that see and act on the bigger pictures, you are making a difference.

The Break Room

I am strangely including the break room because of the relationships that occur on breaks, although not necessarily in the physical location of a designated "break room." We do have a relationship with the break room, even if yours is the corner convenience store, local coffee house, even if it is under a shade tree while building a house.

The surface, yet still somewhat dangerous, relationship with your break room is the one sitting on the counter in all its delicious forms—sugar. Although I, too, succumb to the sweet, pretty, and tasty poison that will one day further down the road have a warning label on it just like alcohol and tobacco. Sugar is not my friend. Sugar, due to supply, demand, addiction, convenience, desire, and habit, is somehow magnetically drawn to our break rooms. It is how we "treat" ourselves and others. We give it to people to thank them and show appreciation, we celebrate with even more of the pretty tasty crystals or syrup. I hate how hard I struggle with my brain's addiction to sugar. Oh, I am addicted, even though I sometimes go days without it in quantity.

What we now know about sugar is scary, and it is affecting your lives and relationships. We know it causes weight gain, obesity, diabetes, depression, cellular dehydration, fluctuations in energy levels, and fatigue, moodiness, hyperactivity, restlessness, cardio-vascular and vascular disease, fatty liver disease, acne, skin and all cellular aging, kidney disease, dental and oral health, gout, muscle pain, insomnia, headaches, nausea, esophageal burning, even inflammation on a cellular level, and last, but hardly least, it is now linked to dementia. We know all of this, and it is still going to take a long time to get a warning label on it.

We need to give ourselves a partial break about our sugar consumption, yet we also should work harder to ingest less of it. I am addicted to sugar for the same reasons most of us are. The first reason is mind-boggling, literally. Sugar activates your brain somewhat like narcotics do, making it addictive and tough to control our strong cravings. It affects the reward center in the brain, leading to behaviors just like most addiction. Just as a heroin addict knows it is bad for them, we also ignore all we know about its overwhelming harmful effects and consume it anyway. Getting away from sugar can be harder than stopping heroin. I was informed of this surprising fact by a long-time heroin user back in the 1980s, as I was looking to start an IV somewhere in his heroin-used-up veins. He was telling me he has an easier time quitting heroin than he does quitting cigarettes. I was shocked to hear this, and of course, responded with a highly surprised, "Why?!" What an answer he graced me with: "Because every time I stop to get gas for my car I can walk in that store and buy all the cigarettes I want, but they don't have any heroin in there." He was right on; we are inundated with ads and unlimited easy access to consume sugar, and fat grams for that matter.

Since we already know the addiction to sugar is real, let's take a look at signs you might be addicted, these also apply to most addictions. You may be addicted if you have feelings of guilt or shame, you go out of your way to consume it, you know how bad it is for you but you can't stop or even decrease your consumption rate, you use it during emotional stress to calm yourself, you try to quit and actually have physical, mental, or emotional symptoms (this is a well-documented reality not just a perception), you crave salty foods (this occurs because of the dehydration and nutritional deprivation high sugar intake causes), you are always wanting sweet food or drinks and water alone does not appeal to you, you eat sweets even when you are not hungry, you crave more and more sugar and don't stop after several gummy worms but will eat the whole bag, or you hide your sweet consumption.

Unfortunately for me, and many, sugar is not going away anytime soon, so like a powerful addiction to anything, I admit it's a problem and commit to lifelong efforts to decrease its consumption. It requires effort, but I am worthy of my efforts, and always feel remarkably better when I consume less.

Sugar is not the only detrimental relationship we have with the break room. Gossip is not so good for our health either. Gossip even comes with a "warning label," we all know it is unhealthy, but we just can't help it. I don't like it because I've been told I'm "So out-of-the-box that I'm juicy material for gossip." All things in moderation, right?

The Police

I have an unfair advantage in my relationship with the police; I am Caucasian and, statistically, the magnitude of that influence cannot be ignored. All races commit crimes, and Caucasian males kill cops on traffic stops too. I have had many hours of officer safety training, I have watched far too many dash camera videos of the gun being drawn, the shots being fired, and, because the officer is so often still behind the camera because it happened so fast, we only hear the audio of them working to breathe their last labored breaths as the shooter pulls away and the sound of more sirens is getting closer and louder and louder. Officers must keep themselves safe, and they absolutely cannot tell anything about your level of danger to them by any of your outward visual appearances. Race, culture, dress, gender, or age mean nothing to their safety. In my years of making periodic traffic stops, I found a percentage of all demographics to be frustrated by being treated with the same level of caution I treated everyone. Anyone can turn very dangerous very fast, and no one is excluded from officer safety techniques that help keep them alive. So please don't feel you deserve special treatment due to your size, gender, or race, they have no bearing on how little pressure is required to pull the trigger on a gun. Only by immediately and politely following the officer's safety requests or commands will some of their distrust go down. However, until they leave your presence, they have an appropriate need to keep themselves safe. You may know you would never hurt an officer, but they do not know that.

Understanding the above reality is imperative to having safer and more positive experiences with law enforcement across the board. Yes, there is great need for many changes in how law enforcement is interacting with society, including some reevaluation of the standards of officer safety. Those officer safety standards are often based on history and statistics, so the officer that follows them is wise and mostly appropriate. I completely agree, there is much room for improvement from all directions concerning law enforcement and public interactions, including from the side of the citizen in certain situations. I know it is improving and the training is being bumped up to help. Something else critical to this discussion before I continue is that officers are highly trained to go home alive at the end of their shift.

Your relationship with a police officer is for one of four basic reasons: you *may* have done something wrong, and the officer is required to investigate and possibly act, you or your car may resemble a suspect of a crime, you need their help, or they need your help. No matter the reason the contact is occurring, the responding officer does not have a full enough picture of the situation to feel completely safe and won't until they leave the scene. You are most likely a great person in many ways, but there is the potential of instability almost anytime officers are present. Such as, something as simple as the number of things that can go wrong in the human body to cause confusion or altered behavior are endless, and that can cause dangerous behavior. Any of us can become confused and dangerous to ourselves or others from even just a low blood sugar level, or a high or low blood sodium level occurs. It is that simple for anyone to become confused and a danger.

Understanding and tolerance for the extreme danger of that officer's job is the broadest advice I can give you to have more peaceful relationships with the police. Another influence on your interactions with police, especially during traffic stops, is that the seemingly innocuous violation you just committed, and that the officer has pulled you over for, may feel benign to you. "Are you kidding me, you're pulling me over because I was backing up traffic in the left lane? I was doing 65 in a 65, they don't need to be going any faster than that!" But that is not a benign traffic violation, because people are now passing on the right, and backing up traffic in the left lane is against the law in many states. The reality is that forcing cars to pass you on the right increases the risk to all traveling near. While that officer is listening to your attempts to minimize breaking the law, and placing people at increased risk, they are seeing the dead bodies that are the result of poor driving habits.

Cops know that cell phones, entitlement, and minimizing cavalier driving kills, because the blood is literally on their hands, and some of the harder visions stay with us. Cops also know the fact that speeding is the number one factor in all road deaths, because they repetitively see those deaths. You may be late to pick up your child at school or for a work appointment, but that officer knows exactly what it looks like to never make it to that appointment. Your excuses will never erase that officer's visions of the reality of what those excuses cause. The emergency nurse in me also painfully has too many imprinted visions.

At the very moment you are having an interaction with the police, no matter what the cause, reason, your race, or gender, it doesn't matter, even if the officer's behavior seems out of line or disproportionate, cooperate with their personal safety instructions. I cannot, and will not, tell you must cooperate with their request related to search and seizure, that would be me giving you legal advice, and I can't do that. But when a request for the safety of the officers and the bystanders turns into a *lawful* order, then cooperate. At that moment, you don't know if you meet the description of a mom that just beat her child in the back seat of the car while pumping gas five minutes ago that a store attendant called in, or if your car meets the description of a bank robbery that just occurred three blocks away. Most interactions are now being recorded, so do the right thing, and follow their instructions. If they are in the wrong, it will most likely be recorded and you have recourse after the event. Your complaint or lawsuit will also have greater merit because you will sound respectful and appropriate on that recording. Appropriate officer safety is not wrong, we create a safer situation by following their instructions.

Years ago, someone taught me something concerning the cultural influence on some citizen behavior during police interactions. I am not condoning unsafe behaviors, but I admit it is a contributing factor as an influence. I care to address this sensitive subject because the behaviors are costing too many people their lives. A few years back I was taught by someone with a different angle, to help me see wider, that there are two major contributing factors why some people will resist or defy officer direction besides guilt and not wanting to be caught, to either not show fear or not be arrested unrelated to guilt. That this attempt to not show fear of law enforcement by some people standing up to and defying them was described as image protection on both an individual level and a larger cultural, social scale. It was described to me as an influence that is displayed in statements and actions that represent and equals, "I'm not scared of you."

The second influence was much more concrete and influenced by history, facts, and statistics. I was taught that some, even if not guilty, will resist and attempt to elude or resist arrest because the system is stacked against them. Even if they are innocent of what they are being detained or arrested for. Hearing it explained in this person's reality created a higher level of respect for the influence, but the behavior is still dangerous and can even add charges to someone's arrest, injury, or death if the resistance is high enough. This person taught me, whether guilty or not, if someone is unable to afford an attorney, it means they are appointed a public defender, and their past criminal history past the age of eighteen never leaves them, and that history can influence trial outcomes. Not that all public defenders are bad, but top attorneys rarely take on public defender cases. Then the last thing this person shared with me is that I have never known what it is like to have so many racial, social, and judicial cards stacked against me. He closed by saying, "You know how people say, 'Just cooperate with the police,' and if you haven't done anything wrong then everything will be ok?" I said, "Yes." He replied, "Then how come such a high percentage of people of color have been released from prisons, some serving life sentences, since DNA evidence has been used to prove people innocent?" This man's angles left me in a place of greater understanding. But I still encourage everyone to cooperate with lawful safety instructions. It may not be a perfect answer or solution to all our law enforcement issues, but it is the best one we have for now.

Family relationships

Reminding myself that none of us get to choose our parents and siblings helps me with family. After all, fair is fair, they are stuck with me.

The relationship with our family, no matter the configuration, will most likely be the longest, deepest, and potentially bonding or traumatizing relationships we experience. We can become lightning-fast sensitive in our relationships and even our memories with family. Living to 100 is sometimes not long enough to resolve these family pains, history, and more troubling dynamics. Some of these traumas are filled with serious abuse or neglect, while others roughed up our spirit or our feelings of self-worth. Criticism and physical abuse can destroy one's pride, spirit, and trust. As opposed to healthy constructive guidance, reassuring support, and appropriate redirection, by a parent, sibling, or any healthy adult mentor that builds our self-confidence, spirit, and can positively affect one's ability to have healthy relationships their whole life. Our siblings, or lack thereof, mold us far more than we know or admit. Neglect, abuse, or abandonment can create significant, life affecting, and long-lasting issues of distrust. But unless you must literally distance yourself for physical or emotional safety, which I respect, it is still family, and we should expend some energy to decrease the bad bumps. Unlike the rest of our efforts to find ways to suffer a little less in life, family can require some serious digging, and huge pulleys and chains to heal some of the deeper wounds.

Thank goodness some family can also be the people that are there when we need a familiar hand to turn to and hold.

Parents

I know the situations my parents grew up in; they accomplished the task of all parents, to do better than their parents. In their case, they did much better. They made mistakes, and I did too in my relationship with them.

Parents who expect perfection of themselves, because the child is watching, learning, and mimicking can be hard on a child. It raises their self-expectations above human ability, which can create feelings of failure or inadequacy. We are imperfect, and our children need to know, feel, and believe that natural faltering will occur and is normal. The lifelong gift we can give them is to show them that what is important after faltering is to learn from it and go on. I love the answer one of my siblings used to give her kids as they were growing up and asking for advice or hounding for a decision on a request: "Let's slow down, I've never had a thirteen-year-old daughter before, I have no experience with this, and I need some time to figure this out." She was being realistic with herself, and showing her children by example they did not have to have a fast perfect answer to everything.

Because of various social pressures, same-sex marriages have special added stressors, both for parents and their children. Every decade seems to be getting a little better. I don't think it is anything that can't be helped further along with a little more flexibility for the groundbreaking explorations in this rapidly increasing sector of society; patience, tolerance, acceptance, and understanding will go far to make this new permanent way of life easier for all, especially the children. Hopefully, society will continue to show this rapidly emerging culture higher levels of adaptation and acceptance.

Parents and grandparents may not realize their statements are pushing their children and grandchildren away. No matter the sexuality or gender of the younger generation, they are starting to distance themselves from the older inflexible and intolerant. I share this because I care to not see family bonds and relationships weakening because a wonderful, talented, giving, amazing person also happens to be gay, or any other orientation or direction. The series Queer Eye is doing a fantastic job of helping along the greater acceptance that is so needed. Thank you for creating such an important show, and each of you are so humanistic and socially intelligent. The significance of this show goes far beyond the people, families, and communities they so generously give a hand up to each episode. I highly recommend this series to everyone.

Parental mistakes will always be made. I was somewhat lucky coming in at number six, much of their trial and error had been smoothed out by then. But not all. Also, my sisters had a huge hand in raising me, and my brother too, until he headed to college. Dad traveled during the week. Mom was a professional student and pursued her career for interest, mental stimulation, and to help support six kids. By the time I popped out they knew how to guide me with minimal effort. Maybe they were tired of raising kids, or maybe it was the fact that I learned from watching my siblings make mistakes. I am grateful to them for that passive education they gave me. I went on to make a bunch of mistakes anyway.

I have always felt great compassion for the parents that had adolescent aged children when the 1950s rolled into the 1960s. That same first woke period I mentioned that occurred through those few years must have turned the world of parenting upside down and inside out compared to the relatively wholesome latter half of the1950s. Parents had about a three-second warning from the television shows *Leave it to Beaver* and *Make Room for Daddy* to dive headfirst deep into the depths of the Vietnam War and all it brought with it, to the explosion of drug use, a new depth to rock and roll, birth control, and short skirts that made parents beg for the day they thought just above the knee was dangerously risqué. No wonder a percentage of parents started using tranquilizers and Valium like it poured from a soft serve ice cream dispenser. Put yourself in their place for a minute. The same but different type of parental extreme challenge came along in 1990, with the internet. The internet became a vice grip challenge in 2007 with the arrival of the smartphone. With that, the internet left the computer on the desk and fell into the palm of our hands, including into our children's hands.

Since the arrival of the smartphone, our children have been drowned in tech distractions, pornography, Earth's rapid health changes, violence, local and world harsh realities, and social influence by their friends and media all added a thick layer of extreme challenge to parenting, and to the young people's growth and development. These realities, fears, and anxieties too easily fill our children's heads, yet their young minds have not yet developed the tools to cope. Many of us adults, at various times, or the magnitude of the atrocity or catastrophe, have trouble dealing with this barrage in our heads and hearts, even with the wisdom, maturity, and coping tools of time and experience. It was hard enough to be woken in our teens in the 1960s—now they are awoken in their early teens and younger. I have extreme compassion for the parents and families who must deal with, and be shattered by, the escalating suicide threats, attempts, and sadly suicides accomplished, in numbers never seen from such young age groups. Not only has this second wave of extreme awareness created harder and wider issues for parents, but it has also taken away a subjective amount of parental influence and guidance over their children.

It would be impossible to tell what percentage of parental influence has been lost due to so many other strong influences, such as social media, news, peer influence, and their own internal pressures and desires to be an autonomous being. Due to this decreasing influence on their children's growth and development, it makes their remaining influence that much harder, and thus even that much more important. The influences on our youth are strong and often stressful on their minds and hearts. It is important to not give in, don't give up, or stop attempting to have a positive influence on your children. I see how a feeling of futility could cause someone to say, "Oh well." But please keep going, they are hearing a percentage of the goodness you are feeding them, and even more of what you are showing them in your actions. It is worthy, and yes self-sacrificing, challenging hard work.

Our youth need positive influences more than ever in quantity, quality, and frequency. They sadly must learn new levels of self-protection—online luring into human trafficking was not an issue in my youth. Yet, at the same time for balance and the good of all, they also need to learn new levels of *unselfish* behavior right after new levels of self-protection and self-care. It is at moments like these that I take pause, stop typing, stare at the screen, unable to write, also overwhelmed with the magnitude of our times. Until the 1960s, the generations would judge and tease the newer generations for how tough they used to have it, "When I was a kid . . ." I am of the generation that should be saying that too, but I can't. They may have screens in their hands that we didn't have, and a larger number may have family wealth, both making some things easier for them, and some things worse. But these younger generations are not pampered in a lack of hard awareness. Compassion flows to both the youth and their parents that must guide and calm, and yet, still safely and with empowerment, push them out into these overly exposed and hazardous times.

Siblings

I appreciate my siblings for everything they did for me, even the tough love. It wasn't easy, but it paid off and helped me. The sister training started early. I had no idea what a toilet was for, still in diapers, but I knew that seat went down. Shortly after we moved to the bayou, when I was eight or nine, I remember I was watching *Gilligan's Island* on our three-channel television set when I made the mistake of asking one of them to fix me a peanut butter and jelly sandwich. They literally dragged me on my back by my arms into the kitchen, held me down, tickled me, roughed me up for a good minute or so, stood up and told me something along the lines of, "Never again ask a woman to get you anything while you are watching TV. You wait until a commercial and get up and get it yourself, and it is polite to ask anyone else in the room if they want anything also." About thirty minutes later, I was reprimanded for leaving crumbs on the counter and was told, "Making dinner for your lady means nothing if you don't clean the kitchen afterwards, so don't think you did anything special if you make dinner but leave the dishes for her." You heard correctly, I am nine, and my mom and sisters are feeding me these rare and important jewels. The only break I got from my sisters is that they didn't dress me up in their clothes. I guess the last thing they wanted was another sister, they must have figured five women in the house was enough.

It didn't stop there. When I was eleven, I was told to start doing my own laundry. There was a laundry commercial at the time that taught me to separate the dark, colorful, and the white clothes, and wash them separately. That took too long. I also realized if I pushed the clothes down in the wash, it held more. One load every two weeks, and I was set!

The toughest part was when they found out I was about to go on my first date, with an older woman. Yep, I was in the fifth grade and a sixth grader at the big junior high asked me to a dance. A week or so later I climbed into the back seat of her dad's car with about 200 things in my head that my sisters told me not to do, but I had no idea what was actually okay to do. I bet I was a rather polite boring date.

My brother is the oldest and ten years my senior. He spent a little time with me as a kid, and I remember he and his girlfriend took me to the zoo once. I will also be forever grateful for him teaching me to play chess at such an early age. Then, playing with me regularly until he left for college when I was eight. We started playing chess again online together a year ago, which is meaningful to me. He is still incredibly good at the challenging mind exercising game.

My siblings were quite different in personality, and still are. I learned at a young age that each of them was going to have different expectations of me and would treat me differently. Fast forward thirty or forty years, and adult sibling dynamics kicked in, which at times is just like the adolescent personality dynamics, except magnified. The times I have had conflicts with them as an adult I felt like an emotionally arrested teenager again. I am embarrassed looking back on the adult breakdowns in communication with my siblings. It was not the adult in me driving how I felt and what I said, it was more of the younger unsettled teenager inside of me driving my emotional reactions.

Yet, I cannot rationalize those embarrassing words away. I was not an adolescent, I was an adult, and I faltered and failed, and let the immature teen get upset and answer. I, the adult, should not have let that happen. Yet, that teenager remains strong and vocal in all of us when it comes to adult interactions with both siblings and our parents. I apologize to you, my siblings, for allowing my teen to again argue with you. I am sorry. It is amazing how when it comes to siblings and how we interact with our parents as adults, it seems so often to time warp us back to our younger years. Poof, where did my calmer older me go?

There are so many great, simple wise sayings about adult parents and siblings, too many to list, and all too simplistic for the magnitude of adult family dynamics. I will share one with you that helped me move on from the sticky stuff that was at the bottom of my family dynamics cooking pot. I know it is not this easy at times, but maybe it will help you too: "If you are still angry at your parents and siblings you haven't really left home." That does not excuse continued harsh words and actions as adults to our siblings. Although, appropriate self-protection with distance may be needed from varying types of abuse or thievery. I hate that the death of parents, in relation to inheritance especially, causes so many families to fall apart. After grief, that is the number two subject people want to share with me concerning the death of their parents. Family will hurt family.

The pull and power of the sensitivities which family creates in us does deserve respect. Keep finding the ability to accept your part of the breakdown. If you have tried and accepted your part, but the aggression, judgment, and anger keep coming, then step away and keep yourself healthy. If someone can't look in and see they too are faulted, and inflict their humanness on others, even if it is a sibling or worse a parent, sometimes we must step away for short or extended periods of time.

There should never be a need to feel guilty for stepping away from any relationship, family included, if it is for the purpose of appropriate self protection. Family can overdevelop our ego, and the trouble continues.

It has been difficult for many that the political aggression and inflexibility of the times is starting to divide families. I have known adult children who have had to protect themselves from the aggression of their own parents' political judgment and aggression, often aggressively regurgitating what they heard on their news channel. I have known grandparents who have had to ask their grandchildren to go a little easy on them about environmental issues or the habit of using old pronouns. Siblings are also politically polarized, and are aggressively torn apart as stressors mount. Family can be the toughest relationship in our lives, even if it is not so bad.

Our sibling bonds are also capable of providing us with powerfully important growth and goodness. I know mine have helped me, both actively and passively.

The Children

We all need a little help with protection from the world's bad, but our vulnerable, actively-seeking-information young humans need it the most. They are clean slates waiting to soak up what we feed them, so please be cautious, as they are hearing, seeing, and recording our words and actions into their powerful ever-questioning minds and spirits. Every one of us, directly or indirectly, is a continuous contributing influence on who they become. They are counting on all of us.

I have seen the role of parent-child interaction take a drastic turn just by observation in grocery stores and restaurants and when I talk to kids. An example of this change is that I rarely see parents teaching their children in society anymore. I just don't see as much conversation between adults and youth as when I was younger. It's not completely our fault, they love to tune us out at times, and the technology devices don't help either. I like to ask our youth of all ages the open-ended question of "What do your parents do?" Not "mom and dad" but "parents," because so many parental relationships are now same-sex, or one parent, or a grandparent situation. I also like this question because the child often says it in a boasting way, finding their parents special. Twenty years ago, I would get responses such as, "They cook for me, they teach me manners, they clean the house and I have to do my room too. They go to work, or they play with me." Because of the negative aspects of our modern times of technology, more recently I hear, "they talk on their phones, they play video games, or they watch TV."

Children need only one invested, supportive, interactive adult in their life to make an incredible impact. Interactions between children and adults provide opportunities to build trust and to learn important social skills. Children that have a healthy attachment with a parent or trusted adult have a better chance at developing happy and content relationships. Please let us remain committed to helping them fill their being with hope, goodness, and a strong desire to grow. Start with consistency in as many directions as you can because watching is how they learn the greatest and longest. We teach them passively through our behaviors and actively through our instruction. Yes please, let us keep up these caring positive influences.

A letter to the powerful energy teens and twenties

Dear Younger Fellow Humans

The very first thing I want you to know is even though I am writing this book for all ages who care to learn from my pains, trials, mistakes, and humanness, I am also writing for you, the younger beings heading into your tomorrows. Which will be my good night, but I still want to help it be the best we can make it for you. I am hoping to help a speck today so your tomorrow will benefit. Because I will not be here for your tomorrow's, I think your generation's needs, words, and issues are very important.

One reason I am dissecting a rather large part of my being in this book is in hopes you will be gentle and comfortable being human. I care to not have you waste your time, experiences, and missed humor working to be perfect, or fretting during those moments you discover you are also beautifully faulted. Being human is a tough, amazing, scary, exciting journey. I am also saying things that need to be stated for you, and people may be angry with me for that. I feel you and your children's tomorrows are worth it. So, I risk it.

I want you to know your parents, grandparents, and all generations before you, did not get everything wrong. Yes, mistakes were made, some huge. But please, check your judgment and anger, because you and your generation will make many mistakes too. If you get honest on the inside, you will see you have already made mistakes yourself. We humans tend to do that— we make a bunch of mistakes. What is important is to keep trying to resolve them as we discover them.

I also completely understand that you have many reasons to be angry. Please try to work with that anger and set it aside. You have much to accomplish to correct some of the problems we created in our periodic failures. Anger will only slow you down. I can give you this example: every argument I ever had was pushed by some real or imagined level of anger, frustration, or injustice, often driven by passionate emotions. Whether I was wrong or right, I wasted valuable time with those arguments, and worse, I sometimes did damage to a situation's progress. Arguments and anger, without calm, organized purpose, accomplishes extraordinarily little, and sometimes can even increase the distance to your goal.

Discussion, respect, flexibility, and compromise, on the other hand, accomplished a great deal in my life. Those keys will most likely take you far in both your personal and occupation life, especially if you will expend energy to practice using them more. If you read the newspaper or watch the news, and I recommend you do, and you don't, I am sorry you are seeing so much wheel-spinning without traction to accomplish more forward movement in balance of solution-based answers. You are correct, the wheel-spinning is at its worst in not only our government but around the world. I refer to the US because I am a citizen and product of this country, yet the inability to compromise is a problem around the world. There are many keys to discover that will help your level of calm, exploration, and accomplishment besides discussion, respect, flexibility, and compromise, such as acceptance, tolerance, forgiveness, and understanding. Some may try to tell you that many of these keys are a sign of weakness. One uncomplicated way to know they are not weaknesses, is how much strength it sometimes takes to apply acceptance, tolerance, forgiveness, and understanding. Especially during stressful times.

Too many people, races, and cultures want their own way in this world. But this world has become an amazing, irreversible patchwork of cultures and races, so all of us getting our own way is more complicated. Thank you, young adults who have trusted me over the years with your thoughts and fears about these subjects. You are right, many of the old ways are dragging us down. My grandfather warned me this was going to happen a few years before he died, and that was several decades ago. It must be frustrating for you also; I know it is for me. I know why your generation is screaming, because the talking alone does not appear to help, especially when some of that talk is filled with rationalizations, self-serving gains, and deception. I do respect your anger; I too have felt varying levels of that anger since my teenage years when I too first began seeing bigger pictures. I respect your anger, but again, the anger alone will not move you towards your goals.

You are right, some of the talking not only does not help, but hinders, delays, and even takes us in the wrong direction at times. The issue is not the talking, the issue is why is someone talking. The right talking will accomplish much more than screaming ever will. Anger and screaming are what too many are doing right now. It is like trying to get a stuck car out of the mud with the accelerator—we are going nowhere and getting more stuck. I encourage you to read the chapter on politics, it will complete the rest of this paragraph.

Politicians lying and cheating has always been an issue because many humans manipulate for selfish reasons. But I am sorry it is so prevalent right now from every direction. It was hard enough growing up with a moderate amount of it. I can't imagine trying to figure out which way is up with this many people hollering at each other and calling each other liars, and misinformation from too many directions. I have such respect for the challenges you are swimming in. Try not to propagate them. Not all media is bad, so try to find sources that weave through the middle not too far to either side—it's your best chance for more facts and less special interest influence. I apologize for something I have no control of. My apology is from compassion, not due to responsibility for it. I am sorry it is so hard to tell what the truth is today. You don't deserve that, no one does.

Your internal, and sometimes actual screaming, will calm a little in the late teens and through your twenties, but it never goes away. You hopefully just get better at turning the volume down to calm it. Part of the screaming, both internal and external, is because you are in the painful beginning, and fantastic phase, of meeting yourself. Meeting yourself will be an endless life task, but an exciting and difficult wild journey. It is normal to be confused, scared, and excited to see who you will become. Who you become is much more important than what you will become. It is in who you become that you will find the richer, deeper, wider, calmer, peaceful, and much more rewarding you. You may find accomplishing external projects can be fairly easy, yet being self-aware, introspective, and exploring your being is how life is truly and deeply experienced. You do not have to meet yourself to exist, but to be your best for yourself, to thrive, and feel alive, then continuing to meet yourself will help. This is a concept that requires application, but so worth the comforts and exploration it helps provide.

Attempt not to use others, or to have only transactional relationships. Self-gain is hard to completely enjoy when it is at the cost of others. Living a life of only, "What's in it for me," is not as necessary as these me oriented times make it seem. Using others requires a lot of internal energy and is also somewhat self-damaging. Being honest with yourself first is the key to great relationships. Yes, being honest with yourself is one of the hardest and scariest things you will ever do. It's also amazing, because once we accept the humanness of ourselves and others, life becomes even more peaceful and rewarding. Enjoy your extensive and rewarding lifelong explorations.

I encourage you to slow down now and then to listen to others, and history. It will save you much time and energy for other joys and problem-solving. Quickly learn the difference between infatuation and love. Learning the difference will decrease a huge percentage of growing pains and save you a few major heartbreaks and blame-filled arguments. Learn the magnitude of love's meanings, true words, actions, deceptions, and omissions. You will change and grow rapidly through your twenties, so give yourself permission to sacrifice who you are for who you can be, repetitively.

Walk your own roads. You will experience great freedom in slow cautious independence. True autonomy is not doing everything your generation does, it is doing what is right for you, independent of others. You get to paint your picture how you wish. Autonomy has nothing to do with dress, but a great deal to do with the pauses you take to process your thoughts and awarenesses. You get to be you, unrelated to fashion, media, advertising, or peer pressures. That's a big deal, protect it.

The last thing I need to ask is a favor from you please. It is not a small favor either, but you will also benefit from it. It is important you know you are not the first woke generation. The 1960s and 1970s were a major generation of woke, and just as you are paying for your woke period, we too paid for ours. All periods of rapid acceleration of awareness and growth are hard and painful. We discovered everything from the fact that people will push a war for profit, to your grandparents literally having anchors dropped on their boats in the middle of the ocean while they were trying to save endangered whales. They fought to get tuna fishing boats to release the dolphins and sea turtles from their nets and not heartlessly kill them with the rest of the catch. They organized and accomplished international law changes to protect those whales and stop needlessly killing turtles and dolphins, and those populations are returning. Please don't stop fighting their cause. The scientist told us about climate change, and we started reusing and recycling. The scientist told us the aerosol in our spray cans was eating away the ozone at the north and south poles. We listened, banned their use, and those holes filled back in. We learned big things for you. But we are not done, and we need to do better as we walk out and you walk in.

Here is the favor I am respectfully requesting: please know that many of us have already accepted the generational changes and unique needs of your time. There is much going on. To all generations, it can be confusing and painful, but many of us support your many journeys of further awakenings. Some of your great-grandfathers were some of the first people to say, "here I am," and walk out their door in drag, or maybe your great-grandmother burned her bra. We remember, we get it, but we have old lifelong habits to break that don't make us insensitive or less caring. Just because we ride a tractor, or just because our abdominal girth has a direct correlation to our gray hairs, don't assume because we are old and more set in our ways, that we don't support you and are not trying to learn to say "They" instead of "She," or "Them" instead of "He." Many of us are walking with you, we just walk slower.

Now, if you are screaming about your core beliefs, by all means scream away. But if it's an uncle or grandparent that just can't get the new terms and pronouns pushed into old habits of our time, please go easy on us. The same goes for us older generations towards you younger humans—we need to listen to what they are screaming at us; it is both real and will be their reality after we are dead. I again apologize to you for the adults that say it is not their concern because they won't be here to see it. That exact mentality was one of the driving forces of our past generations' negative contributions that got us this far in the hole. You are angry for some great reasons.

By using discretion in picking your battles, you will be more effective. I understand there is no longer room for much compromise in the area of ecology. However, it might still be more productive to flex away from an all or nothing stance in many subjects. It is hard, never give up. I don't plan to give up attempting, because I believe in the many that are doing the right things for the right reasons. But we need your help to keep helping you. Many of us are trying to help you. It just may not always feel that way when you look at the world.

Believe in yourself, your abilities, your goodness, and your tomorrows. With deep respect for your times and stressors,
Vincent Dodd

Random relationships, seemingly unimportant but not

I have struggled with what good could have come from the past years of such turbulence in our social and political realms. Well over a year ago a friend of mine said to me, "The good that will come from these past years is they ripped the scab off of our social, racial, and political issues, and now all we have to do is not waste the opportunity to heal from the inside out." That brought me further needed peace, and the courage to write about these hard to hear issues that can be healed from the inside out. You may not think saying hello to a stranger in the grocery store line is important. You may not think doing something polite and slightly out of the way for a stranger or light acquaintance could make a difference. But these relationships are what can help glue our society back together. We take this for granted because we think we don't need each other anymore. But we do, and these random relationships have the potential to turn so much bad around.

We should never take for granted the fabric of our social structure, which is made of all of us. For the most part, social structure is not made of one race or culture, it is not made up of the wealthy, or the laborers. Our social structure is weakened by allowing fast easy labels to separate us. Saying hello to strangers when you have the appropriate opportunity is how we remind each other that the world is not completely selfish, inconsiderate, or prejudiced. It is how we help each other feel like someone cares.

I know this is tough to do when the world seems so full of "me" people doing their "me" things. But keep doing it anyway. Keep giving back, saying hello, making periodic eye contact, making a self-deprecating joke in a line with others so that being human becomes welcomed again. If it is right, say hello to someone who may not expect a hello from you. Let's reach across the aisles in every direction possible. Let's start to dissolve the "us and them" mentality of society, because each of us holds a speck of that answer and ability.

This is not limited to individuals; groups also have this ability to help. Businesses, church groups, social clubs, and volunteer organizations perhaps arrange group projects or a get-together with diverse people out of your demographics. We can't wait for something big to come along and fix our issues, it is up to us to also start to heal our racial, cultural, and political divides. Let's accomplish these important cross-cultural/racial gatherings, whether two people or two couples go to dinner, or large groups complete a community project together. A few guidelines will increase mutual respect and productivity. Such as, stay away from what you don't have in common and find what you do share. Maybe attempt to stay away from conversations involving converting related to any subject, from politics to religion. Meet other races and cultures where they are, and then accept them as they are, rather than attempt to get them where you think they need to be. Continue to work to see what is different as just that, different, not wrong. History and past issues from any angle or direction can be tricky. Let us look at the present and to the future, that is where we find the most commonality and teamwork. Work to let people finish their sentences, even when you don't agree with the sentence. We all want to be respected enough to be allowed to finish our sentences.

Acknowledge the people around you, those random relationships are magnificent opportunities to heal self, others, communities, and beyond. Our relationships with each other are the glue of our social fabric and bonds, and the stitching that prevents further unraveling.

If we keep staring in the rear-view mirror, we are going to keep hitting the things that are in front of us.

WIDER ANGLES:

THE MANURE THROWERS

Not all my simplified wider angels are designed to help me work with something inside of me; a few are designed to help me accept the external world over which I have little or no control. Unfortunately, we all have a little manure thrower in us.

I think there might be a huge catwalk system way up in the sky, like the catwalk system above a theater stage, that the stagehands of a theatrical production use to accomplish the scenes and special effects of a play. Except this catwalk is painted blue, is very hard to see, and it crisscrosses all around the earth. Walking on it are a few thousand big, tall hunched-over hairy beings, each with a long burlap sack across their shoulders and dragging behind them filled with manure. Their job is to randomly fling cow manure far out from the catwalk at a very steady slow pace, just to help fertilize the earth. In a lifetime, each manure spreader gets to walk all over the globe many times. They look and smell a little rough, but they are great at world geography. They are so high up that we can't see them, and they can't see us—they don't even know we are down here. Unless we are highly alert looking out for it, we don't see the manure coming. No one escapes the fallout. Boom! And we have a flat tire. Ouch! And we hit our head and must go get it stitched up. Zing! We need a new washer and dryer. Or Bam! A company gets a lawsuit brought against them. Double zing! We have a cancer cell cluster starting to divide faster than our immune system can fight it. Yes, we can be preventive by trying to avoid some of these hits, but we all get hit anyway. Sometimes moderately, but sometimes we get hit by one so heavy it knocks us far over, such as with cancer.

Painfully for us, they are all fantastic at their simple job—to reach into that manure bag and fling handfuls over the side. Unfortunately, it randomly lands on us. It is not completely a curse and even has a few gifts, such as motivating us to be more preventative, and to even help us to not fling it onto others, at least not more than we already get on each other by normal humanness. Getting smaller random hits is important to get us ready to handle the periodic big ones that are guaranteed to hit us a few times in our lives. If we change how we see things, then even the sudden random manure strikes can have their place.

Since the throwers have poor sight from too much unfiltered sunlight, and are too high up to hear us, this should remind us that we are not being picked on. That does not mean that sometimes there is not a period where that manure just keeps hitting you more often than you expect it should. That's a valid reason to feel you are being singled out, but you are not. The catwalk extends around the earth is a helpful reminder that I am not alone; the manure throwers are randomly hitting everyone. Whether we are poor or rich, no matter the color of our skin, or the sound of our voice or accents, none of that can be observed from that high up. We all get hit, dealing with it without letting it steal our moments or days is how we win. Getting upset over your random hits, even being angry at someone else to pop off the frustration, is willing giving your periodic random hit your day and even a part of yourself.

We do have varying levels of ability to sidestep some of it. Some, but not all. This absurd, imaginary vision is just another way to help me through my day with a little more peaceful acceptance. It's incredibly helpful when I realize my spare is flat too. Pow! Pow! A double hit on the side of the road!

CHAPTER 8

ARGUMENTS, ORGASMS, AND LOVE

"If sex were meant for procreation alone, and not also for pleasure, the creator could have made an orgasm one tenth as pleasurable, and the world still would have overpopulated."
—Unknown

"The words of the tongue should have three gatekeepers: Is it true? Is it kind? Is it necessary?"
—Arab proverb

Saying "I love you" is not enough

It doesn't mean that's all, I'm not done.
It doesn't mean I don't have to say or do anything else.
Half of I love you is what I don't say or do.
It doesn't mean that is all the energy I have to expend to love you.
In fact, it means nothing without the following.

I love you means I'll love myself first, otherwise I'll just be fooling us both.
It means I'll try my best to pay attention.
It means I'll try to love you how you wish to be loved,
Not only how I think you should be loved.

I love you means we won't ask each other to compromise ourselves.
It does mean I'll be willing to make some changes for you.

There's a difference between those two.
I love you means I'm willing to adapt for you
If I see you will do the same for me
Otherwise, I am compromising myself.

I love you means if I say or do something non supportive, I won't defend it.
I won't say, "No, I didn't do that," or "No, you took that the wrong way."
I love you means I can say "I am sorry."
I love you means I'll accept responsibility for my shortcomings.
It means I wish I had not said it.
I can't say it won't happen again, for I am human, it may happen again.
It does mean I'll expend energy, time, and self to try not to let it happen
again.
It means I'll forgive you also for doing or saying something non-supportive
of me.

I love you means I'll trust your opinions, even when they are about me.
Even when they are pointing out my weaknesses, flaws, and mistakes.
It means I'll accept you for who you are.
It doesn't mean I won't want you to do better and grow.
I love you means you will want the same for me.

I love you means I'll accept and welcome your emotions, all of them.
It means I won't see you as ugly for being angry.
It means I won't see you as weak for being depressed, or soft.
It means I won't see you as a slut for being healthy and lustful.
It means I'll stand by patiently, in silence, even if you don't know what
you're feeling.

I love you means I'll see you as the whole person you are.
I'll accept your strengths, faults, weaknesses, and vulnerabilities.

I'll praise the positive ones and not take advantage of your other human
ones.
I love you means I'll show you all of mine too.

"I love you" is only words, only sounds, only a membrane.
But that "only," if genuine, with actions and omissions. . .
Then it holds almost all of life, that being our love.
Saying or hearing, I love you can be the greatest tool and reward we have.
Healthy love enriches everything and everyone to the greatest potential.

Love and intimate love relationships

I don't think hate is the opposite of love. I think fear and indifference
are the opposite of love. I know love is real, a mother's love proves that.
There is no greater love on the face of the earth than a mother's love for
her children, provided that mental unhealth, abuse, or addiction are
not overriding the maternal love. The proof is not only the care of their
infant, although that is also beautifully bonded love, the proof of true
love is in the tolerance of the adolescent. Infants don't tell their mothers
to go to hell and slam the door. Infants don't roll their eyes at their
mother's wisdom and innate drive to teach and protect or think a hug
from the woman who brought them into this world is uncool.

Even though love is, for most of us, our deepest non-vital reward and
drive, it is also a serious liar. The lies of love, whether for a person, money,
pleasure, or power, have the ability to damage or destroy relationships,
drive homicide and suicide, eat us alive from the inside out, dangerously
distort our perceptions of reality, or force us to dominate, control, and
manipulate. True love does not do those destructive things to us, not on
abusive levels anyway, but even healthy love can be a little messy all on
its own. But if it is actual love, not love's lies talking, it can wrap us in the
warmest, sweetest, safest feelings and become life's most invigorating

exploration one could ever imagine. Separating love's lies and truths is a lifelong pursuit that will draw out our tears and laughs, our pleasures, and our screams to our awakenings, or it can be the impetus to our self-destruction or our greatest blossoming.

Because love's lies and deep stabbing pains can cause us to bleed so much, and it is incredibly capable of being so core-shattering, painful, and misleading, some feel they must turn their backs on love and walk away forever, saying, "It's just not worth it."

We know love is hard to define in text because so many definitions fall short of ever getting close to the feelings of giving or receiving love. We know it is important, and healthy love is proven to be good for us. Blood pressure can be lowered by healthy loving relationships, even healthy friendships can decrease health issues. Healthy human contact is good for us period, therefore healthy loving human contact, whether physical or just emotionally supportive, is fantastic for us. The research on love and its benefits are extensive. But that is only textbook; by the time we take our last breath, we have spent a lifetime studying love up close and personally. How do we define something that is so many things? Compounding attempts to define love are the many types of love, such as intimate love, family love, the love of friends, the love of plants or animals, the love of objects, self-love, even the love of exercise. There are scary loves too. The most dangerous love of all is the love of power, pleasure, money, food, and intoxicants.

Unconditional love is an incredibly dynamic, challenging, and completely unattainable love that is highly worth striving for anyway. We can get better at it, but we all have a limit, even dogs can't obtain unconditional love. The love of a dog is as close as we will ever get to unconditional love. Yet even they will eventually actively or passively protect themselves. We should be careful with unconditional love; it can become the chant of the masochist. A martyr of yesterday was considered noble, but a martyr of today is a fool. I must be a fool and a masochist; I expend energy to get better at unconditional love. That includes the love of those I don't agree with. Just because I don't agree with a person or group, should not mean I have to fear, hate, or discard them.

The love of the orgasm is probably one of our first true loves and infatuation. I would say it is unconditional love, if not for some early guilt and shame, which adds conditions. Unfortunately, it can also share a blurry boundary with an unhealthy love of pleasure, capable of destruction on too many levels to list, if not respected, for its equal ability to lie. Oh, but the love of the orgasm is a sweet healthy love also.

The love of pleasure, power, money, food, and intoxicants are the loves that lie big. But they are solid loves, too often toxic love, but love nonetheless. Perhaps those are infatuations? Except infatuations fade, and some spend their lives in an unhealthy intimate relationship with these five dangerous loves. That is not infatuation. These are the loves that cause self and outward thievery, deception, and partial or harm of ourselves and the people around us. These are the loves that are destroying our families, communities, governments, and the earth. These are the dangerous loves that we rationalize to tell ourselves it is okay to remove limits and the checks and balances of ourselves, of governments, of societies, which are so dangerous to everything and everyone.

If the love of pleasure, power, money, food, or intoxicants is the subject, then I'm not sure I could use the words damaging or destructive too many times. From a work mate to a love partner, parent, politician, and even up to dictators of countries, these five dangerous loves can dissolve and overpower a person all the way up to an entire country.

But this section is about the all-powerful and beautiful intimate love relationship. The holy grail of relationships. The one that can make us wonderfully sweet and stupid, puts us in a hole we helped dig, or shoots us to the moon and past. It is because intimate love comes with so much luggage that it deserves its own chapter. I hate the times love made me stupid and stupid, but I wallow in the times it made me sweet and stupid.

Some of the work required to attempt to keep love healthy

"Anyone who can drive safely while kissing is simply not giving the kiss the attention it deserves."
—Albert Einstein

One way the love of an orgasm can lie to us is its quick, easy deception into infatuation over love. Infatuation strikes fast too, especially in most of our first relationships during our adolescence and twenties. For some, fast-striking infatuation can remain an issue throughout life. The look, the laugh, the first appearances of commonality, and the desire for, or actual touch, the first hug and kiss. Infatuation at first sight is often assigned love at first sight. Be gentle with yourself, it's dangerously powerful, and we all want it to be loved. Who can't respect that hope and want?

Starting with the understanding that love and infatuation are quite different is paramount to healthy intimate relationships, and to having realistic expectations. Quickly followed by the understanding that intimate love cannot be put in a box and does not always involve physical intimacy. These are only a few of the massive dump truckload of reasons love won't fit in a box. It can't be made nice and tidy, it involves the human brain's 80 billion maligned neurons; then add in the heart, emotions, innate powerful drives, and now add a second person doubling all those extremes. Now attempt to fit two people's love into a little box. Or, in this day and time, since polyamory numbers have been climbing for years, attempt to place three or more people in that box.

Infatuation can be a fantastic start for love, if a couple is lucky enough to have infatuation blend into true healthy love and support. Infatuation is that beautiful powerful first connection that is like an explosion in your head and heart. Oh yes, and there too. Infatuation means enough is lining up between two people to cause our bodies to release adrenaline, causing that wonderful funny feeling in your chest. Infatuation doesn't have to involve intimacy; the ease of discussion, humor, and like-mindedness are all that is required, and are actually the stronger foundations to it turning into longer lasting love. Infatuation can be a great start to a long loving relationship, or it can be the perfect setup for a severe storm, filled with hate, anger, and blame when it fades.

Because infatuation in unhealthy relations eventually fades, if nothing else is there to bring the relationship further, then respecting that was what happened helps preserve our sanity and respect for each other. On its own, infatuation fading deserves no blame or anger. Yes, unfortunately, sometimes one or both sides mess up so badly that peace is difficult. When we mix in ego, false pride, insecurity, and punitive poisons into a relationship that is ending or has ended, the odds of a painfully rough ending increase. But, if you safely can, continue to care about the person, even if from afar, you will find faster peace and reward, even though the relationship has ended.

If the relationship stops working, attempt to let people go with your true pride. If there was goodness, then hold onto the gifts that you connected, shared, and grew. Great growth and faster calm can come from not roughing each other up with ego, anger, insecurity, or jealousy because infatuation alone cannot carry a relationship. Be even more gentle because this stuff is hard; intimate bonds connect deep and into the heart, and they are painful and difficult to end and let go of. This is a hard but appropriate time to expend energy to keep our ego out of a breakup. Our ego may be angry the relationship is over and may want the end to look more like kicking and screaming than the gentle ending with respectful closure it most likely deserves. Infatuation only turns into hatred if we allow our ego to control the end. Ego loves to blame and hates to admit partial fault.

Another good reason to allow relationships and acquaintances go with as little ill will as possible is that most likely the 40–60% rule is in the picture. Meaning, far more often than not, both sides probably contributed to the relationship's demise. It is a great time to show respect for what wonderful things occurred between two people, not what did not last. Unless control and abuse were involved, this should hold true for as many relationships in our lives as possible, whether infatuation was involved or not. This is even more necessary when children are involved.

Not letting someone go with peace and self-reflection about the two-way street of the relationship, and what you may have also negatively contributed to its demise, is asking to repeat the same behaviors in your next relationship. It also denies opportunity for growth. Doing the hard work to find those painful truths is how we love first ourselves, then our past, and finally even our future partner with greater clarity and self-awareness. It also creates a greater potential for less strife and longer lasting relationships in every department of life. This is probably one of the more important and functional paragraphs of this chapter for self-growth, peaceful endings, and healthier easier relationships tomorrow. Some feel looking in to find our part excuses the other person's behavior, but it does not. It means we are also doing our work to create ease in all our relationships.

In some relationships the responsibility percentage does widen out from 40–60% to 20–80% or, every now and then, 10–90%, 100% of the blame belongs to one person when extreme control is used, or a preexisting advantage was already present and acted on. When there is abuse involved, a much higher percentage belongs to the abuser because the other person is being torn down from their full potential, and is often forced to move into the best defensive mode they can muster. Sometimes abuse is being inflicted from both directions in a relationship. Owning and exploring your percentage of the breakdown in all relationships will get easier, and help make life easier also.

That same self-evaluation applies to the issues within an ongoing relationship. Most bumps or arguments are a shared responsibility, finding your part and working with it will make the relationship you are in healthier. Admitting to your part also builds trust in relationships, which is deeply romantic. It is my ego and self-defensive habits that hinder my growth, progress, and peace in communication and relationships. Not only does that get in the way of my growth, but if I don't accept my part, then I am asking someone else to. I have been realizing that asking someone else to accept my part of a breakdown is not only wrong, but it eats a bigger hole in my conscience than the little bruise for just saying, "I did do that, and I am sorry."

"You are not the person I met!"

I noticed a fast and detrimental behavior in relationships that I had to learn to pay great attention to. The behavior is wanting the other person to change for us and the relationship. Consciously or subconsciously, we all have a speck of this behavior ingrained to some degree. Some of us gain moderate awareness and control of it, and a few get very good at not acting on it. But wanting, expecting, or manipulating someone to change is another wrecking ball to relationships. Wanting the other person to change in its lighter forms is human, normal, and manageable with self-awareness. In its heavier forms, it is another foundation of abuse. Wanting the other person to change is another human thought process and behavior that falls onto a continuum, depending on the degree. Low levels on the continuum are normal and we all work with them, whether we are sending or receiving the change behavior.

However, higher levels are control and abuse, and it requires work to get under control.

Although we may not always be aware of it, I think it is ingrained in us to attempt to get the person in front of us to be like us or to mold them into our vision of a perfect partner. We all know it certainly is a repetitive theme in unhealthy relationship conversations. The greater our control issues are, in general, the more powerful our drive is to change the other person. Give yourself a break here, too. I think it's second nature, but just attempt to remain aware of it and attempt not to act on it. Many people are keen to this human threat and know to run fast when its level rises above normal flexible requests. Normal and flexible can be something like preferring to wash dishes always on one side of the sink, because they designated the other sink for food preparation. That is the type of little habit or preference of daily living we should all care to learn if we are going to spend time in someone else's space. There's a difference between asking someone to be flexible for you and asking someone to change who they are. As I love to say, in humor, it is the difference between the flexibility of putting someone's toilet paper roll in the same direction they do, as opposed to wanting them to change their core being by asking them to switch toilet paper brands altogether.

If someone wanted you to change your core being, you may have had this argument a year or so after meeting someone. Your partner says to you, "You are not the person I met!" How could you be, if they asked you to stop doing the things you did when they first met you? Due to their issues, did you give up the friendships that made you the person they had originally met? Have they guided you away from something that was a healthy habit of yours when the two of you first met? Or have they redirected your political views, or manipulated you away from your friends or from spending time with family? Are there insecurity or distrust issues in the mix?

"You're not the person I met." How much of that statement is the person stating it responsible for? The couples I know where both partners are good at not trying to change the other are noticeably more peaceful happy couples. If you liked the person that you met a year ago, then everything that person did, or the friends they had, helped them be the person you were attracted to and fell for in the first place. Even past loves helped make them the person you are attracted to. It is unfair and a setup for relationship difficulties that we want and expect them to cooperate in erasing their past. Good or bad, our partner's past led them to who we were initially attracted to. That deserves respect, in either praise for their good past and gentleness for their bad past.

If someone wants to attempt to erase someone's past, they will be attempting to erase a part of that person. To inorganically change someone produces an unsteadiness in the person because their core being was taken off its naturally time-built balance. Resentment can occur also, because too often one person becomes flexible, and one person does not. The relationship now carries another added issue, resentment, which is caustic acid to relationships. Poor outcomes may indicate a fundamental incompatibility, or that the infatuation period is over. Please remember, if core incompatibility or infatuation are the cases alone, it's no one's fault and walk on. You are worth more than the tricks that love's infatuation can play. However, if the relationship has a high level of expecting someone to fundamentally change and give up what made them who they are, then be incredibly careful.

As we head into relationships, change is going to happen; the question is how much will be organic, and how much is being demanded or manipulated? How much of the demise was infatuation not turning into true love and compatibility, and how much was a lack of healthy flexibility and acceptance?

Flexibility is a major characteristic of healthy compatibility and long-term stability. Healthy relationships require flexibility, and our intimate love relationship requires a special type of flexibility. The more personal something is, literally the closer to our internal being, the more we want our idea of "right," also known as our way. We want it even more if we think it is going to be in our lives for a long time. A material comparison but it correlates: if we are renting a car for two days, then the color might not be that important, but if we are buying a car that we hope to have for many years to come, we might have a certain color in our heads that we want that car to be. I am not excluded, flexibility has been a lifelong exercise for me, and looking back, I feel I owe some apologies for not knowing this sooner in life. I still falter, but I accept more and more with time, and I carry less stress because of it.

If core compatibility is not present, expecting someone to compromise their core being is going to create resentment and extreme feelings of unfairness. Even if someone attempts or accomplishes core changes for another person, as opposed to voluntarily wanting to for self-growth and ease, it often won't last. Or it leads to a loss of respect, which often leads to a loss of attraction and trust.

This core remodeling in relationships is normally one-sided, and the dominant personality will dominate. Compromising your core being is true incompatibility being covered up and suppressed, and it will eventually resurface. This is why it is not uncommon to see someone who is no longer flexible after leaving a controlling abusive situation. We become hyper-vigilant to not allow that to happen again. If you are in a relationship with someone whose last relationship forced them to become hyper-defensive to protect their core being, hang in there. This initial hyper-protection is now on guard for a good reason; but with time many will start to relax once their core being returns, especially if you show them, and they feel, you accept them for who they are.

There is an exceptional book, inspired by a famous murder, that I believe is one of the most enlightening and hands-on helpful books out there about domestic violence. After the murder of Nicole Brown

Simpson, her father, Lou Brown, Francois Bubau, and Merritt McKeon wrote, *Stop Domestic Violence, An Action Plan for Saving Lives.* I highly encourage everyone to read this book for a handful of reasons. It is an easy read as far as understand-ability and application. The topic itself is not easy for a few reasons, and one will surprise you. The first of course is the subject; this book explains the pathology of abuse. The other reason is how scarily easy it is to have controlling behaviors that don't necessarily fall into abuse. I have not heard one person get back to me, who I referred or loaned one of my copies of the book to over the years, who did not say it helped them help someone they knew who was in an abusive relationship and help them personally. Most agreed with me that they now needed to pay more attention to their own behaviors. I wish I had read it sooner for that self-knowledge. I thought I knew how to help victims of abuse, but I was not always on the right track. Even if not this book, take some time to learn about the pathology of abuse and control, and how to support yourself and others that are victims.

Sitting with yourself for a few

The drive for pleasure, companionship, and to procreate is so powerful that the world's population is now past 7.5 billion people. I repeat that number a few times because it is so important for realistic big pictures and true problem solving. Our drive to couple is an enormously powerful relentless drive, and our drive to avoid pain is equally powerful, especially the pain of the broken heart. These two forces often cause us to get into or stay in relationships that are not good for us. When these two drives, to couple and to avoid pain, combine, or an addiction to relationships or love, it causes us to do something else that is detrimental to long-term loving relationships: That being going from one long-term relationship right into another.

I am not talking about the dating periods where you are going out on dates with people looking to meet the right person for higher levels of compatibility. When we are relationship jumping, or dating immediately after a long-term relationship, we deny ourselves the gifts of self-love, internal peace, growth, and the joy of meeting our new self. We are also potentially sabotaging the health and well-being of our next relationship. I always appreciated the scene in the movie *The Witches of Eastwick* when Jack Nicholson and Cher are having lunch underneath the tent in his backyard. Nicholson is slowly seducing Cher with empowerment and understanding for how hard men are to be in relationships with. I do not believe what I am about to share from the scene is gender specific; we are capable of doing this to each other when in relationships, gender has no bearing. Nickelson shared the concept that no matter how hard men try not to stifle a woman in relationships, they do. He describes it as once one of the three Ds occurs (death, desertion, or divorce), the woman can then again grow, bloom, and blossom. They pulled the scene off with a little more flare than my two-dimensional words can accomplish, but it still relays the gist: in relationships, even with great effort not to, we accidentally suppress each other. That is another reason not jumping into another relationship is a healthy idea.

Yes, relationships can also enrich each other in beautiful and healthy ways all day long. The growth, blooming, and blossoming that occurs after a relationship, if one can get past the pain and trauma, is where we meet ourselves again. The person we are is influenced by the other person we are in a relationship with, even if they are a healthy influence. As opposed to the person you are when not in a relationship, when you are the main and mostly only daily influence on yourself. That is what is meant by meeting our "self" again. Can that person be autonomous, sit quietly with the self, reflect with clear glasses, not the rose-colored ones, and just be you for a spell? After a long-term relationship ends, sitting with the self can be hard, of course we want to soften those hard pains of grief, emptiness, loneliness, and the self-doubt of self-review, with meeting someone else. I get it.

The blooming and blossoming of a being after a relationship should grow the flowers of the autonomous self. By going from one relationship to another, we deny ourselves our stand-alone self, a recalibration of you. If years have passed in a relationship that changes our core being, that relationship was an influence on our being. If we jump right into another relationship without spending some time with ourselves, we once again have another person influencing our being, and we deny ourselves the opportunity to meet our new self. We have also denied ourselves the healthy grieving of the past relationship. Even if the relationship turned sour, it deserves grieving. Hopefully it was a good relationship on several levels at some point. If it was abusive, then a healing period may be needed even more. This is not only about healing or meeting yourself today, but it also has positive benefits for your next relationship.

That independent and autonomous time on your own is vital to become a whole person again. Your next relationship has such a better start and strength because you walk into it more whole, healed, and have greater tools and learned experiences, because you processed the good and bad from your past relationships. Please always find this courage and strength, our ego is horrible about not allowing ourselves the gift of honest self-review. The ego wants us to paint ourselves angelic and the other person a monster. Rationalizing our part away will only increase our chances of committing the same mistakes in our next relationship. This clearer self-review is not easy, and sometimes anger and defensiveness creates a huge block in this department. Self-review is not excusing the other person for their negative contribution; it is only finding the courage to look and identify your percentage.

We argue to be right, win, or get our way; but we
scream to be heard

We have all heard the most common subjects couples argue about are sex, money, and kids. I looked it up and those are the first three listed out of the top ten. I don't care what the subject is, I hate to argue. "Fighting" is the next level up and has a much worse intention. When there is a fight, it means neither side is interested in compromise and both sides want to hurt the other. Think of two people fighting in a ring, compromise is not a word on their minds at that moment. Even arguing is leaving the realm of discussion and compromise. We have discussions with our rational mind, we often argue and fight with our emotional mind. The other reason I hate arguing is if I look back on my life with unfiltered honesty, I can clearly see that not only have I not accomplished anything with argument, but by arguing I only damaged the relationship by unraveling the bonds of trust and respect. Our egos and false pride both encourage arguing, and I can easily assign them as the pusher of my past arguments. This delineation between discussion, argument, and fighting is very empowering to help keep communication during conflict in the much more productive, respectful, and solution-based realm of discussion. Which is sometimes so much easier said than done. A wise mentor once said to me, "Would you rather argue to be right, or discuss and be loved?"

Once a discussion turns into an argument, our ego, emotions, and dominant self, have emerged, and are taking over the communication. I admit I used to rationalize arguments as discussion with passion. In doing the research to write this section, I also did some internal self-digging to find out what still pushes me to argue. It was not any of the remaining seven reasons listed. The first three I have argued about, and I am embarrassed, because arguing about those three is a lose-lose situation. But arguing about sex is embarrassingly some of my less than shining bright moments that displayed a lack of basic common sense on my part. I never once had more sex after an argument about frequency. However, it was accomplished by doing the exact opposite of arguing; allowing sentences to be finished without interruption, not invalidating that which I do not agree with but rather finding commonality, a willingness to compromise, and listening with respect to understand her ideas, goals, life's understandings, and to hear and act on the needs expressed.

I truly cannot think of a single time or subject that leaving discussion and escalating to argument ever helped, but I can see how it damaged trust and respect every time. Removing little chips over and over eventually equals a chunk of damaged trust and respect, and those two are very hard to rebuild.

With further unfiltered digging, I discovered what in my past pushed me to argue, still embarrassed that I wasted my time pushing for these. But I have realized my emotional, non-rational mind takes over and argues when I am not being heard or validated. A big one for me is when I bring up a need or concern and it is immediately turned around into me being the issue. In other words, I argue to be half of a relationship and not steamrolled, and I argue not to argue. One of the many reasons you read me chanting acceptance, tolerance, forgiveness, and understanding is because they are great empathizers in helping me not argue and carrying them into stressful discussion helps keep discussion productive and prevents escalation.

The other big seven subjects of why couples argue are also powerful subjects: big event timing, romance, how much time is spent together, triggers, the in-laws and family, daily living maintenance energy or what I call the work of life, and the big mean dangerous one, jealousy.

Big event timing subjects are the ones you look back on and call milestones: choosing to be exclusive, meeting parents, your engagement and wedding, having children, and when or where to vacation or spend a holiday. These are the arguments that should most definitely be discussions not arguments, because these positive beautiful events should be surrounded by goodness, not argument and resentment. The tough thing about these subjects is the feeling or issue of control. The person wanting the big event often feels the other person has too much control over it. If one wants to get engaged and the other doesn't, the person wanting to get engaged feels like they have no control of the situation. At the same time, the person wanting to hold off begins to feel pushed and prodded by the person who wants it now. Both of those feelings can move discussion into argument too quickly when one or both people are being driven by emotions and a desire to get the other person to agree with their reasons. The tough thing about this one is that all these events should be exciting joyful events, unrelated to the concepts of control. These milestone events should never be forced. If force is required, perhaps the core compatibility should be further examined?

Romance is nothing but goodness, unless we have to ask for it, or if we don't find the same things romantic. Romance issues can range from not dressing up for a planned date to forgetting an anniversary. Some people deserve a break on this one because it is also related to everyone's strengths and weaknesses of their mind. There are those who think planning a romantic gesture is like pulling teeth, then there are those who exhale romance with every breath. No matter what your romantic strength level is, there are very few excuses not to have a little romance thrown into even longer relationships. I just did an online search for "100 romantic ideas," and received 66,000 returns. As long as we don't argue about romance, only goodness should come from it. Romance is the opposite of being stifled in a relationship and should first be shown as general respect before it can be shown as an invitation or gesture. Romance is the nutrients, water, and sunlight of an intimate relationship; it helps everything bloom and blossom.

How much time a couple spends together is another one of the top ten reasons couples argue, and it has more angles to it than one would think. Our cell phones have become a huge issue in spending time together. Are you spending time with someone if you are in their proximity, but are on your phone? Often one wants more time together, which is a warm compliment. If you don't find your partner wanting more of you a compliment, it is again time to examine core compatibility. Work however must come first, and unless someone is addicted to their work and is spending more time in that balance than is healthy, partners should be understanding of this one. Sometimes work must come first. Yet, it is also not a good sign if one is using work to avoid their relationship. What to do with that time together can also be a difficult call. One wants to hike, the other wants to work together on some projects around the house. Then, with or without friends or just the two of you gets thrown into the mix. All should be compromising to get to that 40–60% fluctuating fair split. When we feel balance and compromise is a two-way street, it helps us feel connected and respected. When balance and compromise are gifted to us, it builds trust, respect, and equality, "What would you like to do with our weekend?" That small gesture shows how easy it is to weave a little romance into almost anything.

Triggers, also known as pet peeves, refer to having our buttons pushed. Conditioned reactions are how we often react to triggers, as opposed to having a slower rational response. The tough part is that our partners get far too good at pushing them even accidentally, and with our partners, we become even more painfully sensitive to having them triggered. Arguments over conditioned reactions can be retrained just like the conditioned reactions themselves. It takes some work, but it can be done. It all gets easier when we work to slow down reactions, because we can't get words back once spoken. We can't.

Regarding arguments about in-laws, I just encourage everyone to remember family relationships can be complex and painfully raw. Oftentimes our partners can see dynamics we have with our own families that we cannot see, but have the potential to really help us grow. They can also judge our families too harshly. Be gentle with each other and remember, your intimate relationship is between you and your partner, not their family. Yes, families are package deals, but you fell in love with an individual, not a family. Love that person, and exercise acceptance, tolerance, forgiveness, and understanding if the family is not at. . . let's say. . . how about a. . . high-compatibility level. Yes! That's the term I needed to find high-compatibility. Whew! For good or bad, active influence or passive influence, you fell in love with the person who is a byproduct of that family. Yes, loving your partner's family can be hard, or an easy flow if it fits, but your partner is most likely experiencing the same growing pains with their family and now with yours also.

We have such a rare, mutual, and wonderful opportunity to help our partner out with family. Our partner will, and should, have some protective and judgmental input because they care for us, and because judging someone else's family can be just too easy. Their view can greatly help you also. They are living amongst your family, but seeing it from a new angle, that can be extremely helpful. Their input is highly worth listening too. Remember, input and criticism are both hard to hear, but the input will be the helpful part. At different points in life, we can be emotionally arrested with how our families affect us, which is why going home is often partially going back to our adolescence.

If there is a lack of tolerance, acceptance, or our deep-seated resentment with our parents or siblings, this is another time seeking professional guidance might help. So many of our lasting pains or troubles stem from family. Usually, it is a combination of what happened to us, how we looked at it or dealt with it, or did not deal with it, and how we carried it through life. I don't think it is ever too late to do a little more digging inside ourselves concerning family, and our partner might be of immense help, especially if they are doing the same work with their family.

Arguing over the work of life, the chores of daily living, such as laundry and the kitchen, can be so grinding to the spirit and persistence. Who does the dishes, and how long do they sit before being done? Who leaves clothes in the washer to back up progress? Who needs the back of the kitchen counter wiped down, and who could care less? I could list a hundred things. The wild thing about this is all of life is teamwork, fair is fair, and too high of expectations disappoints many. The repetition of life's maintenance can be an albatross around your neck or a blessing with the potential to bond a relationship with teamwork, and a welcomed expenditure of energy.

Disclaimer: Not all this maintenance of life subject is meant for parents of kids under the age of leaving the house; that diversion of extreme energy and fatigue falls into its own special pocket of respected difficulty.

Over the years, I worked in intensive care units, some patients I worked with would say something that is worthy of sharing to firmly ground this subject, "I used to complain about the dishes, laundry, and how I had just got so tired of the routines of life. I would give anything to be doing the dishes right now or folding clothes. What I took for granted I would so welcome back now." The first time I heard this was from a mother of three. She was still in the ICU after recently suffering a spinal injury causing paraplegia, unable to move her legs. The ability to physically carry out our daily chores is not the only gift of our life's work to maintain self and home. It also keeps us alive and feeling alive. For thousands of years, we had to expend a huge amount of energy to survive; we could not turn a knob for water, rotate a dial for heat, push buttons to cook, or turn wheels and push on accelerators for easy distance mobility. It has only been a mere 130 years that less energy expenditure to stay alive has been pulling our energy down to self-damaging levels. We walk into gyms and go for jogs because our bodies, minds, and spirits were designed and engineered for the daily expenditure of massive amounts of energy. Many aspects of our life and society are paying for this change. When everything in our lives really only benefits from increasing the amount of energy used in a day. Keep going and doing every day for as long as you can. I wish for you equality with your partner in accomplishing the work of life. It is goodness in action, good for you, and builds respect and teamwork with our partner.

Argument, control, and the damage and pain driven by jealousy

Jealousy is one of the top ten reasons we argue since the beginning of time. It is the big one because of its potential to control and damage self and others, on top of being a natural emotion. We are not the only complex organisms that appear to experience jealousy; puppies, dogs, primates, and even young calves jealous of higher ground will play king of the hill. We want what others have. We also fear its reverse consequence, that others want what we have, so we guard what is ours or what we assign as "ours." Some may ask how can I assign jealousy to other animals' behaviors if we don't know their emotion around it? If the behavior is for survival reasons, it is not jealousy, yet these animals sometimes want what another animal has, even when they don't need it. Sound familiar?

Jealousy in human relationships, especially our intimate relationships, can do everything from causing us to dominate and control each other, to murder each other. Jealousy kills. It kills spirit, it kills trust, it kills attraction and desire, it kills relationships, and unfortunately it kills people too. I have seen far too many bullet and knife wounds, assaults, family violence assaults, and last breaths of life, in the name of jealousy.

I did not really understand jealousy until my high school girlfriend started seeing someone shortly before I left for college. I know I shared that with you, but I did not share what I learned about jealousy from it. I had called to ask her if I could come over and make her dinner. I remember so vividly that I was going to prepare shrimp scampi; but instead of saying yes with the usual excitement, she remained quiet. I asked her if everything was okay, and she remained quiet. I asked if someone was there and then she said "yes," in the quietest, softest tone ever in our two years of dating. That was my first moment of true deep jealousy in my life. Everything went very fuzzy, my chest tightened, and my stomach pitted. I think I remember accepting it in shock, partially getting it, and being accepting in the brief conversation that ended quickly. I foolishly drove by a few hours later and saw a strange car still in the driveway. My mistake, it only caused greater pain, and I never again felt a need to know such a detail, it didn't help. So why did I do it? I already knew she was seeing someone else; she had just been honest with me on the phone a few hours earlier.

Before that, I didn't really feel much jealousy in life and thankfully I still don't. As a kid on the bayou, I wished we could have afforded a boat, but I didn't feel that I was missing out. My friends had boats and that kept me on the water. I wasn't jealous of doctors because I wanted to be a nurse, I wanted the bedside contribution. I've never been jealous of people with money because yes, it supplies comforts, but the research shows it does not increase the feelings of joy or happiness. I have been jealous of dogs with great owners, that would be a great break from the stress of humanness. Jealousy is such a natural old emotion that the first humans probably experienced spearhead jealousy.

That night, jealousy wrenched my heart and being. But as I shared, I did the work to realize that I, and the inexperience of youth, were mostly to blame. I was going away to school, and she was staying in the area for school. I had also not discussed the closure of the relationship with her on a healthy level, I was sweeping it under the rug. How could I be mad at her? I had done this. Or how could I be mad at him? She was intelligent, funny, and a strong, capable person all around. I had a natural, appropriate emotion, but I worked within my rational mind, even though I did not know the concept at the time.

I had more academic and practical experiences with jealousy through sociology, my relationships with both my own feeling of it and jealousy being inflicted on me in a few relationships. Then it left the realm of academics and personal experiences and moved into the end results of our unchecked jealousy. At the age of twenty-one, jealousy took on a more dangerous, tragic, stark, in my face, and on my hand's, reality; I hung a stethoscope around my neck and started to see and touch the physical assaults and dead bodies of jealousy. Then friends and colleagues started to share the levels of jealousy and possessiveness in their relationships, and worse, displayed in divorce actions. This barrage of harsh human dominance and control over each other greatly influenced my feelings about jealousy. Even if not that physical level of abuse, jealousy still is a horribly powerful impetus for controlling abuse. Even its less damaging milder forms can still wreak havoc. I had a trusted friend in college whose partner would accuse them of cheating if they bought themselves a new pack of plain wide comfortable underwear.

The amount of domestic abuse that emergency departments see due to jealousy is shocking. It is not specific to gender or sexual preference in either those abusing or those being abused. Sexuality or gender do not negate the irrational damage of the uncontrolled emotion of jealousy, it destroys and damages across every combination of relationships you can conceive, including friendships and occupational. The conclusion

I have come to after over forty years of feeling and seeing the effects of unchecked jealousy is that we don't own each other. Married or not, regardless of religion, race, cultural views, or norms, we don't own each other. It is that feeling or belief of ownership that leads to the entitlement to control or kill another person in the name of jealousy. Would you not rather be loved because someone wants to love you?

The same wise person who said to me, "Would you rather argue to be right, or discuss and be loved?" also said to me, "When we are threatened by a relationship our partner has with someone else, it is not an opportunity to be mad at either of them for threatening our security or inflaming our insecurities. But rather, it is an opportunity to see where we can grow and do better within ourselves and for our partner and relationship. The only person we should be mad at is ourselves for either not accepting that we all need diversity in healthy friendships, or our partner having a relationship that we both may benefit from, or because we have failed to provide something they need and even most likely repetitively asked for in the past."

It was one of the hardest bites of reality I have had to sit with and process, because that person was correct. I also had an amazing professor in college teach me that no one person, while all parties still respect their sexual monogamy or agreement, can fulfill all the dynamics of an individual. This professor also taught me that we all need male and female friends to help keep us grounded, well-rounded in our views and understanding, and most likely opposite sex friendships will even help the other partner. Since we do not always accept the exact same input from our partner, but we will from a friend. Free will and choice are also incredibly important for the health and well-being of a relationship. I know for me, I want my partner to wake up with me every day because she wants to, not because I have not given her a choice.

Acting too harshly on the natural emotion of jealousy is control and abuse, so let's cut to the chase. If you are arguing and fighting, and jealousy is the subject or the driving force, and it is getting worse not better, seek help. I say this quickly because jealousy, like anger, is a powerful and destructive emotion that, if growing, requires professional help. Again, getting someone to seek help is often challenging, but continuing to argue and fight about jealousy without improvement is a red flag to seek help or move on. From low levels to high levels, jealousy is potentially a very dangerous emotion with deeper issues in control, fear, and insecurity. Please be careful, the emotion of jealousy too quickly can move into punitive or vindictive actions, or dangerous physical rage. First keep your own jealousy in check and balance, then protect yourself from what others are doing with their perfectly natural, but still potentially dangerous, emotion of jealousy.

Healthy argument?

Argument has its tiny place. Even in the courtroom, the term argument is used to describe each side's information they are presenting. Outright fighting, on the other hand, has almost no place, and has accomplished very little in most relationships. If an issue cannot be handled with discussion and occasional rationally controlled argument, escalating to fighting is most likely not going to help find resolution either. Fighting and war will create an endpoint, but that is not achieving a resolution to a problem. If you get your way because you are large, loud, persistent, or manipulative, then you did not find compromise or resolution with your partner, teammate, or opponent, you only dominated and controlled. Size or gender does not make a difference; any person who gets their way by wearing someone down until they give in is also controlling and potentially abusive behavior. Fighting is what we do to conquer or suppress in the name of power, fear, or actual or perceived need, and on some occasions, it is even appropriately used to suppress those wishing to take away freedom. Except for consenting play, conquering should have no place in an intimate relationship. Respectful discussion, with all its wonderful respectful criteria, will accomplish over fighting or emotional argument anytime. The win is a solution-based and agreed-upon result. A bonus, since it was mutually decided on, it also shows teamwork, respect, or love.

Just as we must evaluate the big picture when entering any new relationship in life, we also must look inside ourselves to ask what arguments are going on within ourselves. This inward look helps decrease the defense mechanism of projection. Projection is when we take our own internal issues, struggles, or behaviors, and assign them to someone else. Some of our politicians are unbelievably blatant about projection but, as it's a basic defense mechanism, we all use it, even if just a little. All relationships create a possibility for this behavior, but our intimate relationships can often increase our ability to project.

One of the most useful bits of information I ever heard was from a friend that is also a highly respected family counselor, "Arguing in a relationship is not the indicator of whether a relationship will last, but what is an indicator is whether the arguing styles are fair, respectful, and compatible."

Orgasms, infidelity, our drive for pleasure and escape, and our near insatiable natural need for more

The natural drive and struggle between what we have and what we want can be a healthy drive or become the cause of not only great unhappiness and cause us to miss a little more of life. I'm going to rapidly give you a handful of self-honesty questions. They are a little raw, but might help you find a little more of your core you. I intentionally use the word "you" rather than "self" to remind you that you are a whole unique being, and that you get to be you as you choose, not as you are being influenced. I often begin to feel uncomfortable inside when I allow too much of society to influence my wants and drives. Be gentle, society, advertising, and our peers and cultures are strong influences. See if these questions help you calibrate your you.

Ask yourself what drives you, what motivates your drives depending on the subject? How much of your being is driven by autonomous thought, and what percentage is driven by external influences such as media, society, religion, the people close to you, your upbringing, or past events or traumas? Or are you driven by the healthy motivator of your many potentials? Are your wants your own, or are they ones that have been fed to you by the media and the masses? Are you spending too much time, money, and energy pursuing the things society says you must have? Does that leave you time, energy, and money to obtain, discover, or create our deeper autonomous wants and wishes? Are you allowing the judgment of others, and the expectations of "normal," to keep you from pursuing your true you?

Our drive for more never leaves us, and never completely should. It is only how our free will and choice decides to feed these drives that we have some level of control. Even the world's most self-actualized people have a need for more. Their needs are just not for material things, pleasures, power, money, or self-gain. Some of the happiest and most peaceful people I know have shifted their drive away from those servings to feedings of knowledge, self-awareness, caring, and contribution. In so many ways, less is more, is accurate. Having and wanting less brings with it a grounding that is filled with practical application to bring us more ease. Purchasing, and the drive for more, can easily become an addiction. We have partially become a society that has replaced our deeper fulfillments with purchasing and eating. As opposed to fulfillment via experiencing being alive, awareness of the moment, communication, connections, and the joy of seeing others as our teammates in life. We have learned so much about purchasing over the past twenty years. Research has shown that shopping also stimulates the same rewards in the brain that opioids and other pleasures and addictions can activate. I do not share that same finding with each addiction to make you feel weak or bad, but rather to empower you to be gentle with yourself while you courageously look at your normal humanness.

The well-done movie *Moonstruck* does an adorable job of presenting a fantastic case of balancing family, love, relationships, our drive for love and partnership, and looks at the fears and pains of love and infidelity. Olympia Dukakis spends the movie trying to figure out the deeper reasons her husband is seeing another woman. I will not give you the exact conclusions she comes to, but the gist is the drive for more, and a well-known fear. The movie assigns this behavior to men, but the movie's fantastic reason for why men are unfaithful is one of the contributing factors to why we all want more, unrelated to gender or affairs.

I feel strange that I feel the need to specify that our human behaviors are not gender specific. Even though my two years of sociology, and a lifetime of human and societal observations, taught me the value of demographics; for the most part, stereotyping any demographic is often unnecessary and specifying gender related to topics of humanness is also not required. At times, genders may express themselves in separate ways, or may not, but the internal drives and needs are the same unrelated to gender. Men don't have affairs, humans have affairs.

Our drive for more is another aspect of ourselves that has the necessary balance of good and bad, or productive and non-productive. We get to choose how much of that drive for more we use to provide us with greater knowledge, experience, and peace, to name a few. One of the bad, non-productive effects of this drive is infidelity, and can greatly hinder our lives and all our relationships, especially, but not limited to, our intimate ones. With that said, it is important to know that infidelity does not always come from our drive for more, sometimes it is driven by basic human needs for touch, sexuality, connection, self-worth, reassurance, humor, and ease. Yes, humor and ease are also needs. Ease in a relationship indicates security and trust, also known as one of many forms of peace. Peace is a human need, for it is well known that living in strife has many layers of damaging effects on us physically, mentally, and emotionally.

Our need for more, including the need to have basic met for basic survival, is known as need fulfillment. These normal needs can potentially drive and help improve our current intimate relationship. By communicating and acting to meet those needs together, it helps build another great foundation layer for a better relationship. In one way or another, we humans work to have our individual and shared needs met, and we are going to actively seek to obtain both our need for more and our basic needs to be met, period. How respectfully and openly that is done is where our free will and choice again comes in. If in a relationship, teamwork comes into play to meet those needs in a sustaining healthy way.

There are also those who choose to turn away from intimate love relationships in various ways for various reasons, sometimes completely turning away. Some continue to have their physical needs met by others, but they leave love out of it. Many forms of relationships, sexuality, levels of fidelity and infidelity, and alternative expressions have existed from the beginning. The acceptance of alternative relationships, and the fact that "infidelity" is relationship specific and not an across-the-board standard for all relationships, is completely changing the dynamics, norms, and morays. Although a much lower percentage practice polyamory, about one-third of US couples do admit to beliefs that some level of polyamory is a part of their "ideal relationship." That number increases in the younger generations polled. "Swinging" also falls into the realm of polyamory.

Fifty years ago, the numbers showed alternative relationships had a low probability of lasting, but those numbers have changed. More people are coming to terms with an alternative relationship that has worked fine for them. Whether choosing monogamy or polyamory, sticking to your agreement(s) is a major key to the peace, longevity, respect, and the outcome of your individual and shared choices.

But you Cheated!

Sexual infidelity gets assigned the lead and pinnacle of all bad, or harsh destroyer of relationships, if one of the partners is having an outside of the agreement relationship. Also known as cheating or an affair. Yes, sexual infidelity is destructive, hard to forgive, and even outright dangerous, life threateningly dangerous. The number of innocent partners who died in the 1980s and 1990s due to their unfaithful partners transmitting AIDS to them is staggering. If not AIDS, the array of highly communicable diseases spread to innocent partners is high. But I have known just as many people driven to sexual infidelity because of abuse, neglect, or suppression by their partner as I do those who just outright committed infidelity due to other reasons, such as a sex addiction or general promiscuity. That means a percentage of the time a partner gets to use the old, "But you cheated" coup de grâce, it was the partner using it to not look at the mass destructive contribution they made to the action. "But you cheated," often sprung immediately after the person that broke the fidelity contract attempting to tell their partner the reasons for their behavior. Notice, I said reason, not excuse. If your partner is not respecting your contract of monogamy, it is not the easiest time to do it, but it is the bravest and most crucial time to look for your 40–60% of the relationship's issues.

By using that final blow of "but you cheated," we decrease our opportunities to grow, or we may just be bringing the same equally contributing behaviors into our next relationship. If the health of the relationship is your goal, then both sides admitting and working with their contribution is the greatest opportunity to save the relationship. If it is savable, and you desire to do your work also to save it. This is going to piss many people off, but it needs to be stated: your partner's sexual infidelity may not have occurred without first your infidelities of daily respect for the person they are. Find your percentage, it is rarely zero. Yes, the pain of sexual infidelity is deep and powerful, but it should never excuse the other partner for their part of a negative contribution to the destruction of the relationship. If the partner who is breaching the monogamy contract can also be self-honest, even more growth is possible. Relationships can make it past infidelity, but it requires *mutual* work. This is another valuable time to perhaps seek professional help.

Is monogamy even realistic for you? If not, be honest with your partner. Please show each other as much respect to get to the other side of infidelity, or maintaining fidelity, as you can. Infidelity is a huge problem, but our messy humanness is the real foundation of this issue.

If children are involved, everything about infidelity gets tougher. For their wellbeing, work to keep your words and actions as rational and non-emotionally driven as is humanly possible. This sensitive, difficult, complicated, and thorny issue is hard on the spirit of children to be in the middle of. Parents choosing to part is hard enough on our children; anger, vengeance, and blame only add to their already high stress levels.

Attempting to keep emotions in check at the end of a relationship is always a good idea across the board, but again, when children are involved, it requires the deepest most painful self-honesty we will ever know. Immediately followed by trying very hard to not act on the emotions that infidelity causes. However, no matter what the discoveries of self or partner reveal, stalking, vengeful and punitive actions, or physical, mental, or emotional abuse have no place. A partner's sexual infidelity does not give the other partner a green light granting unrestricted permission to retaliate. When children are involved, even greater restraint is required, or the children pay the consequences immediately and in the long run.

"Emotional affair" is a term that I have been hearing more and more. We may be setting ourselves up for damage, failure, and even further isolation in some relationships by using it. One reason is already understood: one person is not capable of fulfilling one person's emotional and intellectual needs. If the issue is the gender of the person supplying emotional support, that too might be unfair. The reason is that every time I have heard the term "emotional affair" complained of, I knew the person accusing their partner was also turning to more than their partner for friendship and emotional support. Emotional support could even just be one of humor alone. Please be careful using the term emotional affair, it has a lot of highly unnecessary jagged edges. Labeling your partner's friendship with someone you feel threatened by as an "emotional affair" could be real trouble. That friendship could be good at keeping your partner grounded and more aware of your feelings. We must always be careful with the black and white labels we want to throw at issues, because they often deserve softer shades of gray.

One more important balance to consider concerning being threatened by a partner's external friendship is a double-sided edge. You cannot be all things for your partner, but if your partner is turning from you too often for support and reassurance, there may be a basic compatibility issue that is no one's fault. The infatuation stage may be over, or in time you just organically grew apart, neither is one's fault. Getting angry at the outside person is rarely the answer, and none of those reasons deserve blame on your partner. I know that when I did the work concerning my high school girlfriend, I quickly discovered it was mostly my fault. Had I allowed my first emotional reaction to lead me, I would have been angry at them and not myself. It was certainly not the last mistake in a relationship that was my fault, admitting that helped everything get easier. I can see how the term emotional affair could have its place, but for the most part, turning to many for emotional support is not a horrible thing. It could mean potential goodness for your relationship.

The two pains we must all walk with

Returning to the emptiness and loneliness inside all of us, that never completely goes away, should be mentioned here again briefly as one of the deep core reasons we look for love and quality friendships. It is with such irony, in writing a book to help find less suffering, that I fill that very book with raw, painful, deep reminders of our suffering. Yet, accepting that we periodically get our emptiness and loneliness cavity in our chest sometimes partially filled, but never fill completely, is so important. Although some colleagues, friends, family, and partner(s) do fill a part of it, we should accept that it never completely leaves us. That is normal and okay. Yes, that simple of a word, "okay," does describe some remaining emptiness and loneliness we all may at times feel until our last breath. That accepted awareness, to stop trying to completely rid yourself of all emptiness and loneliness, can truly make life richer in every department. The unrealistic expectation that we can rid ourselves of all emptiness and loneliness is where much of our unhappiness comes from, in the form of addictions, infidelity, unnecessary anger at our partners that we still feel some, and a myriad of cyclical returning emotions that hinder the wider experiences of life. This includes our intimate love. Attempting to remove all emptiness and loneliness gets in the way of life and love.

This is not to negate the fact that emptiness and loneliness are huge problems around the world. There seems to be a surprising reverse correlation between the number of people on Earth and the amount of people experiencing higher levels of those two emotions.

This escalating number is one reason I encourage all of us to extend ourselves to others as we can, as well as safely and appropriately for each individual. It is important to delineate the difference between learning to walk with a little emptiness and loneliness in our relationships, and the huge issue of isolation leading to emptiness and loneliness chipping away at individuals, communities, all demographics, and society. The number of people who have so little human contact is too high, leading to depression, addiction, anxiety, and suicide. No matter what your relationship status is, stepping out of ourself to give back to others is beneficial in so many directions.

In any relationship, whether you are single, looking or not, involved, or in a family with kids, getting out and volunteering in society is good for all. Couples I know that volunteers together seem to have gained because of the experience together. Volunteering, it's good for relationships. It is also a great way to meet people if you are single. Extending ourself to others is not only good for alleviating other people's emptiness and loneliness, it helps the giver feel less of those also.

Four more solutions: finding greater peace in the exploration of love and lust

If you were looking for a technical manual to heighten orgasms, I am going to partially let you down. No physical technique advice is going to be given. But sadly, sarcastically thanks to the internet, not even young adolescents need that advice anymore. Kids can now give the birds and the bees talk to their parents. But the beautiful reminder we all will benefit from is that all the pornography online has absolutely nothing to do with love or making love, and it can damage our love relationships.

We are inundated with visual and auditory sex overload and addiction. The percentages of all genders and sexual orientations that have viewed pornography in the past thirty days, in developed non-internet-censored countries, is over 60%. Yet, for the sake of the health and well-being of our intimate relationships, we should strive to remember what is behind the physical techniques of pleasure and touch that makes everything so much more powerful. Pornography is only stimulation, but love and making love is shown, enhanced, and delivered through the act of stripping your being naked from the inside out, unrelated to taking your clothes off, and showing your love partner acceptance, tolerance, forgiveness, and understanding.

I may mention those four concepts often, but they are how we live and breathe respect, peace, calm, growth, and love. Those four in action are how we turn our partners on from the inside out. Those four words in action is how we build trust. We trust and respect the people who accept us for who we are, and who we are not, and who will tolerate and forgive our humanness. We further trust, respect, and are drawn to the people who show those four gifts first to themselves. Understanding is what ties respect, trust, love, and making love all together and grounds us. Through first understanding our imperfect self, it only follows that we would show understanding to others. Acceptance, tolerance, forgiveness, and understanding are not only the four keys to greater stronger love, but they are also four more keys to suffering less in life and work.

We also trust and appreciate the people who show us those gifts and yet want us also to do better. If they show us those four gifts first, we know they aren't criticizing or judging us, and without those four gifts first, someone's input is criticism. Our partners know us better than we think, accepting a fair amount of their healthy, caring input is mostly going to be beneficial to every aspect of our being. Wanting ourselves and another to do better is not the opposite of acceptance, tolerance, forgiveness, and understanding, but rather it is encouraging and caring. I know I want to be accepted for who I am, but always encouraged to do better, please help me.

Acceptance, tolerance, forgiveness, and understanding are how we make love to our partners all day long, even when we are apart. They are the foreplay that intensifies everything, including the strength, sweetness, and melting of every hug of returning to each other's presence, and everything between those hugs. Acceptance does not always mean you must agree with someone; it sometimes means you don't discard, judge, or even attempt to persuade them because you don't agree. We are having a huge problem with this in our society and relationships today, in every subject and every direction, with political and religious differences disrupting families and social progress to sad and dangerous levels. No one wants to be discarded or feel unaccepted in any aspect of their life's, especially in our intimate love and family relationships.

The difference between sex and making love is a beautiful, fun, and powerful delineation. Sex is an act of pleasure. Making love is the culmination of true, respectful connection. When we have sex, we have only had sex, and the joy and benefit of it often doesn't last long after the act is over, as opposed to the all-encompassing, intimate physical, mental, and emotional exchange of making love. Sex is only sex, but the lusciousness of making love is beautifully wide and broad. Making love is also about all the actions that occur between moments of intimate sensuous touch. The bonus is when you make love, you get to have sex too! Sex alone is still a big deal and can be an amazing release of tension and stress like no other and fills some of our touch and intimate needs. Sex happens, but making love infuses your days, life, and relationship.

Making love the next time starts the second you become alive again after an orgasm, or even just an intimate exchange that did not culminate. Post-play is just as much a thing as foreplay, it should be hard to know when one stops and the other begins. Sex is a moment, making love is a beautiful long walk. One of the French terms for an orgasm is "La Petite Mort," meaning little death. When we make love, the foreplay begins the moment we recover from our last little death. Yes, foreplay can be a way of life in a healthy, loving, respectful relationship displayed by far more than touch; foreplay is our words and actions, and often our omissions.

Foreplay is not only the twelve listed steps that the classic movie *Summer '42* so humorously taught us. Foreplay goes beyond touch; it is also how we treat our intimate partner when we are not sharing physical intimacy. Do we let them finish their sentences? Do we respect their opinion? Do we allow them to falter and express needs? Do we listen to them when they talk, as if we truly care to hear? It is humanly impossible to always be fantastic at these. But doesn't it feel so right when we receive this type of respect, to be encouraged to be ourselves, and feel validated? In this day and time, to receive that type of welcoming of who we are is like the entire being having an orgasm. Although I know of no foolproof or guaranteed way to always give or receive this level, it sure is a turn-on to be respected as a whole person when it does happen.

Focusing on those same four extensions of ourselves, acceptance, tolerance, forgiveness, and understanding, should first begin with ourselves. We should always care for ourselves before we attempt to care for another. There may periodically be a fine line between self-care and selfish behavior, but for the most part, those shades of gray rarely fall on the middle shades. The reason we should first accept, tolerate, understand, and forgive ourselves is because it is first how we show authentic self-love and self-respect, and then it makes showing them to others so much easier.

Peace, love, lust, and exploration; found in the title of this subsection are the rewards of doing this work inside ourselves and in our intimate relationships. Some of our deepest, richest, and longest-lasting joys and explorations are found in true love. I can even still feel love from and for friends and family who have died. That is how long true love can last.

If love is real, not fooling you, and respectfully carried out, then please let your spirit wallow in that sweet and beautiful mud known as love.

CHAPTER 9

EXPECTATIONS

"Why toxify a relationship when you are not going to
change their mind."
—A respected anonymous friend, in reference to arguing
with people over politics or religion.

The Apology

There are those who cannot or will not say they are sorry
There are those who say it when they should not
There are those who apologize to pacify or manipulate
There are those who are willing to apologize
Then there are those who do

Those who won't or can't
In some ways they are easier
At least we are not fooled
But it is still sad if they won't
If they can't, be gentle, we know not why

Those who sorry too often
Having their reasons too
Abuse in the past or present is not uncommon
Apologizing for what is not in their control
Sometimes it is just nervous sweetness

Then those we must be weary of
Those who apologize to pacify or manipulate
To only get past a rough with no intention of change
Without actions even if stated
It is void

Then there are the willing
Prevented and blocked
Perhaps anger or other
But on the road, they are
Now to just say and mean it

To say and mean I am sorry
Is a gift to self and all
It says I did that not you
I am sorry
Now let me show you

The first time I flew alone, I was maybe eight or nine. It was the early 1970s, and airlines still gave out little bags of peanuts for the in-flight snack. I finished my bag and was still hungry, so I got up and walked down the aisle and asked people if they were going to eat their peanuts. I remember the people on the plane were laughing about it, but I taxied back to my seat with about five bags of peanuts that I did not have when I started. When I got off the plane in Houston, my mom and a cousin by marriage picked me up. During the drive, I offered them both a bag of peanuts. After answering their question of how I obtained them, my mother was "mortified," as she loved to say, and my cousin was cracking up. He kept saying I was, "assertive" and "ask and you shall receive." Then he told me if I wanted more peanuts, all I had to do was ask the flight attendant and they would have given me more. I am grateful I was ignorant to that simple fact, or some good laughs would have been missed. My family teased me about it for the next thirty years or so. It even lightened the day for the people laughing on the plane as I worked the aisle for my alms.

A few years later, one of my sisters, I don't remember which one, was adding to the pounds of information they and my mother piled on me about dating and treating women with equality and respect in relationships. She referenced the peanut-begging and said, "Asking women out is like working the aisle on the plane for those peanuts, you're going to get some yeses, but you must be polite and respectful about the many times I will be told no between the more rare yes." She said, "If you have a realistic expectation of the rejections, the no won't hurt so bad, and it will give you the courage to ask." Although I was too young and not able to label it, the gift she gave me was the grounding and highly applicable concept of realistic expectations and polite energy-saving responses to unmet expectations. That was a huge gift.

Years later, in a sociology course on family and relationships, I was handed this subject again with a wider scope of explanation. The professor said, "Although it is unrealistic because we all have expectations of each other, and though some are necessary, such as following laws or doing your job well, if you don't want to be disappointed by people then don't set unrealistically high expectations." She then handed us the balance of the concept of realistic and unrealistic expectations, with the example of one of our greatest unrealistic expectations—expecting perfection of ourselves and others.

To this day, expectations continue to be a detrimental issue to our peace and progress, but it has expanded from a personal issue to a larger social issue. We, as both individuals and as a society, have big and increasing expectations. Because a percentage of these expectations are unrealistic, failure is sure to follow. Periodically, the expectation alone is the actual cause of the failure.

The "it can't happen to me" syndrome

Through my thirty-five years in front-line public service, I've developed a belief that we, myself included, often live with the belief that "it can't happen to me." This syndrome, an expectation related to denial, is not meant to increase anxiety. If anxiety is fear of the unknown, then looking at what is known, and applying that information to ourselves has the ability to decrease the chances of bad things happening to us, which should help decrease some fear and anxiety. I think the "it can't happen to me" syndrome really gains strength in our teen years and then never really goes away. Looking back at my life, I can see my first confirmation of this detrimental syndrome was my truly naive belief that I could not possibly cause a car crash. Two weeks after I started driving, I hit two cars stopped at a red light, directly in front of me.

I was driving under the expectation that I could not cause an accident and, boom, I caused an accident. It was while standing outside the car talking to Sergeant Young of the Slidell Police Department, that I realized prophylaxis is a way of life. Had I not had the "it can't happen to me" syndrome, I would have been more preventative, and not have been driving so cavalier. Even the fact that in the 1980s the healthcare field stopped using the term "motor vehicle accident" and started using the term "motor vehicle crash" validates this. Because "accidents" are not preventable, but all car crashes at some point before the moment of impact are preventable.

The "it can't happen to me" syndrome starts in our teens with driving and other grossly reckless actions. Younger than that, I think it is a more general naivety of cause and effect, not an outright "it can't happen to me" mentality. I don't know how I lived through my teen years. We used to jump off an abandoned conveyor belt into the bayou from so high up, that we had to wear tennis shoes, or the soles of our feet would hurt from hitting the water with such speed. We would plunge so deep our shoes and calves would sink into, and be covered with the disgusting, slimy, stinky, and outright nasty sludge on the bottom. We all knew of someone who had died or been paralyzed from diving into the extremely murky waters of the bayou and breaking their necks on a partially submerged object. But hey, it can't happen to me. Or the teen pregnancies that occur thinking of any number of "it can't happen to us" scenarios. But it doesn't go away with age. The number of adults who still drive under the influence of intoxicants, thinking it can't happen to them, is staggering. Hospitals are filled with people who believed the injury or illness could never happen to them. We all have at least a little of this syndrome, and a little will never go away, because no one can pay attention to everything all the time. That is impossible, so we must accept a percentage of the syndrome. I knew a trauma surgeon that would wear a full-face helmet any time he got in a car; I get it, very smart, but I can't live that level of prophylactic actions. But if we all spent a little energy to decrease this syndrome, even a little, then we and the people around us would indeed suffer less.

During my years in law enforcement, I was always surprised to hear so many people being so honest with me after causing a car crash, "I only looked at my phone for a second. It all happened so fast." It is not just with driving, either. We know if we go too fast in life in general, we make more mistakes, but we keep going fast in life too. If we know this, what stops us from slowing down?

Having unrealistic expectations for ourselves is not only a setup for the "it can't happen to me" syndrome, but they are also the setup for its twin syndrome, the "I can't possibly be a part of the problem" syndrome.

As soon as we all acknowledge that we are all a little part of the problem the sooner we can individually and collectively start to decrease our negative contributions and increase our positive ones. I communicate with other humans, and I know I am incapable of communication with perfection; thus, I am a part of communication breakdowns with other people. I drive a car, so I am a part of the carbon issues. I create material trash, so I am adding further to the ecological footprint of us humans. I want love and intimacy, which is never perfect, so I add some level of issue to my relationships just by being an imperfect being with wants and needs.

It is through acknowledging those two highly simplified syndromes, which we are all a part of cause and effect, negatively as well as positively, that we can find greater peace. By being even a little more aware, then proactive, in responsibility and prevention, we find greater peace through less conflict or disruptions in life. Professionalism in action is one tool used to accomplish this. Accomplishing this is also professionalism. The personal and outward rewards and benefits of accepting our part of cause and effect are immeasurable, educational, preventative, and rewarding. Yes, it can feel hard at first. You may perceive some self-compromising or any myriad of feelings around admitting higher levels of culpability. It will easily become second nature and eventually require minimal effort. Self-honesty is not a compromise, it is a gift to the self that can help make everyday easier.

An example is the gentleman who ran naked out of the emergency department. By me reviewing that preventable crisis, meaning learning where we could have done a better job of preventing a potentially dangerous event, fewer crisis situations occurred. That post-crisis review is something I continued to do during thirty-six more years of frontline work. The teams I worked with at first did not always understand the need for a post-crisis event review. But within no time at all, they found it non-threatening, nonjudgmental, and they too saw crisis as often preventable. The team saw that their action, or inaction, at some point escalated, deescalated, or altogether prevented crisis, and fewer crisis

events occurred. It takes a lot less time, energy, and decreases danger
and liability exposure to validate what you can for someone who is
escalating; bring them a warm blanket, a glass of ginger ale to get their
likely low blood sugar level up, and get some X-rays ordered, than it is
to have to physically restrain someone once they have become irrational
and dangerous to those around them. This can be applied in all fields
that provide any level of customer service. Even if their escalation
started with them insulting and cussing, it is still beneficial for all to
check our ego, respond from rational thought and professionalism, and
extend yourself to get them to the other side of the crisis. I only know of
one nurse in twenty-one years who just could not get this bigger picture
and be able to self-review. In this day and time, having the expectations
of "it can't happen to me" or "I can't be a part of the problem" is another
setup for more trouble than will already be randomly thrown our way.

Trusting people

"Most people don't want to have conversations; they only want you
to agree with them. If this were not true, we could all finish more
sentences without interruptions."

—The same friend that knows not to
argue with people over politics or religion.

Attempting to peddle puppies and Easter baskets in a conversation
about trusting humans would be insulting to you and lying to myself. A
few years back I had a horrible thing happen to me related to trust. I see
how someone reading my work could think I am out of touch, asking
yourself questions like, "Does this man live on the same earth as I do, he
seems out of touch with how bad and cunning this world is?" Or "Does

he really think if I am nicer to a few people every day the world will turn into Disney?"

Many unjust things have happened to all of us in our lives, and I know life is populated with a small percentage of scary humans. I was once asked in an oral law enforcement interview, "As a nurse, you have just spent twenty-one years caring for the needs of people and attempting to help them stay alive, will you be able to use lethal force if needed?" It was the moment I realized I was being seen with a white nursing cap on my head. I validated that indeed I'd just spent twenty-one years caring for people, but to please never forget that eighteen of those twenty-one years were in high-volume teaching hospital emergency departments, and that I have seen too many holes in bodies, both the living and the dead, from stabbings and gunshot wounds, to ever be naive to the magnitude that people will kill each other in an irrational second, and that if I hesitate to use lethal force for even a second if needed, that I or another innocent person may end up dead. I then shared that I also believe those who are being granted society's trust to become an officer should also realize the public is expecting those trusted will also take on the added danger of using an extra second, *if that extra second is available*, to make damn sure that deadly force is appropriate at that split second.

Hesitation kills, but the emotion of fear can also unnecessarily kill. There is a harsh saying in law enforcement, "I would rather be judged by twelve than carried by six." I have a hard time agreeing with it 100%, and I feel it is a *part* of the mentality that has law enforcement in such trouble today. But the painful balance is that too many officers have died because people want to kill them in one-tenth of a second, and the officer hesitated for two-tenths of a second, a dangerously and intractable two-tenths of a second longer than they should have. Law enforcement is too often a no-win situation, but they are rightfully trained to stay alive, which is a split-second instinct in *all* of us, trained or not. There are wrongful shootings, but what is also unfair is a sector of society labeling all shootings wrong. People will hurt and kill each other. I share this to remind you of my lack of naivete, the reality of balance, and more encouragement to not give up. It confirms that life is a balance of taking safe care of yourself first, and then taking care of others. Both are achievable.

Yes, I sometimes overly trust people then get disappointed. I recently trusted a group of people, and they used what I trusted them with to judge and discard me. I shared with them my fears, faults, and hopes of a goal I was working to accomplish. I trusted them to brainstorm with me and that caused a breakdown in communication. I accepted my responsibility for my part in the mutual breakdown in communication. I admit, it was all somewhat painful to my spirit. Yet, I refuse to give up on people; I refuse to become distrusting of all, past the normal self-protection we should all have. I refuse to stop caring and trying. I would be surprised if this group ever contacted me again, but if they did, I would ask them, "How may I help?" There are dangerous people and groups in this world, but this group is only self-serving and intolerant of what does not line up with their views and beliefs.

I refuse to give in and stop trusting the deeper goodness of my fellow humans because I know so many amazing, caring, contributing people. I also know they too periodically have bad moments, and they don't deserve to be judged by those moments. I also don't give up because I would be giving up on all the others trying to do more of the right and positive, and they deserve continued efforts to believe in them. We are a team of human beings who also refuse to give up on people and will not completely discard the people and groups that do not line up with our views either. I don't want to give up on believing and trying, it has and delivers too many rewards.

Judging unfairly

"We judge ourselves by our intentions and others by their
behaviors."
—Stephen Covey

One of the starkest tidbits of hard truths I have heard in the past
few years about us humans is the above quote. The complete unfairness
of that quote's truth humbled me for several days while I worked with it.
I became embarrassed of a life where I am guilty of this unfairness that
I had shown to others. Our judgment, or assessment, of self and others
needs to be a mix of both intention and actual action. Considering both
certainly affected the shades of gray. Yet, since most are guilty of this
unfairness, assessing both intention and action becomes a much more
mutually realistic and fair approach. Expecting to be only judged, and
then forgiven, based on, "But I meant . . .", yet I judge others on what
they did or did not do or say? That is a blatant double standard that
requires and deserves serious redirection. This truth really affected me
in magnitude and my guilty history of what I hope is only an average
amount of this blatant unfair double standard.

When I heard this assessment of how unfairly we skew our angles
of judgment towards ourselves, I thought of too many arguments where
I fell right into this human behavior, both in actions, and just my poor
command of the English language, especially during more sensitive
exchanges, also known as argument. "But I meant . . ." or "My intention
was . . ." covers the attempted softening of judgment towards the self.
But then I sum up my own double standard by saying to the other
person, "But that is not what you said or did." This reality in my face
was life-changing for me, and I really was kind of quiet for several days.

The duality between thinking we don't need and affect each other and that we are not responsible for each other's feelings and well-being contrasts with how sensitive we are to other people's words and actions. If others are not responsible for our feelings, then why are we becoming more affected by the words and actions of others? Our levels of resistance, personal strength, and immunity to the behavior of others, and our abilities to not allow it to affect us also fluctuate. Some days we are far better at it than others.

Since we know we can upset each other, and that the closer someone is to us, such as our intimate partner, the more sensitive we can be to their words and actions. What do we do with this knowledge? We cannot be responsible for the whole world's happiness, or even for the total happiness of one other person. That would leave no time to breathe and nourish the self we should always take care of first. We cannot be living and breathing human goodness and perfection all the time, and constant vigilance would exhaust anyone, even if it was possible. Helpful to caring for ourselves in a healthy and balanced way, is to pay attention to the differences between our appropriate self-care and even our accidental selfish behaviors. We all drop into selfish behavior at times, that's normal, but staying away from the dangerous or abusive higher levels is caring in action. I know this sounds strange, but being flexible in a healthy relationship is also self-care. As much as care of others is good and important in many directions, care of the self must come first. That is not selfish behavior, that is healthy self-care.

Yes, please, take good care of you

We absolutely must take care of ourselves first. It is the common sense of survival, and we should never feel guilty for self-care. Quite the opposite, we should strive for it with pride. The pursuit of having our physiological, emotional, and psychological needs met is an inalienable right.

Self-care is appropriate and sustainable with the rewards of a healthy life, growth, and exploration. However, selfishness is our ego again lying to us and preventing the true health of our entire being. When our healthy self-care pushes past appropriate self-need and into selfishness it prevents us from experiencing the most complete and amazing life we can experience. Selfishness may get an immediate need met, or even a life of riches, but selfishness is a thief in and of itself; and the self is its first and greatest victim. Self-care accomplishes having our needs met without the thievery.

Please don't get discouraged thinking the selfish in the world outweighs the good. It is partially an illusion that the bad is winning because it only takes one bad to make the world seem all bad. It is just that selfish actions unfortunately dominate good actions in our minds. No one has trouble going to sleep because they can't stop thinking about the person that politely and professionally helped them find a product in the grocery store, but we sure remember a lack of customer service that unfolded towards us.

We all accidentally or intentionally periodically carry out actions that fall into some lower level of selfish behavior, and hopefully even less into higher levels. I have accidentally cut people off. I have also carried out selfish actions, and I have made choices in personal relationships that I can look back on and easily now label selfish. I have at times, protected myself with defensive or aggressive communication to a perceived or actual threat. Sometimes the line can get a little blurry between selfish behavior and self-care, but for the most part, the gray area is not too wide. Using the exercise of stepping out of yourself to look at your action or inaction from another person's point of view will often help decrease that gray area even further. It is painful work for me when I look at some of my past personal and occupational relationships. I also know love can turn us completely upside down, and all perspective is skewed when hanging by our ankles from the heartstrings of love. I am sorry for my selfish actions, but I am not sorry for those that were appropriately self-protective. Those fall into the category of self-care.

Protecting ourselves, getting our needs met, dealing with unhealthy team members or partners, or just pursuing greater compatibility and peace in relationships, of course, requires energy. The large amount of our energy that it takes from us to accomplish selfishness is one of the reasons selfish actions rob us inside first. The initial rationalization alone, to justify selfish behaviors, takes a huge amount of energy. Then the maintenance of continuing to justify selfish actions after they have been carried out is an even larger waste of our energy, because it literally can last a lifetime. But sometimes, if selfishness is on a really high level, we have to outright lie to ourselves to live with our behaviors. These higher-level lies may be subconscious, or we may be knowingly living the lie to accomplish attempting to be okay with something we did or did not do that our core knows was outright wrong. Work to accept and forgive yourself. Even if total forgiveness for yourself is not possible, still try, there are many positive actions that can help lighten our internal burdens.

Selfishness is wasted energy and wasted exploration of the self. This is especially true considering the rewards of healthy self-care are so great.

I owe a man an apology who I don't owe an apology

Expecting others to think as you do, or assuming you always communicate with perfection, are two more expectations that increase the chances of more frequent life bumps. Because no two minds have the same layout, and no two people will ever have the exact same perspective, even if they are standing next to each other, total and constant alignment of anything between two or more humans, past agreeing on a time to eat lunch, is near impossible.

When the right picture is not received, it is not always one of intentional deception or even a poorly sent communication, it is often the innocent perspectives of the human mind. A fast example is two people standing next to each other looking at a three-dimensional box, if one is at just the right angle, that person will see a two-dimensional square, even though the person inches away sees the factual three-dimensional box. Individual perspective is a constant that should be celebrated. After all, you could be the one standing at the point you only see the square, not the box, so thank goodness there is another perspective.

The basic two angles of communication in a conversation are well known yet taken for granted. When communication is taking place, a message of some sort is either being sent or received. We have a high percentage of accuracy between sender and receiver, just look at the sheer number of sentences we get right, and people receive correctly. Those uneventful sentences are not the issue. However, sometimes the message received is not the same as the message sent or intended. This can happen for many reasons—everything from a poor message sent, to a listener not paying attention, to a language or accent issue, or maybe even a noise level in a restaurant. The basic statements most of us have heard are "The message received is more important than the message sent," and "The message received is the only one that counts." It is the job of all parties to do their part to help communication be as clear as it can be. The sender needs to expend energy to send a clear message and the receiver needs to expend energy to receive the message sent. Even then, sometimes it just does not fall into place. I had a painful confusing failure in communication happen to me that sums it all up. It also reminds us not all communication is verbal.

I live in Austin, Texas, a beautiful, fast-growing, diverse city that has a huge cycling community. There are too many bikes painted white around the city chained to a bridge or a road sign. These bikes are called "Ghost Bikes." Each one is a memorial that represents where a biker was killed, it is also a stark reminder to drivers to pay attention. They are memorials to the biker that was killed, and they are also a stark symbolic reminder to us drivers along the lines of, "Please don't kill us bikers for wanting to exercise." The bikers are rightfully angry; there are a lot of Ghost Bikes around this city, each one killed unnecessarily and preventable.

I was once on a walk in a quiet, unrushed neighborhood, and I took my phone from my back pocket just to see what time it was. I had to pay attention to the time for a scheduled appointment. In the five seconds required for that to occur, a biker rode by and started yelling at me because so many of those biker deaths occurred due to drivers looking at their phones. But I was walking in a sleepy neighborhood, not driving, and only glancing at the time. Still, I partially respected his passionate release, even if it really was undeserved aggression for the total picture. He had slowed and made big circles, not leaving my presence. Being the person I am, I put my phone away and thanked him for the reminder, but he wasn't done, and I discovered where the anger came from. Before he rode off, he cussed again, but I could feel it was not at me, and said, "G. D. . . . He didn't have to die." Compassion for his pain and forgiveness for his release of that pain onto me. I did not mind being his pop-off valve for some of his justified anger and grief. His rightful emotions only allowed him to see someone looking at their phone, not paying attention. Respected, trouble avoided, my ego was not in control, my rational thought was. He is not the person I wish I could apologize to.

Much more recently, I had another biker present me with an interesting challenge. I arrived at a red light, in a left turn lane, with one bicyclist in front of me. He immediately shot out his left arm to inform me he was making a left turn. He then turned his head to his left to make sure I was acknowledging his intention. I gave him both thumbs up really big on top of the steering wheel and nodded my head with exaggeration to let him know I have him covered! I am hoping I gave him a gift, and he is hopefully thinking, "This is one left turn I do not have to fear, this guy sees me, thumbs-ups me, and nods his head big and clear: great, there are still people out there acknowledging and protecting us bikers."

The light has not changed twenty seconds later, and I think he is looking to his left again, so I don't forget. This time I only nod my head big so he can clearly see I still understand. The light changed and we both began our left turn. I'm giving him plenty of room. He moves to the right-side bike lane, and I stay to the left side of two lanes, to stay even further away from him. As I get next to him, I wave because I see he is looking at me. I throw him a big smile and wave. But he is furious with me, giving me the long finger and yelling obscenities, with a face filled with dangerous anger, I can hear FUs through a rolled-up window. I slow my waving and am perplexed by his clear and solid "I could kill you" aggression. Although a few would turn that into a back and forth and maybe worse, I don't see a need to take it further even though I am completely perplexed and drive away. By two blocks later I can't take it anymore. I am not mad but curious; I thought I was a protective bike angel that had just fed my codependency a three-course meal. I'm going to pull over, keep it in gear, roll my window down and very nicely tell him I am sorry I upset him, and I just want to know what I did wrong. Now I am second guessing myself. Could I be looking at the two-dimensional square when it is a three-dimensional box? How can I do better is my intention for wanting to make peace with this fellow human that I clearly, highly, and dangerously upset.

He must have turned off at one of the two streets I passed before having the idea to attempt a friendly hello, and hopefully learn and connect. He never appeared, and I was racking my brain, struggling to review what I did that was either wrong or misinterpreted. It takes me a few weeks to come to my best conclusion; it must have been a different message received than I knew I sent. I think from his point of view, looking around his left shoulder, is where the innocent breakdown in the message sent occurred. There would have been an hour or two before the sun set, getting lower behind my car from his angle, but still maybe in his eyes. So rather than him seeing the message I was sending, two thumbs to represent a few positive things, in his glance, window tilt, lighting angle, and the sun behind me, he saw me giving him the long finger, times two! Not to mention he sees me nodding my "yes" big and exaggerated. What he must have thought? I feel horrible someone received such a hideous message when I was sending such a reassuring one. Sadly, it is also telling of the message some people are expecting to receive in our trying times.

By placing myself into his thought process, I can see how, if the angle is just right, it could have looked like my guess. I can't do anything about it now, and although he thinks I am a horrible person, I did not think the thumbs up could be interpreted another way. Still, to this man I would apologize anyway if I could. In this case, both my intentions and my actions were giving and highly appropriate, but none of that mattered to what he received from his position. He was very mad at me. So, I feel I owed an apology to someone I did not need to apologize to, and I am good with that. I am sorry for the horrible message he received was not the positive message I sent.

This reminded me that even when I think I am sending a good clear safe message, it could be misinterpreted by the receiver for a multitude of reasons. No matter the size of the miscommunication, or the intensity of the relationship, having the expectation that you always communicate perfectly, or that what you send well will be received that way, is unrealistic. Although most miscommunications can easily be resolved if caught, how many will not be caught until the miscommunication causes an issue? The frequency of our miscommunication, and the imperfections of all parties, are the main reason to always strive for greater sending and receiving skills, as well as to be patient and understanding when breakdowns occur. Decreasing the frequency in bumps on both the sender's and receiver's side, being gentle during correction, and walking on when miscommunication does occur, will bring greater ease to your relationships. Arguments over miscommunication are like arguing over sunset happening, they are going to occur.

Our biggest, deepest, and necessary expectations

We can stay alive by only meeting basic needs, prison proves that, but to feel alive, we need to aim a little higher.

Maslow's Hierarchy of Needs was developed by Abraham Maslow in 1943 and introduced in an article in *Psychological Review* titled, "The Theory of Human Motivation." In the years since it was introduced, there have been those who disagree with Maslow's order or the importance of some levels. However, far more agree with the model and it is now more accepted as a truth of our needs more than theory. Maslow's Hierarchy is not just question number forty-seven on an introductory sociology final exam, it is a blueprint for learning the healthy needs, drives, and normal expectations of individuals and, thus, societies' needs and health also.

He used a pyramid to explain this hierarchy of needs, but he also created a pyramid for our hierarchy of motivations. The pyramid of needs has five levels, the pyramid of motivations has three more levels.

Just as with the five levels of the needs pyramid, these drives and needs motivate us to not only stay alive, but to feel alive.

Part of feeling alive means having some higher questions and needs met that help close the gaps created by our big questions of "What is the meaning of my life, why am I here, why is life hard, and do I have a purpose?" The lower levels of both pyramids are the needs and motivations that keep us alive: food and shelter. Yet, this does not mean everything above the first few levels is only icing on the cake. It is a lack of pursuing these higher needs, or futilely pursuing them from the outside of ourselves, that is contributing to our increasing feelings of hopelessness and helplessness. The pursuit of these higher-level needs and motivations greatly assists the longevity, peace, and continuation of both individuals and society, also known as thriving.

Our concepts of successful thriving should not be larger cities, meals to our doors, cars, gadgets, garments, or interstates and jets that move us to our next thing faster. Healthy, sustainable, and truly nourishing thriving should first be how we treat ourselves, then how we treat others, and unselfish planning for our future generations. More and easier is only filling us with empty calories, which only force us to pursue more and more in a frantic futility that only supplies us less and less. Our riches are not in more financial wealth or material possessions, but in what we do within ourselves and how we treat and help others. I have friends who are so busy keeping busy that it is hard to watch, some have money, and some do not, but I am saddened to say they seem to be the most unsettled and unfulfilled friends I have. External busyness may keep the inner self distracted, but it does nothing to truly nourish our inner spirit's healthy growth or our inner peace. This has nothing to do with the subject of keeping busy, active, and exercising to maintain healthy minds, bodies, and spirits. I am talking about the busy that is intended to keep us from our thoughts and feelings. The busy that is used to keep us from taking a few minutes to just sit with ourselves.

These levels are indeed a hierarchy that somewhat need be filled from the bottom up, but that is not set in stone. Firming up these needs from the bottom up helps build a more solid, longer-lasting base. By blending the needs and motivation pyramids and by working on all the levels at the same time we are reminded how interconnected needs, motivation, and expectations are. Maslow's Hierarchy of Needs from the bottom up are physiological, safety, love/belonging, esteem, and then self-actualization. His Hierarchy of Motivation levels, also from the base up, are physiological, safety, love/belonging, esteem, cognitive, aesthetic needs, self-actualization, and transcendence at the top. Let us combine them into one, since need and motivation intermingle between the two pyramids anyway.

The first two levels and base of the pyramids are your physiological needs, the needs that either you meet, or you die: air, food, water, sleep, health, body temperature, and shelter. The next level up is our need for safety. In this day and time, safety can be broad, but includes safety from identity theft, violence, natural disasters, extreme weather, war, family violence, neglect, abuse, financial insecurity, and anything that can damage or threaten your safety or general well-being. Moving higher up the pyramid, we enter the levels that are required for longevity, health, and well-being of the emotional and psychological health of the person, community, and even our tomorrows. The first of these levels, but the third level up the pyramid, is love and social bonding needs: sex for both intimacy and procreation of the species, intimate relationships, and community groups, making contact and forming healthy supportive relationships with those around us, true friendships, contributing to your community, and making fulfilling human connections. All these bonding actions are not only required for procreation and to accomplish the teamwork to make the big picture of life happen, but are equally healthy and important for the individual and community to stave off loneliness, isolation, and depression. We do need each other, and we are definitely stronger and more capable of accomplishing when woven together in united teamwork.

The multidirectional importance of these higher needs is vital to a meaningful life and future, but too often are under-prioritized. We are rapidly losing our pursuit and even feeling the importance of these vital higher-level needs and bonds to our rushed, busy, often isolated, and perceived independent lifestyles. I use the term "perceived," referring to the changes that have occurred in the past 130 years, and especially the last thirty years that have created a detrimental attitude that is rapidly chipping away at the fact that we need each other. The good news is this trend is reversible. If negative beliefs and actions, both small and large, chipped away at our understanding of life's teamwork to stay alive and thrive, then embracing the belief and accomplishing those positive actions can rebuild our healthy bonds. This unraveling of individuals, communities, and society is too easily confirmed by our skyrocketing numbers of addiction, depression, anxiety, attempted and accomplished suicides, since we turned into the 2000s years. The increasing strife and conflict in our communities, across nations, and around the world, are the larger signs we need to strengthen our foundation and our belief in first ourselves and then each other. These higher-level needs we all have are the core of our spirit and our community; having those needs met increases strength and stability. It does not stop there; the strength and stability of the individuals affects the strength and stability of the communities. That is only the first step; the strength of communities increases the strength of the region. Regions make up countries, and the strength and stability of countries contributes to world peace.

Our part as individuals is to keep ourselves, each other, and our communities and businesses healthy and strong. Highly simplified, the role of all leaders, administrations, and officials is to protect and nurture from the people up. It is how both directions keep stability and longevity underfoot. Which correlates to peace, profit, and productivity. Productivity also means functional, balanced, cohesive, and stable human living systems such as infrastructure maintenance, healthy commerce, bonded communities, multicultural peace, balanced economics, uncorrupt governments, and all held together by solution-based collaboration on every level, from local to international.

It is just these types of individual and group interrelated dynamics that inspire me to encourage you so deeply to never forget you and your actions do count and do help or hinder. Maslow's lower levels and our vital organs may literally keep us alive, but it is the benefits of the awareness and achievement of the higher levels that keep us feeling alive. Working to meet these needs also feeds tomorrow's goodness for ourselves and our children's children. Each one of us has the power and ability to help turn it around. Although "I don't need anyone" and "I am only responsible for myself" have become our new chants of self-protection, we do need each other.

Moving up the combined pyramids comes the level of cognitive needs, meaning to stimulate and exercise the mind; the ability to learn, recall information, and solve problems helps us stay alive and heightens our everything with endless benefits. It also reminds us that our brains welcome and thrive on mental exercise, now of immeasurable importance with our increasing rates of dementia. Stimulating the mind meets and strengthens an endless array of needs and supplies the tools to accomplish life and stave off general boredom.

Another level up is our aesthetic needs, basically the need to ground ourselves with immersion into nature. It is through this connection that we become a part of a bigger picture, that our world, life, and spirit connect with and become a part of something much greater than ourselves. When was the last time you walked on the earth barefooted, laid on the grass and drank in the sky, or just sat and watched birds? The research shows that after only fifteen to twenty minutes of spending time in nature, our blood pressure drops, and that is only the tip of the iceberg of the benefits of leaving the concrete. I remember in my childhood, maybe ten-ish, I enjoyed lying on my back on our dock, with my head completely upside down hanging over the edge, just above the water, wondering why the water in the bayou did not fall down into the sky. I need to go seek out that upside down connection soon. In this day and time of devices, it is more important than ever to get our children spending time in nature.

The next level on Maslow's Hierarchy of Motivation and the top level on his Hierarchy of Needs is the wide and self-expanding need and journey into self-actualization. Self-actualization is a push and drive to be the most complete person you can be, to strive for and attempt to obtain your full potential, which includes high levels of peace, contentment, self-acceptance, and self-love. Self-actualization spreads much wider and further than a textbook definition can ever surmise, it even includes contentment with what one will not see, do, or accomplish, it is knowing and wallowing in just being. That has become a difficult task in this day and time. Self-actualization also means growth and peace inside yourself and with the world around you. It is a little like happiness, fleeting and never completely secure, yet thankfully more and more obtainable with the application of more goodness and self-awareness. Self-actualization does not require anything external; it can be maintained in prison or following a diagnosis of terminal cancer. However, in contrast to that statement, the rougher side of balances, meaning the tragedies in life, can set back an obtained level of self-actualization in seconds, such as becoming homeless could affect one's level of self-actualization. But the richer the level of self-actualization obtained, the harder it is to disrupt. Accepting that nothing in life is permanent or guaranteed alone is important to building a solid foundation for self-actualization. It is the cows' peace, calmness, chewing of cud, observing a potential threat while still chewing, then going back to pulling grass once they see no threat, that I am referring to when I jokingly say cows are self-actualized and possess the answer to all world problems. I know they are more self-actualized than I am, because I swallow my food before I'm through chewing it.

Self-actualization is not a state of total peace or nirvana. It is being able to stay close to or return to those easy places inside yourself, despite our daily obstacles, or even high-level tragedies. It is a peace and serenity inside oneself, even when the manure lands on you, that allows us to experience less turbulence inside ourselves, no matter the magnitude of the force pushing on our being or spirit.

The top and last level of Maslow's Motivation pyramid is known as Transcendence Motivation. These are your spiritual needs and your spirituality. This level gets to be highly individualized and can weave throughout all the other levels. Yet, the significance of this level is that it reinforces the importance of maintaining your individualized spirituality in both strength and action, no matter your level of religious affiliation or rejection. Holding onto your spirituality provides you a wider base and guidance that is not external and with you every moment. Your spirituality is your own constant, that only you can challenge or shift. Your spirituality is yours.

The higher levels of need and motivation are not so easy to meet, or even care about, if someone is hungry, homeless, or a victim of domestic violence, to name a few. Someone who has no food and is about to be evicted into the cold of winter may not really care to contemplate their place in the universe. But I have also witnessed people that are handed life's greatest tragedies and pains, from major burns to an eviction onto the street, that calmly accept their fate and meet it with a level of self-actualized and acceptance that lets me know peace and serenity are obtainable, unrelated to the forces on our lives.

Obtainable expectations achieve greater results

I respect not wanting to experience pain, but the balance of good and bad, tears and laughter, and yes, pleasure and pain is a constant that can never be eliminated. Our innate drive to want more good and only less bad is a realistic expectation, and even an obtainable goal that we should never stop striving to maintain. However, accepting the universal law of balance; that all good and no bad is unobtainable, provides a realistic and grounded expectation of life. Our drive for more good and less bad, hopefully encourages us to learn, grow, and explore the knowledge of the self and the world and people around us. That is a great tool to help create more good and less bad in your life. We have a fairly easy time utilizing the knowledge from the external world to decrease pain, injury, and discomforts. Yet, it is looking inside ourselves to gain and utilize that knowledge that we have a harder time accomplishing. As if we convince ourselves who we are is who we must remain, rather than being a springboard for who we can become.

We need to be careful that we don't set ourselves up for failure with our expectations, especially the higher ones. Looking for external fulfillment such as habit scrolling and purchasing, overeating, or the excessive pursuit of excitement will not fill these internal needs. We should also not stop pursuing higher needs due to having accomplished a life of comfort and abundance, or because of uncertainty in being able to meet one's basic needs for food and shelter. Whether not feeling the need to pursue higher needs fulfillment or the interference to pursue them due to circumstance, not pursuing our higher needs feeds our feelings of hopelessness, futility, emptiness, or just general internal discord. Our escalating numbers of suicides among the middle and upper class are indicators that helplessness and hopelessness are not a financial security issue.

Pursuing and holding onto our higher needs provides a wealth of benefits to our spirits and human ease that financial wealth cannot provide. Grabbing the less nutritionally dense cereal is easy, but it does not feed our spirit what it really needs. There are contrasting differences between grabbing the empty cereal and spending the time and energy to feed our deeper being the nutrient-rich fuels known as your higher needs.

A hodgepodge

Spending a little energy to be gentle with ourselves and others concerning how difficult life is, and yet to not give up in exasperation, and still pursuing higher needs is a great use of our energy and exercising of our optimism. Do not wait for something or someone to work towards more peace. Working on more peace today helps with even more peace tomorrow. Higher needs are worked and fulfilled inside our heads, hearts, and in our daily positive actions anyway, so they can be worked towards daily. Having first accomplished the work in our head and heart makes the follow-through in action so much easier. Easier comes out on its own, not forced. Moments, such as not missing a blue heron in a pond because you are arguing with someone, or yourself inside your head, while you drive, are beautiful real moments that are available and obtainable.

Our one hour ago is gone forever, and our next hour is not guaranteed, live to strive to help this moment be the richest moment it can be. Another way not to lose moments is to accept that unpleasant things will occur and trust you can handle it as it comes. Otherwise, we lose this moment to our fear and anxiety. I too lost moments to the stories I create in my head about how scary tomorrow will be, then it arrived, and it was usually so much easier than the story I conjured.

Yes, unpleasant moments are coming. Accepting that is grounding and doesn't waste time and energy waiting for and fearing them since most of our scary stories never happen.

Of equal importance to keeping your moments is not wasting them rehashing what has already happened. I admit, injustices are not that easy to process away. Yet, this awareness alone can help you decrease past events continuing to steal your here and now. Your actual life *is only* this very moment. Blue herons are beautiful, and I hope you see many in your life.

A power tool

Many influences want to lead us down big wide easy paths to attempt to fill our higher needs. It is no one's fault for these misleadings, or should I say our susceptibility to these misleadings. It is the job of corporations to sell their products, it is the job of advertisers to grab us, it is the joy of humans to share their happenings using today's vehicle known as social media. It is no one's fault that our human minds are susceptible to these influences that are created with our normal susceptibilities in mind. I know I can want a flame-broiled hamburger too after watching that well done commercial that makes me want meat. The worst part is, even though every aspect of my being tells me to eat less meat, and we know large amounts really are not good for us, I want it after I see the commercial. I could get mad, but the corporations, advertisers, and my mind are just doing what they do. I do get disappointed in myself a little when my free will and choice doesn't make healthy choices. Because I am aware, it is my weakness, not the fault of the corporation pushing to sell their product.

Redirecting myself away from external social influences is not as hard as it used to be, it takes work, just like all of life. Never stop exercising your mind to use your free will and choice. Talking yourself out of a bad choice is worth it, especially the really bad ones. Above all it requires self-forgiveness, so I love myself enough to keep trying. I know I am not alone in this one either.

Don't stop loving yourself despite your faults and weaknesses, despite your body size, despite a mistake you made, because then we stop caring enough to keep trying.

Spill it

There is a difference between processing a past event for the purpose of calming it and letting it go, and only talking about your problems. Talking to talk with that being the only goal, to verbalize it over and over, is not processing to lighten the stress of an event. I will sometimes remind someone who is about to tell me about a painful or stressful event to, "Let some of it go while telling me, give me some of it while you share it, in the hopes their burden will be even a few ounces lighter when they finish." It is just a slight awareness that helps, as opposed to calling someone, telling them, not having or listening to an exchange of support, then calling someone else and doing it all over again. Talking to talk, as if the goal is not to decrease or alleviate the internal pressure via healthy processing, but rather to articulate the upsetting event. The functional and helpful option is to share it, process it, and listen to and absorb good healthy input from a caring friend or counselor, and to get some more of it out of your being. Attempt to share with the people who want you to let some of the pain and stress out while you talk. As well, share with the friends that won't always agree with you. A true friend will help you see the wider angles of a situation, not just your angle. Try not to get mad at a friend's healthy insight that also is hard to hear. It proves they care on a deeper trusting level. Tell yourself that when you finish talking with this trusted friend, you are going to be a speck lighter with this burden. You may not yet be unburdened, but lighter is achievable.

Finding more peace and joy

It is our internal work and motivations that help us become the person we choose to become. If the growth is wanted and from the inside-out, then that wanted change also stands a greater chance of lasting.

Even if another person's humanness is the cause, allowing the near daily small inconveniences or annoyances to block your joy is often simply in the angle you choose to see it. I know the waitstaff may have forgotten to bring me a condiment I asked for when I ordered, and even though my food is getting cold while I wait. I will advocate for myself and ask again, and I have a choice to not allow that to ruin the meal or lose peace and energy to judge, then criticize the waitstaff for being human, new, busy, or out of their control short staffed. Because some of those reasons are out of their control, I may even verbalize when the requested fresh sliced jalapenos are finally delivered, and they start to apologize, I work to see the bigger picture, "I can see you're short staffed, and I couldn't handle it as well as you are. Good work." If it is a blatant lack of effort or customer service, I still don't want to buy what they are selling. What is a healthier choice for me is to enjoy the already fantastic enchilada and taco. At that moment, another human's behavior was about to knock me a little off my track. Exercising choice and flexibility allowed me to eat my meal and talk with a friend in peace. I also do not have the full vision of the wait staff and restaurant's big picture either. If it was high level poor customer service or rudeness, I may talk to the manager on the way out. It means you leave fed and walking on from someone else's accidental or intentionally less than par humanness, and you didn't get any on you. It is rational detachment applied. Knowingly or not, some people we pass near or interact with will want you to give up your calm moments for them, you often have a choice.

Expectations of conformity to ideas and beliefs is also a block to our peace and joy. Valuing others' autonomous thoughts and actions, if it is not dangerous or infringing on the rights of others, can increase our peace. Sure, we can become sad or disappointed in the actions or beliefs of others, that is normal. However, if you give away parts of yourself because others won't line up in perfect synch-step to march with you, you will be frequently giving away little parts of yourself.

I know I got tired of allowing the behaviors of others to overly affect my day. That was when I decided to expend preventative energy in that direction. I realized I would spend my entire life unhappy if I was going to wait for others to always do and say what would make me happy. I realized it was narcissistic of me to think I knew what was right for others to be doing and saying any further past basic human respect and job competency. Blaming others for giving us so many reasons to be unhappy steals too much of our life. If our life is filled with people, and a percentage of people are angry and blame, then we will benefit from not giving them too much power to affect us.

Action over words

When I hear or read someone say, "Go back to your country," I wonder if they have forgotten their ancestors had, or wanted, to come here for either growth or to stay alive. How quickly we forget the indigenous people of countries all over the world wanted the first invaders of their lands to go back to their country. Just because a culture has the resources to forge steel, and make gunpowder, which was a major indicator in early history of who conquered whom, does not give that culture a right to someone else's land. Unfortunately, that truth is now a moot point, and for the most part, none of us are going back to where we came from. Brute force in our backyards or between countries and cultures, whether driven by hatred, diverse political reasons, resource grabbing, or religious violence, are all still perpetrated around the globe. Muscle, money, steel, and gunpowder are still perceived as the hall pass to retaliate, power grab, or invade. This wide range of actions over words, neighborhoods to nations, is why our words and actions are what brings us both peace and stability.

Your thoughts, beliefs, attitudes, and actions are your tools which you have control over to turn expectations into accomplished outcomes. We have much to work on in this day and time, problems abound to the point that hopelessness is starting to win. We should never accept allowing a vicious cycle of hopelessness to take hold, not in ourselves or society. The passionate are screaming louder about the issues at hand. If actions are the most important steps to accomplishing, then turning the screams into positive contributing actions are important. Then there are those screaming passionately with no solutions, only more blame-based words, with immediate opposition to even solution-based discussions. Thus, hindering finding solutions. This not only relates to national and world progress, but it also relates to personal and occupational blame versus solution thinking and actions.

The world over, we may not be able to get governments to always do the right thing, but we can always do a better job of getting ourselves to do more of the right thing.

I was used to this more functional solution-based thinking and action methodology while nursing, especially in the teaching hospitals. In law enforcement, I observed less, let's find the origin of the problem then fix it from the problem up. There are solution-based thinkers in law enforcement, however, I found more of the find someone to blame and only place a bandage on the surface of the problem thinking and actions. Before I went into law enforcement, I may have heard the term "thrown under the bus" fifteen to twenty times in my life. In law enforcement, I unfortunately heard that term a few times per month. Effort spent on blame is that much effort not spent towards solution, repair, and then continued prevention. Energy is limited, so how we spend that energy is crucial.

My dad placed it all into action the night I hit the two parked cars at a red light only two weeks after I started driving. Of course, that night I had to tell my parents I caused a car crash. Now remember, I am the youngest of six kids, so my dad is fairly seasoned at this point. I get home and my mom is awake. I tell her, she freaks out a little but is also seasoned at this point and can see I am okay, and so is the car. She says, "Go tell your father." Dad is already asleep, "Dad, are you awake?" He rolls over but keeps his arm bent at his elbow over his face and eyes as he always did throughout my childhood if I woke them, so the light from the hallway doesn't shock his eyes. He gives a soft "Yes." "Dad, I caused a car crash about an hour ago. I hit two cars stopped at a red light." His whole life's experiences, awareness, and knowledge comes out in the simplest, most beautiful of action. He raises his arm just enough to see me, he wants to know his offspring is unharmed. He asks, "Are you okay?" "Yes," I responded. His next soft few words, "Is everyone else, okay?" "Yes," I responded. "Good. We can talk about it in the morning," and he rolls over and goes back to sleep. He did not ask a single question about material damage to the car or anything else. He knew the only true important questions had been answered. He knew nothing else could be done at ten o'clock at night about a damaged car. He applied his life's experiences into that simple, caring, appropriate, yet minimal action. He did not waste energy by jumping out of bed to change nothing at that point. Their response was equally a big deal to me as the car crash. Allocating our energy can be productive, calming, meaningful and rewarding. A gift to yourself can be found in how you wish to use your limited time and energy.

Realistic expectations and positive actions are gifts to yourself and everyone. Trust is one of those expectations and actions that I still believe in. I have thirty-five years of harsh frontline work that wanted to beat that trust out of me, that wanted me to discard all trust in my fellow humans. But I refuse to give up on us. I know for a fact most of us do not want to hurt each other, do not want to steal, and even want others to find joy and success. I will not give up my trust in the rest of you because of the few that want to hurt and take. Bad people are out there and deserve our caution, but there are far too many negative consequences of not caring about, or worse discarding, the vast majority, who are giving, contributing, caring, law-abiding, hardworking people of goodness.

Every day, you have many opportunities to give to yourself and others in your positive actions and negative omissions. Yet please, always take good care of yourself first.

A surprising answer to a trusting question

Many years ago, I started to enjoy talking to wealthy people about what it was like to have money. I always waited until a year or two had passed into the friendship, so they knew me from the core out and that I did not judge them for their money, but rather our friendship was because of who they are. After achieving this point of trust with wealthy friends I would enjoy having conversations about what that meant to them. I would often start the conversation by asking, "What is it like to have so much money?" The interesting thing is I often found them wanting to talk about it, at least with me. I observed, and a few just came right out and told me that they were excited to have someone neutral to talk about it with. One of the recurring themes I heard was how draining it can be talking about money with other people that have money; showy, competitive, one-upping in subtle and sometimes direct ways. One financially comfortable friend of mine once said, "Instead of it being like keeping up with the Joneses, it is more like keeping up with the Rockefellers." Yet, they can't talk about it with people who don't have money, because they would tell me they would then have to deal with anger and judgment. Don't ever think wealthy people do not also receive discrimination, that discrimination creates some level of shunning effect for them also. As long as someone did not steal or cheat the system, we should never be angry with someone for being born into wealth or being good at making legitimate money. But I have had some jaw-dropping amazing conversations with wealthy people about what having money was like for them. I have heard the most amazing and interesting answer to my simple open-ended question.

My favorite answer of all time came from someone I met while in my thirties. I had known this person for well over ten years when I asked them the question. This person did not have to work but continues to do so, I think to stimulate their powerful brain and spirit. This person had a healthy suspicious side too, so I started by asking them if they knew money was not my drive in life. They even answered, "Oh, I know, helping people is your drive. I have no idea how you are always so nice." So, I asked my question, "What is it like to have so much money?" The answer was magnificent, initially funny then profound, "Vincent, you know that old saying, money can't buy you happiness?" I said, "Yes." This person immediately said with a fair amount of force, "Well, let me tell you, that's some bullshit!" When I finished laughing, this person immediately followed with, "But I don't mean that how you think. Yes, I am not dumb. I know my life is easier than many others because I do not have to worry about money. But what I mean is, it's what I do with it that brings me my deepest reward. Such as, I recently knew of a poor family in town, with a bunch of young kids, and their house needed a new roof, it was leaking. I hired a crew to put a new roof on their home and had the company owner promise they would not tell the crew or family who was paying for it. Vincent, I will tell you that brought me so much joy. They still don't know who gave them their new roof. It is not having money that will bring anyone true lasting joy. It is what they do with it." About two minutes passed in silence as I contemplated the giving action and the shock and joy to the family, when this person said, "Life is the same way, it's not only being alive, it's what we do with it."

WIDER ANGLE:

THE SPECK

Our level of fascination with the tall powerful human beings has always intrigued me, and I get it. This is not one of my hypocrisies, Earth's human giants have always captivated me. I have been tossed around by a few in the emergency room like I was a piece of wadded tissue paper. Comparing non-human sizes: whales are wow, our huge sun, our massive galaxy, the unfathomable size of the universe.

When I am having trouble feeling like a helpless human in relation to anything I have no control over, or my problems feel too heavy, I like to remind myself I am a speck. This helps me with the truth of what I can and cannot control far more than trying to convince myself I have control, when I don't. An earthquake or a lightning strike is a perfect example. This helps me further reduce fear and let go of worries about big picture subjects, such as tornadoes or meteorites hitting Earth. This also helps me not see people as their bodies, but as their inner being. Four-feet or seven-feet, ninety or four hundred pounds, we are specks, yet each a living feeling life.

Have you ever looked at one of those charts comparing the size of Earth to the size of our largest planet Jupiter, then to our Sun and then other suns? On the first frame, Jupiter looks like the size of a basketball and Earth the size of a marble; Jupiter appears huge. Then compare Jupiter to our Sun, and now the Sun is the size of a basketball and Jupiter is the size of the marble, and Earth is the size of a BB. Let's then go back to imagine the magnitude of a human to the size of now little BB Earth. If you compared a human to the size of Earth, if Earth was the size of a hot air balloon, we humans are smaller than a piece of dust on the balloon.

Ready to get even smaller? Astronomers know we can only see a small fraction of the Universe. They can see stars that make our Sun look the size of a BB. Then there are yet larger stars that make those stars look like a BB. Again, and again, they found a larger star to dwarf the previous ones. Earth and our sun are now both dust specks. To date, one of the ten largest stars known to astronomers is a red hyper-giant named VY Canis Majoris. The explanation they used to help us grasp its size is difficult to fathom. They say VY Canis Majoris is so large, that if you were even able to get near it in a jet that travels at the speed of light, it would take 6 hours to circle it once, whereas circling our sun would only take 14.5 seconds.

To help you comprehend just our single little-huge galaxy, The Milky Way, and the Universe's size, they estimate there are well over 100 billion stars in our galaxy alone, and they estimate there to be over 100 billion galaxies in the Universe.

This knowledge allows me to let go of control, it lets me not fear storms, it helps me avoid getting wrapped up in what I think is a big deal. When I change my angle and think of what would really ruin my day or life, I see my big deals are only specks my troubles get just as tiny, and that brings me further comfort. Yes, I hope to be a good contributing speck, and this speck does want to experience life. I do not believe we are insignificant by any means. I believe the exact opposite on Earth; we are all giants capable of intentionally or accidentally stepping on those around us. We are not specks when it comes to our ability to hurt or heal, to help, or to hinder. We might feel like a speck in that department because of how we are sometimes treated, but we are not specks to each other.

At the speed of light! 14.5 seconds for our sun, and 6 hours for VY Canis Majoris! Yes, my troubles are tiny. Accepting that calms me, then I let go, and just be.

CHAPTER 10

RELIGION VERSUS SPIRITUALITY AND YOUR OWN MORAL COMPASS

"If you are going to write a book about suffering less you have to include a chapter about religion and one about politics."
—A few of my close friends from diverse backgrounds.

"But I don't like discussing those subjects openly."
—Me

"Then you will be leaving out two major subjects that cause great suffering for many of us."
—The same correct friends

Ok, here I go, breathe Vincent breathe

Our times have become so tense that even our religions, which are meant on many levels to increase our acceptance, tolerance, forgiveness, and understanding for each other, are painfully separating, dividing us, and even killing us. Anything that is dividing us is hurting us.

Unrelated to our religious conflicts and thanks to its true goodness, our spirituality is not interested in blaming, labeling, and creating fear of diverse ways, ideas, and religions. Our spirituality is and should be separate; it is our relationship with our god or greater power and most importantly how we show that relationship to the world around us. Religions talk about their god, while our spirituality is each individual's relationship with their own concept of a higher power, and equally important is how one shows in daily actions their spiritual relationship to the world around them.

I started pursuing the difference between religion and spirituality when I first started questioning. A few years later I really started to dig in when people around me started talking about the bad things they have seen or experienced in their religion, or with religion in general. A huge part of the world is painfully affected by the negative actions that people or groups do in the name of religion, such as a fantastic, contributing, and giving person, rejected, or worse, assaulted, because of their sexuality. Or, falsely hiding behind religion, manipulating religious doctrine for self-gain, or using people's goodness and their trust in their religion in order to accomplish bad. My frequent use of the word "Bad" is indeed vague and simple, but I think the great majority of the world understands bad. I also think we know, for the most part, that the core philosophy of religions, all religions, are filled with goodness. What people, subgroups, and cultures do with those philosophies for personal or political gain, or control of an individual or the masses, is where the trouble starts.

The huge numbers of those tortured and killed during the long years of the Inquisition and the Crusades were not small numbers. It was not the entire religion of Islam that on September 11, 2001, committed a terrorist attack on the US, but rather a small violent subsect of Islam. On that day, nineteen terrorists committed four violent acts in one hour seventeen minutes. But the 25% of the world population who identifies as Islamic, often called Muslim, of which the overwhelming majority are wonderful well-rounded people, paid for it with a new level of religious, racial, and cultural persecution. It is not the good people of the Islamic faith who are terrorists, it is the sector of a small percentage of the second largest religion on Earth that is violent. These examples show that the people of religions are not bad, but rather bad people are bad people. Unfortunately, many of those bad people use religion, and peoples need for a higher power connection, to do their bad.

In 2017, Anthony Cordesman authored a fantastic article entitled, "Islam and the Patterns in Terrorism and Violent Extremism," that I found published on the website of the *Center for Statistics and International Studies,* that perfectly summarizes the above redirection in relationship to the labels we gave to an entire religion and its people. I am only going to quote a small section of Mr. Cordesman's article:

"The end result is to ignore the reality that most extremist and terrorist violence does occur in largely Muslim states, although it overwhelmingly consists of attacks by Muslim extremists on fellow Muslims, and not some clash between civilizations (Cordesman).

If one examines a wide range of sources, however, a number of key patterns emerge that make five things very clear:

- First, the overwhelming majority of extremist and violent terrorist incidents do occur in largely Muslim states.
- Second, most of these incidents are perpetrated by a small minority of
- Muslims seeking power primarily in their own areas of operation and whose primary victims are fellow Muslims.
- Third, almost all of the governments of the countries involved are actively fighting extremism and terrorism, and most are allies of Western states that work closely with the security, military, and counterterrorism forces of non-Muslim states to fight extremism and terrorism.
- Fourth, the vast majority of Muslims oppose violent extremism and terrorism.

- Fifth, religion is only one of many factors that lead to instability and violence in largely Muslim states. It is a critical ideological force in shaping the current patterns of extremism, but it does not represent the core values of Islam and many other far more material factors help lead to the rise of extremism."

Mr. Cordesman's summary, and what history teaches us about the smaller percentages of extremism within most religions, should teach us that most religions are mostly good. If the philosophies of religions are good, and supposedly only a small percentage of people abuse and manipulate those good philosophies, then why are so many people so unhappy with religion? The influences on that question and the answers are not so easy to summarize.

I would rather not write about religion and spirituality because my personal beliefs are that if your beliefs are working for you and those beliefs are not forced on you, nor are you forcing them on others, then not only go for it, but I will speak up to protect your rights to believe in and practice your chosen religion. Then I remembered one of the initial reasons so many came to the United States in the first place: religious persecution. This is one reason the courageous Founders of the United States wrote into the first ten amendments, appropriately known as *The Bill of Rights*, a protection of state and people from the church, yet at the same time protecting your right to practice your religion of choice. "Congress shall make no law respecting an establishment of religion or prohibiting the free exercise thereof." Some people take great pride, and others take great anger, in the statement, "In God we Trust," being on our money and found in other places that could challenge and blur the line between the separation of church and state. But for me "God" is a wide-reaching title. The currency of the United States does not read "In the Christian God we Trust" and it never should specify a god. There are many higher powers that can meet the needs of even the agnostic or atheist in some situations.

An exceptional example of finding higher power outside of an expected or traditional god-figure is found in the answers I have heard from atheists or agnostics who are staying sober through following the twelve steps of Alcoholics Anonymous (AA), or by some considering turning to AA for help, because AA has such a high success rate of sobriety. As a nurse, I referred hundreds of people to their meetings. If alcohol consumption somehow lands someone in an emergency department, it could be an indicator that they need help. Following a referral, I often heard "But I don't believe in God or a Higher Power, isn't that required in one of the steps?" Yes and no. Step one is, "Admitting that one is powerless over Alcohol and that life has become unmanageable." Step two is, "Came to believe that a power greater than ourselves could restore us to sanity." Step three states, "Made a decision to turn our will and our lives over to the care of God *as we understand him*." "God" is mentioned a few more times in the twelve steps. I shared the first three steps to get to number three, "As we understand him," leaves a lot of leeway. In conversations over the years with agnostics and atheists, some have told me their higher power was, "The wisdom, strength, and experience of the people in the rooms of the meetings." I once knew a wonderful person who had been sober for over thirty years before their death. This person told me about their higher power was life, nature, and science, then told me "God" is still how they express that belief, "because most people don't like it when your god is not their god." I understood him, including science, because when I really started to learn about the finer aspects of the human body's anatomy and physiology, it definitely helped strengthen my spirituality.

The defending and pushing

"Religion is at its best when it makes us ask hard questions of
ourselves. It is at its worst when it deludes us into thinking
we have all the answers for everybody else."
—Archibold Macleish

I admit, by writing about and publishing this tender, painful, and
sensitive subject, I am scared. People are passionate about their religious
beliefs, and history proves there is no limit to what lengths some people
will go to protect and even propagate their religious beliefs. I'll be judged
and labeled for only sharing what I have learned; identifying issues that
cause so much internal pain and core-questioning in so many of us and
sharing what I have witnessed seems to help people. Many will forget
that just two paragraphs above I stated that I support people's beliefs and
will even stand up to protect those beliefs. It is the same with politics,
I don't want to write about politics. I try so very hard to keep politics
and religion out of my writings. I work to keep it strictly in the cause
and effect of human and social dynamics, and that sometimes includes
politics. I am one of us humans, therefore I will fail at times.

To me, the most amazing thing about this subject is that from the
beginning of recorded history, on cave walls, we have documented an
innate need to have a connection with a higher power, God, supreme
being, or force. This need or pull is in us. The proof is how many
people have believed for so long and how they will fight for it. There
is much human and social pathology so deeply ingrained in religion
and spirituality that an immeasurable number of books and doctoral
dissertations are written on the subject. Just look at the number of
books written around the world dedicated to each of the major religions.
Then why does it cause so much pain and trouble? There are many

individuals, groups, cultures, governments, and yes, even religions themselves that have used and manipulated the functional beliefs of goodness and respect (that all religions lay out in one form or another) for nonspiritual gain. Such as personal or group special interest or general control of individuals or the masses; to shape abortion, alcohol, Sunday purchasing laws, even the books we read, or to con away power, money, or pleasure. It has gone on since the beginning of human manipulation, it is still going on today, and will continue for as long as the human factor is involved and used for special interest gain over applied goodness. Religion is not the big picture issue, but rather these issues are caused by humanness. The not so good humanness is not limited to religions, and can be found within some individuals, groups, institutions, businesses, or governments. But it is a special higher level of bad humanness in religion, because of its ease to manipulate both the doctrine and the people trusting in the words and representatives of a religion.

Innumerable books are also written on the abusive sides of religions. If you need some backing to that statement, do some research into the history of violence in relation to various religions—any of them. The results are humbling across the board. Some aren't so intense, Buddhism is one of the least violent, but still not completely innocent. Although, many within Buddhism prefer to call it a philosophy rather than a religion. As Buddha himself stated not to take his word as law it may not work for everyone, and that he is not a prophet or representing a god, but only human. Hinduism is not at the top of the violent list either. Other major religions, well, how do I finish this sentence? Let's just say learning of the torture and deaths that have occurred in the name of religion will take you a long time to read. Unfortunately, violence and manipulation for gain remains a huge issue around the world, whether perpetuated by religion, politics, organized crime, or individuals.

The common factor is still that too many humans will place self-gain far above the common good of all. This is no different from the rest of human behavior, nor is it new to religion. One example is the push to give money still too often seems to be pushed as a correlation to how much you respect and love your god. The money push is one of the repetitive complaints I hear from people. Yes, just like our healthcare field and all businesses, profit must be made to continue to function, that is not the issue. The opulence at the top is fatiguing to many; diamonds and gold, designer clothes, high-priced cars, mansions, and let us not forget those famous gold bathroom fixtures. How many poor families could be fed and clothed for a year for the price of one Rolls Royce?

For balance, some of the arguments made by those with much more knowledge on the subject can be very generalized. Many present beliefs that only place the blame of the bad, manipulation, and violence onto the responsibility of individuals, rather than the religion. There are major examples in history, such as the burning of "witches" at the stake, or such mass violence and actions of torture and death, in the name of admission of guilt to "sin," alliance to the religion, "just punishments," purification, or to suppress evil. Other examples, such as the Inquisition or the Crusades, challenge the arguments that attempt to move blame away from the religion itself and back onto the people who committed the violence. Further, if a particular view holds no responsibility for the bad actions of its administrators, representative clergy, and members' bad actions, then out of responsibility for past and present religious action atrocities (and to prevent future ones), we must ask ourselves this crucial question. How quickly does a religion's silent acceptance of bad actions, whether by not speaking up or acting to stop the actions, create accountability for that bad right alongside the individual actors' primary guilt? The Inquisition and The Crusades both lasted for two-hundred years. Is it not the role of the religion to guide to higher moral ground? What are many religions still passively condoning today by not speaking to us against the behaviors of its representatives and members? I do not ask this question to attack any one religion or subject, I only ask to protect and prevent.

It has its goodness too

"I do benefits for all religions; I'd hate to blow the hereafter on a technicality."
—Bob Hope, 1903–2003

Healthy-practiced religion has the potential, and often does, play a huge part in the strength of individuals, community, and humanitarian efforts around the world. Most all religious philosophies are mostly filled with functional goodness, and if applied without the wide influences of our human imperfections, then most of the not so good in this chapter would not be occurring. Religions are not bad, their human manipulations for various gains are the core problem. The overwhelming majority of the people of religions are not bad; Christians are not bad, Muslims are not bad, Catholics are not bad, Jewish people are not bad, even most of the followers of Jim Jones in Guyana were not bad. All human beings can be manipulated on some level, towards good or bad, but the manipulation of religion can be a special kind of bad.

It is special because of that deep innate desire for thousands of years to have a connection to a higher power, and our deep trust that expects the people who represent those beliefs to operate on a higher level of good. If we are going to title someone a representative of their god, a rather high title indeed, and we know a large percentage of the people are going to give them more credence and blind trust in their word, then should we not hold them to a higher level of responsibility with that trust? People turn their lives over to the word of these high titles, often turning to them in times of need, personal weakness, or the malleability of youth. Often, they are appropriately guided to safety and strength, but sadly and criminally, are too often manipulated and abused for personal control, or a pleasure, or monetary reward. The power, sexual, and financial manipulation of religion is a huge issue, and again, the driving force for so many turning their backs and walking away. I hear often, that if religions would police themselves greater, the people's trust would return, and membership may again increase.

A conversation I once had may have nothing to do with the negatives listed in this chapter, but I am sure it will give you the same pause it gave me concerning the subject, structure, and location. It may have just been a perfectly happy, obviously younger couple for a few blatant reasons. Or its reason may be some of the bad things we are talking about. One of the handful of times I was lucky enough to live in the country, I hired a company to pump out the septic system. I was fascinated with the entire event and had huge respect for this man's contribution to society; just like me, he was a nurse, except for houses. After he took the lid off the tank and started the pumping and backwashing cycles, I asked this well-seasoned man what was the strangest thing he ever found in a septic tank? Before he answered, being in my mid-twenties and not really thinking what his answer might be or if he would probably rather not recall the vision, I asked him if he ever found a body in a tank. He said in a slow, rough, and rusty voice as he perfectly threw his cigarette butt into the center of the little round tank opening hole in the ground. "Nope, no bodies, but I once found two inches of assorted colored condoms floating on the top of a tank at a little, tiny, old, wooden church sitting all by itself, way out in the middle of the country. White steeple and all." I was struck silent as about thirty seconds passed as I contemplated the magnitude of that information from ten different directions. He followed with, "Yep, all those colors, it was the first and only time I ever looked in a septic tank that I thought it was kind of pretty. Didn't smell any different, but it was kind of pretty."

Finding and applying our own moral compass

My parents did not force religion on me, but we went to Mass on Sundays and the big holidays. What my parents pushed on me was an attempt to do the right thing for the right reasons. They both taught me that moral, ethical, and respectful social structure, unrelated to the wrath of religious doctrine, was the reason to do the right thing. Both admitted they, too, had some issues with the church and religion when I started questioning. Both my parents thought the chastity rule with priests was a setup for disaster. Why wouldn't they? They had six children in ten years! My mother was more vocal about it, "To think that we as humans, with only the words of a religious doctrine, can attempt to suppress an innate desire to express our core sexual beings, or our innate and beneficial desire for intimacy and touch is inhuman, unrealistic, and those normal healthy needs and desires will come out in other less healthy channels." But she adhered fairly closely to the Catholic doctrine. She kept encouraging me to attend Mass, and I am grateful for the balance of being a product of both Catholic and public schools, but she always told me she would not force religion on me. She did a little throughout life, but for the most part, she didn't. Both my parents encouraged doing the right things for the right reasons, with the encouragement of autonomy in thought and respect for all. They both agreed showing God's love was more important than talking about it. Past the melodious chant of eight people saying grace sitting about the wooden picnic table in our kitchen before a meal, religion and God were not a daily discussion in our home. I feel I had a healthy balanced introduction to both religion and spirituality. I have always enjoyed learning about all religions and philosophies.

Like most young scholars of life, I questioned on a higher level around age eleven or so. We attended a beautiful little church on the bayou, just right, with an easygoing priest that taught of love and goodness, not sin and shame. I always figured he knew downtown New Orleans was only an hour's drive away, so he might as well keep it real.

It was not long after these deeper questions started to not be given concrete answers that I began to walk out of church and sit on the dock that was maybe 150 feet away from the church. If I am going to be told that the answer is "Divine Mystery," or "Sacred Mystery," then I better go start looking for those mysteries. I was having a challenging time connecting with what was going on behind me in the physical structure, but I did not have a tough time connecting with what I was seeing and feeling outside. I will trust you. Sitting on that dock is where I found my relationship with spirituality and first connected to the world around me with an alert and excited awareness. Before that I was an instinctual kid on autopilot.

It all started with the one-lane bridge to my left as I sat on the edge of that little dock. I did not know this at the time, but the old human crank bridge was built in 1941. It had a little tiny one-room wooden structure where a family of several lived right next to the bridge. Sometimes two or three times in the hour I sat there, a boat would need to pass and one or two of the family members, often the teenage sons, but sometimes just the mother, would come out of the little wooden structure to open the bridge for a boat. They would manually close the guard arm near the home first, then walk to the other side to close that guard arm also. They would walk back to the middle and lift a metal pole that had a ninety-degree angle hanging on hooks on the inside of the railing. They would insert the short end into a hole right in the middle of the bridge and start pushing the pole as they walked around in a circle. The bridge would slowly rotate open. Once open, I would hear the boat engage back into gear and slowly pass. They would then walk in the opposite direction, pushing the pole to close the bridge, hang the pole up on the side, walk to the far end, and open the guard arm. The cars on that far side would always get to cross the one-lane bridge first after this delay, as they slowly followed the person walking to the other side to lift the other guard arm before heading back into their little home. I had watched this happen many times from the car, but not from a dock so close. It was even more real and quaint hearing the old wooden structure creak and groan as it slowly swung open and closed. I could hear their footsteps back and forth and round and round on the loose wood planks on the roadway surface. I could hear the boat motor pick up power just a little once the bridge was open, then quickly accelerate once past the structure. All the drivers halted by this old bayou tradition across the state knew it took a while, would turn their engines off, and put their windows down. It was quiet. I was slowing down enough to see life and people happening. They appeared peaceful, but I knew they all had a not so smooth story, our home had some not so smooth too. Just under the waterline under the dock was often a blue crab, just sitting there, its claws such vivid blues, orange, and red with white and yellow here and there, its back a greenish-blue-brown. There, in those color changes, I could visually see a higher power that before was only words: it breathes its oxygen out of the water. Looking at the crab I recalled the local king snake, the speckled king, a dark blackish blue with small bright yellow-whitish round dots everywhere. I had held one a few times, and I always wondered, how does half of a scale know it's supposed to be light and the other half dark to create all those little round spots? One scale, two colors? Now I am finding tangible mysteries I can work with; my spirituality was forming a foundation.

These color changes in nature were a wonder to me, and I thought science actually helps strengthen my beliefs, the two are not in conflict. Everything I saw out there seemed more like the work of a creator, a higher power, science, the smooth glide of the people of the bayou and culture, who have lived in relative peace and harmony, with all races and cultures, since before the French Acadians were forced from Canada by the British in the mid-1700s. The French had already settled the Louisiana Territory since 1682. Although I saw some race riot violence in Baton Rouge during the late 1960s, for the most part the cultures and races in South Louisiana got along openly. There were issues there too, but a culture that has been shunned and sent on its way is often a more inviting, welcoming culture. That region has always been a cultural melting pot.

I felt a connection with the people and all the living forms around me. I could hear the people talking in the cars as they waited for the bridge to reopen, the family that tended the bridge, and bigger pictures started to develop than just my picture. Sitting on that dock, without fishing, swimming, or getting dirty in my church clothes, just watching and processing; it was my moment I realized my story is one of many, very many stories. I was a child, but I needed more application than theory, and I needed more concrete answers to my questions. I found out I wasn't alone; I was learning that other kids and adults had the same trouble with the words being more important than the actions. For some reason, even though I walked out of church, my weekly Sunday time on that dock sparked and strengthened my spirituality. I needed tangible to embrace a higher power, and that which my five senses could experience was all I needed to launch.

It was the early mid-1970s and my father read *Time* magazine weekly from cover to cover. I used to look at the pictures and read the description below the picture. The entire article was always daunting to me, to this day, political articles still are. So, I was well aware people were dying still in the name of religion in the middle east and I knew the conflict in Ireland was between the Protestants and the Catholics. With time I learned that conflict was seeded in wider and deeper issues than just religion, as many religious wars are often not only in the name of religion. All of it was not adding up for me anyway, and all of everything drove me to walk out of church in the first place. The last straw for me was watching one of the altar boys. He was a bully, and I knew it for a fact, so it was hard for me to accept that a robe and a ritual is what made people good, or completely trustworthy. I sat on that dock a time or thirty more after walking out. Mom and Dad didn't really say anything; we would go to church, I would sit in the pew for five minutes or so, walk out to that dock, then meet them at the car after church. Mom told me years later that they had a feeling I was going to be okay in the spiritual department because of how I was always challenging doctrine with questions, then contrasting that to people's words and actions. A few years before she died, she said to me, "You may be one of my least religious children, but you are very spiritual in how you treat others." I was just grateful she didn't worry about me—in that department anyway. Oh, and she had big hopes for me in that department, my middle name is even Paul. She wanted a saint, but she got me instead.

After my arrival at college in North Louisiana, I was quickly surprised that even though the North and South of that state are not officially divided into two, they are so quite different. The South is a cultural blend, that thinks any day that ends with a "y" is a good day to have a party and invite the entire community, and that easygoing Catholic way for the region was predominant. The North is considered the "Bible Belt" region and is a little more, shall we say, upright. North Louisiana still has some parishes, counties to the rest of the country, that only allows the purchase of beer, and not on Sundays either. I quickly found out it was not only people who had walked away from their religion, who were eager to talk. I also started to have conversations with people from all walks of life and religious backgrounds. One of those differences were that in South Louisiana I personally knew; we did not really talk too much about church or religion during the other six days of the week. In the southern part of the state, I had never had people attempt to convert me. In the North, they wanted me to be baptized again, they wanted me to be born again. This was all new to me, but I slowed down, no arguments, and I had a few interesting conversations with the devout attempting to save me.

I was fascinated with this contrast; it was also my first experience with ethnocentric religious views. Proselytizing was not a big thing in the southern part of the state, cold beer and fresh boiled crayfish was bigger. Catholicism has a strong hold in Bayous. I had talks with both fellow students and older adults, many of whom were still members of their religion, and they too sometimes admitted to me they have problems with some of what their religion was trying to force on them. Many puritans of all religions feel it's an "all or nothing" belief or you are not a true devotee of your religion. That is a level of conformity too many people started to have problems with. There are those who would walk away from their original religious beliefs completely, and there were those who stayed but were comfortable with turning away from that which went against their core autonomous beliefs. There is a lot of harsh labeling that gets stuck on these partial followers, such as "lazy" or "not wanting to be inconvenienced." In discussions, I found it was more that they eventually had to draw a line between their core beliefs and their religious doctrine conflicts.

Hence the term "cafeteria practitioner." Picking and choosing what works for the individual like walking through the line in a cafeteria. Choosing those items that are not against your core beliefs of what you feel is right for you and leaving the others. When I ask about the feelings of others, from many cultures and religions, about this subject, I always work to ask open-ended questions. I have known many Islamic followers who are tired of the way their mother, sisters, and daughters are looked upon and treated as women, and I know a huge number of Catholics and Protestants who think abortion should be a choice. We could pick any religion and a percentage of its followers may have core issues with parts of its doctrine. I have heard the most scary, sad, and amazing things in these discussions. From tears, to laughter, unnecessary shame and self-doubt, into frustration, and too often, back to tears, with anger thrown into the second round of tears. Usually, the emotional spectrum patterns these conversations would weave through were endless.

Of course, religions have also been for the good. The people who do receive positive support and a belief that works for them is huge. The number of people across the earth who are fed, clothed, educated, and sheltered due to religion is beautiful. Mission work has its place, I just wish it could be done without the need to convert. The atrocities in the name of conversion or obedience to religion are beyond a few-word description. Yet, I know many happy, amazing, caring, humanistic people from all religions that understand, benefit, and share the pure goodness of their religion. I know a substantial number of wonderful religious people who do the right thing for the right reason helped by their religious doctrine. Some common traits I see in these happier people are that they are cafeteria practitioners, and they do not feel a strong need to actively convert others. I have found in the healthiest people that are religious, when they believe in converting others, they think it should be passively; meaning show it, share it, but don't push it, if it works for the person, they will hop on board with you. These are the people that are also spiritual in their spoken words, actions, and omissions.

The more common themes I have heard over the years as to why so many people leave their original religious beliefs are physical/sexual abuse by either clergy or spouses in the name of religion, general manipulation of people or groups, financial manipulation, failure to truly keep up with the times, abortion, an unhealthy push for conformity or money, the unrealistic and rushed marriage practice of no sex before marriage (leading to so many failed or unhappy youth marriages), misogynistic behaviors, blatant hypocrisy and double standards in action, racism, nationalism, and the attempted or accomplished infliction of shame, guilt, and fear. A fair percentage also had a problem with what I touched on above: the past and present violent history in the name of religion. The way many are taught to recruit, or the ethnocentric indoctrination to tell others their beliefs are wrong, is also distancing people from their own religion. More and more people are becoming omnistic in their views, as the cultures of the world must learn to walk next to each other in our ever-increasing multicultural societies. Omnism is the respect for all religions or someone's choice to not believe. All these issues are a lot of strain on a being and society. These major complaints are not on a lower trivial level.

Omnism was yet a term when the Founders of the United States were working to design a safer, fairer, and more balanced government, but you can freely thank your god, of your choice, because they understood the need to protect the concept. Hopefully, we will all continue to work to protect that freedom.

Not letting go of an important support

In over 40 years of discussions with people on these subjects, most informed me they either walked away from religion, or have core conflicts with parts of their religion, but did not walk away from their spirituality. Most people that I have shared these trusted talks with, not only stated they remained spiritual, but also stated a deeper and more practiced connection with their higher power and their fellow humans than ever before. Most said their religious and spiritual confusion decreased once they resolved their contradictions. Distinguishing the difference between religion in theory, and spirituality that is shown in practiced application, gives me great comfort. Meaning the difference between talking about the written words of your religion and showing your god's love, or your spirituality, in actual daily outward words and actions.

I have had negative and positive religious influences in my life. But there is one positive influence that stands out: a friend of the family and my tenth-grade religion teacher, Brother Eldon Crifasi, a member of The Brothers of the Sacred Heart. We would have discussions, which I now realize were not discussions, but were me asking rapid fire, tough, highly challenging questions. I am now laughing, realizing how hard that must have been for him. I respect him for always either giving me an actual helpful applicable answer, or he would say "I don't know," when he did not know. He once ended a conversation with a three sentence slice of wisdom that has helped me ever since, "Oh, Man! Vincent! God doesn't care about all the subjects you want to cover. God just doesn't want you to be horrible or stop trying to be and do better. That's all God cares about."

Some of the more frequent and loudest complaints I hear of organized religions have had to do with hypocrisies, double standards, and the manipulation by all parties for personal gain of any sort. Even while I was still young, having no idea what those words even meant, I kept hearing them in adult conversation over and over. What I heard and felt was that it's hard to hear those beautiful words of the doctrine in your chosen house of worship, but then witness so many uncaring actions and words once people leave the physical structure of their house of worship. The hypocrisies and double standards, from the street corners all the way to the highest halls of governments, are wrenching to hear, disappointing, and destructive to the spirit and health of individuals, communities, nations, and religions themselves. It is one thing to be a normal average hypocrite, it is another to outwardly judge with such righteousness when each of us is standing in our own blatant puddles of humanness. It also seems that the ones who judge the loudest are the ones who are defensive on a higher level, blind to honestly see the magnitude of their own hypocrisies and double standards in their judgment and faulting of others. I respect the frustration and futility that has repetitively been expressed to me in how people deny seeing their own faulted self through religious rationalizations, and the manipulation of doctrine. I only partially apologize for writing the paragraph with the same strength of passion that it was released to me so many times. I am human too; I just don't want to "be horrible or stop trying to do better."

"In my diverse reading of the writings of the world's religions, I have discovered that the vast majority of it is designed not to give us permission to judge others, but rather is meant to highly encourage us to judge ourselves."
—Another friend requesting anonymity

There have been so many wonderful people and cultures around this world that have known how to worship their chosen god in not only words but actions. Unfortunately, some societies often labeled many of them with simple terms for not having more complex philosophies because they were simple in their beliefs. But these people also show a functional and, above all, respectful and sustainable thank you to their higher power. The Indigenous people of much of the world know this. They thank their higher power for the goodness given to them by the act of showing respect to the part of the earth that gave it to them. Such as they would thank the river for the fish by not taking more fish than needed. Or, to show thanks to their higher power for the fruit, caribou, vegetables, monkey, grain, bison, or gazelle, they would not take or kill more than required to live. Then to show further respect by using every ounce of it they could find a needed purpose for. To thank the forest for wood to cook and keep warm, they would only use the wood that was already on the ground, seeing the fallen branch as a gift. Forward thinking and true respect for what one has been gifted.

There are two simple life guiding rules, that in one form or another runs through most religions. These two gems sum up the goal and the tools to obtain that goal of most religions. Those two simples have a highly rewarding bonus: individual, communal, and world peace. To generalize the two: treat others as you wish to be treated, and if you judge yourself first you will see you have no right to judge others. In referring to those two truly golden rules, a mentor of mine told me something close to this years ago, "We don't need thousands of pages of written confusion and outdated doctrine to over-stimulate us and contradict itself. All we need to do is focus most of our spiritual energy, and minute-to-minute communication, into daily practice of those two basics, and our lives and interactions would become so much easier and more rewarding." The hardest part for me, is that those two beauties do bring both the provider and the receiver less suffering, but too many discard them.

People will be angry with me for stating these observations and retellings. But I should not be blamed for the failure of religions for their lack of self-policing, or their inconsistencies between words and actions. I should not be blamed that people often hear beautiful words in the houses of worship that cover the face of the earth, then leave those words behind and walk out the door to treat and judge others as they wish not to be treated or judged. My intentions are not to damage faith, but to help restore faith, it is needed now more than ever.

Most of us want to believe in a higher power, people want to see the good, the comfort, and the bonding of fellowship they feel while they listen to those words inside their chosen house of worship. Religion can be love in action, or it can be a wolf in sheep's skin. The human factor will always be the common denominator. However, the self-honest and introspection of every person making up a religion, then followed by the will and courage to carry out positive actions and suppress the more negative ones, will always be the key to sustainable, healthy, and supportive religions. Is that not also the key to anything healthy and sustainable related to us humans?

Steady yourself with something of goodness that you get to design

I highly encourage all who feel they must walk away from religion to please not walk away from your spirituality also. Please hold on to a belief in a higher power of your choosing, whether that higher power is your God, the Universe, or Science, because this desire or need for a connection with something higher is innate. Holding onto your spirituality is a grounding of your being and life. Your own healthy spirituality is also a springboard to higher levels of self, social contribution, and yes, peace. I hope you will never get tired of me referring to greater peace. Peace is not just a saying and hand gesture left over from the 1960s and 1970s, it is also at times an obtainable goal worth pursuing to higher and higher levels. Peace be with you.

Fellowship is also one of the repeated positives I hear, the bonding of humans, the strength and security that is capable of being created when weaving humans together in the name of all goodness. Yes, research shows that fellowship, feeling a healthy and trusting connection with others, a group orientated towards positive actions, and believing in a higher power, is good for us. The research even shows people heal faster when they have healthy and frequent visitation. Prayer and all forms of meditation, including just stopping and reading something positive, enlightening, or encouraging for a minimum of fifteen to twenty minutes per day, has been proven to improve the health and wellness of those who will stop for a few minutes a day to drop your shoulders, expand your breath, and sit with yourself, whether sick, injured, stressed, or healthy. Prayer, meditation, sitting with yourself, call it whatever works for you, but know it is good for you.

People rarely leave their religions with ease due to the innate pull for that higher something, and the guilt and shame religions are so good at instilling. They struggle and try to bond, they keep trying to fit their core being into the doctrine, until a limit is reached. Still, guilt and doubt, follow many. It is a painfully lost feeling to have been told something is the only way your whole life, and then must reject part or all of that way. It can leave someone flailing without a base. Of course, that hook, "The only way," is part of what is the basic blueprint of most religions, it is even what pushes some people's aggression to both defend and to recruit, and to kill another human. But many are tired of the singularity their religion preaches, and it confuses them. It is not making sense to many: their next-door neighbors are Muslim or Hindu, they are raising a beautiful, respectful family. They share their food and you are loving their cuisine, the wife cut your grass for two months when you broke your leg. They brought you groceries during the ice storm when you couldn't get out, but what my religion tells me is they will go to hell for not worshiping my God? No wonder people are confused and Omnism is on the rise.

Teenagers, oh my goodness, the way the teenagers want answers is so beautifully passionate. Once they see they will not be judged for questioning or shamed for not blindly accepting everything they are handed, they admit confusion and frustration just as fast. Then they turn to those they trust to help them with their screaming internal confusions. They share with me their confusion between what they are told, what their bodies and beings are screaming at them, and what they are seeing in their house of worship compared to the actions they see in society also causes them to question. Talk about being stuck between a rock and a hard place, for both the teen with their big picture questions, and me being questioned.

I never want to contradict the doctrine of their parents, so I say to them the same thing a helpful person said to me when I was a mid-teen and asking these questions. It was the simplest, wisest religious statement ever made to me, "Religion and spirituality are something you have to figure out for yourself." I asked further after hearing that far too simple and way too vague for a fifteen-year-old. I asked for even just a little more clarification. I remember every word, "Okay, let me put it this way then, religion and spirituality are something you have to figure out for yourself." For the most part, other than validating their great questions, that is all I pass on, too. It's not my place to answer those questions for someone else. It is why a little cafeteria style is probably the wisest for many. It may be a major contributing factor to why I see the cafeteria religious at such greater levels of peace and acceptance. It also may be a contributing factor to why I see cafeteria practitioners showing actions to words with greater consistency, ease, and follow-through. Guilt and fear should never be a part of leaving something that has become unhealthy for you, even religion. That can be easier said than done, when so many religions have instilled such deeply rooted guilt and fear that we will be lost if we leave.

Since my youth, one of the main issues that was personally upsetting to me was how autonomous independent thought was suppressed. I also had trouble believing that good people get sent to bad places for being normal humans. Such as the number of teenagers who have asked me if it is really a sin to masturbate. That is one of the few questions I will answer. No, it is not a sin to learn how your body works and enjoy a little pleasure. Yes, any, and all, sexual outlets can become an addiction, but almost anything can get away from us and become an addiction. Asking someone to follow doctrine and suppress their independent autonomous thought to question has never sat right with me. A teenager once asked me if it was true what her church had taught her in a "Marriage" class for teenagers. She said they taught her she can only have one-thousand orgasms in her life, and not to waste them on masturbation. When I told her that was not true, she said, "Good, I was scared I only had a hundred so left."

The immediate rewards of doing the right thing for the right reason

Are good people really bad, wrong, or going to a hell for being alive and not doing too bad a job of walking through life fairly peacefully? If we have all made mistakes that hurt ourselves and others, if someone's sexuality can be called a sin, if it is now acceptable to rationalize knowingly spreading lies for political or personal gain, if self-righteous purpose now justifies unfair means, and a male family member can kill his sister for only believing the woman has brought dishonor to the family for falling in love; then who does go to heaven and who gets sent to hell? Does our impetus to do better and to not be selfish and damaging to those around us still need to be a scary hot place at the end of our life? Should we just not be selfish and damaging to others because it is the right thing to do at any given moment?

For too many, hell is here on Earth. Our words and actions, or our lack of actions or words, is what brings us our hell. The largest and most blatant example is prison. A lesser example, but still real, is the loss of a weekend due to unkind words between a couple on a Friday. Even the criminals you think don't pay, or the intelligent narcissist you think gets away with every selfish action they inflict on those around them, have their own hell on earth. I have known those people, poor or rich, who pay with one of the greatest hells that could ever be self-inflicted: the waste of a beautiful, precious short life.

During my years in emergency nursing, it was not uncommon for me to work with large numbers of in-custody or incarcerated people. Being the teaching hospital in the region, we were usually responsible for evaluating and clearing any trauma that occurred before or during an arrest before they could go to central booking and lock-up. We also were normally the facility state and federal prisons had a contract with to treat those incarcerated who had higher levels of care required than a prison infirmary could handle. I had a standard that I never asked someone what they were in for. We would often know why someone had just been arrested, because it was either significant to the care, or it was volunteered by the person or officer. My role was to nurse them through an illness or injury, not to ask about their incarceration. Most of these people really enjoyed open discussion, as open as it could be with a guard in the room. I broke my own rule once around year eighteen because the person was just so articulate, funny, and out there. You could tell even the guards genuinely liked this person. It got the best of me, and I asked. The person answered so completely, what, where, why, and how, followed by remorse. The only thing I am going to share with you is it was an instant crime of passion and the last thing they said, "If I could only get that moment back, I would, because it wasn't worth this."

I have had many amazing conversations with incarcerated people. Although I wouldn't ask them the reason they were in prison, I did enjoy having them teach me about other angles of their lives, thought processes, influences, and hardships. So rich with views and experiences from other directions than my medium middle class, down the middle of the road life. They could feel I was talking to the person and not their convicted self. I have experienced some of the most heartfelt words of appreciation and goodbyes parting ways with a handful of these people when they were discharged, especially the ones that trusted me. They had gone from one of our hells on earth, where they can never drop their shoulders, to a safer environment, where, for a few minutes or hours in the emergency department, or days in the ICU, where they could have conversations and not be judged. I would never ask direct questions about their religious or spiritual views in relation to their crime, but I would ask open-ended questions about influences on their lives. They often brought up religion, some stated positive and some negative, I say half and half on that.

The few times I had discussions with people incarcerated for a life term, the conversations were quite different from any other conversations I had in all of life. Once someone is removed from society for the rest of their lives, they no longer feel a need to filter a conversation. These rawer talks reinforced my belief that the immediate positive rewards or negative consequences of an action are a far greater motivation to many than eventual eternal punishment or reward of an afterlife. It reinforces the minute-to-minute positive reasons to do the right thing because it brings goodness to this very moment and then to our tomorrows. Or, if it is a negative action or statement, it may bring an immediate or soon-to-follow negative consequence, such as the fear of being caught or the lies that must be lived. Even if someone is a drain on others, such as a psychological or physical abuser, criminal, or the abusively high-level narcissist, and never goes to prison or receives the general consequences, they are still paying. Instead of the courts or other textbook consequences handing down a tangible punishment, their self-inflicted punishment consists of paying for their actions with parts of their being, the loss of a full healthy life experience, a plethora of inward and outwards lies, and some level of dampened exploration of their life due to the manipulation required to carry out their ways. It may look like losing great partners in relationships one after the other, self-inflicted business or occupational issues, or self-inflicted anxieties that are eating away a part of their being or life. People that lie and thieve are doing the same to themselves. The level of convincing one may have to tell themselves to justify their cunning actions alone, is a self con. The size of a home and boat are only material gains, not a guaranteed heaven on earth, but if those material gains are bought with ill-gotten gains, they are also a lie.

We may want the person who stole our tools from our garage, the cunning online scammer who cons our elderly, or the thieving business artist to be caught and punished. Yet, even if they are never caught, they still receive consequences. Even if they never become self-honest enough to allow themselves to be aware of their own self-inflicted punishments. We all know at least one of these people, possibly hiding behind their religion, a con artist on many levels, using others, who often appears to be doing well on the surface. These people are sometimes rather charismatic, convincing to many, and often manipulate religious ideology to aid their self-appointed piety, even though they are basic thieves. They will carelessly use people for personal gain for much of their life.

Most of these people have other abilities to make a living, but they waste life and energy convincing themselves what and why they are doing it is justified. Just like the really bad employee, they often spend far more energy walking that far off the path to carry out their ways than just staying on the path in the first place. It is often a steep rocky path, too. We all end up with some hell on earth that is not cause and effect from doing wrongs. Such as our fluctuating level of normal mental peace alone is an example, my severe depression when younger was a hell on earth. But many actively choose to create hell for themselves, and others, with a life of selfish choices. We all know these people. Although most of the people I had met enforcing court orders for twelve years were good people tangled up in the courts, a percentage of them were these exact cunning thieves. It always amazed me how much energy some people will spend convincing themselves, and me, during our first introduction. Self boasting that they are wonderful people, and often telling me of their deep religious convictions in the first few minutes. In those twelve years, and a few thousand cases, I saw clear patterns of initial pious statements followed by their avoidance to meet the responsibility of the court order against them. It was a painful consistent correlation to witness repetitively.

Unrelated to the people that quickly told me of their religious convictions, was a different type of consequence in life for one's actions. Periodically I would find a lack of up-to-date addresses combined with blatantly avoidance to meet with me. Even though I had one phone call with them, and they knew they were not in criminal trouble with me. That combination is a red flag often indicating extensive civil litigation history against this person. I would then have no choice but to fall back on knocking on family members' doors to track them down. Too often their own families would directly verbalize, or indirectly but clearly indicate, very little respect for the person I was trying to locate. Often grown children or parents were protecting themselves from their own parent or adult child; that alone is a hell on earth consequence for life choices. I have much proof that staying on the path is easier and rewarding.

I once had a defendant who took weeks to agree to meet with me in a coffee shop. After about fifteen minutes of discussing the court order, and the person fully realizing I only wanted to help them get the issue out of their life, they admitted fatigue of the huge amount of energy spent living a life to avoid paying the civil case they had lost in court. This person admitted to me how difficult their life was because of this chosen lifestyle. Admitted to losing track of who they really are and talked of the daily fatigue wasted on the negative rather than using good energy on the positive they knew they could create. It doesn't have to be a big grandiose bad, we all experience a powerful consequence, even little parts of our life wasted in even momentary short self-created jails without physical walls. It is the immediate consequence of a negative. It may be a small and not so great action that your conscience is now working with, or it may be someone's poor or unjust treatment of us. It most often just looks like thinking about it for minutes, hours, or days.

Past the thought of self-review to learn from whatever happened, even if you have zero responsibility but want to evaluate to prevent in the future, past that review we are giving up a part of us and our life.

This happens to my mind too; I also have thoughts that keep re-entering. Using this awareness helps me to shut it down faster, then I get me and my peace back sooner. My spinning thoughts do not magically go away the second I remember this gem, but it moves me into "letting-it-go" thoughts, because it has already occurred, and I can no longer change what happened. Maybe prevent or decrease in the future because of reviewing to learn, and then I get my moments back. I think reviewing to learn, with learning being the key step, speeds up healthy functional "processing" to let something go sooner.

What may have the higher-level bad actors accomplished had they used their charisma, intelligence, and energy turned into productivity and social contribution? I have known many who have proved it is never too late. The open and trusting person who admitted fatigue in the coffee shop chose to work with me! After over ten years of playing the game to avoid paying a six-figure judgment, which they admitted they owed, and all the negative consequences that go with having a judgment on your record; they made a percentage offer on the six-figure judgment. The plaintiff accepted the offer, I collected, and they walked out of their no-wall ten years self-incarceration.

I saw this person years later, they joyfully shared that by removing the judgment from their record, everything got easier, including finally being able to get a business loan to start a now healthy, thriving business. This person got honest and resolved their self-inflicted hell on earth, creating immediate positive rewards. What are some of your smaller to medium self-incarcerations in your day: anger with other drivers or poor service, or maybe allowing something a coworker, family member, or our partner says to take away our joy or moment?

Immediate rewards and consequences

People break the rules and laws of society for many reasons. Hunger and basic human needs, such as shelter, must always be stated first, and I respect that basic need. After basic human needs comes a few of the other reasons people will commit crimes or break the expected standards of a civilized society. As I have shared, a few of those categories are excitement and pleasure, greed, feelings of entitlement, addiction, and even an addiction to the rush of committing various levels of crime. This also covers only a few of the wide range of reasons why some people will do the wrong thing, knowing they are doing the wrong thing, but can rationalize the behavior as justified. Once we rationalize, we often no longer feel we are doing the wrong thing. There are a few people who have a part of their equally imperfect 80 billion-neuron-cell brains that just does not register right from wrong, or even concepts of guilt or remorse.

There is such a range for the reasons some people will steal tools from your ten-minute open garage, or the package thieves canvassing for packages on the front porch, to the habitually dangerous and aggressive driver, all the way to the business world's million-dollar deals that are not as moral or ethical as the textbooks on those subjects discuss. I have been reminded of this range of reasons in conversations with incarcerated people, especially as a nurse, on several occasions hearing something near, "Don't ever forget, I just got caught. We the incarcerated are only a small percentage of those stealing from the top to the bottom." Then I am informed, "Don't be fooled. What I am about to tell you is how most people who don't care about using others were raised and think."

Some of the more common influences these incarcerated people have shared are that they were raised with pessimism, neglect, or abuse of some form, a lack of any positive words or healthy rewards, sadly often given nicknames at a very young age to denote trouble or an inconvenience to the parents, such as "Here comes Trouble," "She's just such a little bossy brat," or "Little Hellion." They admitted frequent insults and put-downs were not uncommon, even by parents, teachers, and foster parents. A small percentage admitted to sexual assault, but we all know some do not talk about it. If religion was presented in their life, it was often misused, extreme, or not backed up with consistent positive actions.

Most said their parents openly talked about using others in some form. I have spoken to people of all cultures and walks of life, poor and wealthy, races across the board, young and old; a moderate percentage stated an early need to steal to help feed the family or admitted to often being hungry. However, many told of coming from families that met all their basic needs easily. But the one common theme that ran though most of these talks, was no real fear of the afterlife consequence. They either did not believe in the concept, or they did not care or worry about it. Many would share something close to, "It can't be any worse than my life has been and is."

Your spirituality and your own moral compass

The foundation of all religions is to help us with individual morality, societal ethical development, and general goodness. The core of what all religions teach is to be good, treat yourself and others well, and you will be rewarded. But our times have greatly changed, and the numbers show fewer people are following an organized religion. Although the numbers trend up in underdeveloped regions of the world, the numbers are trending down in developed parts of the world. This means the religious motivations to do the right thing in many parts of the world are losing their powers of persuasion. No matter what is occurring with the world of religions, or how distant you may feel from organized religion, remaining a spiritual being within, and doing the right things for the right reasons, as often as we imperfect humans can, is a constant that can both supply and drive continuous healthy motivation and support. Our internal autonomous spirituality creates a constant self-rewarding drive. Do the right thing and something good happens right away or soon, do the wrong thing and something bad happens right away or soon, or we pay for it by compromising your greater potential self.

Our world, and the mindset of the people inhabiting it, is constantly changing. Religions have their fluctuating issues; a percentage of human manipulation will always be there. But our autonomously developed spirituality is something that cannot be swayed by the flux or pressures of the external world, or the manipulation of anyone with selfish motives. If we each build an autonomous functional spiritual philosophy that is built of our own foundation blocks of goodness, that we can completely understand and accept, then that solid base walks with us every minute of our day. If your spirituality is built from the foundation of your chosen religion, that will always be with you. If it is not for gain or manipulation, then there is no need to question, challenge, or reject parts of our own spirituality that you build for yourself. Our independent spirituality is steady, solid goodness that is unwavering to bring ourselves and the world around us peace, productivity, and safety. Your own spirituality will never take or talk you out of anything.

No matter what your religion, or your level of devotion to it, or the percentage of acceptance of its philosophy you feel; the choice to develop, strengthen, and practice your own spirituality will not only enhance your chosen religion, but will hold true no matter what your religion or your feelings towards it do. When your religion is not creating a consistent relationship between the philosophy and its actions or omissions, then your spirituality will help create greater consistency, or at least bring you increased peace in the wake of personal religious discord. Or, if you have turned completely away from religion, nurturing your spirituality will still walk on with you, if you welcome it. I hope you will never stop developing and leaning on your spirituality for strength and goodness.

However, it is definitely something you have to figure out for yourself.

God's Spiritual Forest and The Maps of Religions

My subjective expression, just my truths, not facts
The actual paths of my life and spiritual journey
Laid down for all, to be interpreted by each
By the loving, giving, non-judging hands of your God

God has asked of us to walk these trails
To grow, to experience, to give back
To experience the joy of giving than receiving love

Many wise and wonderful humans have explored and charted these vast,
endless, complex, yet simple worlds of spiritual pathways
Their time and efforts, thousands of years of theological discussion, shared
through the written and spoken word
I have no doubt helped more than hindered our collective consciousness
These charts and maps are only the representations of the endless and
ever-changing forest of God's expression

The maps are by humans, the forest is by God
Humans, all so fallible
I believe God inspired these brave people, but I do not feel God stood
behind these explorers to say, "The path turns sharper here" or "Do not go
off the path to see the beautiful flowers there"

These maps can be valuable
They give us a general understanding of the spiritual wilderness
They hold our hands in our youth, or times of weakened being
The less we fall, till we have the coordination that comes with individual, firsthand experience on these balanced, beautiful, yet perilous trails designed by God, known as our life.

I feel God's interest, awareness, observations of me, as a being, on this journey has much more to do with my interactions and experiences with the forest.
Not my intricate understanding of the maps.
Am I respecting the forest
How can I do better

My God first wants to know I have food, water, shelter, rest, and love along the path of my life
God wants that for all, and wants all to help provide for each other
To know I will not rush through a field of flowers, but will walk, smell, touch, and experience the glorious expressions….
This is what is on my God's map

To know I will not rip up the flowers mindlessly
But will experience them with respect, love, and appreciation for what a flower truly signifies in all its majesty.
That is what is on my God's map

To know in daily life, I will not use the gifts laid out for me, even the human ones, consciously or unconsciously, for my own selfish goals.
That too is on my God's map

My God wants me to become gracious and conscious
To do the work from my heart, from love, from giving
God wants me to walk off the path, experience the woods, pick some
flowers, swim in the river, and gather for my needs
God expects my energy will be used, but replaces it with more
Contributing to goodness is how I show my deepest appreciation

The maps are by humans
The forest is by God
I respect the maps
Yet I am walking the trails
I am walking my spiritual paths
I am standing in God's Forest

1997

CHAPTER 11

ADDICTIONS AND THEIR CONTROL, PULL, AND DESTRUCTION

Please always work to reduce, or hopefully stop, your addictions if they are negatively affecting your life. Very few of us do not have one or a few. Some can be seemingly trivial, but they still may have a negative influence on you and disrupting others. Or they can be outright dangerous. In one way or another, they rob us all, inside and out, of every aspect of our being. At least attempt to reduce if you think or feel you should quit. Seek help if needed. There is not a generation that isn't affected by addiction, whether at nine or ninety, they can grab you. Don't beat yourself up for becoming aware and realizing something has control of you; life is hard and painful too. Wanting and hoping to numb the bad and cruel parts with something, anything to ease the scary. I can understand the want. Work to not allow your addiction to become your consolation prize for all the bad, or even a reward to celebrate a success, food being one of our favorites. Moderation is an attainable goal for those hourly in our face ones, such as scrolling, purchasing, and food.

Addictions are so widespread: sugar, dating, gaming, watching the news, even anger and hatred can become an addiction. Be gentle with your messy humanness, find pride in learning to be honest with yourself about it, "it" being whatever addictions you have within your grasp and have their grasp on you. If needed, find an angle to obtain pride in all that makes up your past, present, and your future, including accepting your good and forgiving yourself for your mistakes. You are not bad because bad happened to you. The lack of pride in ourselves is one of the contributing factors to our addictions; so, attempt to break that vicious negative cycle that adds to the bad pull and learn to love yourself. Know that trying to obtain perfection can even become an addiction. Grant yourself permission to build your pride; because all actions that build self-esteem strengthens us further against our addictions.

Please commit to never letting suicide be a choice while addicted or acutely depressed, as that is the addiction or the emotion killing a person. When suicide happens while addicted or depressed, it is really the addiction murdering the spirit first and then the body. Addictions and emotions often kill off parts of our body and mind, whittling down our spirit before they finish us off. Please seek help if you even maybe, kind of, sort of could use it.

Meeting yourself without addictions can be hard and unsettling at first, but the stronger self is worth the initial hard unsettling break from its grasp. Because addictions are a problem in every community in the world, you are not as alone as you may be feeling. If you can't get a hold of it yourself, ask a medical or addiction specialist, or some of the many supportive groups; either they will help you or give you multiple referrals for where you can find help.

You are not alone, please reach out.

WIDER ANGLES

WE TRY TO SLEEP WHILE HOLDING ON

I had an idea that choosing to work twelve-hour weekend nights for twenty-one years would mess up my circadian sleep rhythm, but I was surprised to discover that it would destroy it. I handled it fairly well for the first fifteen years, then it was a little harder for another two to three years. Around year eighteen, I didn't have a messed up circadian rhythm, I no longer had one. By my late twenties, these well-earned dark bags under my eyes might have well been tattoos.

As you know, right out of nursing school, I went to work in one of the most violent emergency departments in this country and all hell broke loose with my inability to sleep. The assault on my rest was multi-directional. My mother could not comprehend that calling me at two o'clock in the afternoon "just to talk" correlated to 2 in the morning for her. I was able to get her to stop by calling her one night from work at 2 a.m. She answered sleepily, immediately worried something bad had happened to me or one of her other five offspring. When I told her, "I just called to talk," it accomplished the goal. She never woke me up again.

I learned the basics to a better day's sleep. I would force myself to find the energy to eat little complex carbohydrates and protein before sleeping, but to stay away from simple sugars. That greatly helped me through the day's sleep—no more low blood sugar crashes a few hours into my rest. I also stayed hydrated during the shift but stopped drinking around 4 a.m. or so. Of course, closing out as much light as possible was important too.

Then I had to deal with the violence and sheer number of patients that invaded my dreams those first few years. The bad ones stemmed from the barrage of assaults, shootings, and stabbings we cared for every twelve-hour shift. Most nights, we would treat four to seven penetrating traumas. On a bad night, eight to ten sometimes if it was a hot humid summer night and intolerance for humanness abounded. Often it was drug turf wars or payback for previous shootings. A few nights were so bad that we had to take the bodies off the "roller" (stretchers or gurneys as the rest of the country calls them) because we needed the roller for another patient and the morgue attendant had not been fast enough keeping up with the transports. I started to have dreams where I was about to be assaulted or killed, slightly disruptive to this young man's sleep. Bullet entry wounds are not always a big visual deal, however, exit wounds can be what nightmares are made of.

The dreams that inspired me the most to develop some strategies for a better night's sleep was a near constant occurrence on the adult medical side of the department. Hospitals from much of the region would transfer patients to us, both for advanced care. A percentage we were not always sure why they were transferred. Funny because aside from the latest knowledge and the ability to handle high patient volume, there was nothing advanced about the physical plant. It was a nineteenth-floor concrete "behemoth," as it was referred to, that was more cave-like and archaic than "advanced." The medical side received so many transfers that the EMS stretchers would line up in the center aisle, like jets waiting to take off from a busy airport, one after the other, waiting for a bed to open. It was the only hospital in my career where I worked that the EMS transport team would not start complaining if they had to wait more than ten minutes to unload a patient. Quite the opposite. They would sometimes have to wait an hour or two for a bed to open. I've seen EMS teams have a pizza delivered while they waited.

It was that line of EMS stretchers invading my dreams that forced me to come up with a plan. I would be sleeping and start to dream that my little bedroom, two blocks toward the river from Saint Charles Avenue on Constantinople Street, would fill up with these stretchers. I am trying to sleep, and I am dreaming there are three or four stretchers and EMTs surrounding my bed, expecting me to help open beds so they can unload and exit my bedroom to go back to transport another patient. I would attempt to tell myself to ignore them, "Vincent, you have to sleep, they are not your responsibility, just ignore them and sleep." That didn't work, and it all culminated the day I dreamed one of the EMS teams was unloading their patient into my bed!

I spent the next two shifts talking with my work mates to see if that happened to them and derived a strategy to keep the line of stretchers out of my bedroom. Since locking the door had proven ineffective. Most of my colleagues admitted to some level of disruption to their sleep, due to roughing up every aspect of our being and spirit by working in that emergency department. The place was so bad that if we were dangerously short-staffed, the house supervisor would send us an ICU nurse from one of the units upstairs to help us get through a twelve-hour shift. Before we would send them to lunch, we would beg them to come back after they ate. A huge percentage of nurses that floated down to help us would not come back after lunch and would tell the house supervisor they would rather be fired than return.

I developed a technique that to this day has helped me. I told myself that my rest is like walking into a dark forest that is safe, the perfect temperature, cozy. The path leading into the dark forest of sleep is an important part. It is a beautiful path with ferns and flowers on the side, well-worn, level, and quiet. Walking this beautiful hobbit-like path is what calms the turbulence of the day, and all of life's stressors. As I get closer to the forest, as the trees get taller and larger so they can protect me once I let go and enter rest. I see the dark gets darker, but it is a safe, calm, secure, dark. But wait, I still have the shift and life vibrating in my head.

Here is the part that took away the stretchers, the patient in my bed, the violent dreams, and the general vibration of all of life's roughs. As I got older those "life's roughs" expanded into bigger worries to disrupt my sleep, such as parents aging, financial responsibilities, friends and family having crises, and my own wasted time of rerunning old episodes of my self-inflicted mistakes or of the injustices done to me. It all wanted my needed and important sleep disrupted. In those discussions with my teammates, I realized many of us are trying to carry a big old heavy sack of problems, fears, and stressors into our night's sleep. That helped me realize we cannot get optimal sleep cooking and stirring our problems while we attempt to sleep. We certainly cannot fix, resolve, or even effectively problem-solve during attempted rest, and most definitely not if we are experiencing repetitive sleep deprivation, because we are mulling, fretting, worried, and anxious over our sack of stressors, worries, and fears. So don't sleep on your problems, but rather set them down first.

I began to imagine myself walking that calming path, carrying a big heavy burden and stress-filled sack over my shoulder, slightly leaning forward because of the weight of my life's troubles filling the sack. But I can't effectively sleep if I take those stressors into the forest. Another positive is, if I get a great rest, I will be able to deal with them with greater strength and clarity in the morning because I slept without holding, looking at, and mulling them over, when sleeping is a healthier choice. Like most of us, if you carry a heavy sack into your rest, or you just don't sleep well, maybe give this a go for several nights in a row, so it has a chance to settle in. Perhaps place a note next to your bed to remind you. After you turn out the lights, start by designing your own quiet calm path to your thick, dark, safe forest. Walk on your path with ferns and flowers covering the sides, it's soft and quiet beneath your feet. As you get closer to the forest, roll the sack off your shoulder. Just set it down off to the side, hidden down in the ferns. It is and will always be only your path, no one is going to take it. I have always wanted someone to take my sack, so my worries would be gone, but that can't happen because no one else will ever be on my path. Who would want my nasty sack of worries anyway? It will be there in the morning; we can pick it up then and restart worrying again after slinging it back onto my shoulder for the day. Better yet, hopefully we won't pick it up and worry, but rather we will start problem-solving what is in that sack with a rested slightly clear*er* head. That delineation is helpful since the concept of worry itself has never solved a single stress or problem in my life, only awareness and action accomplished that. But at night, envision yourself leaning to one side and the sack rolls off your shoulder, nestled down in the ferns and flowers. Such weight is left behind while you release and recharge for your body and your entire being. Take a few breaths, readjust your body slightly to further fine tune your comfort. Now walk into the woods for your night's rest without fears, injustices, and worries. You and the importance of our sleep are worth more than that sack of burdens.

If I am not asleep shortly after quietly walking into the calm forest, I'll imagine a physical sensation rather than a visual image. I will imagine I have no bones. No ability to hold a supported form, to the point I am not laying on the bed, but rather the bed is now holding me up. Accepting that I cannot move, relaxed, heavy, heavy, I then go under and sleep.

"Going under," is another helpful term for calm sleep. It's not good to sleep on top of the storms and stressors of your life. There is no need to ride on top of them, like trying to stay on a bucking bronco all night. Let them buck away up there above in the turbulent storm of life, while you go under into the dark calm of sleep. I found myself calming every time I reread to fine-tune these last three paragraphs Perhaps for a sleep meditation, reread these last three paragraphs just before turning the lights out for a few nights in a row, or when sleep is evading you. Allow yourself to go under for the good of your wellness, rest, and rejuvenation for your next day. Under you go, calm, beautiful, cozy, quiet, and safe . . . Zzzzzzzzzzzzz . . .

CHAPTER 12

NOOOOOO, NOT POLITICS!

"No problem can be solved from the same level that created it."
—Albert Einstein

They sacrificed, they risked, they planned for every angle they could think of, and they knew they would need our help to keep it going.

It is September 1787. Benjamin Franklin is leaving Independence Hall in Philadelphia after signing the Constitution of the United States. He is asked, "What type of government have you created for us?" He replied, "We have built you a republic." Mr. Franklin then added an equally important line: "Now, let us see if you can keep it."

"... And to the *Republic* for which it stands..."

Understanding the difference between a republic and a total democracy is critical to the safe maintenance of a stable and thriving society. I write using the words "paramount," "critical," "most," and any other repetitive words my limited mind can throw out to press important information. But this time, my use of the word critical, is critical, to the peace and longevity of not only the United States, but to every country experiencing political and social unrest. Although the United States will be referenced often, this chapter is about the contribution of our thoughts, attitudes, actions, and inactions in relation to government, politics, politicians, and the peace, stability, and longevity of a society.

In this case, "critical" goes one step past just understanding how a government is set up and how it works. The application of that understanding and the difference between a democracy and a republic into your daily actions is equally critical. It is not only the duty of the government to protect you and your rights. It is also the people's responsibility to protect the government between the times we vote. "If you can keep it," means you have a job to do also. Almost every government, in every culture, has issues that are not so easy to solve. One way to slowly and quietly take a government off track is to bastardize it with many slight changes to protect the ideology, special interest, or greed of a few, placed above protecting the balanced republic. A balanced republic means long-term peace, profit, and productivity for we the people.

History has shown time and again a republic will provide longer lasting and greater levels of peace and personal freedom over an unchecked "majority rules" democracy alone. We are a democratic republic because "we the people" elect our representatives. Our republic gives us far more personal freedom than the loud, angry emotions we hear and feel when some people or news outlets tell us about how bad it is. Some are trying to tell us that our system is not working, which is completely wrong and can be extremely dangerous. The attempted emotional manipulation of our thoughts and actions is trying to lead us to believe that what we have in our current government is bad and wrong. If we continue to allow ourselves to be led by unchecked emotions and blatant manipulations, we are going to lose one of the most well thought-out and well-balanced governments ever written in the history of larger groups of humans. All we need to do is slow down our emotions, increase our rational thoughts, decrease the misleading for the purpose of *excessive* self-gain, and give our country a little overhaul. Then, as Benjamin Franklin stated, "If you can keep it," will become "and we kept it." If our Founders did so much for us, should we not do this for them, for us, and for those who follow? They cared for us over 250 years before we were born. We need more people from every generation and every walk of life that will also do what is right for government stability. Which is a foundation block for our day-to-day stability, and our children's tomorrows.

Our Founders were not perfect, they bickered and divided. Yet, at the time they wrote the US Constitution, they, for the most part, placed their personal financial needs aside and accomplished creating one of the most stable, checked, and balanced governments ever created. Some might say they failed because the atrocity of slavery was initially protected, and woman could not vote. However, as wrong as those two are, those were acceptable norms of the times. Well, at least acceptable to the sector of society that was benefiting from these wrongs. What I am approaching here is a question to you and to society. If the Founders, for the most part, could place their own lives and personal financial self-gain on the line to form this country, can we place even a fraction of our personal financial advancement aside to get this large and amazing beast of a government, society, and thus county, back on the more solid rails which it was built?

I could not have asked for a more accurate, or modern-times appropriate, example to be handed to me than this following. Between the time I initially wrote this paragraph and this last edit, the US Congress started to debate whether a seated member should be allowed to trade stocks. This is a huge issue, basically summing up one of the issues in this chapter. They do have the ability to influence some of those investments for self-gain over what is the right choice for the stability of the government, the people, and the right choice for the right reasons. Statistically speaking alone, whether you are in government or big business, always protecting only momentary profit over longevity and the right choice for the right reason cannot possibly be the best solution for all and tomorrow. We are very capable of seeing and acting on actions that create stability and longevity. It requires unselfish, big picture, futuristic thoughts and actions. The founders of the US proved it can be done for us. Can we do it for future generations as they did?

Ego, power, and profit are some of the more dangerous contributing motivators to pulling social and governmental stability and longevity down initially, and they remain powerful motivators to not want to see a government look for and decrease its areas of room for improvement. All forms of government can always improve their good, right, and fair to higher levels; good over gain is all that is required. Let me ask you a sensitive and self-honesty critical question. If you were sitting in any branch of government or corporation, on any level, in any country, and you had to vote on a policy, bill, law, or decision, and pushing one button would pass a law or policy to promote the peace, profit, and stability of your country and its people, or pushing the other button would further your financial standings, but not help your country and its people; which button would you push?

Part of the United States' republic being created, and its maintenance, involves parts of the democratic process, we vote and the majority rules. This is why the US is referred to as a democratic republic. Looking at a few positive actions that will aid if sustainability is the goal of the formation and maintenance of a government. First, the majority needs to create the rules and vote, with goodness and fairness for all guiding them. Again, if stability is the goal, not only profit and personal gain, then the people must follow those rules, which includes everyone, to the best of human ability and circumstance. Continuing, we must work to maintain those rules where each of us does our part. Lastly, if those rules or policies do need to be changed, the people responsible for making those changes do so for the good of the people and the health of tomorrow. Not their own personal gain, after all, we elected them to represent us, not to represent their financial stability or reelection. The Founders of the US showed, as you will hear, by extreme personal example, that to be a quality representative of the people, only the personal sacrifice of greed and selfish actions are required. Although we are not completely free to do as we please for common sense reasons, we do not have to give up that sacred trinity that a healthy society is formed to protect—life, liberty, and the pursuit of happiness. However, it does not mean you are free to storm our nation's capital, destroy it, bring in restraining zip ties and weapons, assault the officers attempting to protect your federal capital, and be led by emotional unconstitutional speeches filled with uncaring unstable rhetoric about your constitutional rights, just because your candidate did not win. Every four years, a substantial percentage of the US does not get their candidate elected, they grieve, accept, often hyper-ridicule and judge the winner during their term, then hopefully continue to meet their responsibilities as citizens of a free country. It also means we do not allow candidates, or news outlets, to stir us up until we vote with our emotions rather than our wiser, more solution-based rational thought process. Between our votes we do all have serious responsibilities to each other and our government.

Not only is this type of manipulation of the people not freedom, but it actively damages the freedoms that you have been granted. Some see only the sacrifice of young lives during physical threats of war or to protect peace and freedom, but we the citizens also must make some sacrifice to keep a country or community, or even a relationship strong and healthy. Law enforcement's first job, immediately after protecting themselves when they can, is to protect your rights and freedoms granted to you by the Constitution, its twenty-seven amendments, and all the laws and court cases that followed. That responsibility was drilled into us in the academy. I had to pass forty exams in six months to graduate from the academy, and questions about the US Constitution were on a great many of those exams, as well as the state board exam. I was highly trained to protect your rights. I vow to you now that I will continue to work to do so as I write this chapter, just as I worked to protect your healthcare rights in *Suffer Less in Death*. I take my oaths to be an advocate for the people seriously. I too am limited to human fallibility and the skewing of our incapable of perfection human perceptions, as are you, but I vow to do my best. Please remember, this is the other chapter I did not want to write. How would you write a chapter on politics to help to the best of your ability?

Cops, your tax dollars, and your life, liberty, and pursuit of happiness

The Dallas shooter on July 7, 2016, reminded the people of officers' sacrifice on film. News crews and personal videos caught something on camera that depicted police doing what the public often forgets they do for your trinity of rights. This happened at a march, standing up to police shootings. At 8:58 p.m., the gunman started shooting police officers, killing five and wounding nine others. What the videos showed is hundreds of people wisely running away from the gunfire, but in contrast, and trained to do their job, we also saw the officers running towards the gunfire. Officers, soldiers, and periodically brave citizens sometimes must risk their lives in the name of freedom and the actual protection of life. Such as the citizens of Flight 93 on September 11, 2001. A major aspect of the maintenance of a free democratic republic, and the health of all communities, is that we, the citizens, also must sacrifice on hopefully only lower levels to contribute to the daily functioning of that free society. For example, when you are pulled over for potentially infringing on the freedoms of others to safely reach their destination, you are being pulled over for breaking a law. Yet, the bigger picture of that law, and the reasons the police run towards gunfire, is to protect all citizen's right to life, liberty, and the pursuit of happiness. I say, "all citizens", as opposed to only the ones driving near you, because crashes cost taxpayers and everyone's time, money, and sometimes deep grief.

Every year in the US alone there are: six-million crashes, three-million injured, and ninety people die every twenty-four hours. If you drive, you are one of 230-million drivers in the US.

A good and just officer is not harassing you for pulling you over for violating a traffic law. They are doing the job they have been trained and hired to do, to protect. You are right, not coming to a full stop at a neighborhood four-way stop sign is most likely not going to kill another person (although, quiet neighborhood vehicular deaths do occur, just as looking at your phone while traveling through a parking lot also kills people). Everything works together and is far more interconnected than may first appear; we all make a difference, and we are all responsible for helping or damaging each part of the government. It is kind of hard to be angry at "the government" when it is also our responsibility to build, maintain, and protect that government.

The complexity of our political problems and then finding and implementing solutions is so multifaceted due to the social dynamics of these sensitive subjects, with endless influences, and the emotions that go with them. Since law enforcement falls under the Executive branch of the US government, is paid for by tax dollars, and I did enter the field to not only contribute to society but also to study it from the inside out, I am going to continue to use it as a political example of the many angles of cause, effect, and solution.

We do have uncalled-for shootings in this country and around the world. There are approximately one-hundred-forty thousand annually shootings in the US alone. After my years of conversations with law enforcement, I feel safe to say police officers would prefer to retire without ever having to shoot someone, and statistically the great majority do retire without having shot anyone. Even highly justified shootings can damage the life and livelihood of that officer and their family. This is a subject with deep and wide ramifications that stir deep emotions from all groups. However, this social and political issue is an excellent example and opportunity to bring such intense emotional and complex problems into the rational part of our brains to find more angles of mutual responsibility, finding better, longer-lasting solutions, and to decrease all sides from reacting from emotions only. George Floyd was murdered, and his death had nothing to do with protecting the life of a police officer. Yet, that has no bearing on the fact that in other situations, people will kill police officers, and there would be more murdered police if they had not fired their weapon first. I have seen far too many dashcam videos of cops being killed because they were a split second too late. If the officer is fired at first, or their life is actively in danger by powerful, skilled physical force, or another type of weapon, then it becomes self-defense. It is imperative to remember an officer's life can be in danger by an unarmed person. Not resisting a clear and appropriate order, which is an authority granted to police by the people, is also a responsibility of the citizens of a free society. It is against the law to resist a lawful order by an officer, the republic made that law, meaning the will of the people made that law. Not following it is also a form of social chaos. Even if you feel you have done nothing wrong, at that moment the officer most likely has a bigger picture than you. That is why our Founders created a three-branch, and thus a three-point system of checks and balances. Unfortunately, it has failed many times and many people, but that is often a failure of the people making up the moving parts of the system, not the system itself. Although it needs some fine-tuning to rebalance, and always will, our government is not our problem.

Every branch and angle of all governments have room for improvement, accepting and investing self and resources into that is a cornerstone of professionalism will help. Always strive for better, not necessarily easier or more profitable, although with time easier and long-term profit is often a result of achieving better. There is no one group or groups responsible for the chipping away at our republic, and it was done from all directions, the top down and the bottom up. We can all feel, by the tilt we are experiencing, as we walk down the halls of the good ship *The Republic* is indeed listing to one side. Yet not as far as we think, and it can be righted. Preventing and correcting that ship from listing further to one side is an equal responsibility of both the government and its people. After all, balance is the issue when a ship is listing.

I was taught in both the academy and investigation courses in continuing education, that a good cop will work just as hard to prove a person innocent as they will to prove them guilty. If the officers did spend equal time trying to prove guilt and innocence, then most likely a very solid case of guilt will be built once the guilty party is found. With that said, chances are your police interactions are being recorded by the police and possibly by other citizens. If you were wrongfully treated or abused, I highly encourage you to take legal action against the officer or department that wronged you. But if you are resisting or complaining because that officer is appropriately doing their job to keep themselves and others safe, then you are not meeting your responsibility as a citizen of a free country.

Please, do not think I am blindly defending the police, or that I am institutionalized to be on their side because I was in a uniform and a marked police car for those twelve years. Quite the opposite. After working with law enforcement closely in large emergency rooms and riding with them a few times as a civilian observer, talking with officers for hundreds of conversations in the emergency departments, I saw they were headed towards serious trouble long before the George Floyd murder. Although it was the start of change, I was disappointed, but not shocked, that more did not change after the Rodney King beating in 1991. I went into law enforcement for a few reasons at the age of forty-three, one of them being to study it from the inside. I always try to evaluate the many influencing factors on an issue, especially if our mostly subjective humanness is involved. There is no question that multiple influences, attitudes, and actions have created our issues with law enforcement. The relationship between law enforcement and the citizen is only one subgroup of many factors. The bigger picture is all sides are contributing influence on all our governmental and social issues, not just the side of law enforcement. Influences such as the news, social media, entertainment media, including the social injustice levels that are occurring and society's response to those injustices, and of course the actions and attitudes of both law enforcement and citizens. Wrong is wrong no matter who the actor is, but law enforcement, just like every citizen or soldier, has every right to protect themselves too. Police are citizens also, and their rights to further protect themselves as officers of the law are also laid out in the laws of each state. Police officers are already willing to risk their lives for your rights as a citizen, and the citizen's actions should also respect their right to go home at the end of their shift. Because there are so many shades of gray and tough angles to these subjects, accepting that there are no easy answers is a great start to finding deeper and better answers.

The multiple large and small influences whittling away at any issue, especially concerning government, is more encompassing than the actual contributors to an issue care to admit. Even the mostly law-abiding citizen who makes a few blatant dangerous traffic violations that have been clearly recorded by a dashboard camera, perhaps late for an appointment or with children in the car and is late to pick up another child, who then feels they are not a part of the problem to society and berates the officer or fights the ticket in court, has just not met their civic responsibilities. That responsibility looks like helping to supply all of us the freedom of personal safety and not spending your tax dollars by taking it into court to deny the action recorded on the officer's dashboard camera. Please, if you did not do it, fight it, and I hope you win. However, if you committed the violation, own it, pay it, then please pay more attention to meeting that responsibility for everyone's freedom, and drive safer. Thank you to all of you over the years who were able to admit your guilt when you knew you were guilty. Thank you for allowing yourself to be a faulted being, and for meeting your responsibility after you made a mistake or intentionally violated to such a high level that I stopped you. Something seemingly so small is such a great contribution to society, on multiple levels, including to yourself.

Solution-based idea brainstorming

There is so much more than the above citizen responsibility that can be done to further help resolve our police issues. Keep training police to stay alive, but also add in rational thinking training to override emotional responses from fear, anger, or personal bias. I am grateful to have practiced law enforcement in a metropolitan area where all departments did highly train the officers. That training did significantly decrease the issues that need to be addressed. Fear is normal and can be helpful to keep us safe, but acting on it can also be dangerous. Yes, more shades of gray. It would also help to increase education to the public on police interactions. If they don't know why the police do and say some of the things they do, it leaves it up to the public or citizens to fill in the blanks. Create more opportunities for public ride-a-longs, offer free classes to teens and adults to educate and work to change the unhealthy and unproductive attitudes that cops, races, and cultures are not the fast wrong labels that are so easily placed on every group by every other group. It is a negative, unproductive, vicious cycle that is not helping and can be changed.

Our police, but more importantly, all our governmental issues, are not an "us against them" problem, they are a "we" problem and belong to all of us.

The number of times that I was immediately judged for being in a uniform, and the assumptions that were made about how I was going to handle a person or situation was significant, and again, a further part of the problem. No one deserves to be judged for the color of the outside of their body, clothes, or uniform. I worked with mostly caring, holistic, and humanistic officers, who could be forceful when needed. That ability to be forceful does not make a bad cop. No one wants to be assumed guilty without evidence, and law enforcement deserves the same leeway. Being cautious with those fast labels, from and in any direction, is also a part of everyone's social responsibility.

There are many more answers to these problems, but finger-pointing, blame, and holding onto the part of the past that were indeed outright wrong, is not one of those sustainable answers. Solution-based thinking and actions are our way out of our issues. Anything but solution-based thinking will only dig us deeper. It is how our Founders created a well-thought-out complex system. They looked at poorly created or maintained unfair governments and drew from healthy governments. They pooled the resources to create our constitution from both the mistakes and the successes of history. Solution-based thinking, not blame or resistance to change, also meets another responsibility as a contributing steward of a republic. Can you imagine what could be accomplished if our elected officials agreed to place personal and special interest choices aside, and made only true scientific evidenced based choices for four years? Do you think that would be a worthy experiment?

The Founders of the US stated these inalienable rights in the Declaration of Independence, and the laws of most republics guarantee you the right to at least attempt to pursue life, liberty, and the pursuit of happiness. They also attempted to guarantee those liberties for your grandchildren, and their grandchildren, the rest is up to us. I am repetitive with this for a reason. The Founders considered us in forming this government, they knew changes in social standards and views would occur, so they created a government the people can change. If we keep doing our civic work, then our grandchildren will get their life, liberty, and the pursuit of happiness also. In the history of time, a complete democracy has not brought those freedoms for long. Unmanipulated history teaches us that a pure democracy, only run by majority rule, *without the balance of government,* will fall into emotional mob rule and social chaos. Social chaos not only removes your guarantee of life, liberty, and the pursuit of happiness, but it actively assaults those freedoms on every level.

History has also shown that pure majority rule, without laws and a government to help create balance, will eventually turn into a few people gaining and holding power and control over the rest of the people and region. We need to be careful what we wish for, or of what our emotions push us towards. Voters, leaders, and governments led by emotions will never be as fairer, right, and stable as those led by informed rational thought. A healthy, balanced, and protected republic provides many freedoms. We initially had a well-created government with a handful of needed amendments. Then the slow, silent passing of law after law, that had smaller interest gain over big picture good pushing its formation slowly the rails the founders put the national train on has been moved off course. That is only one form of top-down influence. We the people are the bottom-up influence, and the words and actions of both its citizens and those entrusted to run it also have room for improvement. We can move those rails back onto a new, healthier, and more sustainable course.

Attitudes, resentments, injustices, and your free will to redirect them

Take a minute and think about your options. Would you rather live in a peaceful society that requires slight responsibilities from you? Or would you rather be governed by powerful peoples' whims, emotions, and greed? That may be a stark contrast, but history shows us those are our choices. There is not a group, organization, or person that can provide more for the people of this country, or even your special interest group, than this republic is already providing. That is not to say it could not be better. A charismatic and convincing person or group is not going to be able to create, transform, and start a new government that is better than the one we have in writing. I say, "in writing," because we have a well-written government, we just need to bump up our stewardship of that government. Which partially means, if the subject is profit only, it most likely is poor stewardship. That is not only a problem of the United States, but also a serious worldwide issue. There are 350 million diverse people in the US alone, starting over from scratch is not going to create a better government. Many governments are being bent too far, from too many unyielding directions, to be sustainable without some bigger picture choices and actions being accomplished by those who step up to run for office, those influencing them, and we the voters.

Unless you just don't like to play by the rules, most fair and just governments don't ask that much of their citizens for what those requests return in benefits. Some businesses complain about the safety regulations or environmental measures placed on them that chip away at profit, "Government has too much control!" We have a bunch of those regulations in the US, but we have some of the lowest rates of occupational injuries and death, for the percentage of people who will follow them. That saves us from lifelong injuries, such as head trauma, paraplegia or quadriplegia, deaths, families disrupted without compensation, and saves our tax dollars. A company that complains about not being able to dump a byproduct chemical into the water, should visit a country with minimal or no regulations. Another influence on the stability of government and fairness for the people, not paying our taxes fairly is a huge problem that infringes on everyone's rights and freedoms. All the things we complain about, and we think are too much government, are part of what helps guarantee our life, liberty, and our pursuit of happiness. Not getting cancer or toxic levels of anything bad, or not getting car damage because your roads do not have potholes, greatly helps us pursue our happiness.

Dragging an anchor hinders forward motion

I won't completely invalidate pessimism. There are many reasons to be pessimistic, but the attitude of pessimism, or general futility, is getting in the way of us fixing societal and governmental issues. I can completely understand the birth and growth of pessimism, but I also know its negative damaging effects. I will never be able to remove a percentage of the bad I have seen from my memory, and I would not want to. I decided shortly after the barrage of bad built before my eyes in emergency rooms to not allow that bad to morph into pessimisms. It is how I show respect to those people and tragedies, and it also helps keep me grounded as to how lucky I am, and to what is truly a bad day. I am not pessimistic that some people cannot or will not change selfish ways, I am realistic to that fact. Pessimism doesn't have to enter the picture just because a percentage of people will never help or that perfection is rarely obtainable. Negative facts and optimism are compatible, and optimism is an important part of what helps turn the negative into less negative and sometimes into positive.

Attitudes of pessimism, negativity, optimism, or being positive, do spread like the flu. Whether in a home, office, large corporation, or an entire country; you get to decide which one you are going to spread. Our outcome at this point with our extensive knowledge, resources, and abilities to accomplish needed change for the right reasons, really is basic addition and subtraction. When it comes to positive or negative thoughts, attitudes, words, and actions, it all boils down to four factors. Do you want to add or subtract, and do you want it to be something negative or positive?

I respect you have reasons to be angry, that you have a memory of wrongs, and injustice abounds right before our eyes. However, a large sack full of legitimate awareness stirring inside of us is unproductive to solving anything, and worse yet, hinders healing in every direction. These anchors of past injustices can be lifted so our forward motion can progress with much less hindrance. Our anger, hatred, and blame, including both our accurate and false beliefs of injustice done to us, or our people, past and present, is no longer helping towards resolution. Anger and injustice are fantastic motivators, they just aren't so good at evaluation, implementation, and resolution. These tightly held awareness of wrongs committed not only do not help past the goodness of motivation, but they are eating away at us as individuals, groups, communities, and countries from our insides out. The anger also perpetually keeps us divided and feeds a vicious cycle within us, as individuals, races, and cultures. Maintaining, even justified anger, self-perpetuates the anger, hatred, and blame further. Whether a ship or an individual in a kayak, it is hard to glide forward while dragging an anchor.

Injustices, unfairness, prejudice, thievery, and assault have affected all of us. Unchecked human behavior from all races and cultures makes these behaviors an across-the-board human issue, not one that can be assigned to any one demographic. Our problems are not because of these labeled issues, our problems are because of us humans. However, our deeper human social issues do show themself in the problems we can then label as an issue, such as a racial or cultural issues. We are the core issue, not what can be given any other label. Almost every group and culture has inflicted horrible human behaviors towards others and have had them done to them. Often, within cultures, races, and countries. Most likely, the very first unjust emotionally driven human on human atrocity occurred within one tribe or clan. Labeling something cultural or racial is easy, even accurate at times, but our issues are human.

Fast easy labels are a genuine problem which the habits and methods of our politics are perpetuating. Politics is driving too much of our humanness. However, a much greater issue is our messy humanness driving our politics. Yet, if the concepts of government health and sustainability was driving our politics, from the foundation up it would help provide longer and greater peace, productivity, and profit. "Healthy and sustainable," from the base up, would be our humanness working with our humaneness. Ultimately, our human issues are so much more powerful and driving than our political issues, and those fast simple labels we throw on a person's first words are not helping us solve or calm a single problem.

Yet worse, labels polarize us, and that is one of the last things we need more of. This book is an excellent example. I and this book will be given fast labels, even though its goal is to help people, all people, no matter their generation, political affiliation, race, news source, culture, gender, class, or sexuality.

Fingers can be pointed at each other until the end of time, or we can instead see that injustice has been across the board, so let us redirect even appropriately harsh emotions brought forth from yesterday and start working together. Can you imagine what we could accomplish if we took all the energy we spent in anger, fear, blame, and resentment to get us to this tense point, and redirected that amount of negative energy spent and applied it in a positive forward direction? We could spend our entire life angry at the people, races, and cultures that have hurt us, or we can admit that we, too, have hurt others and break the cycle of endless blame and non-forgiveness.

Swing that big heavy sack of you and your ancestor's truths, traumas, and injustices off your shoulder, set it down on the side of your path, and walk on. It won't get any lighter or more productive to carry it to your death, and it gets set down at your death, anyway. You might as well set it down now and pick up a new sack of something lighter and easier that will bring you more of everything good and solution-based, including more calmness and joy. We free up more of our moments and our life by setting down our heavy sack that we have been carrying so long. For many, their parents gave them the same sack their parents dragged their whole life also. I can see how it could be hard to let go of that history, it is a significant and sometimes blood-letting tight grip we have on our sack of wrongs. It may seem impossible to break the grip of our negative, vicious, and justified, but still unhealthy, cycles. So very many of those wrongs are justified too, but that changes nothing towards working to create calmer bridges to social cohesion and teamwork.

Contrary to several famous quotes, we are capable of learning from history

According to even pre-recorded history, from a great many people, cultures, and times filled with the scarred and broken bones of violent conflicts, politics, and aggression have been a fundamental problem for an exceptionally long time. For the first time in history, we have a greater ability to achieve a higher level of good, right, and fairer, more than ever before. However, that higher level of good does not look like the actions around the globe of our escalating emotions driving our politics further away from the cohesive efforts and tangible accomplishments required to steady our nations, solve our problems, and continue international peace. As I type, Russia has built up troops and munitions threatening an invasion of Ukraine. Actions far from the well-thought-out selfless actions, efforts, and goals of the Founders of the US. These large general concepts of goodness are needed in many countries around the world. How long will North Korea kill people for trying to cross to South Korea, while being forced to literally worship their leader, and be rationed meager amounts of food? How long will female genital mutilation continue to take place in some male-dominated cultures? Accomplishing higher levels of good, right, and fair is something this world needs, and are keys to peace and healthy longevity; although utopia is impossible, more good, right, and fairer is always obtainable.

Republic governments have leaders, but they are not kings, dictators, or tyrants. All leaders should keep in mind, and in their actions, that for the years they are in office, whether hired, appointed, or elected, they are representatives of the people. If they choose to apply, serve, or run for office, they should do so with that principle guiding them to the best of their ability. Many public officials serve the people very well and know the difference between a politician and a servant of the people. We, too, have choices, and those choices come with responsibilities— the same responsibilities we expect of our government officials, making the right choices for the right reasons. Learning from the history of us humans is a functional tool to help with our choices of today.

The Founders

To the absolute best of their ability, these courageous people put their personal agenda and special interests aside and created one of the fairest and well-thought-out constitutions ever created. The formation of the government by designing and writing our constitution was the Founders second brave and selfless act.

They first accomplished setting into motion, and then obtaining, our freedom from England. They were not done when they signed The Declaration of Independence. Then they stood up to the mightiest force in the history of time to that point and accomplished that brave and selfless sacrificial feat also. Please do not invite only men into our vision when you think of "Founders." Men may have written the Constitution, but it was women, teenagers, and children, who lost their peace and lives to accomplish the creation of the United States. History shows that creating a healthy country away from tyranny requires great sacrifice. Then keeping that which was created required lower levels of continued sacrifice. Just as is all of life, creating and maintaining requires energy and teamwork. Creating any healthy government requires the sacrifice of many. Keeping it only requires a lower percentage of sacrifice, but still from everyone. Can we accomplish a lower level of sacrifice to rebalance and maintain?

In looking to answer that question, I found another human problem for our modern times. Many no longer see normal respectful personal sacrifice as healthy and honorable to maintain freedom. Many now see it as weakness and compromising their personal freedoms.

"Our Founders." When we hear that term, we should stop and think about the magnitude of their risk, their extreme lack of selfishness, and what they accomplished with personal strength, sacrifice, and honor in making those sacrifices. We know they also did it for us. We need to do the same level of unselfish thinking and actions to get sustainability back on track for our future generations also. Our thoughts, words, and actions are pushing those tracks off their balanced direction. Let us not lose what they did for us. We say, "Place your John Hancock on the dotted line," but do we consider when he signed his name so big and bold to back our separation from England, that he was potentially signing his death certificate? Every signature you see on the U.S. Declaration of Independence is someone willing to die for what is good, right, and fairer. When today, so many refuse to potentially risk *anything* for what is good, right, or fairer? Those fifty-six people who signed our Declaration of Independence knew England ruled the world and were an extremely powerful military force. Yet, in the name of good, right, and fairer they signed a document which most likely meant they would hang from a rope, and if they were lucky, that is all that would happen. If the new first efforts to form the United States had not won the war, their deaths were basically guaranteed to occur. All because those wise brave people who wrote the document, signed it, and then a copy with only two signatures, John Hancock and Charles Thomson, the President, and the Secretary of the Continental Congress, was delivered to England.

What happened to these brave people who stood up to England and suffered the consequences so we could have the joy of freedom and even the honor of our personal responsibilities today that we take for granted? The fifty-six people who initially sacrificed to give us our freedom, did something powerful known as self-sacrifice. We need to truly, and not by adding another surface bandage, get our government, country, and its people back on firmer and more secure ground. Since 1291, Switzerland has understood this fundamental need for active flexibility to achieve healthy longevity; in 1999, they updated their Federal Constitution for the third time. The US is struggling at 250 years, they have accomplished 730 years.

Many of the Founders of the US were comfortable in wealth, but yet nothing of the wealth standards of today, educated, families with children, and many with thriving businesses with so much to lose, pledged in the name of good, right, and fairer: "For the support of this declaration, with firm reliance on the protection of the divine providence, we mutually pledge to each other, our lives, our fortunes, and our sacred honor." In this day and time, how many of us, leader or citizen, would sign a document that ended in those 14 words? They did sign it. . .

- Five were captured and tortured to death.
- Twelve had their homes ransacked, then burned.
- Two had their sons die fighting in the revolution.
- Two had their sons captured during the war.
- Nine of the signers fought and died in the war.
- One wife was captured, tortured, and died in custody. This is just one reason I refer to our Founders, not our Founding Fathers. All gave up almost everything, many lost their family or their life. Also, consider the supply lines in the 1770s to feed and clothe those fighting. Just as all of life is teamwork, every person that believed in the cause that could, helped the troops how they could. From the beginning spark to the completion of the war, and then more teamwork to write The Constitution. Extreme teamwork was required to form this country, and they did it. What will be required today to correct our governmental, social, and environmental troubles? Teamwork and sacrifice?
- One signer was a prosperous merchant that lost his ships to the British Navy, but still sold all his possessions to pay his debt and died poor.
- One had to place his family in hiding, his possessions and property taken by the English, yet he later served in Congress without pay, and died poor. Can you see our legislators saying, "Our salaries and retirement packages or a strain on our financially troubled country, I want to give some back."
- One knew his home was being used as the base for General Cornwallis, reported it to General George Washington, and his home and property were destroyed in the battle. He also died poor.

Not all the delegates agreed on what type of government they should create. Some even wanted George Washington to be our king. Yes, they debated, a few outright arguments occurred, but they settled, chose, then accomplished. You may think such tasks and accomplishments are not possible today. I confess, I can understand why we could feel that hopelessness. But I have watched many people accomplish great feats in my life; this shift away from labeling and blaming and moving into solution-based collaboration can be accomplished. Some of my evidence is small in words but large in gesture, but still proof that people are capable of seeing much bigger pictures than themselves, even in life's critical moments.

John, my friend I have shared stories about, in our nine years of friendship before his death, showed me many times, on many levels, there are still people who will sacrifice parts or all of themselves for the greater good. In his mid-nineties, John fell and fractured his hip. Due to a large oak tree that leaned and stretched across his driveway, the ambulance barely made it to his home, with only inches to spare. Then they had to back out of the long driveway once they had loaded him for transport. From the moment he awoke from the surgery, he always welcomed the several-times-a-day the staff pushed him. He wouldn't stop there, he pushed himself harder with frequent self-initiated walks beyond his two daily physical therapy sessions in rehabilitation. Having returned home weeks after the fall, we were standing in the front yard talking about the night of his trauma, and we looked at the old oak. Always the nurse, I regurgitated the standard humans first type of line and said, "Well, it looks like it is time to take that oak down, so the ambulance can make it to your home and back out." Without hesitation he replied, "My life is not worth more than the importance and beauty of that much older than I am oak tree's life." Years later, the new owners of the property built the new driveway around that beautiful and important oak.

And now the willow

Why is flexibility with changing facts and new findings labeled a "weakness," or "they don't know what they are talking about?" Even worse, we the people label our elected officials harshly if they change their opinions, or just learn new facts. At that point, we should want and celebrate them changing their minds. Although, that is not the way our politics has been going. Yet, with how much is at stake, our elected officials should be flexible with the current information on all subjects. There is a wonderfully accurate saying that is meant to remind us that we are incapable of perfect thoughts the first time, every time, "First thought, wrong thought."

Such a simple, seemingly insignificant saying, but so often true and should be considered far more than we do. To take it one step further, we should encourage each other at times to change our minds if for a better outcome. Yet, we judge the behavior negatively, and even use it against the person that used their strength and wisdom to change their mind. I know I can't get stuff right all the time, and I wouldn't want to, either. That trait is one of the reasons narcissists are so dangerous; their chant is "I'm always right." But I also try hard to say "I don't know" when I don't know. I also always attempt to be open to being told something I said has some latest information, or what I stated was no longer accurate. Please, teach me! The ability to flex and grow with knowledge is also one of the many characteristics of being a professional. The magnitude of judging someone for changing their mind, especially while we have so many major problems that need professionals, and professional methods, to find more appropriate, solid, and longer lasting solutions, is actively defeating solving our issues, and worse, is damaging our progress to solve. "First thought, wrong thought," is a simple wisdom that can save us a lot of trouble. It does not have to be something our ego must waste our time defending. Quite the contrary, we should feel and build pride in knowing we are doing the widest job we can of looking at a problem, implementing a plan that takes the most into consideration, and then evaluating if we accomplished the task to the best of our ability. If we did not completely accomplish the task, then we start over and try again with pride, not judgment. That is not failure, that too is professionalism, and in this case, the most efficient use of government time and your tax dollars.

Of no fault of their own, attorneys are wisely trained and become highly skilled at winning, not necessarily being right. I'm not bashing attorneys for being good at what they do in and out of the courtroom. However, I am saying that bringing these levels of courtroom tactics, win over right, into our government is not solution-based, and is also blatantly self-serving, manipulative, and outright preventing us from finding solid answers to our mounting issues and general stability. But that means both our leaders and we, the people, need to change our thinking and the general attack tactics of our politics. I am intentionally using the negative word "politics" again here because attacking, belittling, or taking out commercials accusing someone of incompetence because they have adopted the wisdom of the scientific method to save our tax dollars, strengthen our government, and resolve more of our serious issues faster is outright sabotage. Attempting to sweep our issues under the rug, to either avoid spending tax dollars or to only protect profit, is just as detrimental and will cost much more to deal with tomorrow in both consequences and greater tax dollar layouts.

If we do not somehow change this blatantly dangerous paradigm, we basically will be knowingly allowing the magnificent, painstaking, and sacrificial work of our Founders to be further divided and weakened. Please, let us stop attacking, judging, and manipulating. We have too much work to do for parties to be actively sabotaging because solution- and longevity-minded people are caring to help on a higher level. I'm realistic, I know a campaign think tank is not going to read this paragraph and only run commercials with puppies and Easter baskets. I know you the voter gets to make choices based on a candidate's intelligence and willingness to solve issues over being led by emotional reactions to commercials, articles, or a news outlet's ability to scare or stir the voter. No matter how good they are at stirring our emotions to get our vote, seeing bigger pictures is the individual citizen's empowerment to greater stability and increased personal and social calm.

Unless you are one of our true, high cognitive ability people, or a professional in whatever subject is the topic, none of us could possibly have the right answer immediately after every question or issue is stated. Same problem from another angle: why is standing our ground so important for some even though they have discovered they were wrong about something? When we block or reject more information on a given subject out of fear the added information might mean we have to change our minds, we are caring more about self-protection of something obviously incorrect, or our ego. When new information proves someone is holding tightly onto information, or ways of doing something that are no longer accurate, they are actively sabotaging solution-based stability and easier longevity.

For some reason, we worry we will be seen as weak for being flexible and changing our minds. Likewise, we the public see people and elected officials as being weak for changing their mind. You have seen me contradict myself intentionally, mid-paragraph as I write. Not to disprove myself, but to openly admit there is more than one angle to consider, especially if humans and our behavior are involved. Not only am I not embarrassed to do that, but I am also being realistic to admit something is not a clear-cut subject, and I am seeing more than one side. Such as right now, presenting why changing our minds can be a bad thing if it is for the wrong reason. Changing our minds too often is not good if we do so only to go with the opinions of those around us, or to pacify, manipulate, or talk someone out of a dollar, or into a vote.

The Founders of the United States knew there had to be a better way to treat people, and that a more perfect government could be formed. For the most part, they checked their fears of change at the door and created a healthy government in a relatively brief period. For our wellbeing and of stability of our Children's futures, can we check our fears of change at the door?

We do need some changes. Not because we have an ineffective system at its core, but rather because it has been taken off its rails by people who did not have the best intentions for the good of all, or tomorrow's stability, in their actions. This slow but steady derailing occurred by the passing of a steady stream of laws and policies since the government was first formed. Special interests for a few slowly nudged a big heavy healthy train from its tracks. If you feel we do not need to get the United States back on track, please ask yourself what motive you have for wanting the off-balance chaos in our local, state, and federal branches of government to continue? One way to show someone gratitude for a gift they gave you, not a store-bought gift, but a handmade gift that involved earnest efforts, risks, wide considerations, and the sacrifice of property, wealth, and their life, is by protecting that gift.

They tried so hard to prevent what we are now doing to each other. We kick, scream, insult, we don't let each other finish our sentences, much less a complete thought, and some will even threaten, assault, and kill those who disagree with their beliefs. Every day we witness these assaults on each other's freedom to have an independent autonomous thought that differs from someone else's agenda or concept of right. Played out in our news and information, on the floors of our legislation, on our streets in protest, and even at our kitchen tables, where we have recently started to discard even our own family if they do not agree with us. Some people want us to be upset, and we are giving them what they want.

By believing the few and persuasive that want us confused and angry we help them meet their ploys for self-gain over some sacrifice and flexibility for long-term stability, peace, and yes, even good healthy well-earned profit. Some use the political tactic of keeping us on edge believing every issue is dangerously urgent. Or convincing people to feel like victims of injustice, that had better act fast before it is too late. The healthy choice is the opposite; we really should be slowing down to be more cautious with our words and actions.

Even if you do have beliefs that the United States is upside down and needs to be wiped clean and rebuilt, what group has the width and background, experience, and true unselfish ability to create a system better than the one our Founders created? An example occurred on January 6, 2021, at our nation's capital. Did they have a plan that went further than their emotions leading them to destroy our capitol, assault our police, and wanting to physically hurt or kill our elected officials they consider the enemy? It appears they wanted to hurt the very people who are trying their hardest to stand up for the people and the republic. They seem to be the angriest with the officials who are trying their hardest to protect everyone's freedom and tomorrow. Now that they have hindsight on their side, they should be most angry with the people who incited their emotions.

That was an action driven by stirred emotions, far from rational. Free countries guarantee the pursuit of the sacred trinity of life, liberty, and the pursuit of happiness. I want those protected, too. It is not the important protection of that trinity that is the issue, but rather the excessive, immoral, and unethical means of near-sighted unconstitutional words and actions that is our true enemy. What makes that even worse, it is from within the borders of our county that this assault is occurring.

Your family also left their country of origin

Our basic human rights have always been threatened by a handful of people and groups that live in our community, are a part of our occupational lives, and from all regions of the world. Since we first formed various independent groups, some humans have had to walk out of their country or across a river to a new boundary, because those basic principles were lacking in their tribe, community, or country. Sometimes so lacking are these basic principles that they must leave before they are killed. People also leave healthy countries for positive reasons, such as an opportunity to fill a need, or the pursuit of a better life. People are still leaving their families, work environment, religions, cultures, and countries all over the world, to find those principles to either stay alive or to thrive. Someone leaving an abusive partner is no different.

As I type these words, the Taliban are again taking over Afghanistan and the people are fleeing for their good, right, and fair privileges, as well as their lives. Humanitarian efforts from around the world are working around the clock to evacuate as many as possible before they are killed or their basic human rights of free will and choice are denied to them with force. We have so many good reasons to slow down. These atrocities and crimes against humanity are why people, to this day, must leave their lands. Many of us and our ancestors, even the ones from European countries, did it for either opportunity or to save their lives. Both are respected. The pursuit of practiced human rights and decency is what drove our ancestors to migrate to what all free countries are founded on. No matter how angry, upset, or appropriately confused about what to believe is our current state of politics and internal social aggression, the goal of trying for better, right, and fairer, is the part we should never forget or give up working towards. Especially today.

The number and magnitude of issues our Founders had to take into consideration were daunting, just as our issues and considerations are today. Please let us learn from them. The Founders of the United States had personal interests, but thankfully and wisely they did, for the most part, set them aside. They knew how important that first step was in forming a more perfect government because they, or their parents, may have fled some region of the world filled with special interest by the powerful. As they declared independence and wrote the constitution they set aside their innate human drive of comfort, power, and profit, and only focused on one big healthy picture: How do we learn from the mistakes, abuses, and misuse of power by people and government around the world, to do the best we can to form a more perfect government than any of us or our ancestors came from? Again, selflessly, they then considered: how do we do the best we can to make sure it lasts for our future generations? I often wonder how they would shake their heads in disappointment if they stepped into our present social and political upheaval. Unlike Thomas Edison looking down from a night flight to see how many light bulbs illuminated a city, I do not think they would be proud and amazed.

The Founders of the United States' brave Declaration of Independence, the war itself, the well-thought-out Constitution, and the formation of the initial government had another invaluable quality: they knew they could not be right and perfect all the time. A quality rarely seen in our politicians today, and a quality rarely forgiven by the media or we the people. It is apparent they knew the inability to be right and perfect in their efforts was evident in how they started the constitution:

"**We the people** of the United States, in Order to form a *more* perfect
Union, establish Justice, ensure domestic Tranquility, provide for
a common defense, promote the general Welfare, and secure the

Blessings of Liberty to ourselves and our Posterity, do ordain and establish this Constitution of the United States of America."

Humble, wise, powerful, and realistic, it does not read "In order to form a perfect union." They also knew it would need to be fixed and changed with the times because they created ways to change the constitution, known as amendments, to alter the Constitution itself, and add or subtract separate laws and policies in day-to-day legislation to help refine what is good, right, and fair. This predicted need to change our government was not set up to slowly dissolve its collective good with little law by little law slowly turning the tracks further from the broad good of the Constitution. Our Founders deserve major credit in the formation of the country and the Constitution. Some of those who followed did care to work towards maintaining what was created for us all. Do you feel we deserve credit for protecting their efforts in our actions today?

Can we again rise to their level of big picture actions?

"The only thing necessary for the triumph of evil is for good [people] to do nothing"
—Edmond Burke, 1729–1797

"But I thought freedom meant being free to do what we want?" The textbook definition is close to that: *The quality or state of being free*. But that vague definition does not cover the width and depth of the subject, nor does it cover the actions required by the people to keep freedom. Despite what is being yelled out on the floors of our legislative building in every state and in our national capitol, despite the poster signs being held up at angry rallies, freedom is not something you yell and scream at people who differ from you in their beliefs, sexuality, religious views, or skin color. Quite the contrary. If you are screaming at someone because you feel they are wrong, you are denying their freedom to peacefully have an opinion that is different from yours. The greatest definition and action required to uphold freedom, I have ever received was a simple and accurate definition: "Freedom is meeting your responsibilities."

Over the past year or so, knowing I was going to write this sensitive chapter, I asked a few older children what "politics" means. I knew for the most part, their answers would be from observations of adults, not the formed opinions of adults. They are so unfiltered and right on, "It means we aren't going to get along" was a hard one to hear. "People fighting to get their way," was another ouch of an answer. My favorite answer was more right up my alley, "What are poly tics? Will they bite me?" Maybe that one was a little too young to ask such a scary word, but strangely gave a rather insightful answer.

Anything can be tipped off balance with a big force or a bunch of little forces. Politics is no longer just debate, it is no longer an argument with compromise, politics has become a huge part of our demise as a nation, and my friends were right, a cause of our suffering.

Our government is not bad, our politics is bad, our system has been slowly manipulated by bad politicians, both those we elect and those with great wealth and power that influence from behind the curtains. Wealthy people and businesses are politicians, too. They just influence from behind with donations, gifts, and lobbyists. Lobbyists are professional persuaders, hired to persuade our lawmakers to pass special interest laws that will help, or block laws that will impede, those who hired them. Some people make bad politics, not the government, our Founders are pure proof of that. Communists are not bad, Democrats are not bad, Republicans are not bad, whatever your party may be, are not bad. People that will lie, cheat, steal, manipulate, abuse, use, and even kill, to hold power and wealth for the purpose of dominance, control, personal profit, or pleasure are bad.

Not all elected officials are bad, but we need more people to become politicians that will not stray from what we and any country needs. It is not only motives that make for bad, but also the difference between confident and competent. We have many confident people in government, but confidence alone is not the same as competence. Confidence without competence can be dangerous. The word politician now has such a negative life of its own, with so many negative connotations, the word alone may contribute to a self-fulfilling prophecy. If we call them elected officials, perhaps it could even slightly help their actions to rise to a higher standard. Calling a percentage of them "representatives," is misleading also, because many do not represent the people; but rather they represent the money that keeps them elected. I am aware that this is the present mode of operation in politics, yet that does not mean it is the healthiest or most sustainable mode we could be using.

Mr. Franklin was correct, but he stopped short only in detail when he said, "Now let's see if you can keep it." The detail he assumed we understood was whether we can meet our responsibilities of maintaining a republic, which then supplies and protects our freedoms. Our Founders' intelligent forward thinking created the US Constitution to form the government that has gotten us this far. It has the capability of getting us much further. The distance any healthy government or society travels is up to the drivers and the quality and maintenance of the parts that make up that government or society. We are all the drivers. Our government needs a little overhaul, for the right reasons, to get it back onto a healthier track. Blaming our "system," rather than seeing our responsibilities as individuals, as those influencing from any direction whether media or money, and our big picture responsibilities as the elected or appointed officials, is only going to keep us from our self-governing responsibilities. That avoidance is not going to help us accurately assess, diagnose, and appropriately correct for greater health, stability, and longevity. That holds true for any government, agency, corporation, community, group, and even a family or couple.

If the actions of meeting your responsibilities as an individual is freedom for that person, then what actions are required of a country to maintain its freedom? This definition may not fit in a country where your freedoms to even meet a responsibility is taken for granted. No matter how hardworking a citizen of North Korea is, they still do not have the freedom to search unrestricted internet as a free countries' citizen does, or buy a car, or even an extra pound of flour. That is only the surface of their lack of basic human freedom; movement and travel is restricted, cars are only for top government officials, even food is rationed, and religious freedom is not a freedom. Those few facts alone should be enough of a reminder of why we need to slow down and protect what we have, including accepting the importance of balance from opposition.

Doing whatever you please is exercising unfiltered free will and choice, but it is not true freedom, unless you live on an island by yourself. Since we mostly ended up with a two-party system, it is important to understand that if one side dominated and always got its way, you would not be living in a free society for long. I can't believe I'm going to recommend this TV series, because it was seriously psychologically difficult to watch, and living it would be inhuman— *The Handmaid's Tale* (2017), based on the book by Margaret Atwood by the same name. It is a harsh example of how society could end up if one side completely got its way. Elizabeth Moss does her usual fantastic job of communicating subtle paragraphs without saying a word. Unlike this series where one far leaning group got its way, we feel frustrated that our opposing parties are forcing us to find balance. However, it is middle ground compromise that keeps us out of the ditches more than it is unhealthy for our freedoms. The problem is, we are losing our wisdom to appreciate the importance of that balance. We appear to be more and more passionate, on a new and less stable higher level, to get our way and only our way. All or nothing too often lands on nothing, and sometimes worse.

"Our side" is not the only side that has truths, key facts, and considerations. Healthy discussion to find the best answers, not the first one that is convincingly and passionately sold to us, fed from the news station that agrees with us and we agree with them as the only source. Or the answer fed to the elected official by heavy contributors or lobbyists. Wise open discussion is dangerously no longer a standard in our political theaters, most news articles, or even discussions at the kitchen table during family get-togethers. An elected official not voting a party line may not always be as bad as the party and its people may assign. A little more autonomous thought from our leaders may have prevented some significant issues in our past and will again in our future. It is our increasing levels of insisting on all or nothing that is preventing progress in resolving our very real and present dangerous issues. It is also ripping apart families, communities, and every single one of us from the inside out. I know a shocking number of adults whose families' have aggressively disowned them and outright discarded their own children, grandchildren, or parents, because they are so passionate about holding onto their views as if they are the only truth. I am so grateful my parents or siblings did not toss me aside when our political, social, or religious views did not completely line up. The behavior feeds unhealthy in both directions. If a family feels it can discard, then it condones it for a nation, and if a nation condones discarding, then families will also feel it is okay to discard a member.

Unfortunately, this all or nothing, agree with me, or you are completely wrong, and get out of my home or off my legislative floor, is moving us further away from finding more solid stability and sustainability. All or nothing is pushing a frustration on both sides that is both the left and right foot helping to peddle a negative cycle faster and faster, that is sending balance and resolution further away from us. It is directly and indirectly assaulting our present-day freedoms and will most definitely damage tomorrow's. Our all or nothing thinking is only going to get us more surface bandages in the meantime, because long-lasting solutions are more often found in the balanced middle than the far outside. We now have 250 years of surface bandages trying to hold this country together. If we want to heal and strengthen this country from the origin of our issues, we will need a few deeper, slower, and well thought out "surgeries." Successful major surgeries are accomplished by professional teamwork, diverse member teams that are educated and skilled, with the goal of healing, health, and wellness.

Why is freedom meeting your responsibilities? If you meet the responsibility of paying your phone bill, then you are free to use your phone. If you meet your responsibility of going to work, then meet the responsibility of doing the job assigned to you well, and earn a paycheck, then you are free to keep a roof over your head. Further, just as our responsibilities to maintain freedom have many levels of action, if you meet the responsibility of maintaining your driver's license, insurance, and car maintenance, then you are free to drive your car, legally anyway. Even if you inherit massive amounts of money, and never actually have to clock into a job again, you still must meet your responsibility of not losing it to poor investments or the addictions that will take that money from you, such as purchasing, gambling, intoxicants, or the pursuit of extreme excitement or pleasures.

If we know this is a universal truth, why do we exclude a healthy government from this truth? Why do we feel that we as citizens, and the people that run a government, can neglect to meet basic responsibilities to maintain a healthy balanced productive society and government, but assume it will keep working? When we know the phone eventually stops working if we don't meet that responsibility.

The power of your vote

An even greater responsibility than if we vote is what we allow to affect how we vote. Our Founders did an impressive job trying to predict our tomorrows, and they got close. Now it is up to us to overhaul it the rest of the way to protect what is good and right concerning today's current issues. They created a government that allows us to do that; they were thinking of us! Even though there is nothing easy or fun about it, too many people and officials do not want to acknowledge the need to address these critical issues pushing on us all. Admitting, facing, and accomplishing this now vital task is also a responsibility of maintaining our republic, or any healthy government. Easy? No. Our responsibility? Yes.

Hopefully, our new batch of elected officials in the next ten years will get on it with a renewed level of selfless professional duty, like we have not seen for 250 years.

The ability to amend our Constitution was created because part of our Founders' wisdom was knowing that change occurs, and to help heal sickness in the nation's social or governmental structure when an "illness" is discovered or created.

Slavery is wrong, and always will be wrong. As wrong as it will always be, slavery is still a wrong of today, but now it is called human trafficking. Human trafficking is rampant round the earth. Just like women not voting was a standard of the times when our country was formed, so was slavery. Wrong, but still a standard of the culture of the time. A huge percentage of the country figured out slavery was wrong. Between slavery and the riches of resource availability, we had a painful civil war, and we started killing each other to settle the matter.

The Founders knew what was acceptable as a cultural standard, such as slavery or woman not voting, may one day not be acceptable to the majority. Social norms and mores do change, and laws should be changed if that is what the majority believe.

Legalizing marijuana is a present-day example. Although many feel uncounted and helpless to effect change, the majority does still get a say-so in the US. It is not only the powerful top that has influence, we the people still can affect outcomes. We voters, if honestly informed, and if we do not allow ourselves to be misled by sensationalism, or our emotions of fear, injustice, and anger, but with valid facts as our critical key, are highly capable of making responsible voting decisions. Working to not vote with our emotions, which is the influencers main tactic, and they are so good at emotion stirring, is another critical key to voting for true stability and longevity of peace, productivity, and profit.

How much peace, productivity, and profit do the people owning businesses in an area that riots for social justice experience?

When we go to vote on an issue or election, we deserve factual knowledge, not slanted input from an ad on television. We should never vote for a person or issue because we have been scared or made angry by advertisements, news, or social media that are good at doing just that. Being emotionally stirred is normal and healthy. Not acting on those emotions is where we get to exercise our free will and choice, daily. Before we vote or tell someone they are wrong because their view is different from ours, move those emotions into the rational part of our mind to assess it for its totality. Assess the total picture for both its good and its bad, not just the scary part that has been shown to you by advertising or media. Our own fears of more than one view can be just as damaging as the misleading advertisements and slanted information.

In the spring of 2019, I had dinner with two people who I have known for many years and respect. It was at Threadgill's in Austin, Texas, the little restaurant on North Lamar where Janis Joplin got her start. The restaurant was opened in 1933 by a lover of country music and bootlegger Kenneth Threadgill. Sadly, Threadgill's did not survive the pandemic, or the escalating cost of taxes and rent in the area and closed permanently in 2020. These two people mean a great deal to me, but what happened during that meal was a painful moment for me and an example of our political and social times. Or maybe I should say antisocial times? I thought I could trust these two people to have an open discussion, and I was excited to hear their thoughts on something that had been building in my head for years. I was hoping to discuss the difference between politics and government, and how bad politics is chipping away at the foundation and goodness of our country. I wanted to see what ideas they might have to fine-tune and update our government from the foundation up. I was only going to talk about how, if a company operated for 250 years and had no changes to structural bylaws, did not change and grow, if they never further developed their product or service, never investigated a better deal on suppliers, or changed with the fluctuating needs of society, that business would not survive. I was looking forward to their opinions, knowing they would be different from mine, but still welcomed. I wasn't going to try and convince them of anything, or tell someone how to vote. I was only seeking good old everyday trusted open discussion. I was not allowed to even finish my first thoughts to lead into the discussion. That is how fast they aggressively shut me down. Both people are professionals who know a company must vary and adapt to have long-term viability. But, that evening, both very quickly told me I was wrong and used the long history of strife in our government, especially the legislative branch, as their excuse for the reason everything is fine with our government, and our blame-filled politics are not an issue. I was looking forward to their thoughts in discussion, but all I got was one aggressive double-team shut down.

If these two people had not meant so much to me that night at dinner I would not have been knocked over by their fast and aggressive status quo system protection. I am not a wimp when it comes to knowing many people will disagree with me. I have known this reality since the first time I stood up for someone, stating an opinion in a college class that was not popular, or wrapped my first dead body in plastic from a human's lack of rational control of the mind when someone feels somehow threatened, whether that threat is real or imagined.

Why should these two people's aggression surprise me? That night, their acceptance of our present day extreme unproductive political strife, was a hard awakening for me that many people actually think this country's level of self-destruction is acceptable. At least as long as your interests are being protected. We have wrongly come to believe in too many aspects of our political follies, that the means do justify the end. Even if present day destruction is the means, and today and tomorrow's potentially avoidable disasters are the end results?

Those two people double-teaming me with extreme unnecessary pressure for our relationship and general discussion, is not about my painful only externally oppressed moment at that table. But rather that moment is a dangerously accurate representation of the harsh yet accurate correlations to our times. Starting with the fact I was not allowed to finish my first thought, and then that neither of them even noticed the rest of the meal I said very little. Representing that if you are not going to agree with me, then sit down and be quiet. Or worse, they noticed but felt okay with not hearing an opinion that differed from theirs. They never even heard what I considered to be the problems, or that I was not going to blame, but had some solution-based ideas concerning the problems. Yes, I could have raised my voice and attempted the futility of forcing my words onto them, but I knew better. If an opinion is forced as opposed to welcomed, it becomes incomprehensible words sounding much like Charlie Brown's teacher or parents, "Wah wah, woh wah

wah." I knew better than to push at that point, but the food was good. I still miss Threadgill's.

Solution-based brainstorming: A simple change that would help us all, except the work-shy or those okay with our manipulation

A few months ago, I was having a political discussion with one of my closest friends. We do not always agree completely on political issues, but the interesting thing is we almost always line up on social and humanistic views. He and I are the pure proof we do not have to have all 80 billion neurons in both brains line up perfectly to accomplish mutual respect and great friendship. Our opposing political lean is not that far, but it endears me to our friendship further that we do discuss our different views and never decrease our respect for each other. His, "Now, I cannot agree with you on that," never damages our friendship and accomplishes expanding both of our views. When we hug, we don't let go for a few seconds, and the squeeze is one of pure appreciation and respect. This is a very special friendship to me, for both my gratitude to our friendship and to him, and especially in this day and time of painful and unnecessary extreme intolerance.

Just after sunrise, the two of us were having coffee on their beautiful front porch discussing political problems and solutions, not pointing out our differences. Even when he and I do differ we do not call the other wrong. Although he will call me wrong shortly after reading that compliment, so he can then enjoy pointing out that he knows for a fact I have printed misinformation. This beautiful calm morning we were discussing the US has over 250 years of bandages attempting to fix issues at the surface rather than deeper at the origin of the problem. We agreed that the country needs a tune-up to catch up to our modern-day issues.

Then my favorite part, the brainstorming, we moved onto throwing a few solutions around.

He said, "Such as we need to give our president on the federal level, and our governors on the state level, the ability to veto line items." Line-item veto means that when a bill has been approved by both the house and the senate, the governor or president, instead of having to sign or veto the entire package of several laws and policies in one bill, they can line-item veto and remove laws or policies in that bill that they do not approve of. I shared with him that a line-item veto is adding another surface bandage to a problem and does not fix the origin of the issue that is causing us serious problems. He asked me to teach him the bigger picture. We both know labeling a view liberal or conservative helps nothing, and we work to stay away from the one side is right and one side is wrong unrealistic and unproductive discussions. It requires us to expend only minimal energy to respect and find the truth in each other's angles. We sometimes disagree, but it does not turn into more than the unstated understanding that our minds don't line up and can't. We have a wonderfully connected sense of humor too, I bet that helps.

Slightly expanded, this is what I shared with him about the difference between a surface bandage, in this case the line-item veto, and fixing a problem at the origin of the issue. The origin of the problem is what is known as a rider. Riders are laws, special considerations, or policies that are attached to a bill to become a law. They are incredibly bad and outright dangerous for you and our system for so many reasons. Work-shy and convenient for legislators, but dangerously bad otherwise for the rest of us and the big picture health of the government. Riders make it easier to manipulate the voter, and potentially hide what we should be seeing and knowing. The fact that riders have been banned in 43 states tells us they are not a great idea.

To start with, this is how laws, policies, and actions that otherwise would never have made it through the process become actual law. It saves time and quietly slips not so good changes through, but now it is a dangerous snowballing menace to us all. Here is a fictitious example of how riding more than one law onto a bill is the origin of a problem that is hurting all of us except for those wishing to manipulate and fool us in both laws passed and elections. Let's say I am running for a second legislative term, and my opponent runs this ad, "Vincent Dodd voted against patting you on the back, Janet Palmheart promises to vote to pat you on the back." Your first thought is, "Well, I'm not voting for him, he just outright did not want me patted on the back, but Janet Palmheart will."

You, the voter, have just been extremely manipulated. Yes, the record shows Vincent Dodd voted against the patting you on the back bill, but that political advertisement does not tell you the reason I voted against it had nothing to do with not wanting to pat you on the back. It was because riding on that bill was also a congressional raise of another $3,000, when last year we just gave ourselves a $3,000 raise. Hell yes, I wanted to pass a law to give you a pat on the back, but I do not feel we deserved another $3,000 raise. But the commercial made me look uncaring. If those two pieces of legislation could not ride on each other, if we overhauled the system and completely removed the ability to ride more than one law, policy, or action onto a bill, you would clearly know what your candidate actually stands for or against. You would know I felt that a $174,000 annual income, which is the salary of a US legislator in 2021, was indeed enough of a salary for me, and I need no more of your tax dollars in my pocket. I also would have voted for you to receive a pat on the back. If this is a change we want, then our legislators, who supposedly represent us, should make the change. That is how my eighth-grade civics book said it worked! Would you not want a simple fix to not be manipulated during elections, and to be able to have less smoke and mirrors in our politics?

The problem with attempting to solve this issue by giving line-item veto powers to our governors and president is that it does not address the problem at the origin of the issue. One bill with one law will increase the work of our legislators. However, in every other aspect of solving this smoke and mirrors issue, especially to the voter and the watchdogs attempting to keep an eye on our elected officials, it is a solution where everyone benefits. This is not a party issue, both sides have benefited and been hurt due to this archaic way of slipping things by the people and making their job easier. Another huge benefit of this one example of how we need to overhaul the old system is election time, you are not going to be manipulated by an ad that says, "Vincent Dodd doesn't want you patted on the back!" with a picture of me looking mean and uncaring when all they did was take a picture of me when I accidentally hit my funny bone on the back of a chair.

I finished this explanation on the front porch that morning and my friend said, "Wow, you are right, and I just wanted to add another bandage."

How good things are, not how bad we are being told they are

I prefer not to watch the news but to read it, watching it scares me more. My other reasons for reading are to exercise my free will and choice in a few directions. I choose to read what I want, as opposed to what a news channel chooses to push on me. The second reason is I choose how much of the scary article I decide to read. I'm also not affected by the facial expressions or the inflections of the news anchor. Those all help me remove other people's personal influence in what I choose to read, and it decreases how I am influenced. That influence is another reason I stop reading after I have discovered the objectives of who, what, when, where, and how. Then I get to skip reading the subjective personal or political slant part of the article, usually not as heavy in the first few paragraphs. About a year ago, I read somewhere, "If you only get your news from one source, you are only half-informed." I told this to a friend of mine and in a split second they said, "Yes, and half-misinformed too!" Mostly, that depends on the source, which is why I get my news in the morning with coffee by reading a few dissimilar sources. Some are harder to read than others, over filled with obvious heavy slant, so I exercise even more free will and choice with those articles. I try to stay away from aggressive, blaming, or fear-based news.

I found everything got a lot easier when I stopped news-hounding myself into depression. I stayed informed, but I now avoid the repetitive assaults of blow-by-blow repetitively watching and thinking I need more of the same news. Our news is much the same too, human behavior and the weather. The weather changes more than some of the human behavior. The worst part is I already had harsh reality jobs in my face, the human tragedy that passes before the eyes of an emergency department staff is overloaded. Then law enforcement. Watching the news for me was like a contractor going home and turning on a house remodeling TV show. Enough was enough. But I figured out a long time ago to stop watching news on the tube, exercise free will and choice, because they are just too good at upsetting us! I recently looked up where the top various news sources fall onto a conservative-liberal scale. I was grateful to see the ones I read are closer to the center. I feel safer and less manipulated by reading only and taking back that control of what I feed myself, as opposed to being force-fed by watching. We are worth more than that lack of choice or sensational manipulation.

We all know there are different types of news: the factual news known as the who, what, when, where, and how, and then there is the sensational or slanted news. One article can hit all three. The sensational or slanted news has a sneakier job to do besides only inform us—to pull us in and keep us there, sometimes to manipulate our views, or to feed us our opinions. Sometimes with blatant fear pushing it on us, and other times still feeding us, but just a little more softly. Sensationalism increases ratings and sells commercials; slant intentionally influences you, and they can overlap. Then there is the very really bad information: the extremely slanted, the ones that want to scare you beyond the everyday already bad enough news slant. Bad information is everything from outright false information, to lies, manipulation, to every ulterior motive past informing us. This type of intentional spreading of false information and fear is what some outright bad people do, and it is a form of terrorism.

Part of the definition of terrorism includes, ". . . intimidation, especially against civilians, on the pursuit of political aims." The definition also includes, "unlawful," so maybe one day it will be unlawful for news stations to use slant to intimidate and ignite our fears. It sure is terrorizing our older generations. They have been convinced that their children and grandchildren are their enemy for having wider views that are highly justified for their times, generations, and increasing issues. Issues they will be dealing with after we have died.

Sometimes it can also be hard to tell the difference between news and opinion. If a station has more opinion than factual news, should it be called a news station, or an opinion station? The good news, pun intended, is that the world and your back door are not as close to collapse as a few news sources want you to believe. Just because someone is selling total fear doesn't mean you have to buy it. Perhaps, consider not watching the news every day, give your spirit a break, go a day or three, or thirty, without assaulting yourself with news. Or at least maybe cut back, portion control?

We are better off than the fears they are selling

Most every country has some major national issues, and then there are the human behavior issues; our environmental systems are strained further than ever in the past fifty years, bad politics, and violence has been an ongoing issue since the first cave-dweller picked up a club or decided they wanted to oversee the tribe because they were the biggest. Back then, and strangely to this day "big" is an influence, it was the biggest in size who ran the cave. Today it is the biggest in bravado, resources, and hopefully, heart and intelligence. Our world is not declining as fast as a few, but significant in their ability to influence, want you to believe. They too might be trying to sell you fear and decline, but you don't have to buy those, either. Here is the reassuring hope and proof we are not circling the drain. That is not to say we do have areas and issues creating instability, and there will always be much work to do.

Every generation thinks the end is near and "the good old days" are gone. We sort of have a hypochondriac syndrome about our society instead of our bodies. As an entire society, we gravitate towards the assumption that everything is sick, and we need our politicians to hurry up and heal all the bad they scared us with. If they keep us scared of the other side, we will keep voting for them. That is the blatant tactics of some news stations also. Most of us are not worse off in the big picture than the previous generations. Those good old days that so many long for, were they as good as we prefer to remember? Our minds protectively prefer to see and remember the smooth more than the rough, but our rose-colored memory can harm us also.

Let's start with the big one to keep us very grounded, everything past this is icing on the cake of gratitude that our world is better every decade. Before 1928, when Sir Alexander Fleming discovered penicillin, we died from pneumonia or almost any infection that could spread and end our life. Ten years before that discovery, the average life expectancy was fifty-four, today it is 78. Clearly, we are doing better there.

Hate crimes still occur. The new Asian hate is pathetic, as if beating up an elderly Asian woman standing on a street corner, would ever change the outcome of the COVID-19 pandemic, or worse yet, as if she is responsible. That is unfortunately unchecked anger and insecurity in action and does not accurately represent the latest increasing trends in general acceptance. Thank goodness it does not represent all of us. Yes, the years of Trump-ism ripped the scabs off many of our issues, including racial. The only good in that department is that healing always occurs stronger from the inside out. Maybe now that the wounds are further exposed, we can decrease our anger and blame and allow some deeper and stronger healing.

Insecurity and prejudice are obviously decreasing through each generation. Gay men are being beaten on the streets far less than even twenty years ago. Two women getting married can invite more of their straight friends to the wedding than ever before. Our commercials are no longer filled with only light-skinned people, now all gender identities, races, and mixed couples are represented in more of those commercials too. Although some racists are getting louder, many people are not as prejudiced towards others as decades ago. Some need to be cautious with the assumption that a person is prejudiced because of their race alone. Not only is that racist also, but that belief is adding to our racial issues. But the world's increasing acceptance is occurring. Unfortunately, that positive sometimes causes those less accepting to get louder, thus we hear and notice them more. Which is their goal. As I mentioned earlier, the world's increasing omnistic views of various religious beliefs is also proof. In other words, more improvement! We are climbing up and doing better in many ways.

Only three decades ago, talking to friends on the other side of the earth was a feat, or at least expensive. Skype helped change that in 2003, and Zoom is moving on into our lives, making it even easier to share relationships, business meetings, and knowledge. I used to play maybe three to five games of chess a year on a board, and now in the palm of my hand I play that many sometimes in one day. I also lose an impressive amount, so I guess progress does not abound in every direction. We have in the palm of our hand's a small device we can seek knowledge or entertain ourselves with. It's unbelievable to those of us that remember before. If you are of the newer generations, please understand and respect both the device's goodness and its extreme potential to be used for bad. Set your devices down and go touch the earth and talk with people in person, it will expand your world in ways the device cannot. We pre-internet people know its ability to destroy self and community, we watched it happen. Trust us, it can be dangerous also. Please use it wisely and with good and right in front of your intentions. As I read somewhere a few years ago, "We hold in our hands a device that literally gives us the knowledge of the world in seconds; but instead, a percentage of us use it to critique on disrespectful levels, scare with false information, boldly dispense hypocritical judgment, and to argue. All with total strangers."

Alternative energy, jaw-dropping incredible! A small stream can now supply power to thirty homes from a system smaller than the size of a small car. We are harvesting energy from the waves of the ocean. More solar energy hits the face of the earth every sixty seconds than the entire population of the earth can use in one year, and we are figuring out how to harvest and store more of that energy. Electric cars and their benefits are moving into the mainstream quickly. I have a request for the fossil fuel industry, please. We will continue to need what comes out of the earth, but please be willing to support the necessary progress of alternative energy. Fossil fuel and its profit are not going anywhere soon, and our future generations will need alternative energy even more than we already do today. They too are compatible in the world.

We have our progress and actions moving towards sustainability. Every solar panel that faces the sun, every wind turbine that completes a full revolution, and every wave, means our fossil fuel will last that much longer, and we slow down global warming. Of coincidental interest: In 1856 Eunice Foote, a scientist and activist for women's rights, placed a thermometer in three jars. She filled one of three jars with water vapor, another with air, and a third with carbon dioxide. She then placed them in the sun, the jar containing carbon dioxide heated faster and higher than the other two, it then took much longer to cool. In presenting her findings, she warned that increasing carbon dioxide levels in our atmosphere is not something we want to occur. Only three years later, in 1859, Edward Drake accomplished the first successful drill for oil in western Pennsylvania. We have shown so much progress in alternative energy that parts of the world are even installing small wind turbines close to commercial truck high-traffic routes, the air disturbance from the trucks turns these small wind turbines creating electricity. More needed sustainable goodness.

Dogs. I know this is a strange one, but it's true. We are better off because of dogs. I've seen too many dog bites in my nursing years, most were preventable. With that balance stated, dogs have been our wonderful friends and extreme helpers for a long time. Over 15,000 years is the low estimate, 40,000 years is the high estimate. They really do have much to teach us, and they are trying. I think it's one of the reasons they don't live long, they give us humans part of their spirit and life in teamwork and love. We do have a dog number problem; we could be more responsible in our choices with them. We cannot override our natural drives to propagate, and neither can they. Let's do everything we can to prevent unnecessary reproduction; please choose to adopt, and have our dog fixed. Why do we call it "fixed," aren't they working to start with, and we really take them to get broken? In that case, please don't ever fix me! I like the broken person I am, literally and figuratively speaking. You don't even have to remember the confusing "spay" or "neuter" terms because neuter is a Latin word meaning to neutralize and can be used for both genders.

Another reason we are better off with dogs in our lives is that dogs watch us and want to learn how to be better companions. If we teach them, they are always trying to do better. Some can't, but you can tell they want to. We are the same, we can also almost always do better. Also, just like dogs, we respond better to positive reinforcement than we do to negative reinforcement. Big dogs, little dogs, slow-moving dogs, hyperactive dogs, addicted dogs, so many types, but still inside a beautiful dog. Oh yes, dogs get addicted; have you ever owned a Labrador or a Belgian Malinois and a tennis ball at the same time? We are so lucky to this day, to have dogs. I am grateful wolves started hanging out near us for our scraps. That was the beginning of the teamwork. We are also better off because of dogs because their lessons for us are endless and important to peace and growth.

Have you ever seen a video of a dog greeting their human who has been a soldier overseas for a long, dangerous time? In that extreme moment of beautiful uncontrollable joy, they are trying to teach a few more life saving things. For one, they show us that uncontrollable joy is acceptable to experience and display. They missed us, and their heart is exploding that one of their humans is back to share more teamwork, love, and support. They are also attempting to teach us, with every bit of excitement, energy, and love they can muster, that if we slow down and do this right, if we keep trying to see bigger pictures, as they also often try to teach us, that maybe, just maybe, one of their humans won't have to go risk their life, and thus maybe never come back to that waiting dog, parent, partner, and children. Dogs know to make the best out of every moment they get, and that's a lesson we all need to be reminded of also. Our dogs know that no matter what another dog looks like, it is still another dog.

Strange I admit, but still a lesson for us: they are also trying to teach us to allow ourselves to feel joy and goodness. I just realized another bond we have with dogs—newspapers can scare both humans and dogs; they can scare and can swat both our spirits.

Knowledge. In every field and every decade, we know so much more. Even better, it is available at our fingertips. Our knowledge is another increasingly positive goodness of our times. Our level of knowledge is an extremely helpful sign of sustainable progress. That knowledge also needs to be used for good over gain. For the most part, our scientists are trustworthy, and they are not putting out slanted facts. However, be cautious, there are those who will slant the scientific findings, that is where our concern and distrust should be pointed.

We have enough knowledge to solve, or at least decrease, many of our world issues. Including our issues related to the human population and behaviors, such as prejudice, racial, and cultural conflicts. Our collective potential is magnificent, if we will just use what we know about human needs and drives, history, the environment, individual and group behaviors, science, engineering, even profit, economics, governments, and cultural dynamics. It will require effort and some sacrifice. Albert Einstein is right, the answers will not be found on the same level we have been doing things. Otherwise, more of the same is going to bring us more of the same.

Another sign of progress is that the world can accomplish a collective action to solve earthly problems. We already proved we can fifty years ago, it required knowledge and then application in action. The proof: in the 1970s scientists discovered the use of CFCs in aerosol cans was responsible for the ozone layers thinning above the north and south poles. The United States banned CFCs in aerosol cans, most of the world followed, and the ozone layers above the poles began to rebuild. Pure proof that we are better off, and that even our big environmental problems can be turned around with effort and application. We have significant issues that need attention, but we are not as bad off as many want us to believe.

We may think we want those "good old days" back because our minds self-protect and tend to want to remember only good things about a period of time or a part of our life. Just like not being able to control what emotions come to us, we do have not always have such good thoughts either. Yet, just like emotions, it's what we do with them that makes the difference. I can't blame anyone for wanting to look back on an era and remember it with goodness only, "Ah, the good old days." We just need to slow down, too much is happening far too fast. We are like a snow globe being constantly shaken. Since the 1960s the snow globe we live in, known as our world, has been being shaken near constantly and extremely hard from many directions. For that reason alone, we should be gentle with ourselves, each other, and our many types of relationships, because all 7.5 billion of us are now in that one snow globe.

No matter how hard our world is being shaken, we still need to remember our past as accurately as our imperfect human minds allow. We should remember the civil rights movement workers, only fighting to be allowed to eat in a cafe or try on a shirt or shoes before they buy them, who were being beaten with nightsticks, bitten by police dogs, or literally killed in the backwoods never to be seen again. That was only fifty years ago. Is this really a time we want back? Do we really want women to live under those levels of subservient standards? Again, I reference *The Handmaid's Tale*, even the wives of the rulers had no say, and all women were denied liberty and the pursuit of happiness with many also denied life. We may think we want the good old days back, but those good old days were not so good for everyone. For many groups and cultures good, right, and fairer were being denied. We should not be okay with that.

Judgment and suppressive actions have and will remain an issue fed by fears, profit, narcissistic and ethnocentric thinking, as well as entitlement. With all the progress we have made in human equality rights, we know we are going in the right direction. Let us attempt to judge even less, and act even more with our words, actions, and omissions, towards further equality. It is time we stop pointing fingers and flinging the fast, easy, and unproductive labels denoting what is different. It is time we mark, celebrate, and work with what is both different and the same to help slow down the hate and blame across the earth.

Thank goodness so many of us are getting along so well now, and that so many want to keep trying. Your efforts are meaningful and are not wasted. You are contributing to not only good, right, and fairer; you are also helping to pour more hope into the mix.

Goodness continues to grow in ways that are hard to see if we buy only the pessimism we are being sold, giving us yet another reason we should slow down, see, and feel more of that goodness that is indeed increasing every decade. If we remove the dirty foggy glasses some people keep trying to get us to wear, we can experience greater reassurance. The people selling those foggy glasses, conspiracy theories, and slanted and outright false information are hoping you will keep buying it. When we buy their false, angry, and scared old beliefs, we help them create and spread the fear, easy harmful labels, and judgment that divides us and helps them reach their goals. Some intentionally want us standing on shaky ground, yet removing the muddy glasses strengthens our ability to see where to stand on solid factual ground. Greater stability and peace follow, then our progress can be seen clearer. So can our goodness.

Something else that brings me hope and reassurance is that we do have an increasing awareness of our behaviors and influences. Many may argue that statement, but again, I am speaking collectively. We do know more and more about our minds and behaviors as humans. This too has shown progress every decade, with breakneck progress in self-awareness and humankind-awareness since the 1960s. People have been examining, charting, philosophizing, and sharing those discoveries about us humans for thousands of years, self and social awareness helps if we will continue to teach and apply it.

It was in the early 1980s, when magnetic resonance imaging (MRI) really started to be used around the world, that we learned even more about the brain and how our minds function. By scanning people while having them see images or other simulations that allowed us to see what part of our brains is being stimulated by a picture of chocolate cake, or the taste of sugar, receiving a narcotic, or being pleased or frightened, we started learning some wild, amazing, and scary things about how our minds work. The MRI helped us learn more about our emotions. We even learned what part of the brain is affected when we live without financial security, wondering if we can keep a roof over our heads. Yes, poverty has been shown to affect a part of our brain. The MRI helped us explore our minds at a deeper level than we ever imagined. Or should I say imaged?

Progress is clearly present, because we do have the ability to change some things about ourselves, both individually and collectively. It may not seem like it, but many of us are learning to slow the intensity of anger, hatred, and intolerance for anyone different from ourselves. Just the awareness alone that a person has zero influence on what gender, race, region of the world, sexuality, level of wealth, or religion they are born into is creating less prejudice and greater equality. Thank goodness many more are feeling and showing less judgment, blame, or hatred for those that differ from themselves. The theme and success of the fantastic series *Queer Eye* tells us we are on track. If we moved that groundbreaking show back forty years ago, it would not have even been produced. Which means, it could not have become the socially important and contributing hit those humanistically and socially intelligent people are creating to help contribute to such needed progress. If we will drop our shoulders, relax our eyes, and stop focusing on the small pockets of loud and scary, we can see increasing goodness is also happening.

Although a stranger may hurt us, strangers are not who want to hurt us, bad people are who may hurt us. That overlapping delineation is to remind us that most of the people in this world that we will meet, interact with on some level, or just stand near while doing are periodically required to wait in public, do not want to hurt. We may speak and dress differently, but inside, underneath those surface observations are whole and equal human beings. Accepting that makes life so much easier, calmer, and extensively enriched. Our increasing awareness that we are all far more alike than we are different also tells me we are doing better and we can continue to be even better.

The gift to yourself known as empowerment

Voting is a powerful thing, the health and longevity of a healthy government and the general state of well-being of its people depends on us voting. Significantly far more importantly than the act of voting is being highly informed about who we are voting for. We have a job to do as well, and the good news is we are not powerless to help correct the issues. We can help in many ways, such as helping to keep the government tab down.

The main tragedy of vehicular negligent homicide is the loss of life, and the devastation to the hearts of the families. Starting in the law enforcement academy, I was informed by a state trooper, and a few times since, about this subjective but understandably accurate or even low estimate. The average cost to all of society for one traffic fatality is estimated at a minimum of $1 million. This includes, but is not limited to, the cost of the healthcare tab, the lost productivity and time involved in the road closure to investigate, property damage, the response of police, fire, EMS, possibly a life flight helicopter, the cost of others also injured, the lost work of the people delayed in traffic, then the criminal and civil litigation, court time, and possibly the incarceration or probation of the person causing the death. We all pay with life, grief, family system disruption, and financially for all major traumas. Whether a fatality is involved or not, so many of these tragedies are preventable by just realizing we do have a responsibility to each other and ourselves to help maintain all our lives, liberties, and pursuits of happiness.

What else does an individual helping maintain a functioning, respectful, efficient society, government, and freedom look like? Many of the same things we ask of our officials, whether elected, appointed, or hired government employees: to not waste our tax dollars, do the job well, and make your choices for the good of all, not just those that get you elected with money or votes, don't manipulate people, and then look out for and help others. Some of those may seem corny, but they are also daily, healthy, and important ways to contribute and not drain. It is also doing what you expect of others. As a nurse, I had a personal guideline that I worked by—never ask a nurse-aid to do something I had time to do myself, especially since we both already had ten to fifteen things on our to-do-right-now list. It was efficient, and extreme teamwork and those responsibilities were also my responsibilities. Should we not be spending effort to accomplish the same tax-saving actions and omissions we expect of our government?

Because the world's corporate industries are so powerful, they also have a responsibility to lead by example, and many do. Which is also why so many of us, no matter your party affiliation, except for big business, think big business has too much control over our politicians with their influences. I recently heard that CEOs, big businesses, and the political influence of the wealthy, referred to as, "the fourth branch of government," because of the huge influence they have on government via politicians. These influences are broad but also include money donated to their campaigns or charities they may be supporting or are even affiliated with, various flavors of favors, their goal to be reelected, and the persuasion of their lobbyists. The lobbyists are hired persuasion, not always fact, which is another periodic setback in open progress towards solid problem resolution. Big business gets no more of the blame than any one of all the other negative contributing factors, they are just self-protecting and maximizing down-the-road profit. I cannot fault that goal, but it can be detrimental if at any cost. Such as government contracts, the price-gouging of government entities is a burden on all of us. I again understand that profit is necessary, and economic health is based on strong profit and growth. Yet, ethical restraint and profit are mutually compatible.

When trying to see the many influences on government, politics, our actions, and the needs of a society to stay alive and thrive, it all becomes so interrelated and daunting that we can feel rendered helpless by the magnitude of its dynamics. I share with you again what I tell myself over and over to help me remain positive and try harder: if actions small and large can pull a large situation down, then positive actions small and large can lift it back up. We all have an ability to help these issues more than we think and feel. It starts with believing, closely followed by positive thoughts, attitudes, words, and actions.

Big business extends a bigger helping hand

Big business has a special and wider reaching ability to contribute positively to our all-encompassing issues. They already make major contributions that are so valued in the realm of well and good, employing people, supplying goods or services, and many take part in humanitarian relief efforts during disasters. If they want to help further, they are already sitting in a prime seat to do so. Big business is in a unique position to make a significant difference in the world far and above profit, employment, the product or service the company provides, and even further than the wonderful nonprofits that so many businesses support. Thank goodness so many caring and powerful businesses are going above and beyond to actively change, help, and make a difference. Walmart and the Texas grocery store chain H.E.B. are two such companies during times of natural disaster. These community active corporations immediately send convoys of their trucks, donating bottled water and other necessities to disaster regions. Often arriving before the authorities will let people back into an area. To those that do contribute, I thank you, and I apologize for my "big business" statements which unfairly appear to include significant socially contributing companies. As well, there are an impressive number of small businesses that support local little league teams and contribute to school functions and academics! Those that are accomplishing extending your hands to help in so many directions, please continue your selfless actions, you are making a difference. As you are about to read, I am hoping many more will join the efforts.

The world is filled with nonprofits known as charities and foundations that are an army of goodness. The overwhelming majority of the world's nonprofits are somewhat like a private United Nations, trying to do good across the face of the earth, to keep peace, feed the hungry, and plain help out. People, animals, and the environment are better off because of the millions of nonprofits started by good people, with good intentions, to do the right thing for the right reasons. Here is how large and small businesses across the earth could do the same thing. Melinda and Bill Gates have over twenty years of proof. As of 2020, their nonprofit's total endowments are over $20 billion.

Big business and industry hold a special place and power to be able to help on an even larger and wider scale than the important giving actions of donating water and supplies during times of disaster. They hold an opportunity to help on an even higher level than the collective efforts of our world governments to become proactive to help us move into a sustainable tomorrow. The stability of community, society, nations, and the world also means sustainability for companies, employment, and community. If the community falls, businesses fall also, and vice-versa. Every town you drive through that has closed storefronts with a failing real estate market is the local proof. So how can business think and help even bigger?

Wealthy corporations such as Walmart, Tesla, FedEx, Amazon, and the next 500+ wealthiest companies, no company would be too small to join, could easily accomplish more than my limited mind can even consider. That is why I wish to encourage them to please help. However, I do know the idea I am about to present is possible. If one couple, Melinda and Bill Gates, have already been proving that since the moment they realized more money was falling out of their pockets than they and their children could use in their lifetimes. They started thinking bigger, of progress, of goodness, of sustainable functional research and development of a better tomorrow, and of everyone's tomorrow.

The top producing countries of the world already have an organization known as G7, which stands for The Group of Seven, made up of Canada, France, Germany, Italy, Japan, the United Kingdom, and the United States. There is more than one G group, but let us use this one as an example. These seven developed nations, that together account for over 50% of global net wealth, and over 30% of global gross domestic product, came together and pooled their resources to help accomplish change, stability, growth, progress, unity, and economic and ecological sustainability. Although the G7 has its limits, issues, and critics, it also accomplishes large humanitarian international efforts to combat world diseases and pandemics, such as HIV/AIDS and presently the COVID-19 pandemic; they also help lift struggling countries and regions through initiatives and financial aid, and are attempting to address climate change through the 2015 Paris Agreement. The G7 did not stop there, they expanded into the theater of international security, human rights, and global economic stability, including financial help to highly indebted poor countries. They wisely realize that world economic stability benefits all. The G7 even helped build the structure to encase the damaged radioactive reactor in Chernobyl, Russia.

If governments can unite to accomplish such feats, I know businesses can too. There could be a B500, for the purpose of uniting the powerful businesses in the world that want to help on a global level. If seven countries can unite and accomplish, I know with the resources, ability, and business's extreme abilities to accomplish a task they set out to accomplish, that with such a powerful capable unity far more could be accomplished than the G7 have, especially if the G7 will provide support on levels and in the directions they can. What is vital to this hopeful endeavor: when the B500 meets once a year, it should focus on how to maximize world peace and stability, not profit. However, as those closed up store fronts teach us: even though increasing profit should not be a part of the B500's goal, the stability and longevity of profit would naturally be a secondary benefit of their worldly accomplishments.

This would also be a wonderful opportunity for the big businesses of the world to take the politics out of their actions, led by example, and take on some of our world issues. No matter what direction the owners, board, or shareholders lean politically, left or right, or how they influence politics to help maximize their profit in their business arenas, they can put all that aside and openly, using the scientific method, help solve these big world issues. I bet the majority of the world would pull for you to accomplish your goals and respect you for the worldly contributions.

The world is already, and has been, working together

In researching the G7, I was saddened, but not surprised, to see there are people strongly against the G7 for several reasons. The one that stood out is their fear of globalization. It surprised me because "globalization," literally and figuratively, has already saturated the earth. Fearing globalization is equivalent to fearing the earth rotating, too late! It is businesses and other organizations developing international influence and interaction, mutual need, a sharing of knowledge, buying and selling each other's products, building, transporting each other's goods, and joint affairs and efforts. Globalization is so much more than international business mingling; sending a hospital ship after a tsunami, ordering a part for a car, being able to travel to tour China, it's the clothes you have on, it's the diversity of people in your grocery store line, or caring for you in the hospital. It is even the international infant and child adoptions that happen every day to help give everyone a chance. I discovered a few have fears of it leading to some type of world order or one government. Too many people know that is a bad idea to allow that to be a worry. Yes, anything could happen, but a great deal would have to occur for that one to line up. One government controlling the world would be horrible; it would remove balance, cultures, and that beautiful diverse autonomy I'm always encouraging. Let's not waste our potential goodness and energy for today on such a thin possibility, we have too much else that needs to be accomplished. The G7 is goodness in action, and a B500 will be more goodness in action.

Accepting that the people have integrated on a global scale will greatly decrease our pain and suffering and is a massive advantage to us on many levels. Although there are those who disagree, except for the opportunity for increased hatred, judgment, and ethnocentrism thoughts and actions, we have all benefited from the blending of the people of the world far more than we have been hurt, slowed, or damaged. As soon as we figured out how to walk long distances, ride camels and horses, and build boats that could cross the ocean, business, racial, cultural, product, and knowledge globalization was a done deal.

Yes, please, let's keep our various countries around the world. Diversity is not our enemy, but rather works to our advantage and adds richness to our lives and relationships. We all like pasta, tacos, coffee, and chocolate, right? Uniting on as many fronts as we can, and the business world has the potential for wealth, knowledge, ability, and resources to accomplish a level of sustainable social, humanitarian, and ecological progress beyond anything any one government or seven governments can accomplish. Especially if governments will cooperate. The top 500 most powerful companies in the world could make a serious difference, I can't fathom what they could imagine then accomplish. The world's pollution, trash, and recycle problems could be a start?

Having a DNA ancestry analysis done confirms that globalization is a fact, not a fear.

They may not be able to fix it, but we can still help

After writing this subsection, I was starting my first full run-through when I began second-guessing myself at the first few lines of a paragraph below. I had written, "We are expecting . . ." I can't say that, was my first thought. You can't place that blame on we the people, was my next thought. Second-guessing myself while I write is not new to me. Yet, I seem to have an inability to keep observations of injustice to myself. At times, I consider it a fault of mine, but some tell me it is a gift. I know a lot of people don't like it. Due to my inability to ignore human or social injustice, I sometimes run things past a friend or three for their new angles, and to check myself.

Again, I asked a few people about the subject and the direction of what you are about to read. This is how I approached it: I introduced the subject, explained my feelings about what I had written telling them the gist, then I asked, "Do you think I should include it in the chapter?" Then I stopped to see how they would answer that medium open-ended question. Two told me to trust you all and share it. One added, "Your audience already knows they don't like hearing some of what you have the courage to say about ourselves." Another friend said, "It validates what many already know, feel, or practice, and everyone likes to be validated." I want you to know I'm sharing it because I care, and because it feels fantastic and benefits all to be nice to people until you must protect yourself, then just step away. My favorite answer was, "Vincent, you shouldn't write half human truths you write, you keep ruining my denial, but it's strange, you say hard things, but they help!" Yet again, my chest is pounding, but here I go.

In these challenging times, it is easy to feel helpless to prevent the bad. Many of the problems we are asking the government to fix we have contributed to the issue. Yet we can also help turn negative contributions into positive ones. Us calling for gun control is a harsh but potentially helpful example. Now you know why my chest is pounding.

We are expecting our politicians to fix problems that we also can help solve. We aren't personally responsible for our past mass killings. We did not take away the free will and choice of the shooters, stabbers, bombers, mass poison attackers, or drivers of vehicles intentionally driven into groups of people around the world. Guns are only one of those five methods to mass kill and injure. However, we have unknowingly, sometimes unavoidably, and sadly even intentionally, contributed to the bad actions that occur in our world. It is a rather large mixed bag of contributing factors, such as: untreated or unrecognized mental illness and its unnecessary remaining stigmas by a sector of society, alienating anyone different from us, bullying, zealots inspired by religion or politics, unhealthy aggressive and manipulative politics itself, and media who intentionally provoke anger and fear, racial and cultural intolerance, and a plethora of generations of other uncaring actions that have led to not only our mass killings, but also our escalating numbers of depression, isolation, anxiety, suicide attempts, and suicides. Our politicians either won't fix a percentage of our current issues, because either their voters, contributors, or the system does not want them to, or they truly can't fix an issue. Since all guns and other forms of weapons cannot be removed from the earth; this is one of those it is up to us to fix issues.

No matter what reason our elected officials can't or won't help, we can help. Helping is achievable. These mass killings and injuries are not only killing us physically, the above signs and symptoms of depression, anxiety, addiction, suicide attempts, suicides, are proof that they area also killing our spirits in mass.

Thankfully, we have control over how we treat each other. How we treat each other does contribute to mass killings, and our own personal internal disruption. It hurts to be treated less than human, and we sometimes do that to each other. Most of us walk through our days with peace and gentleness towards others. Yet, we can be rough on each other as individuals, and in our various roles of customer, driver, management, peer, and even as human created company policy. But from the bottom up, it is we the individual that has the power to help.

We should accept that it is also up to us to help each other stop wanting to kill, hate, shun, or bully each other. These problems are not only a schoolyard, social media, or youth related problem. By the time these issues get to the schoolyards, it is a late sign and symptoms, as we say in the medical field. Such as getting pale, pasty, and passing out on a hot summer day is a late sign of dehydration, while a little dizziness when standing several hours before passing out is an early sign of dehydration.

If left unchecked, dominant and alpha personalities have a natural drive to do just that, dominate. Whether controlled by our own internal filters, or by external standards, expectations, or laws, not keeping dominant tendencies in check is dangerous. Some of this drive is helpful to our growth, development, and safety. However, these behaviors in children are often learned, whether from the home, media, social media, video games, movies, cartoons, and we often either teach it actively because we know some is good for the child, or we passively condone the behavior. They hear us judge and blame everyone but ourselves, they rarely hear us apologize to even our partner or close friends. They need the opposite from us, to let them know our humanness is normal and okay, including that we are imperfect, and we fail. Children thrive when taught and shown these executive functioning skills, humanities, and helpful realistic self-awareness. Even before these behaviors start, children need to see we care about other people, they need to learn that life is now the teamwork of all humans. If not, our hatred, blame, bullying, mass killings, and intolerance are only going to get worse.

Meeting the humanistic responsibilities we have to each other, especially since we are all walking in the same halls, is a powerful and long step to helping decrease the devastating behaviors that contribute to someone's acts of mass hatred.

As an individual may not have the power to prevent all mass killings to suicides, and everything sad in between, but we do have the power to help slow these human tragedies.

Our politics is aggressively adding to the problem. The manifestos of our mass killers are often filled with political rant. Our politics highly encourages bullying, blame, hopelessness, helplessness, and intentional confusion. Too many of our politicians have become schoolyard bullies. Watch their words and behaviors, the only thing missing is the schoolyard. They accomplish scaring and dividing us. If they scare so many they win, so why would they not keep scaring us? It is like the painfully accurate line in the movie *Bombshell,* when Kate McKinnon's character says, "Ask yourself, 'What would scare my grandmother and piss off my grandfather?' That's a Fox News story."

Whether they ever pass laws or not, changing gun laws in this day and time will not stop killings, I've seen too many stab wounds and deaths in my years. Cars can be driven into crowds, and Austin Texas had a serial bomber detonate five bombs, in three weeks, causing death and six injuries. Guns kill, but abuse, neglect, indifference, and uncaring attitudes, actions, and omissions are the true causes of our mass killings.

It is not only the people that own guns that kill people, but we also still kill each other more with cars than we do with guns. Not only are we not screaming "car control," we complain when an officer pulls us over for speeding, but speed is the number one factor in road deaths. I know I mentioned respectful driving ad nauseam, but your car is a loaded weapon, and its only safety is your awareness, alertness, concentration, respect for others, and lack of aggressive driving. I also mention it often because of its anonymity that seemingly gives us permission to drive poorly. It also creates a huge entitlement, that the aggressive or late for an arrival time driver feels their destination is more important than the other people's time or safety on the road. How we drive is also a direct reflection of ourselves, and a general indicator of how we treat each other as a society. How we drive is a respectful responsibility not only to keep ourselves alive, but to keep others alive. If you ever question this, or the need for traffic law enforcement, watch some dashboard camera videos of some less restrictive and enforced countries, such as Russia. See what a lawless, unchecked freedom to drive without respectful safety creates. Be prepared. The aggression in those videos is hard to watch. These videos are exceptional cause-and-effect examples of the benefits of respectful socially minded attitudes and actions that have unlimited positive rewards for all of us.

It all is such a mixed bag of cause and effect in thoughts, actions, and omissions. Whether in a grocery store line, your work setting, the road, or the schoolyard, we have far more power to turn the tides than we are giving ourselves credit for. Our politicians will never be able to stop one angry mind, in one house, that keeps to themselves, that has the resources to hurt many of us by carrying out acts of mass violence, but we do.

"Gun control," are two words most of our politicians only verbalize after mass shootings. Saying the words "gun control" costs nothing monetary-wise so they say the words. But fixing the issues of our day and time is going to cost us all one way or another. Either by what it takes to solve an issue, or the greater cost to all of us of what it costs to not address an issue. A percentage of our elected officials want to spend their time, energy, and our money to fix our issues, while a percentage of the politicians only want to keep things as they are. Find out which is which before you vote next. Then, ask yourself if how we have been doing it has been working?

There are exceptions to what I am about to share, but for the most part, people who are loved, listened to, not cut off on the road, and even somewhat helped to feel respected, validated, and some levels of self-worth, do not walk into public places and start randomly killing people they have never met.

Here is a question that sums up our ability to make a difference. How angry and frustrated does caring and professional customer service, or healthy respectful peers, make you feel?

Back in the 1990s, I gave a talk at a medical symposium on staying safe in the healthcare setting. When I finished and opened the floor to questions, someone asked me, "What do you think is the one most important thing I can do to keep myself safe?" I answered, "There are times we have to do and say things or direct people that will upset them, such as removing a child from a parent's custody or deny a narcotic addict more drugs, but aside from those times, if you don't want someone to hurt you, then don't give them a reason." That's the gist of what I am saying. Gun control may help decrease mass shootings only because there are too many other ways to end a life. However, treating each other with greater respect every day will decrease not only mass killings but will also help decrease the tensions and tiny little nonphysical assaults in all our days. Teach your ego to let that car move into your lane; they may be a trauma surgeon rushing to get to an emergency surgery, or you may help someone's anger lesson. You eased up a few pounds of pressure on an accelerator for 2 seconds, and you made a difference. Maybe a lifesaving difference. You are not a doormat for your goodness, you may be a hero.

Good news, bad news

Because we have become a society that feels we don't need each other to get by, we don't talk to each other for fear it may be taken "wrong," and in general people are sensitive, angry, and defensive, so we now stay tightly to ourselves. I get it too. I recently heard it summed up well; we used to be a society that sat on our front porch and interacted with our community. Now we sit on our back porch and hide from our community. All of everything that divides and isolates us is also chipping away at our spirit. Here are a few questions you can ask yourself to see if you are contributing to yourself, individuals, and community to help with the escalating issues of the past twenty years. Do you drive with general respect and courtesy to those around you? If appropriate, do you ask people how their day is while waiting in a line, or talk to someone you normally would not? How often do you listen more than you talk during a conversation? Do you extend acceptance, tolerance, forgiveness, and understanding? Or do you find yourself more often extending judgment, frustration, and a lack of those four pillars of goodness? When someone is rude, or just off with you a little, do you bite them back, or do you actively extend yourself to them, or passively help them by remaining neutral and getting to the other side of the bump? Do you react with fast emotions or respond with more calming rational thoughts? Do you accept your part of a bump? Do you accept and appreciate yourself from the inside out? That one makes a difference, too.

Have I got some news for you

There is one more influence on the freedom and stability to all societies, governments, and our sanity in general, that holds a great deal of responsibility besides government officials and we the citizens, that being the news media. Our news outlets have a responsibility to not incite us with emotional slant, and to attempt to the best of their ability to provide the news without personal, financial, or political bias. Accuracy without slant sums up the goal. Some news outlets are inciters, while others are doing their best to do the textbook job, but still hold viewers. We have a responsibility here as well. The media knows what pulls us in, if we change our needs from wanting sensationalism and accepting the slant, we would be less pulled in.

I know it's a tall order, but the media is also capable of changing its modality. Can they find other ways to profit? Would we keep watching, so they appropriately continue to sell commercial time, if they only gave us the who, what, when, where, and how but left out the slant? Our news outlets need rightful profit. At the same time, they need to remember their true role in society, that of watchdogs, and not of influencers. News needs to be for the purpose of informing the people and exposing the truth, not to influence by manipulating the bad.

Is their job to inform us of bad scary news, or to scare us with the bad for a special interest goal? Don't worry, the reality is sensational enough, if you feel it in your heart as the human tragedy it is. Many people are very good at knowing how to guide us too easily. We can blame them for using their knowledge, skills, and money to manipulate, but we cannot blame them for all its effectiveness. There are reasons I repeat free will and choice, and all the apparent simple or basic empowerments that I admit redundancy. These intelligent but manipulative actions are powerful, and we have given them a percentage of our free will and choice. We are also not completely to blame that they are incredibly good at what they do. I am already grounded in the fact that the news outlets most likely will not curtail their part just because I have written a few paragraphs stating a need. Which is exactly why we should focus even harder on thinking for ourselves after we hear or read what the news has to say. I still recommend reading more than you watch. Periodically walk away from it for a few days, it will be there when you get back.

Another example of updating our government for our times

The number of people who think the electoral college system is outdated and outright unfair for voting in our president is significant. We have had two elections in the past twenty-year period where a person won the popular vote but lost the electoral college vote.

My whole life I had heard one reason we use an electoral college system is because each state had to ride their state's votes into the capitol on horseback. This does not make sense, of course, because several witnesses could have ridden a popular vote to be counted just as easily as an electoral college vote. I mention it, because the reason being used today for keeping the electoral college is just as outdated as the untrue horseback theory. The actual reason it was created has also proven outdated, and no longer stands up to rational scrutiny. Supposedly the reason we will still have it is so smaller states receive equal representation, with the initial worry being that states would vote somewhat like-minded. This too has proven to be untrue. The population of most states divide their popular votes between two or three candidates. The other reason is surprising: you can't be trusted. It was originally created to form a buffer between the popular vote and who became the president. Just in case the majority of we the people voted in who the electoral college electors felt they were making a poor choice. Hum? It also is not conducive to our system, a *democratic* republic. No one likes it when their candidate doesn't win, but we normally accept it. For that matter, no one likes when they don't win, but the person that is the loser normally accepts that too.

I know the very first argument that is given for the need for the electoral college is, "But it gives the less populated states equal representation in electing the president, otherwise the smaller states would not be represented." I am going to give a handful of reasons the electoral college is antiquated and unfair, but I will start with this actively sought-out observation. If little states needing equal representation were a true concern, then logic would mean that each state, no matter its population, should get the same number of electoral college votes. Since that is not the case, I picked the smallest state, Rhode Island, to start asking the people their opinion. Go to the source, right? Rhode Island has only four of the country's total 538 total electoral college votes, and 270 are needed to win the presidency. But California has fifty-five votes? Rhode Island still does not have equal representation. That would look like every state having the same number of electoral college votes no matter its population. For close to forty years now, every time I met someone from Rhode Island, whether in a hospital or a coffee shop, I would ask them personally if they thought the electoral college was a good idea, did they think it was fair, or did they want the country to go to the popular vote only? In the maybe twenty people I have asked, I have only heard something passionate along the lines of, "No, we don't like it. It is obvious a candidate really doesn't care about winning our state, which means our vote doesn't really count. Even though our population is large enough that if every one of our votes were counted in a popular vote election, we could influence an election." It also does not give equal representation for the people in cities that vote one way surrounded by a state that voted the other way, their votes also end up not counting. Such as Austin, Texas.

Another major flaw in the outdated system is the all or nothing way a state's electoral college votes. California has fifty-five electoral college votes. If 45% of the state votes for candidate A, and 55% voted for candidate B, one would assume twenty-five of those votes would be cast for candidate A on arriving in Washington and thirty of those votes would go to candidate B, right? No, I am sorry, all fifty-five electoral votes are cast for candidate B. It is not even an appropriate division by ratio and proportion, and that is not democratic.

There is another issue with the old system: the electoral college electors arriving in Washington do not even have to vote for the candidate that won the majority of the state! Hence, the loophole that was created because you, the voter, can't be trusted.

In every election, one person counts for one vote, except when we vote for the President of the United States. The entire system is supposedly based on representation of the people. However, in the above example, 45% voting for candidate A in a presidential election, which is a huge percentage of the people of a state of California, being completely ignored, does not equal representation. Even if we did stick with the same system, we could at least get a more accurate representation of your vote by casting those electoral college votes with accurate ratio and proportion for how that state voted. Do we need a new government, or do we just need to fine tune this one?

Careful what we prioritize, there are historic microcosms that should not be ignored

"The only thing we learn from history is that we don't learn
from history."
—George Wilhelm Friedrich Hegel

"Those who don't remember history are destined to repeat it."
—Winston Churchill

A grandparent says to you, "I wouldn't do that if I were you." Maybe you replied, "But, I won't . . . because . . . it won't . . ." The grandparent says again, "I'm just saying. I don't think you should . . ." The next thing you know you are both standing at the kitchen sink washing out the cut, you're crying, and the grandparent says, "I tried to warn you not to do that." Rapa Nui Island and the Rapa Nui people are trying to tell us, "I wouldn't do that."

Rapa Nui Island is now more commonly known as Easter Island. It is owned by Chile and is situated about a quarter of the distance across the Pacific Ocean off the west coast of South America headed towards Australia. It takes about five hours to fly there from Chile. Like most of the islands in the Pacific it was formed by a volcano. It is estimated it was first inhabited roughly 1,000 years ago. Verbal history into written history tells of its discovery and habitation by a canoe party consisting of only a few boats. For a long time, the Rapa Nui had it going on much like we do; resources, riches abound but had more to do with creature comfort than with money, of course. They wanted to thank their god for their bounty, and protect themselves from evil, so they started carving the huge, massive heads known as moai, pronounced "mo-eye," that heavily dotted the island. The iconic heads have dwindled in numbers for several reasons, 887 of the statues remain. Archeologists are good at putting the pieces together about how a culture lived and died. They feel the clues are rather clear concerning what happened to the Rapa Nui, which is another reason the history of these people has something to teach us.

It's a good-sized island, roughly 63 square miles. If it were a perfect rectangle, it would be a little more than 4 miles wide by 15 miles long, which is three times larger than Manhattan, New York. It was covered with lush trees, many palm trees, with a tree count in the millions, and the coastal land could grow ground tuber crops. These people had the land and resources to create a comfortable and modern culture for their time, just as we have today. A couple hundred years passed and a Dutch explorer with a beautiful but hard name to pronounce, Jacob Roggeveen, discovered the island on Easter Day, April 5,1722, and named it Easter Island. The island and its people were already well into serious decline when Roggeveen landed on the island. By 1774, when Captain Cook landed on the island, the Rapa Nui were in even worse decline. The correlations between what happened to these people, and our past and present, is a significant likeness.

Archeologists agree on many of their findings, that when the island was first discovered by the canoe party, it was a lush resource rich island, and it grew to become a healthy and thriving culture that may have been populated at one point by as many as 17,000 people, fed by abundant seafood and agriculture along a percentage of the coastline after trees were cleared. They agree, and the evidence is clear, it was a group of people who became obsessed with carving and moving huge statues with upper torsos, then buried so only the neck and head are visible. The archeologists agree that the people arrived at a tree-filled island, and deforestation took place to the point there were not enough large trees to even build new canoes. Affecting their ability to fish and then to even flee the island. The cause of that deforestation is listed as everything from mass clearing so they could grow crops, move the moai, and build shelters.

The archaeologist agree human actions were the cause of most of the deforestation. Just as we know today that our collective way of life also contributes to our ecological issues. They know they flourished and thrived, then hunger and political division divided the people, and created bands of warring factions. They know their lack of foresight contributed to the imbalances of their ecological and cultural systems which they, like some of us, assumed was endless during their "progress." Those assumptions and their lack of foreplanning ultimately toppled their community. They even toppled each other's statues to attempt to upset and weaken each other's emotional and spiritual strength.

We have everything required to learn from history and change the course of our tomorrows. The Rapa Nui spent their energy and resources to carve and worship a god made of rock. Unrelated to religion, what are we "worshiping" that is causing the self-destruction of our larger "island?" What assumptions of unlimited resources are we assuming?

The lessons of our many microcosms around the world and throughout history, not just the Rapa Nui, are highly worthy lessons. A microcosm is the same as the big picture of Earth, only smaller, but everything else is the same. What happens in a microcosm happens to the world, our world. It is also important to remember the "it can't happen to me" as well as the "I can't be a part of the problem" syndromes. We are the Rapa Nui, our island Earth, still fragile and requiring balance and forethought. The choices we make as individuals, communities, businesses, and governments, will decide whether we have learned anything from the Rapa Nui telling us, "I wouldn't do that."

"People that value privileges above principles soon lose both."
—Dwight D. Eisenhower

What would happen if one side always got its way, and why we should respect opposing views

Visualize every government and country, culture, race, business, industry, your work, your friendships, and even your intimate relationship as its own airplane in flight. Although this would be accurate for any group, company, or relationship in life, let's place societal pull, politics, and government in one airplane. Some countries' airplanes are flying a little higher than others because some countries are more stable than others. Obviously, the fewer the stressors on an airplane, the smoother, straighter, and more level it flies. Some countries' planes will be fighting with sputtering engines and unable to maintain smooth and level flight. Other planes are flying high, straight, level, and smooth. Others may be not too far off the ground, running low on fuel, or serious social and political winds and storms are creating their extreme turbulence. What are some stresses that can push on any person, community, country, race, or culture? Emotions and excessive gain over good always land close to the top, with of course big ones such as anger and fear also causing turbulence. Hunger and a lack of basic human rights are always respected, for that will always push on a society or unjust government. Then there are threats and apparent threats. In this day and time, misinformation and political slant comes in close to the top in reference to true threats. History teaches us that extremely off balance social and political injustices often bring planes down fast. The extreme overload of misinformation is causing our planes to do a lot of unnecessary traveling rather than efficiently getting to our more needed destinations. Why would a pilot waste time and fuel going around a storm cloud that does not exist? That is what the false and misinformation is doing to us. A lack of forethought and preventative choices further add major stress and turbulence to any country's plane's smooth flight. Which would equate to not going around a real storm cloud.

If an airplane is getting into trouble, and it did not have safe altitude or a fine-tuned engine allowing it to power up so it can gain altitude, what would happen if the pilot put one foot down turning the rudder completely to one side and turned the yoke, all the way to the same side? It would quickly lose altitude, stability, even flip over possibly, all causing a crash, unless skillfully corrected. This is exactly what the left and the right seem to be fighting for—total rudder and aileron to one side only.

However, find and maintain balance, even with the constant corrections required if windy, and the plane remains in flight.

That extreme pull to one side is what groups around the world are trying to do. One of the reasons George Washington warned us not to create parties was to increase our choices, balances, and stability of our country to more than only left or right. He knew it would create a constant side-to-side push-pull that would not create stability. He knew extreme polar political tugging would cause great instability. We are proving him correct.

Slowing the forces down that want you upset

The people and groups who outright want to manipulate you only want you to see little pictures. They can manipulate you easier and lead you to believe the answers to our problems are simple and that they have the simple answers. Little pictures are easier to scare you with. They keep you from seeing the true complexity of our problems, and just how complex many of the answers to those issues are. If I show you a picture of a scary clown from 200 yards away it's not going to be too scary. However, if I show you a close-up picture, so close you can see the pores under the pancake makeup and the facial hair stubble, that's scary. Especially if an evil face has been painted, rather than even a neutral one. Some politicians, political groups, and news outlets, prefer that you not see the true big picture. If you see the bigger picture, they don't want you to see, then you would know their answers are not as easy as they make them sound, and that their simple answers are now much less effective. Also, if we are distracted with fears and quick little easily fed concerns, then that stays our focus, and they keep on doing what they do, and don't do.

You have been endowed with highly functional weapons against these smoke and mirror antics. The weapons can be used in numerous directions to empower you to make more informed choices, and to have a much more peaceful reaction to politics, government, our problems, and even the solutions. Using this one tool every time the subject of politics or government is at hand will decrease these stressors' abilities to create an emotional response or manipulate your vote. Your empowerment is your autonomous thoughts.

I used the plural, "thoughts," to emphasize the importance, and strength, of spending a speck of energy to not be led down streets and alleys that keep you manipulated and willfully following the manipulators breadcrumbs. Harsh, but true. Expending the energy to constantly work to have thoughts that are formed by you, that make you who you are, that separates you from even your twin if you have one, is another part of you that makes you special. We are alike in powerfully connected ways: our hopes, dreams, joys, and even our fears and failures often bond us in commonality. Exercising our autonomous thoughts are why we are who we choose to be, and how we choose to think about life, and from what angle you wish to experience your life. Not using your autonomous thoughts is allowing an outside force to guide your autonomous you, such as advertising, news, friends, or politics. Be autonomous in your thoughts as often as you can keeps you from being overly led by others. Other input can be healthy and right for us, just use your autonomous thoughts to decide what is good for you. It can be safer, calmer, and protect the you that you want to be, not the you someone else wants you to be.

The exercising of autonomous thoughts guarantees you are speaking and doing because you choose to, not because you were led to. It means when the commercial states, "Don't vote for Vincent Dodd, he did not vote to give you a pat on the back." You will research that bill that I voted against and discover for yourself that it had a rider for another legislative raise on it, "Oh, I bet that is why he voted against it. It has to be, because I read his book and he is a patting on the back kind of person." Autonomous thoughts mean you will consider much wider consideration than the first thing you read or hear, then make up your own mind and carry out your conclusions, not someone else's.

One of the stages that history also shows occurs when a democracy is falling is mob rule. Often incited by one person or a group of people with the intention of creating chaos. Fear propaganda is a powerful tool, often inciting unnecessary fear-based rebellion. Speeches and now online propaganda, often from within the country itself, use these basic textbook manipulative steps. Starting with blame and divide by creating scapegoats and false fears. Next comes the fix, often thinly veiled appearing to protect the people, but most often its underlying goal is to advance the comfort of a few; they tell how they will fix it and protect us from these ghosts and goblins. Incite those who are easily incited first, then they will do the work for the inciter, by working to upset those around them with this important scary information.

In the United States most inciters are from within our country. Powerful bad players wanting to manipulate our vote. It also is utilized for actions such as incite protest, rebellion, or to push laws that help protect their special interest rather than our tomorrows. Some of our news outlets are inciters. But for some of our politicians, it is all they know.

Utilizing bigger rational thoughts over emotional first fears, will also help calm the waters. Much of what we are so upset about is nowhere near the danger we are fed to believe. We do not have to hurry and destroy your opponents. Vigilance, yes. Action, yes. Many little changes from all three branches of our government, executive, legislative, and the judicial, have slowly moved us off track. It is not as far off as some want you to believe, and it is we the people who have the most power to get it back on track. Our greatest individual core tool to accomplish this is our autonomous thoughts.

Words can be arranged to calm or incite, inform or mislead, heal or hurt, or help or hinder; all can be so convincing, whether those words represent the truth or not. This is a destructive standard of our times. Fight it with your free will and choice, your rational mind, your ability to see both big and little pictures, your ability to partially step out of yourself to see tomorrow also, and then use your powerful autonomous thoughts to form your opinions and choices.

We are lucky, autonomous thought protects both our peace and our freedoms, it costs nothing, and you always have it with you. Every human mind is capable of being manipulated, learning to exercise our independent thoughts keeps our minds more resistant to falsehoods. One of the key ingredients to the longevity of our life, our liberty, and our pursuit of happiness is our ability to daily apply our freedom to think for ourselves. It also keeps the dignity, heart, and soul of our country, community, and ourselves healthy, alive, and thriving.

But I don't agree with that!

Our politics and our times are both lightning fast to label people. Bam, we stick a label on each other before we have even finished a sentence, and even rarer, a paragraph. Bam, quickly label it anyway. Our issues are not that easy to summarize, nor is the fast inappropriate cut-

and-dry labeling helpful. Assigning fast labels to issues or one's beliefs, such as "liberal," "conservative," "socialism," "rights-infringing," and many more are not realistically addressing our true core issues. Nor have those quick stick labels helped us find tangible solutions. Quite the opposite. We seem to be so dead set on getting the labels and blame forced on each other, that the problems are compounding, and the often-unfair labels only further divide us.

This futility to blame and label, when we have all contributed, only forces us further away from sustainable functional actions. The labels are also often wrong, not a full sentence or paragraph has been stated, and bam, you just won a label. Depending on the subject, most people's views are more diverse than one fast label could summarize. I know mine lean both ways depending on the subject, and whether the issue is humanistic, social, or governmental procedural. Keep in mind, some politicians like the labels, they help them divide us.

We have become a society that rewards the ridiculous and those who argue over each other. Some news stations intentionally put people on television that cut each other off mid-sentence, raise their voices, and insult each other. One of the things I was taught in nursing school, law enforcement, and all crisis intervention classes, is also a basic principle of conflict resolution, problem solving, and above all, gracious general social etiquette and human respect: allow people to finish their thoughts and don't interrupt unless needed for safety reasons. We have begun to reward those who discard that basic principle of letting someone finish their sentences. Jerry Springer figured this out a long time ago and capitalized on it for twenty-eight years on his talk show. Correction: it was more of a scream, blame, and physical assault show, with very little talking. The wild and not surprising fact is that he was a politician before that show.

The importance of allowing someone to finish their sentence, even if you strongly disagree with them, has been taught to me from so many angles. Whether you are a nurse busy at a triage desk, or in law enforcement, if they are verbally escalating but not physically acting out, it creates an opportunity to resolve a problem or issue, or even avoid violence. Actual problems I have avoided over the years by not stopping someone from even rambling too soon: admitted a gun was in bags, purses, and waistlines handed over to me with full cooperation, overdoses admitted such as "I just took twenty Xanax in the parking lot," or "If you let me call my mom, I won't slit my wrist in the bathroom." The next thing that person was going to say, that was interrupted by a politician on a legislative floor or by two news pundits on a news channel, may have been the solution to the problem being discussed, especially since both sides do have some correct answers to solving many of our issues of today. Sadly, and selfishly destructive, it is some people's goal to not let problem-solving answers be spoken.

It is not as clear cut sounding as the easy answers we are presented. The only slightly harder to work with the gray, messy middle is where we are going to find most of our sustainable answers. In both ourselves and our politics, some of our political inflexibility is keeping us from achieving better, and yes, eventually easier. All or nothing is not a healthy way to approach most issues, is unrealistic in most instances, often requires force or manipulation to achieve, and is rarely the best answer. Collaboration is the key to peace, productivity, profit, and tomorrow.

Paramount to functional solutions is knowing that factual information does sometimes conflict and overlap. That does not make the information invalid. A rational person, government employee, or official should always welcome all information, whether it agrees with their initial statements and beliefs or not. Many have made flexibility in an elected official a bad or weak thing. Flexibility in a politician is one of the reasons we should elect someone to represent us. Some people get elected because they are inflexible, with the voter believing such staunchness is protecting their beliefs and ways.

We are capable of slowing down our vicious cycle of hurry-hurry. Politics, government, and the emotions of the people, elected officials, and the media of any country are not a mass of energy we really want careening forward with real speed. Our urgency to get our way, or to quickly protect gain over good, is damaging us and our system in many ways and directions. Fast thinking and actions cause more and bigger mistakes.

Are we pulling our elected officials from the wrong field? And a few requests to maybe help make a difference

The number of influences affecting our suffering concerning politics are also immeasurable. Believing that we have an ability to be part of the solution is the first action we can do to help make our lives and the various issues around all of us much lighter. Then there is the daily choice of whether you want to live and breathe the blame and fear game or walk with bigger picture thoughts, and direct that energy into functional multidirectional exploration.

Some of the "few requests" in the title of this subsection are to please run for office if you will protect your government and *the* people, not *your* people. Then, whether you are an elected official voting on legislation or a citizen voting, please vote seeing a much larger picture than the snippets shown.

Double standards and hypocrisies are rapidly assisting in dissolving our social and governmental structures. We almost did not elect one president because he admitted to smoking pot, but we elected another one knowing full and well the magnitude of his colorful history. Please, don't not vote for a good person because they do not always do what you want them to, or because they have a normal human past. Every candidate has human mistakes in their pocket. More important than someone's past humanness is will they vote to protect the people and the constitution to the best of their ability. That does not mean we should condone or tolerate actions that are past humanness, such as habitual lying, non-disclosure, divisive words, and criminal history.

Another key to less personal stress and greater contribution is the willingness to accept change. This is yet again another one that crosses over into every aspect of your life, work included. If we look back at history, we can clearly see that resisting change mostly only delayed the inevitable changes that needed to and did occur anyway, and only created social unrest before that inevitable change occurred; most civil wars are a good example. That is not saying that a percentage of civil wars did not need to occur to defend what is good, right, and fairer. Yet the US's Civil War is a painful example; six-hundred-thousand dead and the needed change occurred anyway. Please be willing to realize the familiarity of the past and how things were done are not always a part of the answers. Resisting change, or refusing to let go of old ideas, concepts, are only slowing our progress to less strife, less instability, and more real and helpful solutions. As one of my nursing instructors used to say, "If anyone tells you, 'But that is the way we have always done it,' remind them that the frontal lobotomy also used to be an acceptable and frequently performed procedure." A frontal lobotomy is severing the connections in the brain just behind the forehead. Some doctors used an ice pick-like instrument, or an actual ice pick, to accomplish this procedure. Thank goodness most changes are for the good if they are done for the right reasons.

Except for now and the period leading up to the Civil War, the US population in relation to political party identification has always looked like a normal bell curve, with the great majority of us, left and right, creating the middle of the bell curve. Due to our lack of ability to compromise and work together, we are no longer on a bell curve. Our political curve now looks more like an "M," with the middle of the M being pulled further apart and increasing, thus weakening it in the center. The two peaks represent the left and right pulling and fighting harder and harder to get their uncompromising way. An unhealthy amount of tension and force is required to turn a bell curve into an "M" shape. Too much force and tension and something has to give. A percentage of us are flexible, and many more do have the ability to change their rigidity before we spread further apart. Hopefully, all groups and cultures will continue to find greater flexibility. All sides pulling harder is not going to keep us in the middle, it is not the balance many believe it to be. Our all or nothing multidirectional pulling from political parties, big business, and various subcultures related to race, religion, or ideology, is significantly decreasing teamwork, productivity, and society's stability. Worse, because it is from the core of our being out, it is tearing us apart as individuals from the inside out to see it, feel it, and suffer its many repercussions. Our lack of flexibility and unity is dangerous and damaging on every level, first the individual, then up through our families, through communities and nations, to international peace.

Thank goodness we as individual citizens hold some of the power also. Never stop reminding yourself the greatest power is not in your single vote, but rather how you cast that vote. Yes, sometimes we vote for the lesser of two less than ideal choices. Our informed vote can help keep positive actions, both small and large, moving us to better. It is important that we attempt not to vote for the person who will protect only our monetary investments or personal beliefs of today, but rather that we vote for the person who will work to keep good, right, and fairer, as well as our children's future, in their words and actions. Finding a way to make another dollar is fairly easy, especially if you already have dollars. Finding a way to keep people, communities, and nations healthily, stable and thriving for our tomorrows, will be much harder.

Run good people run. . . No, I mean for office

Who runs for office? Mainly attorneys. I personally know several attorneys who would make great public officials, but they don't want any part of frontline politics. In my research, it appears that 40–50% of higher position elected officials have law degrees. We already talked about what attorneys are trained to do, protect their clients, and to win. That can be dangerous if they are hired to win when their client is not right. I know many attorneys who care to stick to what is right. We need people to start running for office who have bigger picture visions and greater selfless awareness, who will think of the stability of government, stability of the citizen, and tomorrow over today's high profits. We need solution-based, not blame-based smoke and mirrors, people to step up.

Then, equally important, we need to elect them. Only half of our political health depends on who runs for office, the other half of that long term wellness is who we vote for. We could have a fantastic person run for office, but that is worthless if we won't change what influences our vote.

Why do attorneys dominate in the field of politics? Knowing law helps, and being trained and becoming successful by winning, not always by being right, especially if persuading a jury is involved. Which translates to being good at persuading people. Hence, getting persuaded votes, not informed votes. Then all they have to do is manipulate the people, often via our emotions, and convince us our fears and beliefs are right. This correlates to their donors having become the politician's clients, not we the people, and the jury now equals their voters. We don't even hold them accountable to be right, they only must convince us they are right, or again manipulate our emotions, and we vote for them. Which means advertising agency minds and speech writers win elections, not the hearts, minds, and spirits of the person running for office. These are not traits of only attorneys, all politicians get good at these angles if that is a tactic being used. If it works on us, they will keep using it. Only you have the power to keep your vote an informed vote not a persuaded vote.

We hold some responsibility for their ability to accomplish their goal, by trusting their words and our emotions they ignited, without double checking their factual past actions or our emotions. Whether in practice of law or they become a politician, they are trained and skilled at arranging their words, message, and emotional delivery of that message so it is received by the jury or voter to be what we want to hear or will be emotionally moved by. Not always what is factual or right. Your autonomous big picture thoughts are still your most powerful empowerment to protect yourself from such intentional manipulative convincing. This holds true whether a candidate is an attorney or not, because everyone can learn these manipulations.

So, who does have this special skill to be factual and solution based? If you were going to ask someone to run for office, what skills would you think are more important than being skilled at convincing people? Here is where our younger generations come in. We need people to run for office, please, that will help get our system back on more solid tracks, and then will help to literally reaffirm and maintain all our lives, liberties, and our pursuit of happiness. It needs to be people who weigh all sides of an issue and are not convinced by the first persuasion of only one fact, fiction, campaign contribution, or getting reelected. They won't have to worry about being reelected if we do our work to see the bigger picture, and if they are good at protecting us and our government, we should re-elect them, if that is what they are openly doing. I include one fact, singular, because it needs to be someone who will look at all the facts, not the one fact that supports what their voters or contributors want only. One of the differences between a republic and a total democracy is balance. The side that voted or contributed to your election is incapable of always being right.

No one side is ever capable of always being right, it is statistically and humanly impossible for an individual or a group. Safe balance is not only side to side to keep a ship afloat, but top heavy is also an off balance that can topple and sink a ship.

Our all or nothing expectations of our politicians are causing us issues. Which in actions means we don't vote a good person out because they don't always do what we want. Personally, I think all elected officials should post their reason for voting for or against a bill. I also think they should randomly poll the people in their district on an issue. If you were elected to represent us, then actively ask us. Not just the people who do know to call, email, or show up at your office to express their opinion. That is only a tiny sampling of the people who have a higher stake in whatever issue is involved. That is special interest arriving at your office or committee room, not the opinion of one-hundred people in your district that elected you to represent them. The average worker does not know something important to them is coming up for a vote in a few hours and a handful of special interest people, in your face and present, are attempting to influence your representative's vote later that day. You could advertise and invite the people of your municipality, county, or district, to register their phone number or email with your office, that way they know who is contacting and would answer or reply, and randomly survey fifty to one-hundred people to ask their opinion. I have been a part of one of those large groups, with a common interest to protect, arriving in a committee chamber to influence a vote on a state level. That was not a true sampling of the people's opinions, wants, and needs. There is always a better way, and solution-based thinking and action is how we find better. I hope we will keep spending our energy and flexibility to find those better ways.

Two more solutions to these big issues are supporting more people to run for office who will do the right thing for the right reason, and then we voters start to elect them. I personally know of a few fields that would be good at this. Teaching hospital doctors and nurses comes to mind first, of course. No, I do not want to run for office. I know my strength and weakness, and the government is not how I am supposed to help. Teaching hospital personnel are highly trained to not go with their first thought, but to keep digging. They have all been humbled by complexities and know that illnesses are not always as clear-cut as they first appear. They also know human lives are involved. Don't you think that would be a great base for an elected official? Pathologists would be uniquely qualified; they are great at microscopic details, and they are used to gross stuff. Scientists and healthcare professionals are highly trained to find the truths, facts, and not to place their first thought into action, but to place it into *challenge*. Then it must pass challenges before it goes into the category of factual. They want proof, they don't want to hear what supports their first thought, before they form conclusions. But this means that you, the voter, will be willing to appreciate the same scientific method, *even* if it means you discover your initial thinking was wrong. It is okay to be wrong, especially if it gets us closer to right.

Pilots would also potentially make great elected officials. They are methodical, attentive, constantly ready for the unexpected, and are highly courageous because they chose a career that requires them to argue with the powerful and deadly constant of gravity for their entire career. Statistically speaking, landings to crashes, they are exceptionally good at taking care of the people they are assigned to keep alive.

I would say chefs would be fantastic because they are so creative, resourceful, and they like quality for the people. But they can be moody as all get out. Wait, I changed my mind! They only get moody when people don't do their job well, chefs would make great public officials!

CPAs and accountants would also make for fantastic officials. They are methodical and meticulous, they hate negative balances, they know which tax loopholes are fair for all or just for the wealthy, and most will not risk liability exposure for a shady client and will drop them. It's also hard to hide money from them. They only want the facts, and they are great at seeing and comprehending both the little and big picture. That's it, our perfect elected official is a second-career teaching hospital doctor because they are scientists, too, whose first career was a CPA, loves to cook, and flies on weekends!

Anyone from any field is capable of making a great elected official if they will take care of the republic and us before they take care of image and donors. The gentleman who pumped out my septic tank years ago knew that just because something looked pretty, it might still smell bad. That is definitely a great quality for an elected official to have.

My ideas are to strengthen the individual, so we can find our answers together

As I shared, I didn't want to write this chapter or the one on spirituality and religion. But I do know to listen to my friends, even when they tell me things I don't want to hear. Much like politics, we do not always like what we hear or what happens, but if it is the right thing for the right reason, you don't lose out as much as you think you do. That sentence has the power to heal, calm, and strengthen, immediately and tomorrow. That is why I wrote these chapters anyway, not for me, not because I had thoughts that I felt could fix anything, but to attempt to do the right thing for the right reason. Because attempting to do the right thing for the right reason is doing the right thing. Writing these two controversial chapters was not the easy route for me, that would have been a chapter on my favorite subjects of puppies and Easter baskets.

I know there is some personal slant in this chapter, but I tried awfully hard to stick to big general concepts, as factual information as I could research, and always with examples. Earlier, I mentioned manipulative slant as opposed to openly stated blatant opinion. Removing all slant on this personal to all of us, treacherous, and explosive, subject is not an easy task, thus please, always exercise your autonomous thoughts. I attempted to decrease the slant in how I wrote, or to write so you could also see when it was a blatant opinion. Manipulative slant is when a news article leaves out key important parts of the full picture, or uses wording for intentional manipulation, attempting to lead you.

Disclosure of more information and the ability to admit shortcomings, weakness, and mistakes, would also be an exceptional quality in our elected officials. However, that also means the media and we voters will need to stop expecting perfection from our elected officials. Greater stability will be found in voting for who the person is, not how they sound, dress, their gender, religion, race, or culture. Excellent elected officials may be found from any direction. We even vote for people who have the most signs, coolest slogans, names that appear the same as our race, and who can raise the most money. Which could be a scary indicator, it might mean they have financial special interest behind them. Or the proof that none of this is easy, it might mean they are really a fantastic person. Donor lists can often be researched to help your autonomous thoughts.

The Founders of the United States knew life and government were gray, and they took that into account in many directions. Can we show ourselves and future generations the same gift they gave us? Can we put our cut-and-dry thinking aside to keep, and pass on, the gift they gave us? Mr. Franklin warned us that we will need to expend effort to keep it, but only if we can find the selfless courage they did. I know we can, because I know many people from all walks of life who show selfless courage every day. I know it's up to all of us, because Mr. Franklin did not say, "If your politicians can keep it." He said to a citizen, "...if *you* can keep it."

CHAPTER 13

HATRED, BLAME, AND REVENGE

"An eye for an eye only ends up making the whole world
blind."
— Mahatma Gandhi, 1869–1948 (assassinated)

WIDER ANGLES:

ONLINE DATING AND KEEPING AN EXISTING RELATIONSHIP GROUNDED

In 1995, the far more positive than negative world of online dating launched into a mainstay standard. I have known many who meet via the web who are still in long, healthy relationships. In 2012, it went on steroids, with the first dating app now in your hand. Your thumb can now deliver the action that can brighten, "naaaah," or wrinkle your life up badly, in the dating and intimacy department. Along with all its goodness to fight loneliness and spark love or play, it brought with it just a few buyer-beware worthy notations.

Not exactly online dating's biggest issue, but a time saver nonetheless, meeting online can decrease the initial meeting of three-dimensional people, who put off receivable energy that tells us a great deal about people, and compatibility. We are all such multifaceted individuals, and online dating can turn humans into flat screen words, with hopefully a recent picture that somewhat, kind of, sort of looks like them. Yet, that still can't get close to the dynamics of in person meeting, reading the person's presence, interpreting, then maybe connecting. Our many ways to video call with people has been a great help to further filter initial connection incompatibility. This too is less and less an issue because those that want, often meet in person soon, anyway. Now, with one swipe, sometimes that in person meeting occurs in minutes!

For lack of a more eloquent descriptor, growing up with four older sisters and an out-of-the-box mother was a trip. When people hear that I was the youngest of six with these older sisters their first response is often, "I bet you were so spoiled." Don't I wish! Don't get me wrong, they did some spoiling, but there was also some serious training going on. The magnitude of this influence began while I was still in diapers; I did not know what the toilet was for yet, but they had already taught me the seat went down. I only exaggerate the magnitude of this training slightly.

My sisters read *Cosmopolitan* magazine in the early 1970s when I was rolling into the age of nine or ten. I think that magazine was an influence on them training me. They taught me things such as, "Never approach a woman for a date at the gym or when she is working, especially if she is a bartender or waitstaff. They are friendly for tips but are sick of being hit on." This was before gyms turned into what is now referred to as "meet markets." In humor, I intentionally spelled "meet" incorrectly. I already shared that my sisters taught me it is okay to respectfully approach a woman to ask if they are seeing anyone and would they like to go have a coffee, and yet to gracefully accept "no." One of my sisters taught me, "To never take a girl for pizza on a first date, it's too messy, and the lasting impression you do not want to make is a string of grease and cheese on your chin or shirt." I was over-trained for dating. If there can be such a thing?

I signed onto a dating site around 2006, but it wasn't for me. I have been having dating discussions with friends that do online dating for nearly twenty years to form an outside perspective that stems from hoping we find healthy love. Sometimes it is the third-party's view that helps us see yet another helpful angle on a subject. I have also gone on dates with a few women who were serious online daters. They were not like any other date I had ever been on; they were more like a formal interview rather than the untitled casual interview, a first date already is.

A friend of mine who I have known for a few years is an avid online dater and recently told me that the COVID-19 pandemic has taken this already popular standard of dating into a completely new realm of growth. They taught me it is now almost the only way to date, due to so many changes in society.

I had another friend call me several years ago, completely distraught over being rejected by one of the online dating services. It is one of the services that require you to fill out a rather long survey about yourself and what you are looking for. They were truly upset and told me they had spent an hour filling out the survey, hit the enter button, and the screen replied something along the lines of, they were not compatible for the site to assign potential matches. I know about this person's life, and with shock, and potentially knowing what the problem was, I asked, "Did you answer the questions honestly?!" They replied, "Well, yes, of course." Because they normally have a great sense of humor, I said, "Well that's the problem!" Sadly, it was one of my many failed moments of healthy human support, and they did not find it funny. This person was truly hurt by the rejection, but they asked me to explain why I found it humorous and why I think it happened. Great personal self-review and courage to ask me.

Some people embellish a little on their profile. But people have been known to self-hype in person too, so that's a partial moot point. Except it is a waste of time, we eventually meet our core partner anyway. Of all the times I have asked people to share their pros and cons of online dating I have a favorite. This wisely accurate wisdom had to do with people's profiles. This person did date online and said to me, "I don't think people should write their own bios. It's a perfect setup for failure, because it is never a good start to a relationship when two self-delusional people meet each other!"

They went on to share that people should have their boldest, most unfiltered close friend write their bio, that assures no one is fooling anyone.

Over the years, I have had a few trusting experiences of being in the presence of a friend while they went through their incoming hits. The further trust was that they shared some of their thoughts with me as they went through the list while deciding if they wanted to consider, discard, or reply to their hits. It was amazing how many there were, especially for the woman. Before I continue with these observations, I want you to know I am realistic. No one can give that many hits personal attention. There must be a few screening criteria to thin them out. If you get twenty or more hits a day, it's not like you can send them all a handwritten thank you note. I watched and listened as they went through the pictures and read these bidding suitor's bios, and sometimes a personal note was included. Most are surprisingly fast and make a comment about the picture or then the bio, then click them off the screen. Gone in a click or swipe, with maybe a few staying to evaluate further when I am gone from their presence. What I took away from these observations were questions of cause and effect. Beneath our surface, what does it do to us, and ultimately to how an entire society can feel about people, to discard other humans based on appearance and just a few words? Whether the goal is long-term compatibility, or as some openly use it for, a playground, does this barrage of potentials with a much narrower range of actual long-term compatibility, begin to bend individual and social attitudes and actions?

The need for a thinning process has been a constant since the beginning of time for many multicell organisms, thinning out choices is nature. I think it is fantastic, and a direct correlation to us humans, that some species of female birds will reject a male suitor because either he can't dance or build a suitable nest. I also appreciate the appropriate wisdom of many species, including as it should always be for us humans also, unless near blanket permission is granted; the female has the final say to couple. Because of these many influences on the natural selection process, at some point we all become a "click" to someone and are discarded. Although we cannot avoid being a "click" to someone, or having to swipe people off our screens, our awareness and attitude of its deeper influence could potentially help us with healthier relationships. It just seems too easy to surface judge the person by the tiny cover they present, then discard the whole potentially funny, kind, giving person, who you may be highly compatible with great shared intimacy. In our youth we are guided to believe a fantastic lover has a look, then with time and touch, we learn the connection, compatibility, and feel is so much more powerful. Those stronger and deeper commonalities are so very sexy and beautiful.

Without a little awareness, this next angle has the potential to unground us, then set us up for disappointment: looking for a partner that has A, B, C, D, E, and F to line up perfectly. I see how this could easily happen due to the sheer numbers of hello's online dating provides. If you look at a profile that interests you, and they have A, B, D, E, and F but are missing C then click, off and away they go. Yet, the next person has C but is missing E, click, off they go. If you have thirty hits a day, I see how one could wait for A, B, C, D, E, and F. There is only one problem with waiting: these pictures and profiles are not textbooks, they are human beings, and finding all your required expectations is a long shot. How many of us have all our letters lined up to offer perfection to someone else? I know I'm missing a few letters, to put it softly.

I have always felt people should put their worst picture on their profile, not their best. We already have some trouble being attracted to people and loving each other from the inside out. Maybe that would help a little also? Another pitfall of online dating that seems apparent is too much surface showing and seeking, when all real connections that last with health, mutual respect, appropriate flexibility, and growth, are attractions that are primarily from the inside out. I hear there are dating sites where you can choose to not show your picture until you know there is some compatibility. I get it, that could work to help people meet from the inside out first. Oh yes, physical attraction is important, chemistry is real, we release various chemicals in our bodies from various organs, for various reasons, thus the term "chemistry." But it's the inside attractions that connect us the tightest, last the longest, promotes the most peace in the relationship, and are what makes us beautiful. Our inside.

My caring is not only for those seeking a relationship, but also for those already in one. It seems we are looking for a partner, or are disappointed that our current partner does not have A, B, C, D, E, and F. With time, other deeper letters surface too, "Whoa! Where did that R and Y come from?" But we all have Rs and Ys too. We just may not show them in the early part of a relationship. That is not deceit, but nature, the peacock cannot hold its feathers up and spayed its whole life. That fact of nature only becomes a serious issue when the feathers go down and something we are not compatible with is before us.

I wish you peace, gentleness, and success in either your search for healthy love, or in the maintenance and growth of an existing relationship with core compatibilities nurturing healthy love. I also wish you healthy love and compatibility with yourself when you are walking solo through life either by choice or circumstance.

CHAPTER 14

CHOICE AND REWARDS

"We won't be here forever, so we might as well devote
ourselves to something bigger than ourselves to help
tomorrow. It is the pursuit of contribution, not making
money, that brings us our greatest rewards."
—Dr. James Manning

The Pirogue

I was maybe ten sitting on our dock fishing after school
Gars rolled
Mullet jumped
The commonly seen blue crab holding onto the pylon just below the surface
The silence
All these gifts telling me everything is as it should be

As it should be
Even though my extreme learning disabilities
And frequent harsh migraines are clobbering my small young being
I'll even give up in a few years because the clobbering continued
To this day I am so grateful I failed
Life got much easier after I realized how short and amazing it is
As well I learned to accept the balance of tough joy pain and laughter

A human paddled towards me in a pirogue
Rowing so softly the human was close by the time I heard
Hellos and fishing results were passed between us

We had calmly exchanged a speck of ourselves
My bobber barely moved as the small boat passed
Off the human went with a slow near silent rhythmic forward propulsion

Quickly a motorboat well over the posted and respectful "Create No Wake"
The high-pitched motor bitter angry screaming
It sounded and felt as if a chain was being pulled quickly through my head
The high wake is now waves loudly rolling down the shore
Slapping hard against the bulkhead under the dock
The human is gone but the water remains churned
Our exchange nonexistent
I wonder if the human saw me

I sit and recover
Replaying the contrasting travelers
Both crossing the bayou of life

I am a human and must cross that bayou
I will create a small wake yet sadly larger at times
I will disturb others
I care to apologize for my larger wakes

I would rather cross my bayou in a pirogue

The destruction of yesterday and the rebuilding that can follow

I am not special, what has happened to all of us is hard in various degrees and levels. My childhood had some difficulties, but it was not filled with the abuse and neglect that so many lived through in childhood and throughout life. Yes, my years in the frontlines of public service presented more human tragedy to see, touch, hear, smell, and care for more than any one person needs to experience in life. But again, I'm not special. Too many have had a barrage of bad in their past, and there is more to come for all of us, because various levels of bad are a normal part of all our lives. Yet, we can help decrease the bad, get less of it on us, and even work a little easier with what does hit us. Bad's inevitable arrival does not have to stop Good's hopefully more frequent visits.

I am periodically asked, after someone gets to know me and my past is, "With all the tragedy and death you have seen, why do you laugh so often?" Sometimes the question is worded slightly differently, which changes the answer slightly, "With all the tragedy and death you have seen, how can you always be so happy?" My answer to the first question has always been something along the lines of, that is exactly why I choose to laugh at life and myself as often as I can, because life is hard.

> ". . . Some of it's magic, and some of it's tragic, but I had a good life all the way . . ."
> —Jimmy Buffet, "He Went to Paris"

To say life is hard is an extreme understatement. Yet, life is also an amazing and an unfortunately short, and powerful gift. So yes, I do find the good, the humor, and the laughter as often as I can. My answer to the second slightly differently worded question is basically the same, it just starts with, "I am not always happy...."

We all have legitimate reasons to be sad, anxious, worried, angry, self-protective, distrusting, and yes, even periodically selfish in this chaotic and aggressive world we all live in. Yet, I refuse to give up and give in. That is the gist of why I laugh when I can. The tools and efforts behind that are broad and deep, this entire book is the how. I also have reasons to give up and not strive to live in as much joy, laughter, and assistance to others as I can. One of my major influences on why I did not sink into a deeper hole was my grandfather, who you met briefly in "Wider Angles: Strong versus Tough." I watched, and he showed me another way. He also had many reasons to give up and turn away from people and life, but he did not.

My grandfather, "Daddy Whit" as he was known to my family, was born in 1891 in northeastern Texas. He was a calm, solid, hardworking man, who made a living farming, raising cattle, and driving a school bus. As far as I can remember, he never spoke an unkind word about another person. He loved to tell interesting stories about his full life, and unless the tragedy of the subject would have been inappropriate to do so, he always included humor in those stories. To this day, my grandfather remains one of the more positive influences in my life, through both his words and his actions. When I look back on many of those stories, I realize just how amazing he was to continue to be the person we all knew. In his ninety-nine years of life, he lived through enough tragedies to turn anyone sour, pessimistic, aggressively self-protective, and distrusting of the world; but instead, he chose to remain the opposite. My grandfather embodied goodness.

Whit Yandle fought in the trenches of Europe, mainly France, during World War I. He had physical scars from the war, of which he could recall the trauma of origin, and describe tactfully without unnecessary details. He lived through the Spanish Flu of 1918–1919, which killed over 20 million people worldwide. Another difficult aspect of his life was living through the Great Depression of the 1930s, which was not easy on his family or community. However, rather than telling us how hard it was, he chose to tell us how communities bonded together to feed each other, including the strangers passing through town to find a better life. This focus on the goodness of people continued as he would tell us of his life. When he talked of World War II, he shared of the world's sacrifice at home to support the troops and war effort. We never heard him call those sacrifices for the greater good an infringement on his rights or freedom, he saw bigger pictures.

My grandfather never told a life story without finding something positive and of value to also relay. One of the hardest tragedies he experienced he rarely spoke of, and if he did, it never involved details, was the gas explosion in the school in New London, Texas, in 1937. Before that event, natural gas was odorless, the crawl space under the school had filled with gas and exploded just after three in the afternoon. It is estimated there were five-hundred children and forty adults in the school at the time of the explosion. Two hundred ninety-five people died, mostly children. He immediately got on his school bus and drove 15 miles to New London. He knew his bus would be needed to transport the injured. He never dreamed he would also transport so many dead. Even the rare few times he told me of the New London explosion, he would emphasize the heroic teamwork of the rescued, the recovered, and the outpouring of social bonds that followed in the weeks and months that followed.

Yet, with all the history and wisdom my grandfather bestowed on me, nothing has contributed to how I have attempted to practice my life and influenced me more than one simple conversation I had with him in 1984. He was in his mid-nineties at the time, and we were sitting in his home outside of Henderson, Texas. The phone had yet to turn into a handheld computer, and the internet had six more years to go before it was available to the world. He was well-read, broad-minded, and an unselfish thinker who could see the cause and effect of human actions. In his mid-ninety-year-old soft, slow-paced wisdom, to the best of my recall, this is what he shared, "I have lived through the most amazing one hundred years of inventions and accomplishments in the history of humans. During my life, we have gone from the horse to the car, from the telegraph to the phone, from wanting to fly to the airplane and jet, then the rocket to the moon, from the pencil to the computer, from sure death from pneumonia to antibiotics, from chopping wood for heat to turning a dial, from carrying well water into the home to indoor hot showers, and from the printed word to the television and computer. But I am sorry to say, Vincent, I fear your generation, and the future of all will pay."

I already knew he was right; it was happening already. But I very much wanted to hear his answer after he had brought those amazing facts of his life span to my attention. So, I asked, and he answered, "The people and the world's relationships will not be ready for the consequences of such accomplishments, and the negative effects it will have on the earth, the people, and society. The population growth alone will strain the earth's resources at an alarming rate and force a level of competition that will create a destructive vicious cycle between people. Above all, the lack of the perceived need to help and support each other will break down the foundations of every person, and then society. But sadly, and worst of all, rather than working to change with our times, people will fight to cling to their ways of the past. Those old systems will not only no longer remain functional but clinging to those old ways is going to accelerate some of the trouble."

I remember having little to say for hours.

His forward thinking and accurate words not only helped me care about the bigger picture throughout my life, his words and his life were a considerable influence on why I choose optimism as often as I am able to.

Here is an even more amazing aspect of his life: he remained loving, giving, tolerant, optimistic, good, right, fair, and never stopped laughing at the goodness of life, or himself. My grandfather was an amazing man for many humanistic accomplishments, but also for his daily accompaniments. His calm and steady daily ease and goodness was just who he was. I aspire to his level of consistency in actions over words, and to obtain his level of acceptance and peace even when it was something he knew was upsetting. Today we take bad, and it makes us meaner and more self-protective; he took bad and allowed it to make him nicer, more tolerant, and more giving.

Watching the evening news with him was interesting, he remained neutral, and spoke of solutions, not blame during the commercials. Because of his wisdom and ability to see those bigger pictures, he knew what he could affect, what was beyond his control. I think one of his greatest tools was knowing, and living, that our fear of what is to come changes nothing concerning what arrives. That was the wisdom that fed his gentle calm.

—Whit Yandle, 1891–1990, remarkable spirit, a painful and wonderfully balanced life, never an unkind word, and his internal peace and acceptance proved the rewards of his positive mindset and actions.

It can be easier

There is no one easy answer. I can't eat healthy, exercise, or help others and it fixes everything. It requires daily work and I admit sometimes forced effort, but I find great rewards also. Even the effort itself can be one of the rewards. The expenditure of our energy is good for us, and it keeps our minds, bodies, and spirits stimulated and healthy. Our ways of life and choices to save energy with convenience are actually hurting us on many levels.

I have trusted you on a deeper level in this book to share the pain of my life, as well as some better parts. I shared some mistakes as well as the accomplishments because the mistakes are also my accomplishments. They mean I tried. Some attempts were horrible failures that hurt others, and for those, I am sorry. Strange, I know, but accepting that I am a faulted human is part of my trick to make life easier. Attempting to be perfect, always right, or being unnecessarily defensive chips away at a part of our moments and ease, and our joy and laughter.

We are alive, but do we feel alive? I know I find myself holding my breath sometimes, and I see many others holding their breaths too. The path to less breath holding in life is acknowledgment, followed by a slight expenditure of energy to add the acceptance of balance, completed with increasing the positive beliefs, words, and actions in your life. Those choices also will bring you greater calm and easier breaths.

Not meeting and learning to work with our emotions is also giving too much of our self and potential wonderful experiences away. Take back or increase your life's healthy joys and experiences, they are launched higher with greater self-honesty to greatly increase-awareness. It is only hard at first to bump it up, and the rewards alone start to make it easier each day.

I wrote this book for the same reason I wrote the first one, because I care. I care that our suicide rates are rising at unacceptable rates among all ages. I care that too many feel forgotten. I care that we feel urgent needs to keep up and get ahead, that is costing us energy and days, which again translates to giving away moments of our life. I care that the internet and news is a life-crushing force on all ages, stirring anger, fear, and resentment in all generations. I care that some news outlets can instill too much fear and anger into so many. I care that we are becoming so aggressive in our driving that we forget cars kill around the same number of people every year as do guns. I care that our youth require medications to function at alarming rates, and too many threaten suicide as a primary option to their daily pressures and fears before they leave middle school. Worse, that too many accomplish suicide, cheating themselves out of a potentially balanced tough and amazing life, with laughter, experiences worth living for, and amazing, exciting accomplishments and contributions, not just their fears that push them to end their life. I care that we scream blame rather than calming our voices, and we point fingers instead of finding discussions. I care, and that is why I am putting myself on the line, to let you know you are not alone; you are not crazy for your confusion, anger, anxiety, and depression. I care that you know, believe, and feel your self-worth, and there is hope, joy, and laughter too.

I will never tell you that life is not painful, stressful, and hard work. But I can promise you it is also a short, powerful, and rare ride that is worth the effort. How do I know this for a fact? Because I have lived the tremendous wide range known as a human life, from an attempted suicide to a life of helping thousands in their moment of crisis. I have hurt others and I have been hurt, and I too feel deep sadness and elated joy, and I'm so grateful I still believe in us. The fact that I still laugh, and I still love this hard beautiful experience called my life makes it all much more than just okay.

I have seen inside of too many of us, including myself, that there is a dark place between feeling alive and death that we sometimes get sucked into. That place is emptiness, isolation, loneliness, paralyzing fear, anxiety, depression, anger, resentment, jealousy, even blame, and heavy addiction. It is my hope that none of us have to stay in that not-dead but not-alive place for long. We arrive there when our feelings, perceptions, and sometimes the actual reality of our life, hits a difficult span of more bad than good. That periodic normal to humans imbalance causes the rough and bad to cover more of our spirit than the light of goodness can illuminate. In this day and time that not-dead not-alive place is happening to us all too often.

We also have valid reasons to feel overwhelmed, depressed, anxious, or to question our world and life. But you are alive, and unless chronic or severe, those painful, aware, and sensitive human experiences have the potential to enrich our lives. It requires a cautious balance, aided by actively doing what we know is good for us, and by expending a little energy to address and work with the thoughts and behaviors we know can be unhealthy for us. As pressures mount, this can be difficult, but still obtainable with effort, or professional assistance if needed. Acknowledging how tough and scary it all can be at times is a great healthy start, it is also an exercise in telling your ego to quiet down because you want to enjoy your humanness. However, day after day with the rough and scary thoughts is not healthy either. Daily is an unhealthy level, and perhaps professional help should be considered?

One way I used to validate people in peak acting-out crisis, meaning verbally escalating, angry, or raging, and potentially about to become physically violent, I would actually say to them, "I am scared too, you're huge and angry. I'm skinny and hairy, you could crush me, and you're right, life is hard and unfair at times." I validated their fears because I, too, have fears. That would often help a notch or three, especially if I meet their immediate needs also. I would even ask the other nurses and hospital police to, "Move back a little, they are okay, they don't want to hurt anyone." Because most of us don't want to hurt anyone. They wouldn't leave me or drop their guard too much, but they knew how I worked, they knew I wasn't completely dropping my guard yet either. I am human.

Slight slide here, although I am learning to drop my guard more in general in life, it feels fantastic to turn off or lower "on guard." I am scared, I do have fears and anxieties at times, but I don't care to live half-cocked either, as the world pushes me to be. I have discovered I miss too much of the good when I live half-cocked. Allowing the world to get to me was adding to the bad in my life; I was giving the world too much permission to upset me.

I am alive and I have opportunities to grow, experience, help, and do better. I watched, learned, made mistakes, and I even improved at times. Hopefully, that is a truth for every aspect of our lives, every day, until we die. Stating, reading, or planning intentions is the easy part, the follow-through is the harder part. It can also feel hopeless and defeated when it seems as if we are surrounded by people who are aggressive and just do not care to help in positive directions. Sometimes bad is just bad, yet often how we see it and deal with it only can make it much less bad.

We let the few bad ones overfeed our pessimism

I had been in law enforcement for less than a year when I was northbound on a freeway called MOPAC. I saw a pickup truck entering the freeway from the wrong direction coming onto an exit ramp. I quickly activated my overhead lights, aimed right for the truck, and luckily it slowed and stopped, as I turned my car to the side, completely blocking its path and to create a wider safe lane for me to get out and hopefully resolve the situation. As I exited my unit, I could see the person was in crisis, but their eyes told me they were waking up to the reality of what they just did. Frantic, but attempting to hear me, the person cooperated and turned off the engine and handed me their keys. Traffic was moderate, but of course, backed up fast even though we are only blocking the far-right lane of three lanes and the exit ramp. Everyone is figuring out, moving left, and going on down the road. Maybe ninety seconds into this situation, a driver aggressively honked several times and accelerated with excess to show intolerance for their inconvenience. I was still talking with and assessing the driver and how best to quickly handle this. After all, I was still a rookie. This human who honked was too far back to have seen the incident and was not aware the inconvenience was in their favor, having most likely prevented serious deaths or injuries from high-speed head-on crashes that could have involved numerous cars. This is the world we live in. Without knowing, some judge, blame, and assign; I was a cop inconveniencing someone's day, not someone who just prevented you from a head-on collision. Welcome to law enforcement, and welcome to our world.

Choosing to experience less bad in the bigger picture is how you exercise your free will and choice, instead of focusing on the impatient honker only. I had the freeway back open in minutes. No other officers had to respond, and it worked out for everyone. Well, except for the honker, but that was their choice not to follow their first wrong thought, rather than see a bigger picture. The big picture of goodness that my free will and choice chooses to grab was that out of several hundred cars that were delayed due to a human moment incident, only one acted out. Sure, a few more may have grumbled in their car. That happens. But one grumpy driver acting out to a few hundred, who rolled slowly on and were okay with the delay is a great reminder that we are still an okay society. Maybe four minutes total before I had the road open again, three or four hundred people at the most were slightly delayed, but only one was outwardly angry. As far as the original driver goes, I had their spouse get to us, I talked with their psychiatrist on the phone, and the spouse took them to see that professional.

But the reward was in helping that person and the people who didn't even know they were delayed for a significant reason. The first twenty or so cars that witnessed it were gone, but I would guess had just been reminded of how lucky every day of life is. This is one of those times, as is so much of our daily life, that we can find lessons in what we think is something bad, wrong, or inconvenient. It's all in how we choose to think about everything. Every day may have some bad, but every day we are only inconvenienced is another lucky day.

But they keep trying to sell me magic dust and surface repairs

When it comes to choices and rewards for the mind, body, or spirit, there is rarely a magic dust that works for long. Meeting your basics of healthy foods, not overeating, hydration, exercise, peaceful long nights of rest, and attempting to keep the rougher parts of life to a minimum to the best of your ability, is preventative from the origin of health. The extreme knowledge we already have requires more work and effort to implement, as opposed to taking an actual or metaphorical supplement. I also need a few repetitive reminders to keep doing the right things, and I give great credit to those who show daily consistency in self-care. I feel so much better after only twenty-four hours of better self-care. The basics are everything. Our magic dust cannot arrive at our doorstep the next day, it is already inside of us, we just have to reach in and use it.

Would you rather fix problems after they have occurred or prevent them?

"If you want to go quickly, go alone, if you want to go far, go together."
— African Proverb

Although all the interns, nurses, and residents would teach each other, one particular emergency resident, Dr. Jimmy Ballone, stood out in his desire to learn from and teach in every direction. His humanistic understanding, emotional intelligence, and social awareness, added to his drive to help and teach other residents and nurses alike. Jimmy had a direct yet respectful bedside manner. One rare night in this extremely high-volume emergency system, there were a few open beds on the medical side known as the "MER," for the Major Medical Room, in the D cubicle almost across from the asthma cubical just a little further down the aisle. Each cubicle on the medical side held four to six beds.

Jimmy and I were sitting on the same side of one of the beds, talking, breathing, for a rare moment of calm. The triage nurse was walking a very regular asthma patient back to the asthma cubical. They passed us and turned into the cubicle, and I regurgitated something I had heard other nurses say. Please remember, I was twenty-one when I started working there, learning to grow in both good and not so good directions due to the severity of the work. The only food the department would receive was a cardboard box of small milk cartons and "egg" sandwiches that were nothing more than highly processed "eggs" on white bread. They were a funny color yellow with no mayo, salt, or pepper to cushion the blow. These sandwiches were so bad that we would make quotation marks in the air anytime we referred to them as "egg" sandwiches. This patient, who we sometimes saw twice a day, would always ask if we had any sandwiches left to give to him. After he finished passing, I said to Jimmy, "I bet he wants a sandwich." Jimmy slowly turned his head to me and softly spoke, "Have you ever gone a day in your life without food?" I replied "no" with embarrassment realizing the big picture. "Then why would you deny him one of those egg sandwiches that have been sitting there all day, and you won't even eat? Maybe give him two sandwiches and two milks," he stated as we both got up to hustle away the rest of our night. To Jimmy, and every patient, family member, nurse, and doctor who shared their knowledge, asked me a challenging question, and gave me or listened to one of my in-services, I thank you sincerely for the greatest start and maintenance of a professional, and humanistically-oriented, career I could ever have imagined. Thank you!

There have been thousands of teachable moments in my life for professional and professionalism growth, starting with my parents attempting to teach me manners, and much of what is now known as executive functioning. Executive functioning is our ability to smoothly handle our day's task and interactions with the world around us. It includes our trained thought processes, such as memory, flexibility to adapt, basic manners, the ability to work with our emotions, general respect, organizational skills, and communication. We use these skills every day to learn, work, and manage daily life. School teachers have been telling me for the past few generations executive function is a waning skill. When executive functioning is not developed, we have trouble staying on track, following directions, remaining calm, and in general, more little bumps occur in our days.

Developing these skills first came from my appropriately persistent parents, five older siblings, and then teachers' guidance. Throughout my life, I continued to work with so many people who so generously and trustingly shared their amazing experiences of both their mistakes and growth. Many of these same mentors also showed a personal concern for me and taught me the value of self and peer review without criticism, to point out areas I could improve and grow. There is another powerful, professional, and life-changing experience that stood out as true professional review and professionalism. It also represents, and teaches us, how we as individuals, groups, communities, and even countries and large corporations, can work together.

In 1986, I was invited to an LSU "M and M Conference," which stands for Morbidity and Mortality, in the morgue's postmortem, meaning autopsy, amphitheater. From movies and television shows, I knew such arenas existed to allow large groups of medical students to look down from steeply rising circular rows of seats to watch surgery. This is all now done with cameras and monitors. I did not know such an amphitheater existed for postmortem teaching. They only met in this arena to discuss the exam findings; the actual exam had been previously performed by the pathology resident, who was presenting the findings and leading the discussion with other doctors who had cared for the person who had not lived. This is why pathology is known as "The Truth" or the "The Justice System" of the healthcare field. The postmortem exam answers the questions and mysteries the living body does not always clearly share.

What I witnessed that morning stirred sheer awe and motivation in me to spend my life studying the concepts of professional learning and professionalism in action. It was at Charity Hospital that I learned the difference between the title and roles that we wrongly label "professional" and the earned achievement of applied professionalism. I have known many people with titles we call "professional" who fell far short of the classic criteria of a professional. I once went through a drive-thru to place an order for several people. I was hungry, tired, and confused with my order, but the voice remained friendly and knew that menu like the back of her hand. She even smoothly guided me to meal deals and packages to save money. All with a friendly voice, not put off or rushed, and not so fast I could not hear. At that moment, getting me to the other side of that experience was her only goal. Do not ever think that because someone is in one of the fields we label "professional," such as doctor, attorney, engineer, nursing, or law enforcement, that they are a professional. Nor assume that the person feeding you at the drive-through is also not a professional. Being a professional is not the job we are doing, but rather how we do that job. Being a professional human being in all of life is no different. How you treat those around you every day is professionalism, including customer service, interacting with a call taker, how we treat our employers and employees, and including our personal relationships.

The M and M Conference started with a medical resident presenting the case, starting with the person's age, their physical complaints of what brought them to the hospital, how long the complaint had been going on, their past medical and surgical history, what was found during their initial exam, what studies were ordered, what treatment was provided, and how that treatment was changed as laboratory and studies returned. The resident then ended with a long list of what changed, what they thought the diagnosis was, how they treated those signs and symptoms, and everything that occurred until the very elderly person's body died. Then the pathology resident presented the factual findings on the internal exam of the body. Open discussion followed that lasted for maybe thirty minutes, which was highly educational.

To this day, what amazed me the most was the level of professionalism in that autopsy amphitheater. No finger-pointing in blame, no throwing your colleagues under the bus, no unnecessary protection of the ego displayed as defensiveness, but instead a jaw-dropping articulate open discussion for the purpose of learning and doing better. No one had done anything wrong, there was no negligence or malpractice, only a failing, very elderly human body that can never be put in a picture-perfect textbook, who showed multiple conflicting signs and symptoms until death. All accomplished by an amazing group of professionals only caring to learn *together* and continue to do better.

I couldn't help but to attend a few more M and M Conferences over the next two years. Inspired to never stop learning about the human body, to constantly strive to achieve the difference between being a professional by title as opposed to professionalism by actions as well as omissions, such as blame and defensiveness. This all culminated in the realization that the number one part of me that will prevent the growth of both professionalism and expanding my knowledge is the often-unnecessary staunch protection of my overly sensitive ego.

One of the many reasons I spent almost all my years in public teaching hospitals is because of the spirit of those M and M Conferences somewhat prevails throughout the day-to-day work and collaboration. To have an attending physician ask the room before stopping a resuscitation effort on a dying person, "Can anyone else think of anything we have not thought of before we stop?" is pure professional gold. It is also a great reminder that the care of the human body, and all of society, just like all of life, is teamwork. No one person will ever know or see anything with 100% accuracy, every one of us will make mistakes, and any one of us can catch and prevent those mistakes. Especially, if teamwork, not competition, prevails.

We so desperately need to embrace this professional model in every aspect of our lives and society, whether personal, occupational, government, and the many angles of all our relationships. What we think is right one day, research may show the next day there is a better way, or that the old way was wrong. Because of this, every medical textbook, soon after publication, will have information that is no longer accurate, hence the need for revisions and multi-editions. This is how all of life works, we either learn and grow or we choose to not look for potential improvements, thus we keep making a few of the same mistakes.

Part of being a professional in life is also accepting and working with the fact that no two human minds will ever have the same strengths and weaknesses. Expecting even one person to totally align with your thought process on every subject is impossible. It has become one of the pitfalls of our society: throwing people, groups, cultures, or businesses away completely because of a behavior or view that does not line up with your own. If this trend continues, we will all eventually be discarded. To help combat this, and increase general human professionalism, is to accept input and knowledge from all directions, even the ones that are hard to hear. Our human errors are our learning gifts to ourselves, but we must first be willing to admit to them before we can unwrap those gifts of growth and thus easier.

Can you imagine how much more peaceful, productive, and profitable (both literally and figuratively) all aspects of our lives would be if we blamed and judged others less? It would solve another problem at its origin if more of us realized and accepted that, at times, we are all just as faulted and uncooperative to others as the people or groups we are pointing to.

Turning the page

As I wrote just now, a tear began to slide down my cheek. It formed first because you read my book, which is caring to meet me, and help yourself and others. The tear is also for the joy of you doing the work and then finding the peace I know can follow. Then another tear rushed down to join it when I thought of all the hatred and anger in the world, the sadness, neglect, abuse, and the lack of hope. When the sad hatred tear caught up to the waiting joyful tear, they joined to create balance, and dropped off my cheek. Both tears are beautiful; they mean I am alive, and I can feel. Good and bad, these tears mean I am whole, I am balanced, and I am.

It is painful that we often choose not to learn from our past. That past being both our life as an individual or the conception of humans as a society from the beginning of our beginning. Which means both as individuals and collectively, we are giving up a percentage of our ability to positively affect ourselves, community, and tomorrow. We all have reasons to be angry about yesterday, and fearful and hyper-vigilant about tomorrow. Please don't think the importance of the need to stand up for what is good and right or to protect yourself is ever lost on me. However, it is the anger, fear, and resentment that history creates that prevents us from letting go of the wrongs of our past enough to be able to effectively learn and move on to creating more peace in this moment, more stability, calm, and issue resolution.

Much of history outright sucks. I am not even going to try and word that prettier, it would only do it injustice. However, not learning from history is even worse. Clinging to history for hatred, blame, anger, and vengeance prevents us from dissecting history from a solution-oriented standpoint. Since every race and culture has abused and manipulated others, the issue is a human one, not one that warrants labeling and demographic blame. The pigment level in our skin is not the issue, nor is our culture, religion, or political affiliation, and blame based on these are not only useless and worse, wasting our precious time, but it also sets us back further. Every skin color has done atrocities to other races and cultures, including their own. Holding on to the past atrocities done to you or your people is preventing progress, problem solving, and our reuniting to find higher levels of peace between all races and cultures when it is needed more than ever. I know how long we can be angry with each other, but how long do we need to be angry with each other? One-hundred, two-hundred, one-thousand years? How long will the better people of today have to pay for yesterday's bad people?

Changing our response to history from blame, hatred, and anger to education and issue resolution will move us in the right direction. Blame is too easy, and often attempts to make one side right and one side wrong. When the responsibility of cultural, racial, or political strife, is often a varying degree of shared mutual responsibility. Even when there is no mutual responsibility, the awareness that all cultures have wronged other cultures should help us be cautious with our blame. History's wisest and greatest potential is in our abilities to combine our minds, spirits, skills, labors, and resources to also have a greater percentage of positive outcomes. Scientists, engineers, the field of medicine, musicians, and humanitarian efforts have been great at this for a long time.

I just realized, as I move through this last edit, these fields that are good at teamwork, international collaboration, and the unrestrained sharing of knowledge and skill have all advanced, yet our political worlds which are poor at these positive and productive traits, have hit turbulent waters and are regressing. Together, we are stronger and more powerful. Rope is so much stronger than thread, yet rope is only interwoven threads.

"Stay away from negative people, they have a problem with every solution."
—Albert Einstein

We know we can affect tomorrow without paying attention, so how much can we help it if we pay attention? I do not believe we are worth giving up on, nor is it too late. I've watched so many people in the latter half of life rehabilitate severe injuries with conviction and effort. I've known people who quit smoking in their sixties, lost weight, and ran half marathons. It is never too late to spend energy to help ourselves, each other, or for positive actions on any level in any direction. It is rarely too late.

Giving up on you or your life should only be welcomed at the end of a long life with the arrival of an accepted, imminent, peaceful, and right on time death. Otherwise, keep going, trying, exploring, learning, crying, laughing, forgiving, and giving.

I want to help, but I am only one

How do we feel hopeful and positive when there seems to be so much bad? We have a saying in the emergency department concerning cleaning out traumatic injuries, "Dilution dilution is the solution to the pollution!" We teach and chant this little ditty because it works on small cuts to major open wounds to prevent infection and aid in healing. It is also the continued answer to helping your immediate world, our big pictures, and our major personal, social, and political "open wounds."

Let's say you cut yourself cooking, letting water continue to run into that wound, while you rub it and open it using soap to break up the oils and dirt, is how to get the bad particles and germs out to prevent infection and promote faster, less complicated healing. (Caveat: If you ever think a cut extends into a joint, seek a professional medical evaluation right away, those can be serious infection issues requiring advanced care and antibiotics.) Using hypothetical numbers, let's imagine the knife left 500,000 microscopic particles of dirt and germs inside the wound. Diluting and further diluting with water, even opening the cut to wash out the inside several times, you are rinsing and diluting out the bad. Visualize the first thirty seconds under water rinsing out 250,000 particles, the next thirty seconds another 100,000 particles, and one more minute of letting the water run with maybe a second soaping, and hopefully, the microbial count is down to a hypothetical number of 5,000. Your immune system's white blood cells can hopefully kill off those few thousand microbes. This is also one of those examples where the difference between good and bad pain comes into play. The pain and burn of cleaning out the wound for a few minutes is a good pain, because it is not damaging and is preventing further complications, correlating to the discomforts of some harder changes within us to accomplish a positive outcome.

You are correct, one drop of water cannot clean out a large wound. However, each positive action by every person dilutes and does make a positive difference. Positive actions, and omitting negative ones, benefit both the giver and the receiver, then collectively the good of all. We do make a difference. Actions as simple as telling a new checker or waitstaff, "Welcome and great you are learning, I'll be understanding, it must not be easy," as opposed to sighing and judging a delay. "Dilution dilution" is also the solution to hopelessness, helplessness, and pessimism. Win-win actions first start with a minimal effort change in thinking, then small and large positive actions every chance your head, heart, and energy levels allow. Dilution is also an added easy solution to many issues, and kindness in general should never be discouraged, restrained, or underestimated. Kindness is a very powerful dilution for the worlds bad and is so easy to pour a little out of yourself a few times a day.

We all have bad days and years, and we all welcome a little good dilution when we are being clobbered, so why not extend positive dilution to others? People affect us, and we definitely have the power to affect others. Empowering yourself and embracing this individual and social dynamic is how we further positively dilute both ourselves and the world around us. There will always be those who rudely push past you in a store or who are directly rude to you in one way or another. It may feel like a losing battle. Yet, the reality is we notice the harsher person because they negatively affected us. We forget to notice the hundreds of caring people who continue to positively dilute our lives every day. I won't deny that one person can do a bunch of bad, or even a little bad feels huge when a disrespectful act is inflicted on us or witnessed. Please don't give up, the more dilution that occurs, the more effective every drop becomes.

It is also important to delineate that sometimes we all commit rude or even dangerous acts because we are imperfect beings, and no one can pay total attention all the time. Yet still others commit them because they have higher levels of culpability than basic human error. I bring this up to review that we sometimes judge others on their actions, but we hope to be judged on our intentions. Or worse yet, some only hypocritically judge others, assuming they are not equally faulted and inflicting ourselves on others, also. The proliferation of internet critics and self-appointed judges is a modern destructive example. We all place some dirt and germs onto the earth and society, what is important is to continue to dilute with goodness. Since most of our issues, individual or worldly, cannot be fixed with one answer or in one day, dilution dilution is the greatest solution we have. Please keep pouring it on.

It is so much easier and rewarding to dilute than we may think. The next time a checker appears rushed, or a call taker is apologizing to you for a mere thirty-second hold. Try saying, "That's okay, take your time, you are helping me, I am not in a rush," and watch their shoulders drop or listen to how their voice relaxes. Even if you are in a hurry, it is not the worst thing to slow down even when you feel you can't, your shoulders and voice might ease a little also. That's a choice you have, with a literal potential reward of not having a heart attack or a stroke, and even achieving a calmer present moment while you deal with another human. That human, just like you, may have no choice but to enforce the policies and procedures of the company you have called, is new and learning, or having a bad moment or day. We have all been there, and I promise you will be again. Even during bumps, attempt to extend the dilution you hope to receive when not at your peak moments of goodness. Far more often than not, flexibility in thoughts and actions will win over rigidity.

That tiny positive action, to tell another human you care to treat them with acceptance, tolerance, forgiveness, and understanding took only a matter of seconds. Yet, you accomplished a positive with an observable effect, their shoulders dropped, and their voice relaxed. The hundreds of times I have said that in grocery stores or to a call taker who is helping me with an issue that is not even their fault. I burned more calories with the laughter and fun exchanges that took place because I spent half of a calorie to let a random human know they, too, were being considered and appreciated. That basically effortless four seconds to look someone in the eye, grin, and say one generous sentence can easily become a way of life, a standard of communication, and daily application to aid a little in helping us all heal and reconnect, and it is part of the solution each of us can contribute. When you see your positive actions or negative omissions did help another person to take a breath and drop their shoulders, you also have gained. We only fail when we stop caring and trying, everything else is either an attempt or a success.

Gems to help make it easier

Teamwork

The only people who are not your teammates in life are the ones actively working against you. Other than the few bad people who do want to hurt, belittle, or steal from you in one way or another, everyone else is your teammate in life. They are your neighbors you haven't met, or the person who will help you because they saw you get in a car accident, and they did care to stop. They are the truck drivers we should let into our lane because they are helping get that head of lettuce to your grocery store. They are all races, all political affiliations, all genders, all sexualities, all cultures, and all accents. We all fall somewhere into each of those demographics, we are a team, and life is teamwork.

Random connecting interactions

Unless it is just not appropriate due to time availability or the situation, I love interacting with the general public. It does not make a difference if I am in uniform, nursing scrubs, or on a day off in shorts and a T-shirt, I love sharing with people when I am out and about. I also like to hide, as I call it, because I value my down time in solitude also. Some of my favorite moments having fun with the general public was in law enforcement were in grocery or convenience stores. If my credit card or the checker was having issues getting me through a 7 in the morning grocery line filled with half-awake people trying to get in, out, and to work quickly, I would turn to the line I am now delaying and say with a big-eyed, surprised look on my face, "Oops, I guess it's my turn to hold up the line this time and isn't it just like a cop to slow down or completely stop the traffic when everyone one else just wants to speed on through!" It was great to have a group of people all laughing and joking with me at the same time. It is just not expected from a uniformed officer. Any time I was at a convenience store while in uniform, and time allowed, I would stop and open the door for everyone for a few minutes and say a little loud, "Come on in, you're working hard holding this community together, the cold air in there is free!" As they left, I would say to them what had been told to me a few hundred wonderful times in uniform, "Thank you for what you do!" To have such a diverse group of hardworking people smile and laugh with me was pure joy and connection. Every walk of life had fun with me and would joke back. To have a minority worker, who may normally stay clear of law enforcement, literally reach up and pat me on the shoulder and say something fun and nice was more pure gold. Those five minutes of putting myself out there gave me back so much joy, connected law enforcement in a fun way with the public, got other people laughing and smiling, reminded them law enforcement are just people also, and all of this required so little effort. Every now and then, someone in the grocery store line would give me a mean you're-not-funny look while I was joking with everyone, but it was rare.

Our Job

I would guess I started attempting to have personal snippets of conversations with call takers over thirty years, after I became frustrated with an innocent call taker that was only innocently enforcing their companies' policies that they had no control over. It was not some horrible unleashing. But I did my work as I like to call it, and I realized frustration with a call taker is futile, disrespectful, and even if I need to speak to their manager to get a higher level of service, I don't need to be harsh to the first level call taker. I remember some months later even confessing to the next call taker I spoke to like they were a priest and could absolve my human fumbling. I remember them laughing when they asked me what I did, "I had expressed my frustration without raising my voice." "That's nothing, we expect frustration, it's the aggressive personal attacks that wear us down," was their answer. One question I have enjoyed asking, after I have proved to be a respectful caller and I hear their tone relax in trust, "Please teach me, do you find on the days you feel strong and positive that you have less turbulence with the callers than on the days you are not up to par or under personal or professional stress?" It is significant the number who admitted although some people just seem to want to be cruel, they would agree. Before we hung up, a few stating something along the lines of, "Thank you for reminding me I have the ability to make my job easier by taking care of myself."

We may clock into a job, but we should never stop taking care of ourselves while clocked in. We accomplish better customer service and productivity when we do. How high can our productivity or customer service be if we are dehydrated, have a low blood sugar level from not eating, or are about to urinate on ourselves? Take healthy care of yourself before, during, and after your job, and hopefully you have a boss that understands basic human function, motivation, and health.

Another way we can find greater rewards, no matter what job you are doing, is in granting your pride permission to grow. Not loving your job or boss doesn't mean you can't find rewards in accomplishing the task or providing professional customer service to the best of your ability.

Working our bodies and minds is good for us, but our actual job can be hard on us. A percentage of how bad our job is may be out of our control, but the parts we have control over can be better. The expenditure of energy to accomplish our job is not only for food, roof, and family, it is also for our own well-being in many beneficial ways beyond a paycheck. Physical exercise, mental stimulation, exercising emotions, general respect, increasing customer service, and professionalism are all incredibly self-rewarding to both our mind and our body. The numerous rewards of doing and accomplishing create more self-perpetuating positive energy. The more energy we use, the more we produce. As long as someone is not overdoing it with a chronic stress level of their body or mind, then the more we do, the more energy we create.

I have always wondered why we pick the arbitrary age of sixty-five to retire. At sixty-five, our mind and body still have great abilities and far more energy than our aging attitudes talk us out of. I have no plans to use the "R" word, the research even shows we should not stop. When we retire, all aspects of our being decline faster than when we remain active. Before electricity flowed in the late eighteen-hundreds, no one retired.

We human gather, so let's look at that

I confess in college my friends would sometimes call me a sociology geek, and they were right, I still am. Then they would make fun of my first major of sociology, calling it, "The study of the obvious." Further stating everything they would hear fell into the category of either, "I knew that" or "well, of course." Just like all helpful input we receive; the challenge is in the daily application of our knowledge to make our life easier. Such as the amount of nutritional and health knowledge I have in my head should mean I have a muscular washboard abdomen, but I don't. One of the greatest injustices of our education system, besides the insulting low salaries of our educators, is that sociology classes are mostly only available to liberal arts students, or the wise engineer who takes it for an elective, rather than sociology being mandatory for every field. There are three classes: general introductory sociology, death and dying, and relationships and communication, that should be required no matter what your major is. Unless a student just smirks and dissociates from the material, these three courses can enrich and help every aspect of our lives and society.

To go one step further, start teaching these subjects lightly in middle school and more in high school. How much might it help decrease early judgment, prejudice, fear, anxiety, self-doubt, and depression, while increasing executive functioning and coping skills, and helping to bring more self-awareness and self-acceptance to our brave youth? Would that increase in self-, human-, social-knowledge help to decrease depression, anxiety, and suicide? It would also help our youth to communicate on more effective levels and see bigger pictures of the cause and effect of human actions.

In all ages, instilling the humanities and tools to work with self and others is pure win-win. Those three subjects weave through every one of our lives; people and groups, dying then death, and the ability to communicate, understand individual and group dynamics, to truly listen, and maintain relationships on a more effective level will only ease and enhance our personal, professional, and social lives. The positive ripple effect would be immeasurable.

Why am I here, and please, what is it all about?

One of our vaguest yet most meaningful and helpful pursuits is our quest to answer the meaning of life. Although one of the oldest questions of humankind, it is an important one. Although I love discussing it with others, everyone must answer it for themselves. My answer involves self, society, contributing, and an exploration of life, while walking with as much peace and awareness as possible. Life is the survival and exploration of self, and the creation and health of all the teamwork required to accomplish our life. Not caring to pursue higher goals and questions, creates a stagnancy or emptiness that our being will attempt to fill somehow. Unfortunately, "somehow" is not always the healthiest for us or those around us. One of the basic ways we grow this higher exploration is with relationships, starting with ourselves, then friends, family, and the people we interact with throughout each day. Treating a service person with respect and attempting some level of connection is the respectful pursuit of higher self, and the teamwork of life. Doing the work to find your answer to these big questions includes equal parts solo and communal effort and observation. It is one of the few questions in life that the answer is not found in the formations of words into sentences, but rather how we live each day is where the answer appears.

Keep going

Just because you are hit, knocked down, or have just stumbled in life from any or many directions, keep going, keep trying, and keep getting up, until you are truly at your end. That end is not at the end of hope, low hope can often be elevated. I am talking about the true end of a long-balanced life. As I sign my first book, "May you die fast, but not soon, and please keep going until you are good and ready to quit." It takes a book to explain it, but eventually the mind and body do reach an endpoint, but what is important is not to let your spirit reach its end point. However, the fact that our minds and bodies reach an end from age or terminal illness is okay, sad when too young, but we don't have to waste moments of life fearing death. Just please don't rush it. Life is already a much shorter journey than we imagine. We don't need to fear or to run to our death, because it is slowly walking up to us on its own natural path. Please, keep going, even through the tough parts. You are right, life is hard, and yet amazing.

No utopia, rarely perfect, but there is joy and goodness

Remain realistic that we will never find utopia. Complete peace, agreement, and total resolution of our being, our life, or our shared societal issues will rarely happen. There is no way this many people, with this many and various ideas, drives, and strong significant family and cultural history influencing us, will ever completely align. That is not a reason to become discouraged, disheartened, and it is definitely not a reason to become angry and aggressive. Quite the opposite, the mixing of those various ideas and drives is how we found some of the world's favorite food combinations, and it is how we are going to solve many of our bigger problems. We may not be able to fix them all, but we sure can slow things down and smooth out many of the bumps and ridges. Each of us will periodically help and hinder the concept of peace and progress. The obtainable goal is contributing negatively less and less and positively more and more. The more we work towards this obtainable goal, the more we all will suffer less in life and work. Dilution dilution is the solution.

If you want a big uplifting, watch the videos by the nonprofit Playing For Change. They are inspiring and uplifting, filled with the soul, goodness, talent, and efforts of the people around the earth. "Everyday People" and "Skin Deep" are two of my favorites, but they are all beautifully uplifting and great for the spirit. The children from around the world have such joy on their faces. I love thinking about the further joy they felt when they saw the final video. Yes, life is amazing too.

I am sorry

One of the many keys to obtaining self and mutual respect is having the courage to constantly seek the difference between a reason and an excuse. Not if, but when, I make a mistake and say or do something wrong, I work to accept the responsibility for my part and apologize. My apology may include the reason, "I am sorry I said that it was a tough day, and I had not eaten in hours. But that was still wrong of me." As opposed to an excuse, such as, "Well you bit me first, and I was just trying to finish my sentence." It is also important to remember an apology is worthless without actions to improve or correct the behavior or situation. Knowing the difference between a reason and an excuse is critical to professionalism, avoiding arguments, assisting self-growth, and to help increase the health and trust in relationships. An apology can even be sexy in an intimate relationship.

Learn it, see it, do it, teach it, and setting examples

Giving back and mentoring. This gem is where some of our true core rewards come from. The joy and rewards of a material purchase can fade, the excitement of a roller coaster ride ends, and intoxicants wear off or stop working and steal our lives. But working from the heart and helping others to become more every chance we get are the rewards that last. Positive actions accelerate our spirits, life fulfillment, and the well-being of self and all. When we teach, when we hold out our hand, and even when we ignore someone's mistake, fault, or weakness, we are helping others and ourselves with humanness. Helping others becomes second nature when we are aware that we, too, need help in life. It is exhilarating to accelerate a fine sports car, but that acceleration is over the second you let up on the pedal. However, accelerating our spirits from the heart, in our actions, just keeps the excitement and internal joy growing exponentially with every positive action.

Setting examples and encouraging others to never stop their pursuit of growth and development is one of deeper gifts our spirit will ever know, and another will ever receive. Do you have a mentor that stands out from your youth or adulthood? Did they significantly make a difference in your life? Encouraging education, whether vocational or academic, to our youth is helping them personally and their tomorrow to become more and independent. Take every opportunity you can to encourage them both in words and example, you are giving another person greater tools and the freedom to be more. Adults should not stop either, take classes from your community college or online, sign up for what interests you and go keep doing. If you are a couple, sign up together and grow together.

The sharing of our knowledge or encouragement to seek knowledge is how we help ourselves, others, and society to accomplish. It also helps alleviate some behaviors and omissions that arise from our fears, insecurities, and greed that others will get ahead of us.

If you are growing inside, gaining knowledge of life and self, contributing, and increasing your peace and awareness, then *no one is getting ahead of you.* The flip side: anyone pushing and elbowing to get past you, make more money at any cost, or get a promotion, is most likely not attempting or accomplishing internal growth and awareness on an honest level. We do not have to be threatened by others' achievements, knowledge, or skills. Quite the opposite, since life *is* teamwork, the stronger every individual is, the stronger the team, community, and society becomes. It works both ways; the team needs to work to keep the individuals strong, and the individuals need to work to keep the team strong, that mutual reciprocating support keeps the individuals, groups, and communities at optimal health and strength. It is a positive cycle with win-win rewards for all, including longevity.

Our relatively recent unhealthy belief that we are no longer a team and every person for themselves is part of what is breaking us down. We need each other, and our lives are enriched by the acceptance and nurturing of that fact. I play chess online, and my number ranking is lower than it could be because when I see someone is learning, I ask if they would like some pointers. If they say yes, it turns into a mentoring relationship. While playing and teaching, I will lose a few games to help them advance their strategy, and many eventually start beating me on their own. Their first unassisted win is my true high-ranking number, that I gave of myself and another improved. Giving back and contributing is also uplifting to my sensitivities, awareness, and periodic depression when the load gets too heavy. If you have a few people in your life who encouraged and helped you through caring actions, then you know it works. Doing that for others is one way we can say thank you to the people who helped us.

I know I am lucky and grateful to have had so many strong mentors in my life. Seeking and allowing mentors increases the number you will have. With deep sincerity, I thank my many mentors. Your guidance is throughout this book, you helped me, you calmed me, you are meaningful to me, and I am a better person because of you.

Thank you.

Compliments: giving and appreciating them

Find the positive and compliment it, as we all respond to genuine encouragement and compliments. Compliments can make us feel uncomfortable, just learn to say thank you if you don't want to elaborate further. Remember, humble and true pride are compatible. Professionally and with respect, address the negative and learn from it too, but don't degrade yourself or others for the faults and weaknesses we all have as we walk through life. When I handed my mother something to read that I had written in my youth, I was always grateful she found the goodness of what I wrote and felt no need to point out the many words I had misspelled. Teachers tell me this is a problem today with parents, commenting on the poor spelling or penmanship, and completely missing that their child wrote something rich and beautiful.

In the teaching hospitals where I worked, we complimented each other frequently. However, in law enforcement, compliments were rare and sadly often received with suspicion of its authenticity. Law enforcement has the mentality that if you compliment someone, it has a hidden agenda. They call it something else though. Don't get me wrong, there was a lot of great training in law enforcement. But most was formal, in the classroom, or during official field or tactical training. Spontaneous impromptu sharing of knowledge or general compliments any and everywhere, as in teaching hospitals, was rarer. It was hard to go from one extreme to the other when I changed careers, it was strange and saddened my spirit. For the most part, I worked with a bunch of fantastic, intelligent, diverse people with great senses of humor, and we knew at any given moment we would truly risk our lives for each other and the public. It was an honor to work with such people.

I often wondered how quickly law enforcement could accelerate into the better direction it will inevitably realize one day it must achieve, if only it could learn to be more open with compliments and praise within itself. It happens, it just needs to happen more, especially since the role is near impossible to accomplish with perfection. Most police officer's days are painfully filled with no-win situations, so compliments or a little praise from the ranks and each other, can save a human spirit. Every human could use some lifting.

Don't get that on you

Rational detachment can be the glue that holds our lives together when we are having those rough moments or years. I attempt to protect myself by using rational detachment with life's challenging people and situations every chance I get. I even use it if I read a tragic news article. Don't forget, rational detachment doesn't mean you don't care or expend energy to help. It just means you do the best job you can of not letting that person or situation get on or inside of you. We are all worth more than the accidental or intentional attempts of others to smear their rougher humanness on us. Rational detachment is another great tool to help do the work of letting impersonal messy things go. Using this gem also helps me address conflict from my rational thought, not my emotional reactions.

Work to accept that which you have no control over. Spinning all day about the sun setting at the end of the day is futile and does nothing to stop the sun from setting. Life is hard, so I need to conserve energy. I can't afford to waste energy on issues that I am truly unable to help change. It is important to save that energy for positive actions that will help. We nurses may be codependent at heart, but I have my limits and work to stay realistic about my strengths and abilities as far as what, where, and how I can effectively contribute. Let's call that passive rational detachment.

Keep an eye on yourself

Practicing the application of acceptance, tolerance, forgiveness and understanding holds a powerful place in providing peace and resolution when we humans are involved. Those four are how we show love too. With one last painful reminder to watch out for our inevitable hypocrisies, double standards, and future mistakes, all three are "when," not "if," inevitable. Acknowledging and keeping an eye out is the only way to decrease the guaranteed incidences in frequency and intensity. If we start with showing ourselves acceptance, tolerance, forgiveness, and understanding, then everything gets easier.

Listen to your partner

As painful and poorly wrapped as it can be at times, learn to listen to your partner. Any partner, whether intimate, platonic friends, or a work partner with whom you share a front seat or a low cubicle wall. Chances are they are going to know parts of you better than you know yourself. Ouch, I know, but it is true. Because of this painful fact, learn to listen to them when they have the courage to say something that needs to be said or the professional courtesy to give you professional feedback. These people, especially a long-term intimate partner, know parts of you with more accuracy than you know yourself. Whatever the reason, from anger to sweetness, when a person in your life starts to share something with you that is about you, stop and listen. The longer they know you and the more loving their intent, the greater the percentage of truths they will hand you. Try hard not to close down or wall up inside yourself, become defensive, or feel a need to show them their manure, as you listen to what is hard but will help you. How someone hands you that information can make it easier, such as sweetly handing the knowledge to you. Even if it is the other side of the spectrum and they spew it with anger. Stop and hear it anyway. Even though not all gifts come in pretty packages, they have most likely just given you a gift. All you need is the courage to open it. After we work with what they gave us, we can often see it was a present.

Blame and judgment

Blame and judge one less person today. Repeat daily. Let us please actively grant that to each other. Even just one less per day. Hopefully, you will be extended the same gift on your next messy humanness.

Life lessons are endless

Some of our lessons are negative lessons, meaning we learn what not to do. Attempt to allow everyone, every situation, and every experience to be your teacher. Anything else and you missed the opportunity to grow, bond, and explore your life. In the workplace or any setting, work with true healthy pride to carry out your task and accomplish it to the best of your ability. Try not to allow another person or situation to rob you of some level of lessons in even a crummy job, it is most likely still an opportunity to help people, exercise your professionalism, and continue to learn. Work to share tasks and decisions and realize that the ability to compromise is a strength not a weakness that will be a lifelong lesson. Compromise is also respect, wisdom, and love in action. Our lessons help us work to find the strongest and best solutions, not just your solution or the easiest one. If we seek out our lessons, then we allow them to teach us; they make the next day easier. Every lesson makes life easier.

Don't follow too closely, it may be perfume covering stink

Strive to keep your definition of success off other people's scale. Rich and wealthy go far beyond monetary comforts. It is well known among historians that the cultures that first learned to work with steel and then make gunpowder became the power and financially dominant cultures in the past. That did not make them the most balanced or sustainable societies.

What appears to be someone getting ahead in life may be smoke and mirrors, or it may be actual ill-gotten gains. Be careful what we envy or feel a need to keep up with. The rich usually get richer, but the wise, peaceful, and contributing, often get wiser, more peaceful, and more in many other ways.

> "A calm and modest life brings more happiness than the pursuit of success combined with constant restlessness."
> —Albert Einstein

Every single one of us

Continue or work to accept and appreciate the fact that the races and cultures of the world already have and will continue to blend. Too many of us experience hatred, anger, threatened, and are discriminated against for something we have zero control over. We don't want to be judged for our gender, size, color, culture, religion, or even level of personal wealth, yet each one of us could have been born into the body of another person anywhere in the world. The entire population of the earth has so much more in common than what separates us. I have known wonderful and dangerous people from every demographic. There is some level of prejudice towards and from every type of person or group; some people, races, or cultures may have less prejudice, but few are ever perfect at it. We must be careful pointing fingers towards an entire race or culture and labeling them racist, because that too is racist. I was periodically judged horribly for being both Caucasian and/or in a uniform by people who had no idea who I was, how I was going to treat them, or even the caring reasons why I went into law enforcement in the first place. Most people are just doing the best they can, from where they came, from what happened to them, and from the situations they were handed. Most of us do not deserve the labeling, blame, judgment, and discrimination that is inflicted on us.

Since almost all demographics hold partial responsibility for some level of negative towards some other demographics, it is probably a ripe time to try and stop blaming each other so much. There is bad to be found in every shape, race, accent, and corner of the earth, yet there is a great deal of beautiful goodness to be found there too.

Your peace and productivity

Right after the health and respect we feel and show ourselves, comes the attitudes, bonds, and connections we feel towards the people around us. When we work to help those bonds and relations be positive, they hold us together, lift us up, and contribute the most to our ability to not only survive, but further to thrive.

Unless you are printing your own money, if you are financially thriving in high profit and don't think you are thriving because of others, don't ever forget that profit came from the people. It is how we think, feel, and relate with people that is one of our greatest foundations for not only our peace and prosperity, but also for our personal contentment, exploration, and growth.

Yes, it is we the people that present us with our problems, that cannot be denied. However, you are one of those people, you too will rock and upset other people's peace, and you also need those other people to cooperate on a higher level to help you accomplish your life with more peace and productivity. If someone spray paints the side of your car, if a boss or employee is narrow-minded and self-serving, or if another person is looking at their cell phone and rear ends you when traffic slows unexpectedly, they interrupt your peace and productivity. You hold that same power in the level of respect and consideration you show others. Our understanding and application of positive or negative cycles of reciprocation are major keys to our peace, productivity, and stability as individuals, and in our relationships. Peace and ease create more peace and ease.

Very few people in this world can walk off into the woods and survive without the help of others. Even if someone is capable of surviving alone in the woods, it was the knowledge and wisdom of others that taught that person how to survive alone in nature. Further, if they brought tools that they did not make themselves, it is once again proof that our lives are a team effort. We need each other, and "each other" is now a diverse team of a wide diversity of people. Judging, hating, or discarding certain demographics of people or groups only for their views, opinions, skin pigment, or ways of life only, is negatively affecting all of us. Including, caustically eating a part of the one doing the judging.

You have the power to make a positive difference in your life and to those around you. Never give that helpful power away. Never give up or stop believing in the development and goodness of your spirit. Because your spirit is ultimately how you experience your you, and your life.

Our thoughts, attitudes, and actions hold our power

The benefits of choosing to spread calm, productive, solution-oriented energy is that it starts that positive cycle by first easing life for yourself, then easing it for those around you, which then eases it right back to you.

You are significant, and you have the power to add or subtract to yourself and the world around you. Calm or tense energy spreads like the flu; it is up to each of us to use our free will and choice to decide if we want to spread tension, judgment, hatred, and blame, or we choose to spread calm, less judgment, and yes, also acceptance, tolerance, forgiveness, and understanding.

You are powerful.

The ultimate gift to suffering less

Last night I had a raw conversation with the same wonderful friend who I have quoted several times: "If the answer is easy, it is probably wrong," "Most people don't want to have conversations; they only want you to agree with them. If this were not true, we could all finish more sentences without interruptions." and, "Why toxify a relationship if you are not going to change anyone's mind?" We were having a mutually trusting talk about the stressors in both our lives. They were being vague throughout the conversation. I asked if I would ever hear the details being left out. They went ahead and shared the details, and at the end of the conversation, I was informed they felt lighter having told someone. That is not the gist of the conversation, but it reminds us it is a burden to keep too much bad, or heavy buried inside us.

They admit to being depressed by their predicament but were also sharing signs of hopefulness with a three-year plan to turn the negative situation into a positive one. This person was also still wisely brainstorming and considering more angles and options, and further wisdom to not make any fast, first-thought decisions. One of the potential plans being creatively brainstormed was to empower and reward the team of people they employ to help the situation, with the added benefit of lifting that group of people's autonomy and financial status at the same time. Impressive giving, caring, and stress-reducing solution! Knowing I was on the tail end of completing this book, they asked what is one of the keys to suffer less in life. At this point, I am sure you can easily guess that I told him it is in accepting that every one of us is a wonderful and faulted human, making mistakes, getting a little of our messiness on each other, and knowing that none of us are alone in this messy endeavor known as "humanhood." As usual, this particular friend accurately surmised one step further than I, "So the key to deeper happiness is learning to *enjoy* our messy humanness after we accept it."

My jaw slacked. This person just handed me the icing on the cake. I had just been taught why I was still more than just good with life, why I had not only not given up on people, but still believed in and liked them. Why I had not thrown myself or the rest of us humans away. Why I cared to slice myself open to publish this book. Yes, accept our messing humanness, but don't stop there, learn to enjoy it.

With great self-honesty and accuracy, they trustingly admitted, "That will be hard for me, but I will try."

I had stopped short at accepting humanness. I had found the origin of the problem and other parts of the cure, but not the icing on the cake. I was about to cheat you and leave you the problem, the key to the problem, but not the code to turn the key so the door could open. I am sorry I almost did that to you.

Acceptance is most definitely the vital prerequisite to suffering less with our imperfect humanness and our imperfect, often difficult lives. We try to be perfect because the faults and weaknesses scare us, and then cause us self-doubt and judgment from ourselves and others. If I can't get it right, I think and feel I must be bad or not as good as others.

Between the times we find and feel the healthier middle, we either overcompensate with bravado or outright narcissism, or we collapse with feelings of inadequacy and the insecure self-destruction. Often fed by shame, guilt, depression, or other self-destructive behaviors, such as addiction or giving up on self-care, as if "what difference does it make." Which is worse: bravado or bourbon? Both steal your moments, life, and self. Worse, they both remove our ability to enjoy our imperfect humanness. This longtime friend of mine is right, the key to life is accepting the human condition, but then what turns that key and opens the door is finding enjoyment of our imperfect humanness.

A fantastic way to widen your peace, joy, and productivity is to start to feel and see that unless someone is abusive, neglecting, manipulative, violent, negligent in their work, or otherwise dangerously snatching your free will, choice, peace, and productivity: then we should also learn to enjoy the humanness of others. Always working to find the courage to clearly see how we interact with ourselves and each other is a significant stride to meet and welcome the humanness of self and others.

Oh, I can admit it can be somewhat scary to stop and sit with our unfiltered self, with nothing distracting us in the background to keep us from experiencing ourselves.

By inserting this key to greater human enjoyment, turning it, and opening the door, you are beautifully choosing to enrich your life with infinite rewards and possibilities. Laughing at ourselves is a good start, and it should be our home base and reset button. It also means we learn to enjoy the parts of ourselves we love less. I was doing just that when I shared that I accept my periodic depression, that I consider my mistakes in life achievements because at least I tried, and I was doing it the two times in my nursing career I pulled over to cry, recalling the barrage of trauma I have witnessed in my life. Sometimes the "enjoyment" of the not so good and unpleasant humanness means just not fighting it, letting my being do what it needs. It is knowing and trusting that if it is being handed to me, then I must have inside me somewhere what is required to work with it. It is trusting our own humanness.

I had a checklist of a few more gems I felt I should share before closing, but I think they have all become trivial compared to the ultimate final gem of accepting, *and* enjoying, our messy, imperfect wonderful selves. Choice and rewards, right? First for yourself, then from as many directions as you can receive, then please give it back out to as many directions as you can give.

I hope for you many positive choices and rewards that slowly and steadily increase your acceptance then enjoyment of self, life, and others. Including giving and receiving an abundance of daily kindness.

> "Yesterday I was clever, so I wanted to change the world.
> Today I am wise,
> so, I am changing myself."
> —Rumi, 1207–1273

Made in the USA
Las Vegas, NV
13 December 2022

62188906R00275